Magazine Editing & Production

Magazine Editing & Production *Sixth Edition*

J. William Click
Winthrop University

Russell N. Baird
Ohio University

WCB Brown & Benchmark
PUBLISHERS

Madison, Wisconsin • Dubuque, Iowa

Book Team

Editor *Stan Stoga*
Developmental Editor *Mary Rossa*
Production Editor *Debra DeBord*
Visuals/Design Developmental Consultant *Marilyn A. Phelps*
Visuals/Design Freelance Specialist *Mary L. Christianson*
Publishing Services Specialist *Sherry Padden*
Marketing Manager *Pamela S. Cooper*
Advertising Manager *Jodi Rymer*

Brown & Benchmark

A Division of Wm. C. Brown Communications, Inc.

Executive Vice President/General Manager *Thomas E. Doran*
Vice President/Editor in Chief *Edgar J. Laube*
Vice President/Sales and Marketing *Eric Ziegler*
Director of Production *Vickie Putman Caughron*
Director of Custom and Electronic Publishing *Chris Rogers*

Wm. C. Brown Communications, Inc.

President and Chief Executive Officer *G. Franklin Lewis*
Corporate Senior Vice President and Chief Financial Officer *Robert Chesterman*
Corporate Senior Vice President and President of Manufacturing *Roger Meyer*

Cover design by Fulton Design

Contents

Preface

Magazines disseminate more specialized information and commentary on a regular basis to diverse audiences than any other medium of mass communication. At a time when radio stations are going dark, broadcast television is a mature industry, and almost no newspapers are being established, dozens of new magazines are established each year. Even considering the high number of failures, the net result is an increase in titles that offers career opportunities to recent college graduates, many of whom begin as top assistants or even editors of professional association or company-sponsored magazines.

Although it usually takes longer to reach the top on large circulation consumer magazines, people with some background in magazine editing and production often have the edge for entry positions on these and become productive staff members more quickly than those without this background.

Schools of journalism generally offer magazine instruction in two basic courses, one in magazine article writing and the other in magazine editing and production. We have planned this book to encompass the magazine editing process in all sizes of magazines, from the one-person staff of association or public relations magazines to complex, highly departmentalized consumer magazines. The basic processes are the same for both. Differences in frequency of publication, size, circulation, advertising pages, and budgets account for the degree of complexity and varied staff sizes.

Early chapters offer insight into the magazine and its role in American society in this last decade of the twentieth century. Later chapters deal with editing strategy and functions, production, legal and ethical considerations, and circulation.

Teachers can use this book for courses in magazine editing and production, specialized business publications, specialized magazines, public relations publications, organizational journalism, and similar subjects. Schools with student magazine laboratory courses can use this book in the preparatory course that usually precedes the laboratory course. It is a single source that blends the necessary practical aspects with a sufficient amount of magazine history and background. Earlier editions of this book have been helpful to editors of small magazines who have not had formal course work in magazine editing and as a ready source of information about editing techniques.

The rapidly changing nature of the magazine field has necessitated frequent revisions. Magazine production has changed much more rapidly than we anticipated when the first edition was published. Computers and software programs have made in-house desktop prepress commonplace, and this edition reflects that. New material about starting a magazine and about creative, award-winning editing is included. The chapters on law and ethics have been reorganized as well as updated to reflect changes in those areas.

Our division of responsibility remains fundamentally the same as in previous editions. Professor Baird took primary responsibility for chapters 7 and 9 through 18, and Professor Click was primarily responsible for chapters 1 through 6, 8, and 19 through 21.

Acknowledgments

For material provided for previous editions and retained in this edition, we are grateful to John Goodwin, who drew the illustrations; Peter T. Miller, who photographed printing production processes; and Robert E. Kenyon, then executive vice-president of the Magazine Publishers of America.

Appreciation for providing materials and information is extended to American Business Press; Audit Bureau of Circulations; *Columbia Journalism Review;* Ralph R. Schulz, formerly of McGraw-Hill, Inc.; John McCafferty of *DuPont Context;* Frank Bowers and Larry Werline, formerly of Fawcett Publications, Inc.; Herman Panyard, Athene Karis, and Forrest Still, formerly of B. F. Goodrich Company; John Good of Lawhead Press, Inc.; *Newsweek;* Edward Owen of *Printing Management; Reader's Digest; Redbook;* Byron T. Scott, formerly of Ohio University and now of the University of Missouri; Charles L. Scott of Ohio University; Time Inc.; and Verified Audit Circulation Corporation.

We also are grateful to Bruce J. Boyle of Meredith Corporation; *Columbus Business Forum; The Elks Magazine;* Downs Matthews and *Exxon U.S.A.;* Brenda Floyd of *Aide* Magazine; Peter G. Faur of Southwestern Bell; Herman Duerr; *GO* of Goodyear Tire and Rubber Company; Johnson Publishing Company; David G. Jensen of McGraw-Hill; James Jennings, who took the offset production photos for the third edition; Ralph Kliesch of Ohio University; *The Lamp* of Exxon Corporation; Mary Mitchell, managing editor of *Online Today;* Don Moser, editor of *Smithsonian;* and Joe Bonsignore, publisher of *Smithsonian* and *Air & Space Smithsonian; NCR World* of NCR Corporation; *News/Lines* of Pennsylvania Bell Telephone Company; *Modern Maturity;* Thomas O. Ryder, president and executive publisher of American Express Publishing Company; John J. Tuohey and *U.S. News & World Report;* Robert Vereen, John P. Hammond, and Karen Stewart of *Do It Yourself Retailing;* and Lee Young, emeritus of the University of Kansas.

A number of magazine professionals and university professors made major contributions to the sixth edition, including Eric Schrier, editor-in-chief of *Health* Magazine and vice-president of Time Publishing Ventures; Peter Costiglio, vice-president, communications, Time Inc.; Michael D. Kreiter, president and publisher, *Magazine Design & Production;* Christian Kuypers, art director, *Spy* Magazine; O. Louis Mazzatenta of *National Geographic;* Jean Waller, *Chesapeake Bay* Magazine; Ron Pittman of Ohio University; Sharon Bass of the University of Kansas and CRMA Education Fund; Georgia I. Douglass, director of publications, Wheaton College; Guido H. Stempel III of Ohio University; James Tidwell of Eastern Illinois University; and William A. Fisher of Winthrop University.

In addition, we would like to thank the reviewers for their helpful comments: Karen J. Christy, University of Texas, Austin; Frankie A. Hammond, University of Florida; and Vicki Hesterman, Point Loma Nazarene College.

J. William Click
Russell N. Baird

The Magazine Industry

RACHEL finished a morning of editing copy and writing titles as an assistant editor for the upcoming issue of her trade magazine. That afternoon, she was on her way across Manhattan to interview an executive in town for a trade show. She got a major article and personality profile out of this interview with one of the leading institutional designers in America. Four months earlier, she had completed college in Ohio and conducted her job search. She had taken a magazine editing course and worked on her college magazine. Now she was working in the field for which she had prepared.

"I may have been incredibly lucky," Rachel said. "I had a summer job with a community service agency in New York City, so I was here to interview when jobs came open. I had a good academic record and an excellent internship as part of my undergraduate experience. And I was sincerely interested in business publications. It was great to start in New York City!"

That was 11 years ago. She is still excited about magazines and her career. After 3 years at her first job with a multiple publisher and stints as managing editor of two trade publications, she moved a few blocks to another publisher as managing editor of a larger magazine that deals with interior design, architecture, and the development of hotels and restaurants. Then, when the opportunity arose, she moved from editorial into advertising as the magazine's West Coast representative, covering a 14-state territory from Colorado west and British Columbia.

An English major who took a minor in journalism, including a magazine editing and production course, Jane left campus for a job in New York City, where she started doing editorial layout and pasteup as well as writing and editing. She quickly impressed her editors with her writing ability and initiative, so, when her company decided to launch a new magazine for the meeting and convention field, she was chosen to be its editor. That magazine was immediately successful, and she added the title "copublisher."

"When I started, I had my student magazine project, experience on the campus magazine, a burning desire to work in my home city, and little else," Jane said. "From college I knew about business magazines and was willing to start at the bottom, though I didn't want to stay there long. And I didn't. But I fell into a fantastic opportunity. I had high goals, but I didn't expect to be a publisher so soon after graduating from college."

Five years later, when the company decided to do a spin-off in the travel field, she was its founding publisher, supervising people, conducting seminars and trade shows, and speaking across the country. She soon became vice-president of the company, with broader responsibilities, then recently moved to a new position with another company.

Magazine editing is an exciting, varied, challenging, and rewarding career. It's a people business as well as an editorial quality and product business. It's a leadership and initiative business, and it can lead to other media careers in business, advertising, circulation, and administration.

Before we get too far into the concepts and techniques of magazine editing, let's set the scene with some background about the magazine industry.

America's largest circulation magazine per issue in recent years has been *Modern Maturity,* which is distributed to everyone who pays dues to the American Association of Retired Persons. (Courtesy *Modern Maturity.*)

More copies of *TV Guide* are sold each year than any other American magazine, 15 million a week for 780 million a year. (Courtesy *TV Guide.*)

Early Magazine Era

The birth of the first American magazine in February 1741 was a notable event. Colonists, most of whom were still struggling for survival in a strange land, were amazed at the occurrence. The fact that the birth produced twins sired by two of Philadelphia's most sagacious publishers added to the wonderment.

Primary credit for the first American magazine goes to Benjamin Franklin, a young but successful printer and newspaper publisher. The enterprising Franklin was the first to conceive the idea of a monthly magazine, beginning his efforts in late 1740. The first issue of his *General Magazine and Historical Chronicle for all the British Plantations in America* bore the date January 1741 and was, after a tremendous struggle to get its 70-plus pages into print, finally offered for sale on February 16.

In a different print shop in Philadelphia, however, another of the town's respected publishers had heard of Franklin's intentions, and also had set about the task of bringing forth the first magazine. Andrew Bradford, Franklin's chief rival in the publishing business, hurriedly put together his *American Magazine, or A Monthly View of the Political State of the British Colonies,* and gave it the same date, January 1741. His product was offered for sale on February 13, three days before Franklin's.

Franklin managed to produce six issues before giving up; Bradford produced only three. In retrospect, the experience of these publishing pioneers foretold what was to come in the history of American magazines. Although the lifetime for both their magazines were relatively short, it was only a short time before other magazines, by other publishers, found their niches.

For more than 100 years, few magazines circulated far from their cities of publication. Magazines typically had short lives as a result of low circulation and advertising income. There was no truly national magazine before 1850.

After the Civil War, magazines flourished for nearly two decades. The number of periodicals nearly quintupled from 700 in 1865 to 3,300 in 1885, according to Frank Luther Mott in *A History of American Magazines 1865–1885.*[1]

Mass Circulation Magazine Era

National mass circulation magazines were born in the late 19th century as a result of a number of developments in the United States. In the 1890s, the United States hastened its move from an agricultural to an industrial economy. Improvements in transportation and mail service made it possible to distribute goods, including magazines, over wide geographical areas. The national distribution of products brought on brand names and the national advertising necessary to promote these brand names.

At the time, the magazine was the ideal medium for national advertising, and the sale of space to advertisers flourished. Packaged goods were favored by the chain store merchandisers of the time—Piggly Wiggly, J.C. Penney, United Cigar Stores, A&P, Woolworth. The rotary press was developed, greatly speeding the production of magazines. *Century Magazine*'s rotary press could do 10 times the work of a flatbed press the same size. The perfecting press made it possible to print on both sides of the paper in one press run instead of two. Also, development of the halftone meant that illustrations did not have to be hand drawn or, like *Godey's Lady's Book,* hand tinted. All these occurrences favored the development of large-circulation magazines. Magazines had also been helped in 1879, when Congress provided lower-cost mailing privileges for periodicals.

In the last decade of the 19th century, Americans could buy a wide range of magazines, including *National Geographic* and *Popular Science Monthly.* However, most Americans were not magazine readers.

Cyrus H. K. Curtis bought the weak *Saturday Evening Post* in 1897 and began strengthening it; in 1899, one of the industry's greatest editors, George Horace Lorimer, became its editor.

Competition among the magazines themselves created a situation in which the advertiser, not the magazine reader, carried most of the cost for a magazine. To increase circulation, which in turn generated the sale of advertising space, maga-

One of America's leading farm magazines, *Farm Journal*, dates from this first issue in 1877. (Cover courtesy of Prof. Lee Young, University of Kansas.)

zines offered readers bargain rates for subscriptions; club offers, premiums, long-term discounts, and other incentives. The discovery that advertising could pay the bills and provide a profit was made at about the same time by the era's publishing giants. S. S. McClure of *McClure's Magazine,* John Brisben Walker of *Cosmo-politan,* Cyrus H. K. Curtis of the *Saturday Evening Post,* and Frank A. Munsey of *Munsey's Magazine* all joined in the move to rely on advertising while letting the reader off cheaply. McClure entered the field in 1893 with a 15-cent-per-copy price, only to have Walker cut *Cosmopolitan*'s 25-cent price in half. Then Munsey joined the battle by cutting his newsstand price from 25 to 10 cents. So it went, until a tradition was built among American magazine readers that someone else would bear the brunt of the expense for bringing them quality magazines. This tradition changed dramatically in the 1980s, when publishers raised single-copy and subscription prices to reduce their reliance on advertising revenue and to create a more stable revenue base.

Specialized Magazine Era

After World War II ended in 1945, the American economy expanded, television broadcasting slowly began to span the country, and the age of magazine speciali-zation accelerated. No magazine had ever been for everybody. Mass circulation magazines reached much of the nation's population, but never a majority. All mag-azines had target audiences, though some were broad, such as *Collier's, Saturday Evening Post, American, Life,* and *Look.* As Theodore Peterson observed in *Mag-azines in the Twentieth Century,* "magazines were edited for little publics within the population as a whole," both at the turn of the century and in the 1960s.[2]

Commercial television grew from an infant industry to a national institution in less than two decades, but it did so mostly with new advertising money rather than reallocations of money from magazines and newspapers. Magazine circulation in-creased 21 percent between 1950 and 1960, and advertising revenue increased 86 percent. Some individual magazines, of course, suffered during this period.

The end of the general interest magazine of broad appeal and mass circulation was signaled in 1956, when the Crowell-Collier Publishing Company killed its last three magazines in less than six months. *American,* a general interest monthly with more than 1 million circulation, had lost more than half of its annual advertising revenue between 1946 and 1955, and it was discontinued with the August 1956 issue. That December, the company's two remaining magazines, *Collier's* and *Woman's Home Companion,* each with circulation exceeding 4 million, were discontinued.[3]

The magazine industry was to become a specialized magazine industry. Fledg-ling *TV Guide,* for example, eventually became one of the largest circulation U.S. magazines.

The weekly *Saturday Evening Post* struggled through the decade of the 1960s, and it came as no surprise when it ceased publication in 1969. As the 1970s began, it was clear that new magazines would have to rely on their readers for more of the funds needed to stay in business.

Both *Saturday Evening Post* and the weekly *Life* tried to cut their circulations so they could sell more advertising at lower rates, but neither succeeded. *Life* was discontinued with the issue of December 29, 1972, after having lost $30 million over four years. Many other magazines have succeeded in raising single-copy and sub-scription prices substantially, but not while cutting circulation guarantees.

From its inception, the magazine industry has been characterized by change, which continually produces a better and stronger industry. New magazines appear and existing magazines merge, are sold, or are discontinued, for an overall net gain.

The Modern Magazine

Cursory examinations of magazine racks in bookstores and grocery checkout lanes create an impression of the variety and magnitude of magazines. However, one of the first impressions to be corrected for anyone studying magazines is that these consumer magazines represent the entire industry. They represent only a small frac-tion of the numbers that are available. To begin to develop a true understanding of magazines, we should look at them from the standpoint of their readers. Readers not only form the jury that evaluates the magazines directed to them, but they also are the judges who decide what the spectrum of magazines will be.

These readers are not a mass; they are all individuals, each with an occupation, interests, and problems. Magazines want to earn acceptance and respect from readers that will last over time. All of these readers look to magazines for content directly related to their individual needs.

A doctor, for example, may favor a professional journal, which offers valuable information about new medicines and treatments essential to the contemporary practice of medicine. The engineer, the teacher, the merchant, and the business executive may also think first of their professional journals when they consider magazines.

For the golfer, the hunter, the amateur photographer, and the football or basketball fan, magazines may be a source of joyful reading about their favorite means of relaxation. For homemakers, the arrival of magazines may be a signal for brief periods of relaxation spent reading about ways to make home interiors brighter, more cheerful, and more efficient. One's favorite magazine may be the best and most compact package offering complete television listings.

Children at the beginning reading stages may find their magazines to be storehouses of puzzles, cut-outs, and fairy tales to test and expand their imaginations. Teenagers may choose their magazines to match their interests in music or movies. Some adults may find spiritual support and encouragement from magazines that are extensions of their religious communities.

As readers, many of us can explore the world through magazines replete with beautiful photographs and vivid descriptions of places we want to see or have visited, or we can relive history through lively accounts of the tragedies and triumphs of the past. As we jet from place to place, we spend our time aloft, reading the magazines provided free by the airlines, placed conveniently in the seatpocket in front of us. We explore magazine advertisements to pinpoint new desires for products and services. In the inflight magazine, our attention may go to travel accessories, but in a city magazine we might be looking for new and better restaurants for a special dinner or schedules of plays, operas, ballets, or concerts.

We may visit a newsstand specifically to get a magazine that fully compares the year's new automobiles so that we can make a wise purchase, or we might want to explore the mass of computer magazines to try to get information that will direct us to the correct hardware or software for our needs or tell us how to better use what we have. Still other magazines may tell us how to tile the kitchen floor or pick the best college for study in our chosen field. We are all aware of the newsmagazines that interpret current events.

Obviously, we could go on, pointing to magazine after magazine serving individualized needs and interests of readers. No discussion of magazine editing should begin without the **reader** as the focus. However, we also are concerned here with what magazines are for those in the industry—those who devote their professional lives to the editing and production of these sources of information and entertainment.

Struggling for a Definition

In searching for a definition of magazines, some writers have limited their thinking of magazines to tangible products, such as in this dictionary definition: "a publication appearing regularly and containing stories, articles, etc., by various writers." This definition clearly fits some newspapers as well as magazines.

Weekly newsmagazines have some of the functions and character of newspapers, and daily newspapers such as *USA Today,* with an emphasis on color and illustrations as well as "soft" news and feature material, tend to further blur the distinctions.

Frank Luther Mott, author of the classic multivolume history of American magazines, wrote that the term *magazine* was first used "in the title of the *Gentleman's Magazine,* founded in London in 1731."[4] The term is derived from the use of *magazine* as meaning *storehouse* and originally referred only to contents and not to form.[5] Mott added that, although *magazine* is "defined as a bound pamphlet issued more or less regularly and containing a variety of reading matter, it must be observed also that it has a strong connotation of entertainment. A professional and technical periodical for psychiatrists would scarcely call itself the *Psychiatrists' Magazine,* but rather the *Psychiatrists' Journal* or *Review.*"[6] Others, including Roland Wolseley, a highly respected author of books on magazines, have struggled with the notion of developing a precise definition of a magazine, only to beg the question.

Today, *magazine* refers more to an approach or a process rather than to a format (bound periodical). Television has magazines, and there are and will be more magazines retrieved through computer systems, CDs played through computers or TV sets, and other formats. In the information age, *magazine* more often connotes information than entertainment, and service journalism probably prevails over entertainment when all magazines are taken into account.

The Uniqueness of Magazines

The real uniqueness of magazines stems from the fact that they are more than the total of their ink and paper. They are, in addition, personal relationships that are built among the writers and editors of the magazines and their readers, often over a long period of time. Understanding this intangible relationship is the cornerstone of successful magazine editing. Every step in editing a magazine must be taken with the thought of encouraging and maintaining the relationship that comes only when editors and readers are truly on the same wavelength. Magazines must have characters and personalities that are true to the interests of their readers. The niche for one particular magazine exists because there is an audience that matches that particular niche, and every issue must be targeted directly to that audience.

Much more will be said later about this necessity to match content with audience and to develop and keep the respect of readers. Terms such as *readership studies, demographics,* and *fulfillment* are part of the jargon relating to the essential effort to keep magazines in tune with their audiences. Audiences change, however, and so must magazines. In fact, one constant in the history of American magazines has been change. Old magazines that fell out of step have died, and new ones to match the new marching cadence of a changing audience have started their journeys. Many magazines have enjoyed long-term success by changing with the times and their audiences.

The Media Mix

The typical American does not use one mass medium to the exclusion of all others, so discussions about the superiority of one medium are unproductive. Magazines rate high, along with television, radio, and newspapers, in overall use.

Americans use the media to different degrees. One study found that 21 percent of American adults are heavy users of both magazines and television, 31 percent are heavy television and light magazine users, 34 percent are heavy magazine and light television users, and 15 percent are light users of both media. Advertisers need to use magazines to reach the 34 percent who are heavy magazine and light television users. Magazine advertising also is needed to reinforce television advertising to other magazine users.

Media use varies by education, income, and life-style. In one study, 81 percent of the adults interviewed had bought magazines within the preceding year, an average of six titles per household. "Heavy buyers" are only 27 percent of the U.S. population but account for 58 percent of magazine sales, buying an average of 10.3 titles a year, more than four times the number bought by light buyers, and 59 percent of the heavy buyers have annual household incomes greater than $35,000, compared to 17 percent for nonbuyers.[7]

People use the media for various purposes and respond differently to them. People use radio mainly in the morning, when getting ready for the day's activities and while driving. People use television primarily in the evening and at night during the

TABLE 1.1
Total Adult Reading of Average Magazine Copy

Number of adult readers	4.7
Reading days per reader	2.1
Total adult reading days (4.7 readers × 2.1 reading days)	9.9
Reading time per reader	52 minutes
Total adult reading time (4.7 readers × 52 minutes)	244 minutes or 4.1 hours
Copy kept accessible	28.8 weeks
Percentage exposed to average ad page	85 percent
Per-reader exposures to average page (MPX)	1.7×
Total adult exposures per page (4.7 readers × 1.7×)	**8.0**

Sources: *The 1992–1993 Magazine Handbook* (*MPA Research Newsletter No. 64*), p. 39; 1992 Spring MRI, MPX-A Study of Magazine Page Exposure, Audits & Surveys, Inc., 1981, and Changing Channels, Audits & Surveys, Inc., 1984; TGI 1977; and Eyes On Study for *Newsweek* by Audits & Surveys, 1978.

week. Individuals read newspapers for local advertising and a deeper look at the news, as well as for local news that didn't make the TV newscast. People use magazines for a multitude of purposes, many of which have been discussed.

The average magazine copy has 4.7 readers, with 2.1 reading days per reader. Each reader spends an average of 52 minutes reading the copy, for a total of 244 minutes (4.1 hours) of adult reading time per copy.

Each reader is exposed an average of 1.7 times to the average page in the copy, for a total of 8 adult reader exposures per page. Each reader keeps the copy of the magazine accessible for an average of 28.8 weeks (see table 1.1).

The media are not directly competing against each other because each serves a different primary purpose and involves different kinds of effort by its users. They are competing, however, for the consumer's time and the advertiser's dollar. Television and magazines tend to be national media, while newspapers and radio tend to be local or regional. This is changing as city and metropolitan magazines become strong voices in many places and cable "networks" provide specialized programming, such as sports or movies, much like specialized magazines. Print offers advantages in material that is to be read, clipped, and saved. Television is advantageous for showing action, dramatizations, and product demonstrations. Radio prevails in reaching people who are doing things, from mowing the lawn or washing the car to participating in leisure activities.

Time spent with a medium is another factor to consider. The Television Bureau of Advertising has reported that each day Americans on average spend 179 minutes watching television, 109 minutes listening to radio, 32 minutes reading newspapers, and 21 minutes reading magazines.

The development of cable television, fiber optics, and computer data bases has opened great opportunities for magazine publishers because much magazine content can be distributed in these ways. More and more people are using their home computers to access data bases of helpful and entertaining information. Long-time print readers are likely to remain loyal to printed magazines, which also are more economical than electronic means for disseminating much specialized content. The variety of magazine content can now be circulated in more ways than before.

Types of Magazines

The magazine can aim at a precise audience dispersed over a large geographical area, presenting illustrations and articles in a convenient format that can be read almost anywhere at any time. Although several magazines built tremendous circulations to reach mass audiences, others long ago defined their audiences and have been serving them for decades. These are special interest magazines, the majority of which are business publications. There are also thousands of magazines issued by companies for their employees, customers, stockholders, and other groups related to their communications and public relations programs.

Of the numerous ways to classify magazines, it seems best to discuss a small number of basic groups: consumer, business, association, farm, and public relations. Magazines within these groups can be classified in numerous ways, which are not mutually exclusive. Even these groups of magazines are not mutually exclusive.

Consumer Magazines

Magazines sold at retail outlets are consumer magazines aimed at the general reading public. To many persons, they represent the entire magazine industry, but they are no more than the visible tip of the iceberg. They are consumer magazines from the advertiser's viewpoint because their readers buy and consume products and services that are sold at retail and may be advertised in these magazines.

Basically, a consumer magazine can be purchased by anyone, through subscription or from retail newsstands. Many other types of magazines are not usually available to the general public.

Consumer magazines usually have the largest staffs and circulations, but there is wide variation, and many are put out by very small editorial staffs. Editorial positions on these books may be considered the most glamorous, but there is a limited number of such positions because consumer magazines are fewest in number.

Consumer Magazine and Agri-Media Rates and Data lists in its Consumer Magazine section more than 2,300 titles in 70 classifications, from airline inflight to youth, including groups, annual directory issues, and magazines that are published infrequently. See table 1.2 on page 8.

A few examples of the better-known consumer magazines are *Reader's Digest, TV Guide, National Geographic, Better Homes and Gardens, Good Housekeeping, Time, Cosmopolitan,* and *Glamour.* Perhaps less familiar are *Modern Maturity,* the largest circulation American magazine, *Prevention, The American Legion Magazine, AAA World, Southern Living, Smithsonian, Motorland,* and *NEA Today,* all with more than 2 million circulation. Nearly all consumer magazines today are classified as special interest books, some of which are discussed in chapter 2.

Business Publications

Magazines that serve a particular business, industry, or profession are classified as business publications (often referred to as trade journals). Although the field changes continually, *Business Publication Rates and Data* listed 5,853 publications in 177 classifications in January 1993. Many are issued infrequently, such as annually. Analysis of an earlier issue found 3,200 listings of business publications published four or more times a year.

Many business publications are issued in newspaper format and emphasize news in their content. Some in a magazine format also emphasize news, blurring any distinction between magazines and newspapers.

Three publishing arrangements are used to issue magazines serving business. One is the independent, profit-seeking publishing enterprise that is not part of the field its publication serves. Theoretically, at least, such publishers can objectively view the field, pass judgment, and state their opinions as outside observers. A good example of this type is McGraw-Hill, a private publishing firm that issues publications serving businesses ranging from construction to electronics, engineering, and medicine. Other large business publishers include Fairchild, Penton, Cahners, Harcourt Brace Jovanovich, Medical Economics, and Chilton.

A second type is the professional association that is part of the field served and that issues one or more periodicals as an association service to members. Because they are in the field served, these publications may boost their association or field with less critical objectivity.

The third involves independent publishers that issue official journals of some associations, such as Williams & Wilkins, which publishes the *Journal of Immunology,* the official publication of the American Association of Immunologists.

Association Magazines

No one knows how many association magazines are published. At least 600 business and professional organizations publish magazines that serve as business publications for their fields and are listed in *Business Publication Rates and Data.* Thousands of fraternal, social, and civic organizations issue magazines, from local to national. A number of association magazines, such as *The American Legion Magazine, The Kiwanis Magazine, The Rotarian,* and *Scouting* are listed as consumer magazines

First published in 1922 as a monthly magazine offering "articles of enduring value and interest, in condensed and compact form," *Reader's Digest* carried no advertising until 1955. (Courtesy *Reader's Digest.*)

Long called a "quality" magazine by authors, *The Atlantic* describes itself as an eclectic mix of the thinking and writing from a variety of minds, focusing on contemporary, social, and cultural issues through commentary, criticism, fiction, and humor. (Courtesy *The Atlantic Monthly*/Illustration by Ralph Giguere.)

TABLE 1.2
Standard Rate and Data Service Consumer Magazine Classifications

1. Airline inflight/train enroute
1A. Almanacs and directories
2. Art and antiques
3. Automotive
4. Aviation
5. Babies
5A. Black/African-American
6. Boating and yachting
7. Brides, bridal
8. Business and finance
8A. Campers, recreational vehicles, motor homes and trailers
8B. Camping and outdoor recreation
9. Children's
9A. Civic
9B. College and alumni
10. Comics and comic technique
10A. Computers
11. Crafts, games, hobbies, and models
12. Dancing
13. Dogs and pets
14. Dressmaking and needlework
15. Editorialized and classified advertising
16. Education and teacher
17. Entertainment guides and programs
17A. Entertainment and performing arts
18. Epicurean
19. Fishing and hunting
19A. Fitness
20. Fraternal, professional groups, service clubs, veterans' organizations and associations
20A. Gaming
21. Gardening (home)
21A. Gay publications
22. General editorial
22A. Group buying opportunities
23. Health
23A. History
24. Home service and home
25. Horses, riding and breeding
25A. Hotel inroom
27. Labor, trade union
28. Literary, book reviews and writing techniques
28A. Mature market
29. Mechanics and science
29A. Media/personalities
30. Men's
30A. Metropolitan/regional/state
30B. Metropolitan/entertainment, radio and TV
31. Military and naval (Air Force, Army, Navy, and Marines)
31A. Motorcycle
33. Music
34. Mystery, adventure, and science fiction
35. Nature and ecology
36A. News—weeklies
36B. News—biweeklies, dailies, semimonthlies
36C. Newsweeklies (alternatives)
37. Newsletters
38. Newspaper distributed magazines
38A. Parenthood
39. Photography
41. Political and social topics
42. Religious and denominational
43. Science/technology
43B. Sex
44. Society
45. Sports
46. Travel
47. TV and radio/communications and electronics
49. Women's
50. Women's/Men's fashions, beauty and grooming
51. Youth

A business publication for the printing industry, *Graphic Arts Monthly* circulates on a controlled basis to qualified companies and departments. (Courtesy *Graphic Arts Monthly*, Cahners Publishing Company.)

An association magazine that functions as a business publication, *Do It Yourself Retailing* is published monthly by the National Retail Hardware Association. (Courtesy *Do It Yourself Retailing*.)

A monthly association magazine, *The Rotarian* circulates to 529,000 subscribers. (Courtesy *The Rotarian*.)

in *Consumer Magazine and Agri-Media Rates and Data.* The nation's largest circulation magazine, *Modern Maturity,* is published by the American Association of Retired Persons.

Two of the best-known and most financially stable association magazines are the *Journal of the American Medical Association* and *National Geographic.* Other examples of association periodicals include *The Quill* of the Society of Professional Journalists, *Bioscience* of the American Institute of Biological Sciences, and *Texas Architect* of the Texas Society of Architects. Among the hundreds not listed are *Journalism Quarterly, Journal of Communication Management,* and *The American Philatelist.*

Association magazines' staffs range from unpaid, volunteer, part-time editors who do their editing on their home computers to large, well-paid staffs at such places as the Chicago headquarters of the American Medical Association. These magazines range from small issues with no advertising to thick ones in which ads occupy as much space as editorial content.

Farm Publications

Virtually the same as business publications are farm publications, edited and published for the agricultural industry. Many of these also are published by associations. They often are considered as a separate type and are listed in their own Farm Publications section of *Consumer Magazine and Agri-Media Rates and Data,* where 261 titles are listed in 11 classification groupings.

Farm publications typically deal with state or regional subject matter or with specialties, such as daily and dairy breeds; field crops and soil management; or fruits, nuts, vegetables, and special products. Examples of farm publications include *Farm Journal, Progressive Farmer, Successful Farming, Hoard's Dairyman, Soybean Digest, Wallaces Farmer, American Fruit Grower, Indiana Farmer, The Peanut Farmer, Hog Farm Management, Rice Farming,* and *Wines & Vines.*

Video Systems serves 44,000 video professionals in business, education, and government, with articles such as video and audio technology reports; how-to articles; and articles on commercial, corporate, and institutional production techniques. (Courtesy *Video Systems*.)

Exxon Corporation publishes *The Lamp* for its shareholders. The 32-page magazine carries no advertising. (Courtesy Exxon Corporation.)

One of the largest circulation and most read airline inflight magazines is Delta Air Lines' monthly *Sky*. (Courtesy Delta Air Lines *SKY* Magazine.)

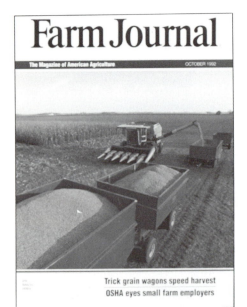

Besides a national edition, *Farm Journal* publishes regional, state, and crop editions and has the largest circulation of any farm magazine. (Courtesy *Farm Journal*.)

Meredith Corporation of Des Moines, Iowa, publishes *Successful Farming* each month for 500,000 farmers. (Courtesy *Successful Farming*.)

Public Relations Magazines

Magazines can effectively win and maintain friends for business or nonprofit institutions. No one really knows how many of these sponsored magazines there are because they do not sell advertising or qualify for second-class postal rates. Many companies publish a number of magazines. In recent years, many companies have converted their magazines to *magapapers, tabazines,* or newspapers.

A public relations magazine is published by a sponsoring company or institution for circulation among one or more of its publics—employees, dealers, customers, stockholders, or another interest group—and usually carries no advertising, unless it is for the sponsor. These magazines are sometimes referred to as *company magazines, house organs,* or *organizational magazines.*

Most practitioners classify public relations magazines by their audiences as *internal, external,* or *combination internal-external,* depending on whether the readers are within the company, such as employees, outside it, such as community leaders or customers, or both.

The airlines' *inflight* magazines started as public relations magazines but have long accepted advertising and are now listed as consumer magazines by Standard Rate and Data Service. They continue to serve a public relations function for their sponsors. Some are published by independent publishers for the magazines' sponsors. Halsey Publishing Company in Fort Lauderdale, Florida, publishes *Delta Sky,* and Pace Communications, Inc., in Greensboro, North Carolina, publishes *US Air Magazine* and United's *Hemispheres,* one of the earliest, established in 1957 as *United Mainliner.*

One-Shot Magazines

Publishers occasionally capitalize on a hot topic by issuing a single magazine about it. Examples range from scientific advances such as space missions, television shows, natural disasters such as hurricanes and earthquakes, and historic events to remembrance books about star entertainers or public figures immediately following their deaths.

Often published by a special projects division of the publishing company, one-shots (or *specials*) may reappear from time to time and eventually become regular magazines. One-shots on crafts, needlework, home repairs, and the like have developed into regularly issued magazines.

The one-shot is risky. Considering the lead time required, it is difficult to sell much advertising, and success depends greatly on timing. If you publish while in-

As a sponsored quarterly magazine for more than 7 million recipients, *Philip Morris Magazine* deals primarily with nonsmoking subjects of general interest and has a brief section devoted to smoking issues. (Courtesy *Philip Morris Magazine*.)

terest in the topic is at its peak and you beat your competitors to the newsstand, you may do well. However, it you are late or existing magazines give the topic ample coverage in their regular issues, you may find it a costly venture. One advantage publishers of well-established magazines have is that it is easier for them to get rack space by using the name of the established magazine.

Magnitude of the Industry

Mere figures cannot convey the magnitude of an industry so diverse as the magazine industry. Raw numbers of magazine titles, combined circulations, dollars of income, advertising volume, and the like may be both impressive and misleading. Also, the magazine industry is more than magazines. Many publishers' operations include book clubs, book publishing divisions, direct mail merchandising, data bases for business, and rental of the magazines' mailing lists. Also, hundreds of associations and businesses that issue sponsored magazines don't consider themselves part of the magazine industry.

Establishing exact dimensions of the magazine field is nearly impossible. Numbers are deceiving. Many magazines are published only once a year. For example, *Better Homes and Gardens* is a well-known monthly magazine, but its annuals on such topics as Christmas cross stitch, Christmas ideas, country crafts, holiday crafts, and prize-winning remodeling and other special interest titles turn it into 35 titles in *Consumer Magazine and Agri-Media Rates and Data,* which in January 1993 listed 2,379 consumer magazines and 261 farm publications. Its sibling publication, *Business Publication Rates and Data,* listed 5,853 business publications. These listings are limited to magazines that accept enough paid advertising to warrant being listed in a national directory for advertisers and advertising agencies.

The International Association of Business Communicators says it has no count of company, corporate, or public relations magazines. As far as we know, no one has counted the number of association magazines regularly published. There are no authoritative figures on the number of magazines overall or in any classification.

The *Gale Directory of Publications and Broadcast Media* lists business, consumer, technical, professional, trade, and farm publications issued four or more times a year. It specifically excludes publications of "primary or secondary schools, or houses of worship" and "internal publications." Under the heading "U.S. Magazines," the 1992 edition listed 2,560 general circulation magazines; 7,678 trade, technical, and professional publications; 471 agricultural publications; 61 black

TABLE 1.3
Magazines Exceeding 2 Million Circulation
Audited by ABC

Magazine	Circulation (million)
Modern Maturity	22.545
NRTA/AARP Bulletin	22.341
Reader's Digest	16.257
TV Guide	14.919
National Geographic	9.787
Better Homes and Gardens	8.002
Good Housekeeping	5.101
Family Circle	5.038
Ladies' Home Journal	5.003
McCall's	4.650
Woman's Day	4.521
Time	4.159
Sports Illustrated	3.573
National Enquirer	3.469
People Weekly	3.444
Playboy	3.402
Redbook	3.356
Prevention	3.273
Newsweek	3.232
Star	3.075
The American Legion Magazine	2.921
AAA World	2.900
Cosmopolitan	2.705
Southern Living	2.395
U.S. News & World Report	2.319
Smithsonian	2.188
Money	2.077
Glamour	2.070
Motorland	2.047
NEA Today	2.035
Field & Stream	2.010

Source: ABC Fas-Fax, 30 June 1992, and supplement.

publications; 245 college publications; 216 foreign language publications; 79 fraternal publications; 88 Hispanic publications; 59 Jewish publications; 554 religious publications; and 159 women's publications, for a total of 12,170 U.S. magazines. For Canada, it listed 294 general circulation; 596 trade, technical, and professional; 60 agricultural; 23 college; 258 foreign language; 2 fraternal; 4 Jewish; 56 religious; and 23 women's magazines, for a total of 1,316 Canadian magazines.

Another table in the *Gale Directory* accounts for 11,143 periodicals in 1992, a decrease of 96 from 1991 and a decrease of 1,166 from 1988. The frequency of publication of the 1992 periodicals listed is 28 daily, 19 semiweekly, 466 weekly, 174 biweekly, 197 semimonthly, 4,326 monthly, 2,143 bimonthly, 3,024 quarterly, and 766 at variant intervals.

Audit Bureau of Circulations studies have shown that consumer magazines average 454,000 copies per issue, farm publications 74,000, and business publications 29,000. Circulations range from small, unreported figures to millions. Magazines with audited paid circulation exceeding 2 million are listed in table 1.3. Smaller circulation magazines include consumer magazines *The Quarter Racing Journal*, 10,177; *Career Pilot*, 14,179; *Palm Beach Life*, 14,198; *Hudson Valley*, 20,016; and *The Blood-Horse*, 20,096 and business magazines *Michigan Roads and Construction*, 1,762; *Cosmetics & Toiletries*, 3,132; *Michigan Contractor & Builder*, 3,136; *Candy Industry*, 3,975; *Construction Bulletin*, 4,073; and *Bobbin*, 7,777.

The *Magazine Week 500* estimates total revenues for the year and reports average total circulation, paid subscriptions, unpaid subscriptions, and single copies sold per issue; the number of advertising pages published during the year; and rates for a black-and-white advertising page, a one-year subscription, and a single copy.

Table 1.4 lists the top 30 magazines in total revenue from the *Magazine Week 500*. It also lists the ranking of each magazine, the category number in Standard Rate and Data Service publications ("C" for *Consumer Magazine and Agri-Media Rates and Data* and "B" for *Business Publication Rates and Data*), and the number of issues per year, or frequency ("Frq"). All but one of the top 30 are consumer magazines. The exception is *PC Magazine,* which is number 11. The top magazine, *TV Guide,* had revenues of $825.5 million from 8.8 million subscriptions, an average weekly single copy sale of 6.5 million, and 2,412 advertising pages.

One of the top 10 magazines in circulation and 12th in estimated total revenue, *Family Circle* published its 60th anniversary edition in 1992. It is one of several magazines owned and published by The New York Times Company. (Reprinted from the October 13, 1992 issue of *Family Circle* magazine. Copyright © The Family Circle Inc.)

TABLE 1.4
Top 30 Magazines in Total Revenue (Estimates for 1991)

Rank	Title	SRDS	Frq	Revenues	Circulation	Paid Subs	Unpd Subs	SCopies	Ad Pgs	BW Rate	Subs$	SC$
1	TV Guide	C36A	52	825,519,807	15,662,154	8,821,725	308,172	6,532,257	2,412	99,700	37.44	0.75
2	People Weekly	C36A	52	526,281,214	3,387,740	1,625,896	152,620	1,609,224	3,297	70,730	79.90	1.95
3	Time	C36A	52	449,417,644	4,455,226	4,000,708	206,661	247,857	2,167	85,000	58.24	2.50
4	Sports Illustrated	C36A	52	439,666,775	3,657,483	3,294,648	240,910	121,925	2,420	79,115	69.66	2.95
5	Reader's Digest	C22	12	427,619,410	16,927,551	15,393,007	621,544	913,000	881	112,660	19.93	1.97
6	Newsweek	C36A	52	290,050,775	3,526,641	3,198,073	106,474	222,094	1,952	69,455	41.08	2.00
7	Better Homes & Gardens	C24	12	275,913,974	8,177,827	7,503,096	174,564	500,167	1,277	112,890	16.00	1.95
8	Parade	C22	52	270,100,000	34,833,588	34,768,088	65,500	0	740	365,000	0.00	0.00
9	National Geographic Magazine	C22	12	255,555,404	10,004,835	9,832,988	83,356	88,491	294	107,140	22.50	2.65
10	Good Housekeeping	C49	12	238,938,039	5,062,587	3,771,318	34,436	1,256,833	1,616	90,055	16.97	1.95
11	PC Magazine	B32C	26	238,762,951	810,278	680,608	0	129,670	7,084	27,980	44.97	2.95
12	Family Circle	C49	17	212,559,387	5,326,605	2,449,355	175,071	2,702,179	1,537	75,470	15.98	1.25
13	Ladies' Home Journal	C49	12	203,242,538	5,280,627	4,154,019	277,727	848,881	1,471	71,300	20.00	1.50
14	US News & World Report	C36A	52	198,664,206	2,460,845	2,273,697	108,923	78,225	2,023	48,500	39.75	2.50
15	BusinessWeek (North America)	C8	52	192,038,408	960,544	857,145	63,741	39,658	3,735	39,720	44.95	2.50
16	Cosmopolitan	C49	12	170,388,355	2,696,712	596,637	17,356	2,082,719	1,954	47,590	25.00	2.50
17	McCall's	C49	12	168,136,347	5,185,339	4,512,072	175,981	497,286	1,083	70,615	18.00	1.75
18	Woman's Day	C49	15	163,429,111	4,825,665	1,416,834	73,688	3,335,143	1,323	66,495	14.77	1.09
19	Fortune	C8	27	156,287,749	898,295	759,409	95,447	43,439	2,950	38,550	49.95	3.95
20	Playboy	C30	12	154,715,174	3,718,636	2,741,486	219,834	757,316	749	48,940	29.97	3.95
21	Forbes	C8	27	153,426,744	795,822	705,720	58,054	32,048	3,572	31,710	52.00	4.00
22	Vogue	C49	12	122,475,864	1,276,893	485,889	40,912	750,092	2,526	32,410	28.00	3.00
23	Money	C22	12	120,855,128	2,069,668	1,591,282	214,242	264,144	1,279	47,430	31.95	2.95
24	USA Weekend	C22	52	118,962,600	16,476,171	16,476,171	0	0	680	174,945	0.00	0.00
25	Glamour	C49	12	117,390,140	2,056,158	930,658	43,853	1,081,647	1,667	42,580	15.00	2.50
26	Redbook	C49	12	113,307,851	3,926,808	3,175,638	84,942	666,228	1,104	57,340	11.97	1.50
27	Southern Living	C24	12	111,030,960	2,439,014	2,215,625	53,956	169,433	1,231	42,870	24.00	2.50
28	Life	C22	12	107,962,739	1,997,406	1,364,459	86,886	546,061	564	54,110	39.95	3.50
29	Penthouse	C30	12	103,159,200	1,533,487	302,667	31,666	1,199,154	752	27,970	36.00	4.95
30	Rolling Stone	C33	24	94,445,152	1,247,661	983,570	40,399	223,692	1,718	32,305	29.95	2.50

Source: 1992 MagazineWeek 500, *MagazineWeek*, June 22, 1992, p. 59. Reprinted by permission.

Media Conglomerates

Much strength in the magazine industry comes from multiple publishing and diversification, which spread risk among more operating divisions. This permits the temporary support of a money-losing magazine with profits from other magazines or divisions until it becomes profitable again or is discontinued or sold.

Time Warner Inc. is one of the best-known media conglomerates that publishes magazines. Well known for *Time, Life, Fortune, Sports Illustrated, Money, People, Entertainment Weekly, Sports Illustrated for Kids,* and *Martha Stewart Living,* its subsidiaries include Southern Progress Corporation, publishers of *Southern Living, Progressive Farmer, Cooking Light,* and *Southern Accents;* Sunset Publishing, publisher of *Sunset;* and Time Ventures Inc., which has a 50 percent stake in *Health, Hippocrates, Parenting, Working Mother,* and *Working Woman.*

Other publishing divisions include Time Life Inc. (formerly Time Life Books); Warner Books; Little, Brown; Book-of-the-Month Club; Children's Book-of-the-Month Club; History Book Club; and Crafter's Choice Book Club. Its Warner Music Group is the leading music company in the world, with 29 labels, such as Elektra, Nonesuch, Atlantic, Reprise, Warner Nashville, Qwest, and Capricorn.

The Filmed Entertainment division comprises Warner Bros., Warner Bros. Television, Lorimar Television, and Warner Home Video. Home Box Office claims to be the most successful cable programmer in the world. Time Warner Cable is the second-largest owner and operator of cable systems in the United States, through Warner Cable and American Television and Communications Corporation.

Time Warner owns 37 percent of Whittle Communications, has 50 percent partnerships in Columbia House; Six Flags Corporation; Comedy Partners; and Cinamerica Theatres, L.P., and a 44 percent stake in EI Entertainment Television, Inc.

McGraw-Hill, Inc., publishes *Business Week, Aviation Week & Space Technology, Byte, Architectural Record, Chemical Engineering,* and 25 other titles. It also has a Financial Services Division, which operates Standard & Poor's Rating Group, MMS International, Commodity Information Services, and Compustat. Its Educational and Professional Publishing Group includes healthcare and legal publishing, and a Broadcasting division operates four television stations. McGraw-Hill also is involved in a joint venture, Macmillan/McGraw-Hill School Publishing Company. In 1991, 24 percent of McGraw-Hill's profits came from the Information and Publication Services (magazine) division, second to the largest portion, 43 percent, from the Financial Services division.

Capital Cities/ABC, Inc., has several divisions, which publish 63 business and 3 consumer magazines, including Fairchild Fashion and Merchandising Group, Financial Services and Medical Group, International Medical News Group, Agricultural Publishing Group, Chilton Company, Hitchcock Publishing Company, *Los Angeles* Magazine, Nils Publishing Company, and Word, Incorporated. Titles include *Multichannel News, Video Business, Clinical Psychiatry News, Automotive Industries, Food Engineering, Institutional Investor,* and *Women's Wear Daily.*

Professional Organizations

Concerned with issues and problems facing magazines as an industry, a handful of professional organizations binds together publishers and editors. The most prominent is the Magazine Publishers of America (MPA), established in 1919 as the Magazine Publishers Association. The name was changed in 1987. Membership includes association, religious, business, scholarly, metropolitan, and professional magazines, as well as consumer magazines. MPA sponsors and publishes industry-wide research, and it attacks industry problems such as proposed postal rate increases.

Affiliated with MPA is the American Society of Magazine Editors, founded in 1963 as a way to give magazine editors a leadership position among magazine executives, to be a forum for discussions on professional problems, and to develop public relations programs of long-range benefit to magazine journalism. Chief editors and their senior associates of consumer magazines, business publications, and farm publications are members.

Professional programs for editors include seminars and round tables on current operating problems and luncheons on topics of interest to editors. Public relations programs are the National Magazine Awards and a magazine internship program that sends students to New York and other publishing cities each summer to fill junior staff positions on participating magazines.

The National Magazine Awards are presented annually to honor editorial excellence and to encourage editorial vigor and innovation. They were established in 1966 at the invitation of ASME with a grant from MPA and are administered by the Graduate School of Journalism at Columbia University. In 1970, the single award was expanded to 5 categories, and later expansion brought the total to 11 categories in 1992.

The American Business Press (ABP) traces its beginnings to 1906 and the Federation of Trade Press Associations, later called Associated Business Publications. The group established standards of practice for the industry in 1913. Membership was limited to publishers whose circulations were audited by the Audit Bureau of Circulations.

The growth of publications using controlled (free) circulation to persons who met certain qualifications within the industry led a group of these publishers to found the National Business Papers Association in 1940. The name was changed to National Business Publications in 1948, and the organization accepted members with both paid and free circulations.

In January 1965, Associated Business Publications and National Business Publications merged to form American Business Press, Inc., with headquarters in New York City. The merger was a natural outgrowth of business conditions, with many publishers issuing both paid and controlled circulation magazines and some belonging to both organizations. To be eligible for membership, ABP requires a publication to be audited by an independent, nonprofit, tripartite auditing organization; to be independently owned and tax-paying; and to adhere to ABP's Code of Publishing Practice (see chapter 20), which places the interest of the reader first. Publishers of about 390 titles are members of ABP. The name was changed to the Association of Business Publishers, Inc., in 1985 and back to American Business Press in 1990.

Annually since 1954, ABP has presented to individual editors the Jesse H. Neal Editorial Achievement Awards in several editorial categories to reward excellence in audited, independent business publications. In 1988, ABP began a Publishing Management Institute in conjunction with Northwestern University, and it awards the annual McAllister Fellowship to a top executive of a member company. It helped found the Business Press Educational Foundation, which offers internships to college juniors and helps universities start courses in the business press.

The burgeoning field of metropolitan, regional, and state magazines has its organization, the City and Regional Magazine Association (CRMA), with headquarters in Los Angeles. Its White Awards for Editorial and Design Excellence and its educational foundation, which conducts professional education for CRMA, are based at the University of Kansas School of Journalism and Mass Communication.

Editors of public relations magazines may join the International Association of Business Communicators (IABC), which had its beginnings in the 1930s as the American Association of Industrial Editors and the 1940s as the International

Council of Industrial Editors. The two groups merged to form IABC in 1970. IABC sponsors an annual Gold Quill Awards competition, which includes categories in internal magazines, external magazines, magapapers, design, and photojournalism. It also conducts an annual convention, presents educational seminars, has an "accredited business communicator" program, and issues *Communication World*. Its headquarters are in San Francisco.

Other organizations with involvement in the magazine industry include the American Society of Business Press Editors, the Agricultural Publishers' Association, and the Society of National Association Publications.

The Future for Magazines

Our need for knowledge, entertainment, and ideas assures the magazine industry of survival, probably in a greater variety of formats and forms. The electronic magazine is likely to develop in on-line and CD-ROM forms. In 1992, *Movies USA* was advertising in *Consumer Magazine and Agri-Media Rates and Data* as "now playing on computer monitors everywhere!!" with IMS on line code M007. In the same issue, Prodigy was advertising itself as "The Next Big Medium," with "unparalleled response rates for the likes of BMW, Panasonic, United Airlines, and Columbia House." These forms seem more likely to catch on than magazines faxed into the home or received on videotapes or audiotapes.

Regardless of new formats, the future of print seems assured. Most of these new formats will pass greater costs to the consumer than printed magazines do. Small-circulation magazines are almost certain to find print less expensive than electronic formats. Thus, association, public relations, and many special interest magazines, such as *Railroad Model Craftsman*, probably will continue in print format.

As the use of CD-ROM and on-line services grows, magazines in these formats may multiply, especially if postal rates and printing and paper costs rise significantly. Alternate delivery systems, which have been tested since 1972, may develop further to reduce magazine delivery costs. New magazines, especially, are advised to set subscription rates high enough to lure only readers sincerely interested in the editorial product. It is more difficult to raise subscription rates successfully after readers have become accustomed to a certain price range.

In whatever form, magazines will need editors who can process information, entertainment, and ideas into effective communication packages and distribute them efficiently to consumers. In spite of economic challenges, the future for magazines is bright. The magazine field is strong overall and offers writing, editing, photographic, design, and production opportunities to intelligent, skilled, creative people who have a never-ending curiosity and a desire to do things excellently.

Conclusion

Although there have been notable changes in individual magazines, the magazine industry as a whole is stable, and more new magazines are being established than current ones discontinued. Americans are reading magazines as a significant part of their overall communication use. The vast majority of magazines are business or public relations publications, but the largest circulations are claimed by consumer magazines. Variety in content, circulation methods, and income sources makes generalization about the magazine industry extremely difficult.

In the United States, magazines have evolved from a form of popular entertainment and nationalizing influence in the 1800s and early 1900s to a specialized form of mass communication, emphasizing the information function, especially since the development of television in the 1950s and 1960s. Magazines always have provided information, but informative ones grew more rapidly in recent decades. Magazines now meet specialized information needs that cannot be met adequately by television, radio, or newspapers.

Notes

1. Frank Luther Mott, *A History of American Magazines,* vol. 3: 1865–1885 (Cambridge, Mass.: Harvard University Press, 1938), p. 5.
2. Theodore Peterson, *Magazines in the Twentieth Century,* 2d ed. (Urbana: University of Illinois Press, 1964), pp. 13–14.
3. Magazine publishers announce "suspensions" rather than deaths. Sometimes the suspended magazine reappears years later as a semblance of itself or in a different form.
4. Frank Luther Mott, *A History of American Magazines,* vol. I: 1741–1850 (Cambridge, Mass.: Harvard University Press, 1930), p. 6.
5. Ibid., p. 7
6. Ibid.
7. *The Study of Magazine Buying Patterns* (Port Washington, N.Y.: Publishers Clearing House, 1991), p. 13.

2

Special Interest Magazines

F ROM fly fishing to flying, flower gardening to model railroading, gun lore to philately, there's a magazine for almost any interest. A family's magazine reading may cover the spectrum from a home and garden magazine that takes no stands on controversial issues through children's magazines, women's magazines, business magazines, a fraternal magazine, a travel magazine, and a hobby or craft magazine, to a fiercely controversial journal of opinion.

Special interest magazines have long been on the American scene. *Harper's Bazaar* dates from 1867, *McCall's* from 1870, *Sports Afield* from 1887, *National Geographic* from 1888, *Vogue* from 1892, *Travel/Holiday* from 1901, and *Flying Models* from 1927. However, the rapid expansion of the population, markets, and family income since World War II has aided their great increase in numbers. Having emphasized in chapter 1 that nearly all magazines throughout history have been special interest magazines, in this chapter we will discuss several, both consumer and business.[1]

Ever since it was established by E. T. Meredith in 1922, *Better Homes and Gardens* has been a leader in service journalism, as well as one of the largest circulation consumer magazines. (Courtesy *Better Homes and Gardens*®.)

Magazine Classifications

People in the business often talk about types of magazines as if there are clearly defined categories. For the most part, there are not. Standard Rate and Data Service lists 70 classifications of consumer magazines and 11 classifications of farm publications in *Consumer Magazine and Agri-Media Rates and Data.* Numerous magazines pay for duplicate listings in classifications other than their primary one. The same is true in *Business Publication Rates and Data.* Not all magazines fit neatly into clearly defined categories. With that overlap understood, we will move on to discuss a number of major groups of special interest magazines. Consumer magazines will be discussed first, then public relations magazines, and finally business publications. Not all classifications of magazines can be discussed; that would be another book or more. We will attempt to give you indications of some significant segments of the industry and its breadth.

Consumer Magazines

When magazines are mentioned, most people first think of consumer magazines. Recall from chapter 1 that consumer magazines are sold at retail like other consumer products, and most advertise consumer goods and services to their readers.

Women's and Home Service Magazines

Long the strongest portion of the American magazine publishing industry, women's and home service magazines continue to have large circulations and large amounts of advertising. Similar in many respects in their focus, home service magazines appeal more broadly to the family than do the women's magazines, which slant toward women, including their interests outside the home.

Six of the 11 largest circulation magazines are women's and home service books: *Better Homes and Gardens, Family Circle, McCall's, Woman's Day, Ladies' Home Journal,* and *Good Housekeeping.* Each has more than 4.5 million circulation.

Ladies' Home Journal was the foundation of the Curtis empire. Prior to its founding, Cyrus H. K. Curtis had indifferent successes with a few publications operated on small budgets. He was editing the women's department of the *Tribune and Farmer,* a four-year-old weekly in which he was a partner, in 1883, when Mrs. Curtis took over editing it after telling him his material sounded funny to a woman. The department grew to a page, then an eight-page supplement, then in December 1883 it became the *Ladies' Home Journal.*

Following a difference of opinion, Curtis gave his partner the *Tribune and Farmer,* which soon failed, and kept *Ladies' Home Journal.* When Mrs. Curtis retired as editor in 1889, the *Journal* led all women's magazines, with 440,000 circulation. Her successor, Edward Bok, was a 26-year-old Dutch-born bachelor, who also became a great editor, guiding the *Journal* for 21 years. He told his readers about venereal disease and civic planning, started a lovelorn column he personally wrote, and had a doctor answer questions about the care of children. Under Bok, the *Journal* was one of the first magazines to reach 1 million circulation. Bruce and Beatrice Gould followed Bok and presided over what some term the silver age of that magazine, although it began to lose money before they retired in 1962.

Both *Cosmopolitan* and *Good Housekeeping* are Hearst magazines. *Cosmopolitan* has long been known for selling most of its copies via newsstands (76 percent). Those who choose to subscribe must pay not only the full cover price of all 12 issues, but also the added cost of mailing. *Good Housekeeping,* edited in recent years by John Mack Carter, sells three-fourths of its circulation by subscription.

Most women's fashion, beauty, and grooming magazines are in the 500,000 to 1 million circulation bracket, except for *Glamour,* at more than 2 million. Condé Nast publishes *Glamour, Mademoiselle,* and *Vogue.* Hearst issues *Harper's Bazaar.* Fairchild publishes *W.*

Usually called shelter books in the trade, the home service magazines cover a wide range of topics: food, appliances, decorating, gardening, health, autos, family entertainment, travel, home maintenance, and consumer buying. The circulation leader in the field is a relative newcomer, *Better Homes and Gardens,* established in 1922 by E. T. Meredith of Des Moines. From the beginning, his magazine aimed at men as well as women readers and stressed service to the point of insisting that each article help the reader do something. Both *House Beautiful* and *House & Garden* preceded Meredith's magazine (1896 and 1901, respectively), but both have always been class-oriented.

The Southern Pacific Railroad started *Sunset* in 1898 to promote rail travel on its Sunset Limited and to extol the virtues of the West. Its employees bought it in 1914 and made it into a regional literary magazine. L. W. Lane, an advertising staff member of *Better Homes and Gardens,* bought it in 1928 to make it a homeowners' magazine for the West Coast. *Sunset,* the Magazine of Western Living, is now distributed nationally to more than 1.5 million circulation and is owned by Time Warner. *Southern Living,* begun by *The Progressive Farmer* of Birmingham, Alabama, in 1966, now has a circulation of 2.3 million and is also owned by Time Warner.

Leisure Time and Avocational Magazines

A trip to any well-stocked newsstand reveals a variety of leisure time and avocational magazines. *Consumer Magazine Rates and Data* has more than a score of classifications for these magazines, ranging alphabetically from art and antiques, automotive, camping, and crafts and hobbies to romance, sports, travel, and TV and radio. It lists more than 70 automotive magazines, and 17 motorcycle magazines.

Four coin publications circulate an average of 75,500 copies per issue. *Lapidary Journal* circulates 35,000 copies per issue, *Tropical Fish Hobbyist* 58,000, and *Flying Models* 23,000. These circulations are small in comparison with the circulation giants, but coin collectors, rockhounds, and other hobbyists are intensely interested in their publications, making them the most efficient means for reaching potential customers.

Robert Petersen of Los Angeles and his partner Robert Lindsay started *Hot Rod* in 1948 on $400 cash and credit with a printer. They hung around race tracks to sell copies, and within a year the magazine was making money. Petersen's other

One of the largest circulation women's magazines, *Ladies' Home Journal* dates to 1883. It is now owned by Meredith Corporation, publishers of *Better Homes and Gardens* and several other magazines. (Courtesy of *Ladies' Home Journal* © Meredith Corp. 1993.)

A bold new cover design greeted readers of *WildBird* in January 1993, the beginning of its seventh year. It is published by Fancy Publications, Inc., which also issues *Cat Fancy, Dog Fancy,* and a dozen other magazines. (Courtesy WILDBIRD®, © 1993.)

magazines include *Car Craft, Circle Track, Dirt Rider, 4 Wheel, Guns & Ammo, Hot Rod, Hunting, Motorcyclist, Motor Trend, Photographic, Pro Football, Skin Diver,* and *'Teen.*

Two duck hunters waiting in a blind got the idea for *Field & Stream* and established it in 1895. It is edited for outdoor sportsmen and their families, giving them advice on hunting, fishing, camping, boating, archery, conservation, sportsmen's dogs, and travel. *Sports Afield* was started in 1887 and *Outdoor Life* in 1898.

Aiming at the gun enthusiast is *Shooting Times,* published by PJS [Peoria Journal Star] Publications. In the same vein are *Guns & Ammo, Guns, Gun World,* and *Handloader,* all issued by magazine publishing companies. *American Rifleman* is the official publication of the National Rifle Association. *Skeet Shooting Review* serves members of the National Skeet Shooting Association, and the Amateur Trapshooting Association has *Trap & Field* published for its members by the Indianapolis organization that publishes today's *Saturday Evening Post.*

Outdoor magazines focusing on specific regions include *Western Outdoor News, Western Outdoors, Southern Outdoors, Salt Water Sportsman,* and *Midwest Outdoors.* A number of state publications serve outdoor interests, too, including *Florida Sportsman, Michigan Out-Of-Doors,* and *Texas Fisherman.*

Several attempts at publishing senior citizens' magazines failed because the potential readers wanted to read about and identify with young people, and advertisers were interested in reaching a younger market. Most successful magazines in this field have been aimed at professionally organized groups of senior citizens, such as the American Association of Retired Persons. The rapid increase in the number and wealth of older citizens has expanded this market, and AARP's *Modern Maturity* is now the largest circulation magazine in the United States. Everyone who joins AARP receives the magazine. The National Association of Retired Federal Employees publishes *Retirement Life,* and The Reader's Digest Association issues *New Choices.*

Metropolitan and Regional Magazines

Originally bland chamber of commerce puff publications, metropolitan magazines have developed over the last two decades into an independent, vigorous portion of the magazine industry. Some credit for leading the way belongs to *San Diego* mag-

Modern Maturity goes to 22.5 million members of the American Association of Retired Persons every other month, making it America's largest circulation magazine. (Courtesy *Modern Maturity.*)

One of several magazines for associations of retired persons, *Retirement Life* is published monthly for 449,000 retired federal employees. (Courtesy *Retirement Life,* official publication of the National Association of Retired Federal Employees.)

The Retired Officer goes to 379,000 officers of the seven uniformed services and their families each month, reporting on developments in defense and military retirement matters, officers' rights and benefits and veterans' affairs. (Courtesy *The Retired Officer* Magazine, Illustration by Eric Westbrook.)

azine, which was started by an independent publisher in 1948 and became the liberal voice in a conservative city served by conservative newspapers.

Philadelphia distinguished itself by helping to update the city's airport and blowing the whistle on questionable real estate maneuvers under the guise of urban renewal. It has won National Magazine Awards for specialized journalism, public interest (twice), and service to the individual. A respected voice in the nation's capital, *Washingtonian* has been honored with National Magazine Awards for reporting (two), public interest, service to the individual, and feature writing.

One of the most interesting and creative magazines since its inception in 1973, *Texas Monthly* has become known for overall high quality and investigative reporting. It has received National Magazine Awards for general excellence in its circulation class twice, reporting twice, public interest, photography, and specialized journalism.

Consumer Magazine and Agri-Media Rates and Data lists 190 metropolitan, regional, and state magazines. *Honolulu* dates from 1888. *Philadelphia* goes back to 1908. However, the majority were established since 1970.

The City and Regional Magazine Association has its own competition, the White Awards, based at the University of Kansas. Winners in 1992 included *D* magazine for general excellence in circulation above 50,000, *St. Louis* for general excellence under 50,000 circulation, *Milwaukee* for commentary, *Washingtonian* for general criticism, *Chicago* for investigative writing, *San Francisco Focus* for public affairs reporting, *Atlanta* for service to readers, and *Arkansas Times* the White Medal for writing. In design categories, *Toronto Life* won for feature design in color, spread design, and special projects; *Atlanta* for feature design in black and white; *San Francisco* for cover design; and *Tampa Bay Life* for fashion.

About 20 states have state-aided travel or outdoor magazines. Although obviously promoting their states, they strongly appeal to their readers, and several are known for their excellent photography and color reproduction. The leader is *Arizona Highways,* a monthly started in 1925 as a black-and-white bulletin of technical engineering information. It later developed into a state travel magazine world renowned for its color photos and reproduction. Closest in circulation and editorial quality is *Vermont Life,* a relative newcomer begun in 1946.

To make up losses incurred in publishing the magazines, *Arizona Highways* and *Vermont Life* both sell related products: calendars, engagement books, copies of pictures, and bound volumes of magazines. Most similar magazines require some subsidy.

Washingtonian has had a distinguished record of editorial excellence since its founding in 1965. (Courtesy *Washingtonian.*)

One of the most successful—and award winning—regional magazines is *Texas Monthly,* based in Austin. (Courtesy *Texas Monthly.*)

One of the largest circulation regional magazines is *Yankee,* published in the 6″ × 9″ format. (Reprinted with permission from the April 1992 issue of *Yankee* Magazine, published in Dublin, N.H.)

A weekly opinion magazine on political and social topics, *The Nation* varies its covers from illustrations, such as the cover about public schools, to the printed word, such as the one dealing with the character of presidents. It also reviews literature and the arts and has been continuously published since 1865. (Courtesy of *The Nation* Magazine. Public schools cover illustration by Robert Grossman.)

A weekly opinion magazine on political and social topics, *The New Republic* also deals with books and the arts. (Reprinted by permission of *The New Republic* © 1992, The New Republic, Inc.)

Several independently published magazines are regional. *Yankee* is a 6 × 9-inch magazine jammed with advertising and several articles on New England each month. Its publishers in Dublin, New Hampshire, say it is "published for New Englanders everywhere."

Opinion Magazines

A handful of magazines that deal with public affairs in a broad sense, usually from a well-defined point of view, have been influential by raising social issues in their pages before the issues become generally popular. These opinion magazines typically have circulations of 20,000 to 100,000 and need subsidies to remain in operation. Although they are similar in these characteristics, they do not agree on their views.

The oldest of these is *The Nation,* established in 1865 by E. L. Godkin, who had immigrated from Ireland in 1856 to write about conditions in the South. He was critical of much of what he saw in America, and his magazine condemned Tammany Hall, the Populists, and the railroad barons, but it also attacked trade unionism and the eight-hour workday. In 1918, after Oswald Garrison Villard had become editor, one issue was held up five days by the Post Office as unmailable until President Wilson intervened.[2]

The Nation is published weekly. Another liberal magazine is the *New Republic,* started in 1914 and issued weekly. The conservative *National Review* of William F. Buckley, Jr., is the most recent entry, 1955.

Three religion-related magazines can be counted in this group: *Christian Century,* a Protestant weekly begun in 1900; *Commonweal,* a Catholic lay magazine begun in 1924; and *Commentary,* a Jewish monthly originated in 1945.

John Schacht observed that the print medium is ideal for discussion of complex issues of human society, and that these magazines are influential as a result of continued repetition of basic themes. "In major issues the journals' views have preceded, not coincided with or followed, government action and changes in public opinion," he said.[3]

These magazines usually keep a major issue in their readers' minds over a period of years, not just when the issue is hot in the other magazines and media. Their approach is usually philosophical, ethical, analytical, and calculated to bring about positive action.

One publisher of an opinion magazine says the magazines in this group don't have to be popular, so they can either say things the big magazines won't say or say them earlier. After an opinion magazine runs the piece, a big book may pick up the issue and do a story. Another publisher claims that the leader or activist turns to his journal for the argument about the issue.

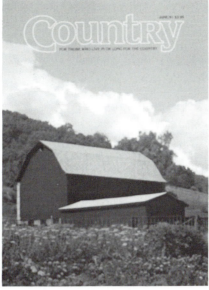

A magazine that steadfastly refuses to accept advertising or to permit advertisers to use its research findings and ratings, *Consumer Reports* serves subscribers with its product testing each month. (Courtesy *Consumer Reports*.)

Country magazine brings beautiful scenes from the countryside into numerous homes without any advertising content. One of a handful of adless consumer magazines, it is published in Greendale, Wisconsin. (Courtesy *Country*.)

Adless Magazines

Thousands of public relations and association magazines carry no advertising, but only an infinitesimal minority of nonsponsored consumer magazines rely solely on subscription and single-copy income to remain in business. A few are worth noting, as are a few that have changed and now accept advertising.

Consumer Reports was established in 1936 to report monthly on the independent testing of consumer products by Consumers Union. The magazine does not accept advertising. It forbids the use of its test findings and recommendations for commercial purposes and has won several suits against companies that have violated that prohibition. It also has won National Magazine Awards for public interest and personal service.

Ms. published advertising from its beginning in 1972 until its suspension in late 1990. After selling a large number of subscriptions for an ad-free bimonthly magazine in 1991, it resumed publication as a totally editorial magazine. Renewals at the end of the first year were unusually high, and the publisher reports that the magazine is making a profit.[4]

Editor Harvey Kurtzman and publisher William Gaines transformed *Mad* from a hardback book into a satire magazine in comic book format in 1955. *Mad* accepted some advertising for a very brief time, but it was incongruous with the overall tone and was eliminated.

When DeWitt and Lila Acheson Wallace started *Reader's Digest* in 1922, it contained no advertising. It operated successfully as an all-editorial magazine for more than 30 years but, facing a $1 million deficit in 1954, decided to begin accepting advertising with the April 1955 issue.

Kiplinger's Personal Finance began as *Changing Times* in 1947 and operated without advertising until 1980.

American Heritage began in 1949 as a spare-time project of Earle W. Newton, publisher of *Vermont Life*. He issued the quarterly with the help of one paid employee and with backing from the American Association of State and Local History. The magazine was sold in 1954 and later began accepting advertising. Currently publishing eight issues a year, it is a division of Forbes Inc.

Two other adless magazines were started by *American Heritage. Americana* was begun in 1958 and *Horizon* in 1973. Both accept ads and are under separate ownerships.

The adless consumer magazine is unusual. Most publishers who have tried to succeed without ads have resorted to them to remain in business.

Little Magazines

Magazines that publish artistic work that is not commercially acceptable to large circulation magazines are called little magazines or little literary magazines. They claim originality, intellectual honesty, and literary influence, and they protest the smugness and security they believe accompany commercial success. Many have been produced by individuals on mimeograph machines or other inexpensive duplicators. Little magazines usually are more for their writers than for their readers. However, a study in 1946 concluded that little magazines had discovered about 80 percent of the important novelists, poets, and critics who began to write after 1912, and that they introduced and remained the basic magazines to publish 95 percent of the poets of this period.[5]

The first modern little magazine in the United States was the short-lived *Dial,* edited by Emerson, Thoreau, and Margaret Fuller (1840–44). There have been at least three *Dials* since. *Poetry,* founded by Harriet Monroe in 1912, has survived. So have the *Partisan Review* (1934) and *Hudson Review* (1948). Most that have survived are subsidized by universities.

The *Sewanee Review* dates from 1892 and is published by the University of the South, Sewanee, Tennessee. The *Midland* of Iowa City lasted 12 years and inspired *The Prairie Schooner* (1927) and *The Frontier,* later combined and published as *The Prairie Schooner* at the University of Nebraska.

The distinguished *Kenyon Review,* established in 1939, fell victim to budget cutting at Kenyon College in 1970. After it was reestablished in 1979, it achieved more than twice its previous circulation record in less than two years. The *South Atlantic Quarterly,* headquartered at Duke University, has published literature and history since 1902. *Southern Review* is published at Louisiana State University, and the *Georgia Review* at the University of Georgia.

Major universities believe that a journal of humanities is a worthwhile venture, by either keeping an established magazine going or beginning a new one. Some of these combine public affairs, politics, humanities, and the arts with literary content.

The Little Magazine in America,[6] a documentary history published in 1978, includes an annotated listing of 84 little magazines with such titles as *Clown War, Evergreen Review, Hearse, Kayak, Kulchur, Mulch, Parnassus, Wild Dog,* and *Yugen.*

A knowledgeable magazine publisher planning to make a profit would not start an opinion magazine or a little magazine, nor would a journalism graduate plan a career editing such a publication. Neither type is conventional or commercially successful magazine journalism.

A university-based literary quarterly, *The Georgia Review* has won the National Magazine Award for fiction. (Courtesy *The Georgia Review.*)

Public Relations Magazines

Millions of American families regularly receive magazines from their auto dealers, employers, or corporations in which they own stock. This area of magazine journalism perhaps started in 1840, when the *Lowell Offering* was begun as an outlet for the literary expression of Lowell Cotton Mills' workers in Lowell, Massachusetts. Other early company-sponsored magazines were *The Mechanic* of the H. B. Smith Machine Company of Smithville, New Jersey, in 1847, and the two oldest magazines extant, one started as *The Travelers Record* of the Travelers Insurance Company in 1865, and the other *The Locomotive* of the Hartford Steam Boiler Inspection and Insurance Company in 1867.

The magazines were issued for general circulation. *The Travelers Record* circulated 50,000 copies of its first issue to hotels, clubs, barber shops, and other gathering places. At that time, *The Saturday Evening Post, Harper's Weekly,* and other leading magazines had fewer than 75,000 circulation. The great growth of general interest periodicals in the 1890s led the Travelers Insurance Company to change its magazine to *The Agents Record* and reduce circulation by limiting it to its agents. It was combined with *The Agents Bulletin* in 1918, and the name was changed to *Protection.*

The first periodical specifically for employees was *The Triphammer,* begun in 1885 by the Massey Manufacturing Company, later to be Massey-Ferguson. *Factory News* of the National Cash Register Company was established in 1890 as a 12-page monthly. It was succeeded in 1967 by a smart, black-and-white, 32-page bi-monthly, *NCR World.*

Many terms have been applied to periodicals of corporations and businesses. The early term *house organ* has undesirable connotations to many in the field, having been applied at a time when those publications often were blatantly one-sided and unreliable. The term still is in widespread use, both by detractors and impartial observers.

When practitioners in this field organized their professional groups in the late 1930s and 1940s, the terms *industrial journalism* and *industrial publications* emerged. The term *industrial magazine,* however, often is confused with business publications that are not sponsored by a single company; in 1961, Baird and Turnbull settled on *company publication* as an appropriate descriptive term. Some editors prefer the term *organizational magazine.*

Because these publications nearly always are issued to advance the aims of a company, and their objectives are compatible with corporate policy, we have adopted the term *public relations magazines* as appropriately descriptive. These magazines are aimed at specific publics of the company in an attempt to achieve certain objectives. They may be issued by the public relations department, corporate relations, corporate communications, or even the personnel department, but their objectives are public relations.

An employee magazine, *Measure* is published six times a year by Corporate Public Relations for Hewlett-Packard employees. (Courtesy *Measure/ Hewlett-Packard Co.)*

Types of Public Relations Magazines

Public relations magazines vary in size, frequency, and purpose. Large companies, such as Ford Motor Company, have a publications division. Very small companies may have an editor in charge of the company magazine, the employee newspaper, and special brochures or other publications. There are at least six types of public relations magazines.

Employee magazines tell employees about employees' achievements, the company's achievements and objectives, company policy and procedure, employee benefits, and other information of interest or importance to employees. Current issues, such as the environment and recycling, usually are included. A large company may assign many of these functions to plant or regional employee newspapers and make the magazine a national voice of corporate policy, objectives, and achievements augmented by general interest content and features that show how parts of the company operate by focusing on people.

A major story in each issue may be how the company is facing a current challenge, meeting its social responsibility, or trying to maximize profits. It may be a negative story, such as downsizing, with emphasis on the long-term benefits for continuing employees, or reductions in employee benefits. Some content concerns broad issues that affect both employees and the company, and possibly the community.

It's sometimes hard to tell an employee magazine from another type, such as a shareholder magazine. Attention to broad issues and general interest content makes them look alike. More emphasis on employees, employee policy, or employee promotions and service anniversaries generally characterizes the employee magazine.

The typical employee magazine recognizes employee activities and achievements, lists service anniversaries, and features company news. Some include a column by the company president or employee questions answered by company officials.

Customer magazines are published for owners of relatively expensive products for which brand and dealer loyalty are desired. Besides providing information and entertainment, a customer magazine reminds customers of the desirability of owning the brand of product, gives ideas for using it and information about its care and upkeep, and introduces new models. Dealers often are required to pay part of the cost of customer magazines to avoid waste circulation and keep the mailing list cur-

BP America publishes *Shield* four times a year for external constituents, such as investors, and BP employees and annuitants. (Courtesy BP.)

Edited for a combination of audiences, *JD Journal* is published for John Deere employees, retirees, dealers, and friends worldwide. (Courtesy *JD Journal*, corporate magazine of Deere & Company.)

Chevy Outdoors covers outdoor recreation and recreation vehicles. The quarterly circulates to the 1 million people who qualify for a free three-year BPA-audited subscription. They need not own a Chevy to qualify. (Courtesy The Aegis Group: Publishers.)

GO, the Goodyear dealer magazine, advises Goodyear dealers each month of successful sales strategies. (Courtesy *GO*, Goodyear Tire & Rubber Company.)

Pace Communications of Greensboro, North Carolina, publishes the monthly *Hemispheres* for United Airlines. United's inflight magazines go back to 1957 and *United Mainliner*. (Courtesy of *Hemispheres*, the inflight magazine for United Airlines.)

rent. Among the best edited and most interesting magazines, customer magazines took a blow at the end of 1992, when Ford Motor Company discontinued *Ford Times* and GM's Chevrolet Division discontinued *Friends*.

Shareholder or corporate magazines are aimed at investors who are interested in earnings and dividends, operating costs, research and new products, and legislation that affects the company. Many of these magazines include material of more general interest to avoid overplaying the company. Many corporations send the corporate magazine to employees in addition to the employee magazine or newspaper. Exxon Corporation's *The Lamp* and *The Texaco Star* are two examples of handsome, colorful, excellently printed shareholder magazines.

Sales magazines tell salespeople about products and how to sell them, aiming to help the company's salespersons operate more effectively.

Dealer magazines maintain a flow of information about company products to dealers, who often sell other brands of the same product. Thus, these magazines attempt to build brand loyalty, pass along successful merchandising ideas, and attempt to increase cooperation between the merchandiser and the manufacturer by explaining and interpreting company policies, such as warranties and return policies. *GO*, the Goodyear dealer magazine, usually features one or two tire dealers, reports on unusual uses of Goodyear tires, and includes some company news in each issue.

Technical service magazines are found in fields in which technical data are important in making the best possible use of the sponsor's products. In competitive fields, the magazine tries to be the tie-breaker in having professionals specify their use of its brand over its competitors' brands, as well as give technical data for their use of its brand. The magazine also may contribute to the prestige of the sponsor and its products.

Clearances

In the corporate setting, editors often find it mandatory to have material cleared within the company prior to publication. In one survey, 20 percent of the responding editors had to go through five or more clearances for some major stories, although nearly 40 percent said they could publish after one or two clearances. Large companies required more clearances than smaller ones. Using 5,000 employees as the point between the two sizes, the survey found that 69 percent of the large companies and 51 percent of the small companies required three or more clearances. A legal clearance usually is required.

Editors within corporations also have to be careful about the use of the company's trademarks and, in employee magazines, about labor law and National Labor Relations Board decisions. In both cases, editors work with company legal counsel and have copy cleared before publication.

Business Magazines

Established in 1783, *Philadelphia Price Current* is reported to have been the first U.S. business publication. It provided wholesale commodity prices and marine information to merchants and shippers. Other early ones were *New York Prices Current,* 1795; *Butchers' and Packers' Gazette,* 1808; *General Shipping and Commercial List,* 1815; *American Journal of Pharmacy,* 1825; and the *American Railroad Journal,* 1832. Their growth paralleled the growth of industry in general, and by 1900 there were about 300 business publications.

The factors that led to national markets for national brands also led to the need to reach wholesalers and retailers with information about their business fields. For instance, businesspeople involved in manufacturing appliances or automobiles need to read about machinery, steel, plastics, management, and related subjects. Engineers read about engineering developments as well as new materials and processes.

The American Business Press, which represents publishers of about 400 business publications, has developed a comprehensive definition of the business press: "independent, specialized periodicals of a business, technical, scientific, professional, or marketing nature, published in either a magazine or newspaper format, and issued in regularly specified frequencies to serve special fields of private or public enterprise and not directed to the public at large." Two key elements of this definition are that it eliminates association- or company-sponsored publications and publications sold to the general (consumer) public. *Business Publication Rates and Data* does not limit its listings to independent publications.

The range of business magazines spans the breadth of American business. *Business Publication Rates and Data* has 177 classifications of publications from advertising and marketing through brewing, computers, electronic engineering, restaurants and food service, and telecommunications to woodworking. The number of classifications changes as new industries become established and others disappear.

Examples that suggest the diversity of business publications include *Aviation Week & Space Technology, Aerospace Products, American Druggist, Appliance Manufacturer, Architectural Record, Automotive Industries, Automotive News, Candy Industry, Candy Marketer, Candy Wholesaler, Discount Store News, Apparel Merchandising, Industrial Equipment News, New Equipment Digest,* and *Women's Wear Daily.* The computer field is served by a wide array, which includes *Byte, CADalyst, Computer Buying World, Computer Graphics World, Computer Technology Review, Computerworld, Datamation, Infoworld, LAN Times, MacUser, PC Week,* and *PC World.* Electronic engineering books include *Electronics, EDN, ECN (Electronic Component News), Design News,* and *Electronics Purchasing.*

Among the magazines for journalists are *Circulation Management, Editor & Publisher, Folio: The Magazine for Magazine Management, Magazine Design & Production, Newspapers & Technology,* and *Publishing & Production Executive.* Advertisers have *Advertising Age* and *Adweek.*

Numerous new local business publications have developed throughout the country over the past 15 years, such as *Business Atlanta, Crain's Chicago Business, Crain's New York Business, Baton Rouge Business Report,* and *The Los Angeles Business Journal.*

Growth in the number of business magazines has resulted from three factors: new industries or businesses emerging to serve new technologies or markets; specialization within an industry, which results in splitting off one or more new specialties; and the regionalization of magazines to serve such areas as the West or South.

Conclusion

There is almost no end to what can be written about special interest magazines. As long as there are enough readers interested in a particular topic and enough advertisers interested in those readers, a special interest magazine on that topic is feasible and likely to be attempted.

Notes

1. *Consumer Magazine and Agri-Media Rates and Data* has a classification titled General Editorial, in which it lists 70 titles, including *American Heritage, American Legion Magazine, CrimeBeat, Ebony, Grit, Harper's, Mother Jones, National Enquirer, National Geographic, Natural History, The New Yorker, Philip Morris Magazine, Reader's Digest, Reader's Digest Hispanic Edition, Smithsonian, Town & Country, Utne Reader, Vanity Fair,* and *Wildlife Conservation.* How general are these general editorial magazines?
2. Theodore Peterson, *Magazines in the Twentieth Century,* 2d ed. (Urbana: University of Illinois Press, 1964), pp. 417–20.
3. John H. Schacht, *The Journals of Opinion and Reportage: An Assessment* (New York: Magazine Publishers Association, 1966), p. 38.
4. Maria Braden, "Ms. Doesn't Miss the Ads," *The Quill* (January–February 1992): 24.
5. Frederick J. Hoffman, Charles Allen, and Carolyn F. Ulrich, *The Little Magazine: A History and Bibliography* (Princeton, N.J.: Princeton University Press, 1946), p. 8.
6. Elliot Anderson and Mary Kinzie, *The Little Magazine in America* (Yonkers, N.Y.: Pushcart Press, 1978).

Starting a Magazine

3

M AGAZINES succeed or fail for many reasons. They succeed if they represent the right idea at the right time, offering information or editorial service that appeals to a sufficient number of potential readers who appeal to a sufficient number of advertisers.

Magazines fail because they lack an editorial reason for existence, lack of sufficient advertising base, undertake inadequate testing to assure a reasonable expectation of success, lack sufficient capital to stay in business until they can become profitable, or lack knowledge of and experience in the magazine field. Edmund Wilson also asserted that a magazine is much like a living organism, growing mature, then eventually growing old, declining, and dying.[1] Contemporary marketing theory, however, suggests that a product, such as a magazine, can be repositioned and need not decline and die.

Special Interest Content

Throughout most of the 20th century, magazines have been edited for special interests. Even the few large circulation general interest magazines of the middle third of the century—the weekly *Life* and *Saturday Evening Post* and the biweekly *Look*— appealed to an identifiable segment of American society. Their demise in the late '60s and early '70s affirmed that the future of the American magazine is in special interests. Even *TV Guide,* for a while the largest-circulation American magazine, is a special interest book.

Statistics cannot tell us enough about the potential for a new magazine to succeed. Most magazines that go out of business don't announce it, and some new magazines disappear before they have been recorded by industry watchers. The Magazine Publishers of America tried to keep score of launches and failures for many years, but ceased in 1972 when *Folio: The Magazine for Magazine Management* started keeping track. *Folio:* stopped in 1979 because it was simply impossible to find out about every launch and every failure. More recently, Samir Husni of the University of Mississippi has been publishing an annual directory of new magazines. Figures from these sources suggest that more magazines succeed than fail, resulting in a growing field.

There are several kinds of magazine launches. The storybook start-on-a-shoestring makes a good story but is a long shot. The launch of a magazine with "almost enough" financing occasionally succeeds by cutting costs and catching on quickly. The carefully developed, tested, and adequately funded idea of an existing magazine publisher has a reasonably good chance of succeeding, and the outstandingly developed, tested, and financed launches of a giant publisher, such as Time Inc., has the best chance, which one expert places at one in two, or 50 percent. A business publication using controlled circulation can be launched with less money and probably a greater chance for success.

Some experts estimate that only 1 in 10 planned new magazines will succeed, and hundreds each year don't even get off the drawing board. Dozens of publishers never produce a first issue, either because of dismal test results or lack of money. Dozens more fail in their first couple of years. It takes a blend of factors to start a successful magazine, but the editorial concept and its execution are the most important. Alan Petricof, a venture capitalist who has arranged magazine financing, said, "One of the biggest problems is most magazines are started by editors and by people who have never started a magazine before. They fail to assemble a team of qualified people."[2]

Henry R. Luce. (Photographed by Alfred Eisenstaedt, courtesy *Life Magazine*.)

Figure 3.1 *Time*'s first cover. (Courtesy Time Inc.)

The Weekly Newsmagazine

Briton Hadden and Henry R. Luce were both 24 years old when they founded Time Inc. in 1922. Hadden and Luce managed the undergraduate newspaper at Yale and conceived the idea of a publication that would present news in a more orderly fashion than the day's newspapers and cover world events more adequately than the day's magazines. Their magazine would organize the week's news into departments, give the news in narrative form, and describe the people who made the news. As Wood describes it, "*Time* would select the facts, tell what the facts meant, and state or strongly suggest what the reader should think or feel about them. The new magazine was to be 'curt, clear, complete,' so written and arranged that each issue would be an orderly and coherent account of the preceding week's news.[3]

The idea was nurtured during their service together at an officers' training camp during World War I and later while working on Frank Munsey's Baltimore *News*. Early in 1922, they quit their jobs to begin raising money for their magazine, which they called *Facts*. With the help of friends and acquaintances, they raised $86,000, renamed the magazine *Time,* brought out a specimen issue dated December 30, 1922, and published the first issue March 3, 1923 (figure 3.1).

Raw news was clipped from the daily newspapers, especially the *New York Times*. Hadden and Luce took turns editing and at times writing 50 to 70 percent of the magazine.

Time lost $39,454 by the end of 1923, and in September 1925 the operation was moved to Cleveland to save money. In August 1927, Luce and Hadden returned to New York, where there was a supply of young intellectuals they could hire for comparatively small salaries and where they could get the *New York Times* 10 hours earlier. The first year a profit was shown had been 1926.[4]

Hadden thought the news of advertising needed to be summarized as *Time* summarized general news, and in April 1927 the company began *Tide,* an advertising trade magazine. After Hadden's death in 1929, executives were more concerned with the company's new magazine, *Fortune,* and late in 1930 *Tide* was sold to Raymond Rubicam of Young & Rubicam advertising agency. Rubicam sold it in 1948, and, after four other ownership changes, *Tide* ceased publication in 1959.

Fortune also was a spin-off of *Time,* whose business section was too small to carry all the material produced by the staff. Henry Luce suggested starting a magazine of restricted circulation to utilize *Time*'s leftover business material, and he suggested the name. The company established a department in 1928 to work out plans for the new magazine. By late 1929, it had produced a dummy, and the first issue of *Fortune* (February 1930) appeared shortly after the stock market crash (figure 3.2).[5]

In 1936, the name *Life* was purchased from the former humor magazine and attached to the company's new picture magazine started that same year. *Life*'s early success could have killed it. Advertising rates had been set on an estimated 250,000 circulation, but its first press run of 466,000 sold out (figure 3.3), and for months the more copies it sold the more money it lost. Because of the high cost of the coated paper required for good picture reproduction, the loss, instead of being small as anticipated, hit $50,000 weekly, totaling $6 millon before *Life* began to pay back on its investment.[6]

Time Inc. developed a "think" magazine in 1947, but it was never published. However, after a year of experimenting with a recreation magazine, the company narrowed the scope to sports and brought out *Sports Illustrated* in August 1954 (figure 3.4). It had 250,000 subscribers from mail promotion before it had a name, and after six months' publication its circulation was 575,000.

Time Inc. had Louis Harris and Associates conduct a survey on six possible magazines that could be bound into *Life* or issued separately. Paul Wilkes mentioned in *New York* magazine January 12, 1970, that the circulation possibilities were *Movie,* 1.5 million; *Your Health,* 1.2 million; *Your Money,* 900,000; *For Children,* 800,000; *Travel,* 735,000; and *Food,* 667,000. The last two were considered unacceptable risks, but *Life*'s leaders decided to test the possible food magazine further because it was well conceived and well edited.

The industry heard in spring 1972 that Time would bring out *Money* in October and probably follow with *Well,* the latest name for the health magazine, by midwinter. Two other magazines were still in the works: *Camera Month,* a photography magazine, and *View,* a magazine of "the moving image."

Money still had not been a smashing success, with its 883,000 circulation, by June 1981, but the unexpected bonanza had been *People,* launched with the issue of March 4, 1974, and in the black within 18 months. *People* has little in common with the other Time Inc. magazines because it is a newsstand magazine sold primarily in supermarkets, is read by more women than men, does not spend heavily on name writers or news bureaus, and has no editorial color.[7]

The first national weekly launched since *Sports Illustrated* 20 years earlier, *People* also was the first magazine Time launched using market research. Two prices and two degrees of promotion were tested in 11 cities in August 1973. A follow-up issue was never published but was printed for testing in October "with a decidedly improved design." The board of directors approved the start October 18.[8] *Time* reported that 85 percent of the test issue copies were sold, spurring the decision to begin regular publication, and that the decision not to promote mail subscriptions was prompted largely by increased second-class postage rates.[9]

Although *Well* and *View* had been under development to follow *Money* onto newsstands, *People* was the one that was introduced and succeeded beyond expectations. Time continued its magazine development and, in late 1977, had a dem-

Figure 3.2 Cover of the first issue of *Fortune*. (Courtesy *Fortune Magazine*.)

Figure 3.3 *Life*'s first cover featured Margaret Bourke-White's photo of a dam at Fort Peck, Montana. (Courtesy *Life Magazine*.)

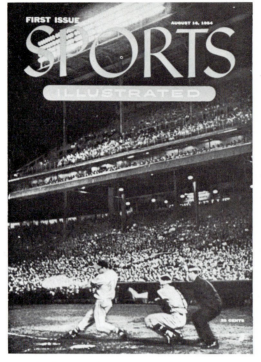

Figure 3.4 Cover of the first issue of *Sports Illustrated*, August 16, 1954. It took nine years and $20 million before this magazine showed a profit. (Illustration courtesy *Sports Illustrated*.)

As a monthly with an editorial concept different from its predecessor weekly publication, *Life* debuted with the October 1978 issue. (Courtesy LIFE copyright 1978 Time Inc. Reprinted with permission.)

onstration copy of *Woman* prepared for reader reaction, based on two years of study.[10] *Woman* was planned to be a pocketbook-sized weekly sold mainly through supermarkets and appealing more to the women who read *Ms.* and *Working Woman* than those who read *Woman's Day* and *Family Circle*.[11] The 92-page prototype issue was the only one produced.

Fortune, a monthly of 627,000 circulation, increased to 26 issues a year in January 1978. As a biweekly, its circulation was 732,000 in 1992.

Life was reestablished as a monthly magazine in October 1978 and was circulating 1.82 million copies per issue in 1992.

Time Inc. entered the highly competitive field of science magazines with *Discover* in October 1980. The first issue carried 62 pages of advertising, and reader demand exceeded expectations to the point that the rate base was increased by 50 percent to 600,000 effective April 1981 and grew to 990,000 by mid-1984. *Discover* absorbed *Science 86* and then in 1987 was sold to Family Media, Inc.[12] It is now owned by the Walt Disney Magazine Publishing Group, Inc.

Perhaps the greatest launch in magazine history was announced by Time Inc. for 1983. *TV-Cable Week,* with a commitment of $100 million over five years to establish the magazine, was to begin in seven markets in April and expand to 20 or 30 cable systems by the end of the year. A separate edition would be published for each cable system that signed an agreement with the magazine.

Conceptually, the magazine dated to 1971 and *View*. It was backed by more than 20 months of corporate planning. More than fifty 10-year business plans were evaluated. The worst one had *TV-Cable Week* losing $1 billion in the first year. *Select* and *View* were considered as names but dropped in favor of *TV-Cable Week*.

The 1971 idea of an entertainment magazine about television, film, and theater was considered to be too costly. A 1978 proposal for a guide only for cable was dropped. However, in 1981, a task force took on the project and investigated a partnership with the cable industry and selling the magazine through cable operators to their subscribers. A production specialist spent nine months developing a system

Using no editorial color, *People* focuses on "the newsworthy rather than just the news." (Courtesy Time Inc.)

In the Time Inc. tradition, *Sports Illustrated* features outstanding sports photography and bright writing. (Courtesy Time Inc.)

Time developed into an all-color magazine editorially, with bureaus around the world. (Courtesy Time Inc.)

to sort millions of cable listings and transmit them electronically to regional printing plants. Focus groups offered critiques of existing cable guides in more than two dozen cities.

As the planning continued, competitors signed cable systems in some cities. A Buffalo, New York, system began promoting *TV Guide,* for example.[13] *TV-Cable Week* got out of the gate in April as planned. It moved into its 18th market in San Diego in September, and it ceased publication with the September 25 issue, having lost an estimated $47 million.

Time Inc. developed into a mass communication conglomerate from a single magazine. Its operations included Time-Life Books, Book-of-the-Month Club, Home Box Office, American Television & Communications Corp. (a cable television systems operator), and a television station. Then, in 1989, it announced a merger with Warner Communications to form Time Warner Inc., "the largest media corporation in the world."[14]

Ben H. Bagdikian, the media critic, wrote that Time Warner

has more technical communication power than most governments. Its assets are greater than the combined gross national product of Bolivia, Jordan, Nicaragua, Albania, Liberia, and Mali. It is the largest magazine publisher in the United States, with *Time, Life, Fortune, Sports Illustrated,* among others. Its aggregate worldwide readership exceeds 120 million. It is the second-largest cable company in the world, one of the largest book publishers (Time-Life Books; . . . Little, Brown; Book-of-the-Month Club), the world's largest video company, and owner of subsidiaries in Australia, Asia, Europe, and Latin America."[15]

Time Warner's own 1991 annual report stated:

Time Inc., America's premier magazine publisher, with 40 percent of the [consumer magazine] industry's profits and one-third of its revenues, led the way in dealing with the profound impact of the worst slump in advertising revenues in fifty years. *People, Sports Illustrated* and *Time* were the three leading magazines in 1991 advertising revenues in the U.S. as ranked by the Publisher's Information Bureau. While continuing to invest in exciting new publishing ventures like *Entertainment Weekly,* our fourth weekly and *Advertising Age*'s 1991 Magazine of the Year, the company moved aggressively on costs, taking a one-time $60 million charge to cover restructuring. Time Inc. developed new cross-media packages that unite our world-class magazine franchises with Time Warner's strengths in video, cable, programming and books. The result is one-stop shopping for our advertising clients that offers a uniquely efficient and powerful way to reach consumers (page 8).[16]

The first national weekly magazine launched in 20 years. *People* exceeded expectations for its success by showing a profit within 18 months. (Courtesy *People.*)

Time Warner again held the top three advertising revenue positions in 1991. 1991 U.S. Magazine Industry Ranking:

	1991	1990	1991 Advertising Revenues
People	1	2	$333 million
Sports Illustrated	2	1	$311 million
Time	3	3	$310 million
TV Guide	4	4	$279 million
Newsweek	5	5	$228 million

Source: Publisher's Information Bureau; Time Warner 1991 Annual Report, p. 16.

Circulation revenues increased in 1991, a difficult year for the industry.

Time Warner's 1991 annual report said the company "solidified its position as America's foremost regional magazine publisher, through combined advertising opportunities offered by its wholly owned subsidiaries, Southern Progress Corporation and Sunset Publishing. *Sunset* magazine was redesigned, and *In Health* (renamed *Health*) continued its robust growth. *Parenting,* the company's first entry in the family category, was joined by four newly acquired baby-care magazines. And Publishers Express, an alternative delivery system, was expanded to sixteen cities as of May 1992." Also, "customized advertising was made possible by selective binding and ink-jet printing. And 37 percent-owned Whittle Communications expanded its innovative Channel One satellite-delivered news and information service to more than 10,000 secondary schools."

Entertainment Weekly debuted in 1990 as a highly departmentalized magazine to review and report on what is new and noteworthy in movies, television, books, music, and videos. By mid-1992, its circulation was 803,000. The regional and new venture magazines included *Cooking Light* (7 issues a year, established 1987, 1992 circulation 1.02 million); *Health* (7, 1987, 1.19 million); *Martha Stewart Living* (6, 1991, 509,000); *Parenting* (10, 1987, 743,000); *Southern Living* (12, 1966, 2.39 million); and *Sunset* (12, 1898, 1.51 million).

Martha Stewart Living, a life-style and home entertaining magazine, was launched in July 1991 as a bimonthly, with plans for video, television, and book extensions. In October 1991, Time Inc. purchased *Baby Talk* and three annual magazines written for expectant and new mothers, complementing *Parenting* magazine.

Entertainment Weekly debuted in 1990. This is the 10th issue, for the week beginning April 20. (Courtesy Time Inc.)

Time Inc. entered regional publishing by acquiring *Sunset* magazine on the West Coast and *Southern Living* in the South. (Courtesy Time Inc.)

John Johnson and *Ebony*

John H. Johnson's magazine publishing success story is both different and typical. He became a successful minority publisher at a time when that was nearly impossible, yet his methods have broad application.

In Chicago, Johnson was editor of his school newspaper, president of his senior class, and president of his student council. Because of his leadership, he was invited to attend an assembly of outstanding high school students from throughout Chicago; at the assembly, the president of Supreme Life Insurance Company of America was the speaker. Afterward, Johnson went to talk with him and told him he wanted to go to college but needed a job. The president suggested he stop by in September.

Starting as an office boy with Supreme Life, Johnson later was assigned to clip articles about black people for the president, who did much of the work in publishing the company's *Supreme Liberty Guardian.* Soon Johnson was promoted to assistant to the editor.[17]

As he clipped newspapers and magazines and gave his company's president a digest of what was happening each week in the black community, he asked friends if they had read this article or that one. Usually they hadn't, so he thought there might be a market for a *Negro Digest.* He approached friends to go into business with him and people with money to invest, but no one was interested. He eventually convinced his mother to let him borrow $500 on her furniture. He discussed his idea with the president of Supreme Life and was offered the company's mailing list of 20,000 names.

Johnson used the borrowed $500 for a mailing to determine how many people would be interested in a black magazine, asking them to send him $2. About 3,000 replied, and he used that $6,000 as a base to persuade the printer to extend him credit. By working nights, he and his wife prepared copy for the first issue of 5,000 copies, which appeared in November 1942 and sold out within a week. Within a year, circulation reached 50,000 a month.[18]

John H. Johnson, founder, president, and publisher of Johnson Publishing Company in Chicago. (Courtesy Johnson Publishing Company.)

Johnson's associate Ben Burns, after putting in a day's work with the *Chicago Defender,* edited the magazine at his home.[19] Circulation plateaued at 50,000, until Eleanor Roosevelt wrote the first piece in a series by white people, "If I Were a Negro." Her statements were picked up by the press, and, following the wide publicity, circulation shot from 50,000 to more than 150,000 within 30 days.[20]

As World War II came to an end, Johnson thought the returning servicemen would be looking for light, interesting reading material, and he had a pictorial magazine in mind, which became the formula for *Ebony.*[21] Burns put that one out with freelance contributions until the first staff was recruited in 1946. *Ebony,* more than any other magazine, demonstrated to advertisers the importance of black consumers.[22]

Johnson points out that *Ebony* has been successful because it has changed with the times and has a commitment to its readers. When the magazine started, success was equated with material things—a Cadillac or mink coat. As the magazine developed and matured, it found that success is accomplishing whatever one sets out to do.[23] *Ebony* plays a positive role, telling people what they can do. Any black person doing a successful job in a unique situation is an *Ebony* story, Johnson says.[24] *Ebony* has helped black people become proud of their heritage and proud of themselves, and it gives them information and inspiration they cannot find anywhere else.[25]

In 1950, Johnson started *Tan,* which was similar to *True Story* or *True Romance.* After the October 1971 issue, the name was changed to *Black Stars,* and the magazine concentrated on the black entertainment world—blacks who have been successful in films, records, night clubs, and the like. *Black Stars* was discontinued in 1981.

Jet was begun in 1951 and was one of the few pocket-sized news magazines that survived into the 1960s. It was designed to give a brief weekly summary of what is happening in the black community, and it was a success from the beginning.

Negro Digest was phased out in 1951 because it was felt to be performing a function similar to *Jet.* Readers kept asking for its return, so it was revived in 1961. Its name was changed to *Black World* in 1971; then the magazine was discontinued in 1976.

Although not the first Johnson magazine, *Ebony* became the flagship of the company after being launched in 1945. (Courtesy *Ebony.*)

Johnson Publishing Company started its book division in 1961 and entered radio broadcasting in 1973, buying WGRT and changing the call letters to WJPC. The company moved into its own, newly constructed 11-story corporate headquarters on Chicago's South Michigan Avenue in 1971. Johnson received the Henry Johnson Fisher Award as the publisher of the year from the Magazine Publishers of America in 1972.

EM: Ebony Man was started in 1985 as a fashion, grooming, health, and fitness magazine for black males. It also deals with financial matters, career advice, relationships, nutrition, sports, and travel.

Essence

Essence grew out of a black capitalism meeting called by a Wall Street brokerage firm in 1968. A 24-year-old New Jersey Bell ad salesman suggested the idea for the magazine, and the adviser steered him to a printing expert, a financial planner, and an insurance salesman. They got volunteer assistance from Time-Life, *Newsweek, Psychology Today, New York,* CBS, Young & Rubicam, J. K. Lasser Tax Institute, Cowles Communications, McCann-Erickson, and Lorillard Corp. and took the name Hollingsworth Group, using some stationery Cecil Hollingsworth, the printing expert, had left over from a graphics consulting firm he once started.

Their original proposed budget of $5 million was cut to $1.5 million, and they eventually sold the idea to First National City, Chase Manhattan, and Morgan Guaranty banks. They got Gordon Parks, noted black photographer and writer, to be editorial director and assembled a full-time staff of 26, including four whites. Eighteen months after the first meeting, the stylish monthly for black women appeared with a May issue in April 1970 and a circulation base of 150,000.[26] Its sworn circulation by the end of 1971 was 162,000, but by mid-1972 it was not yet breaking even.[27]

Media Industry Newsletter reported the March 1973 issue as the first break-even issue, with 42 pages of advertising. Investment had grown from the original $120,000 to $2 million, and in its first three years *Essence* had switched from a fashion magazine to a women's service magazine and had grown to 200,000 circulation. The staff, which had been increased to 39, had been cut to 27.[28]

Jet and *EM: Ebony Man* make Johnson Publishing a diversified and multiple magazine publishing company. (Courtesy *Jet* and *EM.*)

Essence was started to give the black woman a magazine that portrayed her role as it should be viewed in society. (Courtesy *Essence.*)

The magazine idea had come from a historical perspective of how black women had been viewed in American society and what was happening in 1968 in terms of how black women were being used and viewed in older magazines. No one was talking to the black woman about her aspirations, needs, and desires or was portraying her in the role as she should have been viewed in society, as a beautiful and intelligent human being, according to publisher Edward Lewis.

The magazine's working title had been *Sapphire,* to connote the precious jewel qualities rather than the Amos 'n Andy image of the black woman that had to be overcome. However, the negative associations were so great among women interviewed that the title was changed to *Essence.*[29] *Essence* was originally intended to be strictly a fashion and beauty book, but it soon became apparent that that would not be enough for the *Essence* reader. Its content was broadened to include consumer reports, child care, food, health, fiction, fashion and beauty, and some politics and religion. Special theme issues were begun in 1972 on topics such as college and education, careers, travel, and home sewing.[30]

The editor-in-chief who saw the book achieve its first break-even issue and septuple its advertising income was Marcia Ann Gillespie. She came to *Essence* as managing editor in November 1970 from Time-Life Books and became editor-in-chief in May 1971 at age 26. She saw circulation grow to 550,000 and advertising income grow from $557,000 in 1971 to $3.76 million in 1976.[31]

Gillespie left *Essence* after the 10th anniversary issue of May 1980. Circulation stood at 600,000 and, over the next year, increased to 650,000, as first Daryl R Alexander and then Susan L. Taylor succeeded her as editor-in-chief. Circulation was 900,000 in 1992.

Self

Condé Nast's *Self,* launched in January 1979 as a monthly focusing on self-improvement and the realization of individual potential for career women, claimed to be the most successful new women's magazine—in both circulation and advertising—in more than 35 years. Projected to achieve a first-year circulation of 500,000 and 250 to 300 advertising pages, it achieved 900,000 circulation[32] and attracted 521 pages of advertising in less than one year. The magazine was a $20 million venture developed by a full staff for a year before the premiere issue.[33] *Self* could attribute much of its rapid progress to the credibility of Condé Nast, which also publishes *Vogue, Mademoiselle, Glamour, Gourmet,* and *Gentleman's Quarterly.*

Getting Started

If you have a powerful editorial idea that appeals to a large number of people who also may be a highly desirable audience for advertisers, how do you go about starting this magazine?

Organize the most talented team you can, whether they're close friends working with you on a volunteer basis or professionals you have to pay. Work out editorial ideas for at least one year's issues. Creative people should have far more ideas than could be used in one year. Work on layout and graphic appearance. Develop a cover design, keeping in mind whether the cover will have to sell the magazine on newsstands or compete with the other mail subscribers receive. If you can, print a dummy and test it with focus groups, If you get this far, try a direct-mail test to a large number of potential subscribers, using lists rented from other magazines. This test will cost a large sum for postage, printing, mailing list, and mailing house services. Get your seed money as early as possible and spend it as wisely as possible. You'll need most of it for the direct-mail test.

If the test yields 3 to 5 percent positive response, then draft a business plan explaining the magazine, the capital needed—usually $1 million or more to start nationally—and the projected cash flow for the first few years. Next, carry your plan to investors. It is extremely difficult to attract needed investment capital before testing—and very difficult to attract it even after testing.

To get this far could cost about $75,000, including $5,000 to $10,000 for legal fees to form the corporation or partnership and to create needed documents; $5,000 to $10,000 for consultants and to prepare and print a business plan; $50,000 for the direct-mail test; and $15,000 for incidental expenses.

Expect to spend at least a year obtaining your financing. Alan Bennett spent seven years raising money for *American Photographer*.

Finally, hire a hugely talented staff.

Magazine consultant James Kobak says that to get from the idea stage to the brink of publication usually requires a minimum of 18 work-filled months.

The Business Plan

Sophisticated investors expect to see a detailed business plan, which describes and explains the editorial concept, the target market, the organization chart, cash projections, and the assumptions on which they are based. It may be contained in 20 to 30 typewritten pages. Experienced publisher Leonard Mogel recommends that the business plan be entrusted to a skilled magazine consultant, unless the originators have successful experience in all phases of magazine publishing.

The business plan may follow an outline similar to the following:

1. *The Concept.* Concisely state the concept of the magazine. Tell how it differs from existing magazines. Describe the areas of interest it will cover.

2. *The Editorial Need.* Position the proposed magazine against its competitors clearly and specifically. Tell why readers need this magazine.

3. *Editorial Content.* Two levels should be dealt with here. First, specifically state editorial objectives or guidelines. The magazine will (1) inform readers of the latest developments in computer hardware and software, (2) instruct readers how to use their computers with greater efficiency, (3) provide depth interviews of personalities in the computer field. This is very much like the Publishers Editorial Profile in Standard Rate and Data Service publications. Second, give examples of the specific content the magazine will carry—the types by topic of its articles, the special features that will appear on a continuing basis, and the departments that will appear in each issue. Sample tables of contents could be used here, preferably for one year's issues.

4. *The Reader Potential.* Specify the demographic characteristics of the potential readers: the age group, education, occupation, income, and sex. Then specify the psychographics, such as their VALS 2 groups: actualizers (abundant resources); fulfilleds and believers (principle directed); achievers and strivers (status oriented); experiencers and makers (action oriented); and strugglers (minimal resources). VALS 2 is discussed more extensively in chapter 8, "Magazine Research." How many of these people are in the region you will cover, whether it's a metropolitan area or the nation? How many can be expected to buy the magazine?

List the other magazines these people read and the circulation of these magazines. State the circulation objectives of your new magazine for its first three to five years. Much of this information can be inferred from the intellectual conception of the editorial idea and content. Engaging the services of a research firm or consultant, however, usually is required to provide sufficient detail.

5. *The Advertising Potential.* List the primary and secondary types of advertisers and the total amount spent by these groups on magazine advertising the preceding year. List the 10 or 15 most important competing magazines in the classification, such as computers, with the number of advertising pages they published and total advertising revenue the previous year. Inevitably, the new magazine will have to attract advertising dollars already being spent in its field. Remember that advertisers budget far in advance and don't want to be in the first issue of a magazine. Nearly all advertisers want to come on board after success has been established.

6. *The People Involved.* In a creative field, the people involved are crucial. In publishing, the inventory is people. Tell potential investors the names of people involved in this project and their backgrounds. List all key personnel: publisher, editor, art director, advertising director, circulation director, production manager, editorial ad-

TABLE 3.1
Basic Assumptions About Proposed Magazine

	Test Period	Year 1	Year 2	Year 3
Issues per year		6	6	6
Average circulation		100,000	160,000	200,000
Subscription price per year	$12.95	$12.95	$12.95	$13.95
Total mailings per year (in millions)	.250	3.0	6.0	6.5
Average percent return from mailings (gross)	3.5	3.0	2.8	2.7
Renewal percentage (Regular renewal)		52	49	46
Newsstand draw (in thousands)		30	50	60
Newsstand percentage of sale		35	40	50
Newsstand price per copy		$2.95	$2.95	$2.95
Average total pages per issue		84	100	116
Average advertising pages per issue		20	30	40
Advertising CPM, black-and-white page		$75	$75	$70
Cost per copy, printing and paper		$0.85	$0.75	$0.65
Full-time employees				
Mechanical and distribution		1	1	1
Editorial		4	5	5
Advertising		6	6	6
Circulation		1	1	1
General and administrative		4	4	4
Total		16	17	17

visory board, consultants, lawyers, and accountants. Give brief job descriptions and an organization chart. Highly respected advisory board members, consultants, lawyers, and accountants add credibility to the project and could enhance the possibilities of raising the needed capital.

7. *Basic Assumptions.* Investors want to see cash projections for three to four years, or until profitability is achieved. The editorial concept and its execution will make or break the magazine in most cases, and some experienced magazine publishers ignore cost projections when evaluating a proposal. Many magazines' projections can be cut, and the magazine can be launched for far less than the business plan stipulates. Nevertheless, this is an important section. These, of course, are estimates, and even the most successful publishers have made wildly incorrect estimates. Here again, experience is of great assistance.

Three-year projections of basic assumptions about a proposed magazine's size, frequency, price, advertising volume, and other factors on which revenue and expense estimates are based are given in table 3.1. From table 3.1 we can see that the magazine will be bimonthly. The average circulation is projected to increase 60 percent the second year over the first year and 25 percent the third year over the second year. Remember that this is average circulation. Actual circulation will vary from issue to issue. If the magazine is successful, it could increase every issue, but there are low periods during the year when circulation may slump.

The test mailing will be 250,000 pieces, with an expected yield of 3.5 percent. The first year, 3 million pieces will be mailed using several lists, yielding an average of 3.0 percent from the various lists. The second year will see 6 million pieces mailed, with an expected return of 2.8 percent, and the third year 6.5 million pieces expected to return 2.7 percent.

Renewal rates generally are low. That's why publishers spend so much money and effort promoting subscriptions and single-copy sales. The estimates of 52, 49, and 46 percent may be realistic in a given geographic or subject area that quickly develops reader loyalty.

The first year's issues will average 80 pages plus the cover, the second year's 96 pages plus the cover, and the third year's 112 plus the cover. Although the magazine may aim for a 60:40 split between editorial and advertising and maybe eventually 50:50 or 40:60, a new magazine usually carries far less advertising. This estimate may be in the ballpark.

The cost-per-thousand (CPM) for advertising pages must be competitive with the other magazines in the field targeting the same audience. It also must reflect a profit over the cost of production. CPMs around $100 are not unusual in smaller

TABLE 3.2
Cash Projections ($000)

	Test Period	Prepublication	Year 1	Year 2	Year 3
Revenue					
Subscriptions	$5	$40	$492	$764	$800
Single-copy			105	192	230
Advertising (net)			612	1,510	1,885
Other			15	25	40
Total Revenue	$5	$40	$1,224	$2,491	$2,955
Expenditures					
Mechanical and distribution		$9	$215	$300	$400
Editorial		25	160	200	230
Advertising		50	130	180	225
Circulation promotion	$60	15	990	1,100	1,400
Circulation fulfillment			55	85	105
General and administrative	10	50	190	215	245
Total Expenditures	$70	$149	$1,740	$2,080	$2,605
Net cash flow	($65)	($109)	($516)	$411	$350
Cumulative cash flow	($65)	($174)	($690)	($279)	$71

circulation magazines. The printing and paper cost per copy should decrease as the press run increases because fixed production costs are amortized over more copies, even though total costs of paper and other supplies increase.

This hypothetical example suggests that no one will be employed full-time during the test period. One editorial employee will be added as the magazine grows in the second year.

After the basic assumptions have been made, cash flow can be projected.

8. *Cash Projections.* The publisher, as well as the investor, needs the cash projections as an operating tool (budget). These amounts often are budgeted monthly or by issue, as well as for future years (table 3.2).

The originators of this hypothetical magazine believe they have budgeted modestly for 100,000 circulation the first year, realistically for 160,000 the second year, and 200,000 the third. Their projection shows that $690,000 is needed to get through the first year and that there still will be a cumulative net loss of $279,000 at the end of the second year. They plan to show a profit in the third year.

In difficult economic times, they may not be able to raise advertising rates so rapidly to keep the CPM at $75. A higher initial ad rate or more modest revenue projections for years two and three might be more realistic. Advertising (net) in table 3.2 means that the 15 percent agency commission has been deducted. Other revenue can come from reprints, circulation list rentals, mail-order sales, mechanical work done for advertisers, conferences, T-shirts, and the like.

All printing, production, and shipping costs are assigned to mechanical and distribution. The cost of free-lance manuscripts, photography, and artwork is part of editorial costs as well as staff salaries. Advertising sales staff salaries and advertising sales promotion come under advertising expenditures.

Circulation promotion is the cost of mailings, including renting lists from list brokers; these costs increase each year to increase circulation. For the mail test to be valid, it must ask for subscription money. Reader interest without payment is of little or no value. A favorable response of 4 percent would indicate the magazine has a viable concept. Circulation fulfillment covers maintenance of the subscription list, the charge for applying the labels to the magazines, delivery to the post office, and postage.

General and administrative covers administrative salaries and wages, rent, utilities, supplies, insurance, depreciation, and miscellaneous expenses not chargeable to other departments.

The Printed Dummy

After the business plan has been completed, a printed dummy is essential if a large amount is needed for financing. The editors will have to invest a great deal of time and money in the dummy, but it is the recommended professional approach.

The dummy should be realistic in all respects, using four-color only where it would appear in a regular issue, using real article titles and illustrations, although greeking (fake body copy) can be used. The contents page especially should reflect the contents of a typical issue, the topics, variety, departments, usual features. This dummy can be used to solicit financing and to sell advertising. It also may be used for public relations and promotion and to recruit staff, so be sure enough are printed. Reprinting is very expensive.

With a business plan and a printed dummy, the proposed magazine's originators now can seek the financing needed for a full launch. Investors are rare. A magazine has a high start-up cost and little assurance for success. Banks and investment companies generally are looking for something with less risk. Existing magazine publishing companies almost never buy an idea. They probably have already considered and discarded it. Sometimes securing a big-name lead investor attracts other investors. Often the entrepreneurs have to go to friends and acquaintances, selling them small blocks of stock in the magazine.

However the funds are finally acquired, adequate financing is important. An underfinanced magazine faces the possibility of cutting color, staff, printing quality, and editorial quality, and failing because it did not maintain its standards and editorial objectives. It can take three years from concept to publication, and years after that to make a profit. A new magazine is a long-range project.

Developing a Magazine

One methodical way to go about starting a new magazine was described by Bruce J. Boyle, publisher, Meredith Video Publishing and Magazine Development, to a magazine educators' meeting in Des Moines. His presentation was an excellently organized summary of what numerous publishers, consultants, and observers have said in other ways in recent years as well as a description of how Meredith—publisher of *Better Homes and Gardens, Country Home,* and *Midwest Living*—goes about developing a new magazine. Most of what follows in this section are Boyle's words, moderately edited for this book.

There are a number of ways to create new magazines, Boyle says, and there are understandable differences over which work best. "Our charter at Meredith is to create magazines that nourish and serve special interests. We start magazines because somebody recognizes a need and thinks he or she knows how to fill it."

Editorial

Most of our early attention is directed at questions related to editorial, such as

1. Can a clear statement of editorial purpose be made?
2. Who is the reader?
3. What is the editorial content?
4. Do we have the editorial expertise necessary to produce this product? If not, where do we get it?
5. What are the editorial subjects or categories—how do they help legitimize the life-style or activities of the reader?
6. What percentage of editorial should be devoted to each category?
7. What tone and writing style should be used?
8. What should the title be?
9. Why is the content of this product better than the competition?
10. What's the ideal frequency?
11. What should the cover program be?
12. What will the art and editorial cost to produce?

Circulation

At the same time we are puzzling over the preceding questions, we have to find answers to similar questions concerning circulation—for example,

1. What's the potential reader universe for this magazine?
2. How can potential readers be reached easily and relatively effectively?
3. What is the geographic distribution of the audience?

4. What should the subscription price be?
5. What should the cover price be?
6. What's the acceptable level of response to circulation tests?
7. What circulation growth can be expected?
8. What renewal rate can be expected?
9. How can single copies be sold?
10. What alternative distribution methods can be used?
11. What's the rate base necessary to attract target advertisers?
12. What budgets are necessary?

Advertising

Because advertising is an important revenue source, we ask questions like these:

1. Is advertising necessary to the success of this product (magazine)?
2. Is the audience for this product (magazine) attractive to advertisers?
3. Who are potential advertisers?
4. How can advertising response be tested before launch?
5. What ad budgets do potential advertisers have and how are they being spent?
6. Do we have the expertise to effectively sell advertising for the product? If not, where do we get it?
7. What discounts should be offered for charter, volume, and mail-order advertisers?
8. What sales staff is needed?
9. What other means can be used to sell advertising: rep firms, telephone solicitation, and so forth?
10. What should be our introductory cost-per-thousand and how fast can it be achieved?
11. What is the target rate base?
12. What is the optimum editorial/advertising ratio?
13. What research, promotion, and departmental budgets are required?

Competition

To properly position a new magazine in the market, we have to identify and take a close look at the competition, so we start by asking these questions:

1. What and how many competing products are in the field?
2. How successful are they?
3. How much do competing products charge for advertising?
4. Who advertises in the competition and why?
5. How long has the competition been in business?
6. What's their circulation growth been?
7. What's the competing magazine's percentage of subscription sales and single-copy sales?
8. What are the cover and subscription prices?
9. How many ad pages do they carry?
10. What's the advertising revenue?
11. How big is the competition in ad revenues and book size, and how have they grown through the years?
12. What are the editorial points of difference among our products?
13. What are the target market points of difference?
14. How do our proposed advertising rates and out-of-pocket costs compare?
15. What are the demographics of the competition's readers?
16. What basic selling proposition is being used?
17. Why are we a better buy?

Physical Characteristics

We look at the physical characteristics of the proposed magazine and continue asking questions:

1. What quality is necessary: What weight and quality [paper] stock should be used? How much color? How many pages?

2. How can the magazine be produced most efficiently and how much will it cost?
3. Which printing and binding options are open and how much will they cost?
4. What kind of distribution is available and how can we use the various channels?

Focus on Readers

Of all the criteria used and all the questions asked, it really boils down to answering two fundamental questions:

1. Will potential subscribers recognize that they have a need for this magazine?
2. Will potential subscribers recognize that this magazine will satisfy that need?

The Process

"At Meredith we've been trying to break the pattern of major publishers who have been haunted by expensive and unsuccessful launches and start-ups that have cost millions of dollars," Boyle said.

The toughest task facing those of us involved in magazine development has been organizing the testing and development procedures into a systematic and thorough examination of new ideas. What we've come up with is a fairly loose—but still a structured—procedure that lets us identify ideas which seem to have promise while at the same time minimizing the investment of time and money on projects that have only marginal chance of success.

So, here's a quick checklist of the steps and procedures we're using. Based on what we've experienced so far, it seems to work and add some order to what otherwise could be a rather chaotic and undisciplined activity.

Editorial Statement

The first step is to develop an editorial statement or statement of purpose that identifies the specific editorial focus of the magazine, who the intended readers are, and a definition of its personality. Meredith attempts to keep this definition to less than one page, preferably just a paragraph; as Boyle explains, "If we can't write a brief, clear definition, we don't have a magazine that will work."

Evaluate the Market

The second step is to evaluate the market from three points of view:

1. Circulation: From a circulation standpoint,

   Define the potential reader universe.
   Examine appropriate demographic and sociological trends.
   Identify prospective readers, the availability of mailing lists, and alternative methods of circulation solicitation.

2. Editorial: From an editorial point of view, take a look at the competition and prepare a critique, and then structure content outlines for a full year's publishing schedule.

3. Advertising: Study the potential for advertising by

   Taking a look at the competition.
   Identifying primary prospects.
   Defining and projecting potential revenue sources.

Develop a Prototype

If things continue to look encouraging, the next step is to develop prototype materials, which include

   Two or three different covers
   One or two complete tables of contents with both art and set type
   Five or six front-of-book features, with typeset heads, art, and greeked body copy
   Four or five main editorial spreads, with titles and art
   A list of alternative titles to be tested and list of department headings and features article ideas, complete with an explanatory blurb on each

Organize Basic Research

At this point, it's finally time to begin to find out what the real world thinks of the new magazine idea, so Meredith schedules a series of focus group sessions (1) to discuss the general concept of the magazine; (2) to ask the participants to critique logo variations, cover styles, and the overall design concept; and finally (3) to select those articles they find most appealing.

Even though these results are not projectable, the reactions help Meredith refine the idea and get to the next step, which is the first attempt to get a projectable response to the concept with a mail questionnaire sent to 1,500 to 2,000 names that have been selected from the mailing lists it will use in the circulation drop. The questions parallel those used in the focus groups and they ask for responses to things like the editorial statement, design, and article ideas.

Title Test

The final stage is to test the title. Of course, Meredith has tried to get some reaction during the focus groups and with the mail studies, but it places a lot of weight on how prospective readers feel the title describes and defines the magazine, so it extends this research with mail intercept interviews, which are obviously more thorough than the other two techniques.

Circulation Test

Finally, Meredith is ready for the ultimate test, a circulation mail drop. Test packages are prepared that feature different approaches, offers, and appeals, and, for the first time, it finds out what the public really thinks of the new magazine because it has asked people to put up their money for subscriptions.

Pro Forma

If the response measures up to its financial requirements, Meredith can then develop a pro forma that includes informed assumptions and provides a framework for the disciplines it will be living with during the first few years after launching the new magazine.

Strategic Plan

If these pro forma numbers are attractive and workable, Meredith's next step is to develop a strategic plan for the launch and for the first two years' operations before requesting funding for the project.

This 10-step process provides a number of advantages. It forces Meredith to do its homework before investing big money. It provides checkpoints for "go" or "no-go" decisions throughout. It involves readers and focuses attention on their requirements and reactions. It also allows Meredith to examine a number of concepts at the same time, to have several projects in varying stages of development simultaneously. Boyle commented,

I think it's important to point out that we're still learning and experimenting, and we don't have all the answers. It's inevitable that during our shakedown process we're going to miss things, and that probably includes overlooking opportunities. But launching a magazine costs money, and we think this process helps minimize that risk.

Remember, five years ago *Country Home, Wood,* and *Midwest Living* were just a gleam in the eyes of some very dedicated individuals, and the experience we've gained from their successful launchings has helped crystalize the *process.*

Hippocrates Magazine(s)

Eric Schrier and his associates launched *Hippocrates,* since renamed *Health,* with the May/June 1987 issue. There is no typical launch, but this one is an excellent example of editorial concept development by experienced magazine people. Schrier was one of the founding editors of *Science 80* when it was launched and managing editor when it won National Magazine Awards for general excellence in its circulation category in 1982 and 1983.

Schrier had put together a prototype magazine called *Novus* in 1979, the outgrowth of his master's thesis in journalism at the University of California at Berkeley. That led him to *Science 80,* which was published for six years by the American Association for the Advancement of Science before being sold to Time Inc. and incorporated into *Discover* magazine, which was later sold to Family Media and has since been sold to Walt Disney Company.

Los Angeles physician Denis Kollar and his partner Leslie McCurdy were frustrated with the media's health and medical coverage. In 1985, they shared their frustration with a friend, John Klingel, a publishing consultant with whom Schrier had worked on the launch of *Science 80.* Klingel told them he knew an editor.

Schrier recalls, "The medical stories we ran at *Science 80* got a lot more response from readers than did the stories on plate tectonics. With those topics, you have to shake the reader and say, 'This is why you should care.' With health and medicine, the reader already cares."

The results of a direct-mail test asking consumers whether they would subscribe to a new health magazine were encouraging, so Schrier left *Science 85* to help raise funds toward the start-up. He had been through a money hunt in 1977, raising around $12,000 to print 7,000 copies of *Novus.* "I had to sell my 1969 MGB to pay the color separation bills," he remembers.

The funding goal for the new health magazine was $5 million. "We thought it would be a six-month job," Schrier said. "Instead, it took a year and a half." Rejections came from investors uncomfortable with the entrepreneurial set-up, including, Time Inc., then trying magazine start-ups internally. One venture capitalist said, "Let me get this straight. I'll give you $5 million on Monday, and you'll spend $2 million of it by Friday, on 6 million pieces of junk mail? And you don't even know if anyone will pay for the magazine once they get it. And you haven't sold a single page of advertising. That's a helluva business you've got there."

The investor, Doug Peabody of INCO Venture Capital, came through, however. Additional funds were secured from Allstate Insurance's venture capital arm; HEI Corp., a hospital management firm; Century IV Partners (now Philadelphia Ventures), a venture capital firm; and an anonymous private investor. By November 1986, the $5 million was in place.

Next followed selling ads for the first issue (31 pages, a good showing), selecting a name (*Hippocrates* won out over *Health & Medicine* and *Heartbeat*), and filling out the editorial and business staffs for the California-based magazine.[34] *Hippocrates* was named for the ancient Greek doctor known for the physicians' Hippocratic Oath and included a lead-in subtitle: *The Magazine of Medicine & Health.*

The editorial prospectus used to raise the start-up capital and plan the editorial content for the magazine is reproduced below as an example of good editorial planning.

Editorial Prospectus

Here follows the March 13, 1986, editorial prospectus of

The Magazine of Medicine & Health

HIPPOCRATES

Editorial Prospectus

The Niche

It's no secret that America has discovered its body. Best-seller lists are crammed with books telling you how to shape up and stress down. Supermarket shelves are packed with foods advertising lots of fiber and low sodium or less fat. Streamlined department store mannequins sport leotards and sweatshirts. Swimming pools and running tracks are jammed with rush-hour exercisers.

Clearly the health and fitness fad is no fad at all. It has become a life-style. And as a life-style, it has changed what we eat, wear, talk about, and do. It has become a robust part of our economy and an increasingly conspicuous part of our

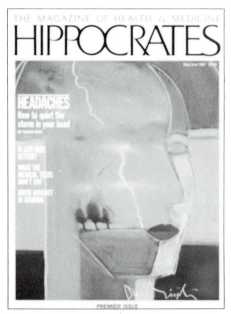

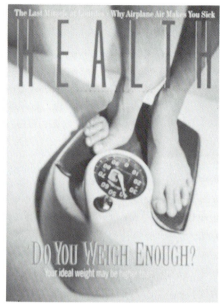

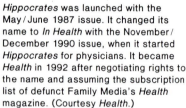

Hippocrates was launched with the May/June 1987 issue. It changed its name to *In Health* with the November/ December 1990 issue, when it started *Hippocrates* for physicians. It became *Health* in 1992 after negotiating rights to the name and assuming the subscription list of defunct Family Media's *Health* magazine. (Courtesy *Health*.)

culture. Virtually no corner of the publishing world has missed the chance to catch these new winds. Magazines such as *Runner's World, Vegetarian Times, Self,* and *American Health* have all made it their business to chronicle various facets of the new health life-style.

Meanwhile, hardly a day goes by without news of some astonishing medical development. In one way or another, these developments dramatically affect our lives, yet only the "big" medical stories make us realize it. William Schroeder gets an artificial heart, and each day we check his chart. AIDS relentlessly and mysteriously finds more victims, and we think twice about giving and getting blood. Jim Fixx drops dead on the run, and we all stop to take our exercising pulse. *Time* and *Newsweek,* along with the newspapers and television, make it their business to keep these big stories very much in the public consciousness.

Such prominent but spotty medical coverage coupled with the sweeping impact of the new health life-style have created a surprisingly empty niche. Behind the medical headlines, beyond the seemingly insatiable appetite for expensive exercise machines and active sportswear, a deeper curiosity has emerged. It is a basic curiosity about the workings of the body human, the people who study and treat it, and just what each of us can and cannot do to make it run better.

The key to satisfying this curiosity is reliable and readable information—content *with* style. There is not a single magazine, newspaper, or television program that delivers both to readers. The existing health magazines, for example, are long on practical advice but short on explanation. Readers may think they're getting their fill of medicine and health information, but it turns out to be a junk food diet.

Hippocrates, the magazine of medicine and health, will fill the empty niche by delivering a high-quality product to a well-educated, affluent audience. It will be written with more wit, reflection, and authority than the newspapers and health magazines and with more warmth and relevance than the popular science magazines.

The audience for *Hippocrates* will be predominantly college-educated men and women who, by reason of their intellectual curiosity or practical interest, want a dependable source of health information and a perspective on the rapidly changing face of medicine. By appealing to the more sophisticated and demanding lay reader, *Hippocrates* is likely to attract doctors and other medical workers as well. To pick up information outside their own specialties, these professionals must either pour through dozens of technical journals, consult colleagues, or rely on the same mass media sources as the rest of us. *Hippocrates* will give them an authoritative alternative and, in so doing, increase its reach and impact.

Hippocrates has the rare opportunity to be both useful and compelling. Useful because the average American spends more on medical care than on clothing, recreation, and education—and because there's a growing sense that good health is as much the province of the patient as the doctor. Compelling because few subjects lend themselves to more drama and sense of awe; few aspects of life affect us so intimately as our health and the health of those close to us. By making the most of this opportunity—in its writing and in its art—*Hippocrates* will have a long and productive life.

The Competition

Obviously we would not propose a new magazine if we thought an existing magazine adequately served the sophisticated lay reader. No magazine does what *Hippocrates* will do, though some magazines cover pieces of the same territory. Early in the magazine's life, people may refer to *Hippocrates* as an "upscale *American Health*" or "the *Science 85* of medicine and health," but what will quickly emerge is a magazine that is memorable and distinguishable to readers and advertisers alike.

Health Magazines   *American Health*'s quick success—it reached a circulation of 800,000 within three years—is testimony to the nation's overwhelming interest in health and fitness. Tailored to a predominantly female, high-school-educated audience, *American Health* is clearly a life-style magazine. Its regular departments, for example, include "Skin, Scent, & Hair," "The Fashion Report," "The Fitness Report," and "Lifestyle." Its features also emphasize exercise, fashion, and self-care medicine. When it does cover the people, research, or ethical issues in medicine and health, its stories are often superficial. The magazine treats the subject this way because its editor and publisher understand how to best fill their niche and serve their audience—an audience that is generally satisfied with a magazine full of snippets of information. But it is not our niche nor our audience. To some extent, *American Health* is whetting the appetite for some of its readers for a richer, more substantial magazine like *Hippocrates.*

Prevention, despite a circulation of nearly three million, offers even less substance than *American Health*. It practices a folksy, simple-minded style of journalism. *Prevention* writers approach their stories with a kind of wide-eyed wonder for the human body and an innocent attitude toward doctors and scientists. Regular departments include "Beauty Network," "Fitness Vacations," and "Your Healthy Pet."

Except for its title, *Health* is indistinguishable from the women's magazines. Recent typical stories include "How to Lose the Seven Pounds You Gained This Winter" and "Miss America Answers Your Beauty Questions." Like *Prevention,* which uses a reduced format and is short on graphics, *Health* projects a dull, uninspired visual style.

Science Magazines   Magazines such as *Science 86, Discover,* and *Science Digest* have gained great popularity in the last five years as the public's interest in science and technology has grown. The combined readership of these three magazines is now more than two million. As part of their wide coverage, each magazine usually publishes one major medical feature in every issue. Although many of these articles are done well, such limited coverage gives short shrift to the explosion of useful and exciting information about health and medicine; it also falls far short of the demand for material in this field. The strongest medical story in a typical issue of *Science 86* comes closest to what *Hippocrates* will offer in every one of its features.

Medical Journals and Newsletters   Under titles such as "Idiopathic Hyperaldosteronism: A Possible Role for Aldosterone-Stimulating Factor," medical investigators report their research findings in *The New England Journal of Medicine, The Lancet, The Journal of the American Medical Association,* and other publications. These journals are required reading for any medical researcher who wants to keep up in the field. But they are also difficult reading—even for experts. *Hippocrates* will be as important for the layman, and for many medical specialists, as these publications are for their audience. *Hippocrates,* however, will replace these journals' terse data charts with vivid graphics, their dry summaries and clinical detachment with vigorous and sensitive writing.

The Harvard Medical School Health Letter is the forerunner of the well-written, authoritative, no-nonsense newsletters about medicine and health. Others include the *University of California–Berkeley Wellness Letter* and the *Mayo Clinic Health Letter.* Always aware of the consumer, these six- to eight-page letters may describe a phone-in medical information service, warn against burning preservative-treated wood, or summarize the latest on caffeine or sugar. Their quiet success—the Harvard newsletter has 300,000 subscribers—is a sign of the need for clear, reliable medical and health information. But, by definition, they can offer no more than the barest bones of any story and virtually no illustration. *Hippocrates* will pick up where they leave off.

Special Newspaper Sections   In the last four years, 20 large newspapers have launched regular sections or separate fold-in magazines on science and health; one of the most recent additions is a weekly health tabloid published as part of *The Washington Post.* Operating under roughly the same constraints on space and production time as the daily newspapers, these sections usually offer shallow stories, each rarely more than a magazine page in length. Most of the medical stories in these sections concentrate on a service angle: nutrition tips, exercise, and dealing with your doctor.

The Magazine

In 65 to 75 editorial pages, *Hippocrates* will focus on the people and ideas at the cutting edge of medicine and health. In its departments and features, *Hippocrates* will make its reputation on reporting that is incisive and revealing. Its stories will entertain its readers as well as inform and challenge them. By tapping its distinguished board of physician advisors and a larger network of experts, and by checking all manuscripts for factual accuracy, the magazine will confirm its image as the source of reliable information about medicine and health.

The photography and illustration in *Hippocrates* will be as bold as that of any magazine in the country. Its visual style will convey the message that the magazine's subjects are not remote, clinical, or technical, but human and accessible. Where appropriate, explanatory illustrations will clarify the tougher medical concepts and summarize useful information. Selected sections of the magazine, most notably the 10- to 12-page Special Report, will be peppered with cartoons to break up solid pages of text. The only magazines that effectively use cartoons in this way are *The New Yorker* and *Playboy,* but the stable of brash and witty cartoonists willing to slice up the nearest medical laboratory, doctor's office, or health club is much larger than their pages suggest.

The following departments and features are described in the order they will appear in the magazine:

Editor's note: Many magazines use the editor's page to congratulate themselves or to formally offer an opinion. In *Hippocrates,* this page will instead give the readers an insider's view of the stories behind the stories.

Reflexes: Letters from *Hippocrates'* readers will confirm the magazine's vitality, accessibility, and importance.

Newsbeat: Few fields evolve as quickly as the medical sciences. In five to six pages, Newsbeat will offer 10 to 15 brief stories on the latest in causes and cures, technologies and treatments, politics and people. Vital Statistics, a regular box in the section, will be the cocktail partygoer's delight, listing numerical tidbits such as the amount of shock absorption provided by different shoes (hard-heeled shoes with inserts are better than crepe soles) and a comparison of the leading causes of death over the years (cancer caused only 3.7 percent of the deaths in 1900 but 17.2 percent in 1970). Case History, another regular box, will recall great and not-so-great moments in the history of medicine.

Food: This two-page department will bring new understanding to the saying "you are what you eat." It will explain the facts, not the fads, of nutrition. This section might cover the dangers of sulfite preservatives in wine and fresh fruit, describe the link between premature puberty and the hormones fed to beef, or discuss how the body uses selenium. Whatever the subject, Food will serve up nutrition information that can be used, clarifying the link between diet and health.

Drugs: Perhaps medicine's most direct influence on us, drugs have become an inevitable and almost unconscious part of our daily lives. In this department, *Hippocrates* will stop and reconsider the world of drugs from some unexpected angles; it will offer news and perspective. It may report on a surprising series of experiments that suggests left-handed people are more susceptible to psychoactive drugs. Or it may describe the obstacles—both medical and political—that have prevented the creation of a contraceptive pill for men.

Rounds: Nothing matches the case history for drama; witness the popularity of Berton Roueche's medical detective stories in *The New Yorker.* In one or two pages, Rounds will include both on-the-heels reports from two medical teams, one in New York and one in San Francisco, and tales of epidemiological sleuthing from around the world. In one issue, for instance, readers will watch as the San Francisco doctors learn, to their surprise, that a patient has a benign heart tumor instead of the more serious condition they expected. In another, the medical detectives will crack the case of "Liver Lover's Headache," when they discover that five chronic headache sufferers have unintentionally overdosed on vitamin A by eating as much as 24 pounds of liver each week.

Stitches: Even if laughter isn't the best medicine, it sure is easy to take. To guarantee a dose of it every issue, our resident humorist will give us a chance to look at sickness and health, doctors and patients, research and treatment through an odd but illuminating pair of glasses. Whether he's taking sides in the great national debate over designer scrubs, describing 101 uses for a personal nutritionist, or administering his very own Type C personality test, this specialist will keep you in stitches.

Features: Each issue of *Hippocrates* will carry four or five features. Here writers will range across the entire breadth of medicine and health, its practitioners and its patients. Some features will satisfy curiosity—describing, for instance, how embryonic cells know what to become. Others will escort readers down the same paths that medical researchers travel to their discoveries and insights, or to confounding dead ends. There will be incisive reports—for example, an examination of doctors whose ignorance of detoxification has caused drug addicts to overdose. Some stories will simply offer useful information on health. Profiles will sketch both the well known—such as Robert Gallo, the discoverer of a human leukemia virus, as famous for his arrogance as for his ability—and the less-familiar—such as David Bresley, whose Santa Monica pain-control clinic is among the most successful in the country.

Clippings: This will be the reader's clipping service, harvesting two pages of excerpts from the finest, quirkiest, most thoughtful writing about medical matters. One issue's fare might include two paragraphs from *The New York Times* in which Harvard Medical School resident Perri Klass draws a searing profile of the macho doctor, a section of a proposal from Brown University students urging the school to stockpile "suicide pills" for use in case of nuclear war, and an over-the-shoulder account of the first operation to use anesthesia.

Business: This country spends close to $400 billion a year on medical care, a figure that continually attracts investment in new ideas, services, and products, usually with healthy returns. This two-page department will report on what's new in the health-care business. It will also examine the companies that control such issues as the way doctors practice medicine, which drugs get made, how hospitals are run. It may, for instance, look at the sugar industry's retaliatory strike at NutraSweet, the quality of medicine at Goodyear Company's cut-rate clinic in Lawton, Oklahoma, or Campbell Soup Company's run at the fitness marketplace. In addition, each issue will carry the *Hippocrates* Health Stock Index—a survey of what the key medical stocks are doing and our expert's short analysis of why.

Sportsmedicine: The days of the weekend athlete are over. According to a recent Gallup survey, more than 50 percent of Americans exercise every day. And while there are plenty of magazines telling them what muscles they should work on, what form they should have, or what food they should eat the day of the big race, rarely does anyone tell them why. From the biomechanics of jumping and the architecture of the foot to the psychology of coordination—*Hippocrates* will cover the whys of sportsmedicine.

Special Report: For every half dozen or so medical developments that demand a feature story, there is another that requires even more special handling. Because of the subject's complexity, because of the depth needed to bring it to light intelligently, because of its importance, *Hippocrates* will give such a story extra space in a 10- to 12-page section. Often Special Report will analyze medical policy—the new standardized pricing schemes at hospitals, for example, that make all related treatments cost the same amount, regardless of how difficult or easy the condition is to remedy. It will provide perspective to topical developments, perhaps analyzing Humana, Inc.'s well-publicized, high-volume, franchised approach to medicine. And it will explore controversial issues, such as the still pervasive threat of asbestos—to factory workers, consumers, even schoolchildren.

Challenge: Sometimes this puzzle page will offer readers the necessary clues and challenge them to solve intriguing medical cases. Other times it will engage them in *Hippocrates'* own research projects. We may ask them their birth dates to test once and for all the old wives' tale that claims more babies are born during full moons than any other time. Or we may survey them to find out what percentage of patients actually take the medicine their doctors prescribe.

Critic: In a few pages, *Hippocrates* will critique books, films, television, plays, museum exhibits—recommending whatever is especially well done and creative, steering readers clear of the junk.

Ethics: We can now experiment on a human embryo in a laboratory dish, we can repair a defective fetus before birth, we can prolong life with artificial hearts and other heroic technology. But should we? Every time medicine takes another impressive step, it stirs up a morass of moral, ethical, and societal dilemmas. In one page, our columnist will take a provocative look at those questions as well as the medical aspects of other ethical issues—should a tobacco company be held responsible for the lung cancer death of a lifelong smoker, for instance, and what must be done to stop the flood of bogus doctors?

House Call: Every issue, *Hippocrates* will satisfy its readers' curiosity by answering their questions in simple but authoritative terms. How do you know if your headaches are migraines and what does it mean if they are? When your dentist says not to worry about regular X rays, does he know what he's talking about? What are those tiny bright specks you see after rubbing your eyes?

If *Hippocrates* had been publishing last summer, it would have run many of the stories in the two sample issues described on the following pages:

Sample Issue #1

Editor's Note: This issue's feature on Spain's toxic oil mystery reveals some curious differences in the ways American and Spanish medical detectives work a case.

Reflexes: Letters from our readers.

Newsbeat: Twelve of the latest medical developments from the months of May and June. Vital Statistics: President Reagan's cholesterol count, the cholesterol count of the average 74-year-old American, and that of the average 25-year-old; the decibel level of an office, an air conditioner, a rock concert, and how long your ear can take traffic noise before it's damaged. Case History: A very short profile of Imhotep, grand vizier to Egyptian king Zoser and the first doctor to receive a degree.

Food: Milk, eggs, and other food can interfere with medication. A guide to the most common food-drug interactions and how they work.

Drugs: The road to a vaccine against tooth decay is paved with good intentions but few victories. A report from 30 test mouths in Boston.

Rounds: It's a big day for Steve Holloday and for the doctors of this New York hospital. It's the first day that 18-month-old Steve, born without an immune system, will eat unsterilized food. The immunologists and surgeons take us on a visit with their favorite patient.

Stitches: Doctors call someone with jaundice a banana, a professional patient a gomer ("get outta my emergency room"). A look at a behind-the-patient's back, unabridged medical dictionary.

Features: (4 to 10 pages each):

DIAMOND'S BRAIN—It began nearly 40 years ago when, on rounds with her physician father, Marian Diamond chanced to see a naked brain lying on a table. Her fascination with that "most esoteric functional mass on Earth" has led the UC Berkeley neuroanatomist to a revolutionary discovery—mental activity can prevent the brain from deteriorating with age. As Diamond puts it: "You use it or lose it." A visit with a brain researcher who plans never to lose it.

TOXIC OIL SYNDROME—On May 1, 1981, people began arriving at hospitals in northern Spain, complaining of shortness of breath, fever, rash, pain, and vomiting. Since then, more than 20,000 have been afflicted and more than 300 have died. Officially, the blame has been put on illegal, tainted cooking oil. But researchers and victims aren't buying that explanation—and still no cure has been found.

BEYOND STEROIDS—It may enlarge their hands and feet, coarsen their facial features, and weaken their hearts and bones. But athletes are taking human growth hormone anyway—on the slim chance they might grow bigger muscles.

A MEDICAL MASQUERADE—Consider the career of Abraham V. K. Asante: Exposed as a medical fraud in 1974, this bogus anesthesiologist nevertheless proceeded to win a medical award from the Army and to work for two other hospitals and the National Institutes of Health before he was convicted for inflicting irreparable brain damage on a patient in 1983. And Asante has lots of company—a federal investigation estimates there are 10,000 phony doctors in the U.S.

DO-IT-YOURSELF DOCTORING—If you want to know if you're ovulating or you're hypersensitive or you have venereal disease, dozens of entrepreneurs are betting you'd rather do-it-yourself. The best and the worst of what's here and what's coming in home health kits.

Clippings: Syndicated columnist Ellen Goodman ruminates on Doctor as God. From *Audubon* magazine, an acrophobic's account of his terror. Gems of wisdom from "Expando-Vision," a computer program that supposedly can subliminally persuade TV viewers to lose weight, quit smoking, or build sexual confidence.

Business: Inside the Red Cross's move to monopolize the business of procuring organs and tissues for transplant operations.

Sportsmedicine: Of carbon fibers and rubber bands—the artificial ligament gets its first road test.

Special Report: THE VACCINE VANISHES—Without the pertussis vaccine 7,000 American children would die of whooping cough this year. But, according to one estimate, the vaccine causes 40 cases of brain damage every year that it is administered. A recent spate of million-dollar lawsuits has scared two of its three manufacturers out of the business, leaving a shortage of pertussis vaccine and the strong possibility that other vital vaccines will soon disappear. Special Report weighs the medical evidence for and against the mass immunization of kids and considers whether the federal government should compensate victims or limit vaccine makers' liability.

Challenge: The results of *Hippocrates'* reader hiccup survey: the five most common situations preceding a hiccup attack.

Ethics: Our columnist argues that doctors should be able to take transplantable organs from all cadavers unless the patient or his close relatives have explicitly forbidden removal. Does the deceased have a right to his own body?

Critic: Spectacular computer graphics make "The Living Body," a new 24-part series on public television, a tour de force.

House Calls: Our readers ask . . . Which is more likely to give me a cold: shaking hands with an infectious friend or kissing her? . . . Is food more fattening if you eat it just before sleeping? . . . Do one-a-day vitamins do any good—or harm?

Sample Issue #2

Editor's note: An MBA "hospital doctor" talks about what one financially sick Chicago hospital could do, besides dumping its unprofitable patients, to get into the black.

Reflexes: Letters from readers.

Newsbeat: The most interesting medical news stories that occurred during July and August. Vital Statistics: The amount of body fat on eight kinds of athletes (the fattest are football linemen; the leanest, gymnasts); the number of people who treat themselves with borrowed drugs or old ones and the annual total of deaths due to using the wrong drug; the number of tests given to high blood pressure patients by U.S. doctors and by British doctors and the success rates of treating high blood pressure in the U.S. and Britain. Case History: A brief biography of the first laboratory rat.

Food: What puts the zing in curry? What makes chili peppers burn? Some new findings on the chemistry of spice, and why some like it hot.

Drugs: E-Ferol, a vitamin supplement, has been linked to the deaths of 32 infants and caused adverse reactions in another 86 babies. It is just one of some 5,000 drugs that a federal loophole has allowed manufacturers to market without proof of safety.

Rounds: In June 1984 there was something special about the sore throats of a certain group of 60 people in seven different states. A sharp-eyed Missouri epidemiologist follows the train to spoiled macaroni and tainted mousse at a hotel convention luncheon.

Stitches: The last word on waiting room etiquette.

Features: (4 to 10 pages each):

NO ADMITTANCE—Patient-dumping is the callous practice of quickly getting rid of unprofitable cases. Skimming means taking only the well-paying cases and leaving the rest for nonprofit hospitals. These strategies are beginning to replace the creed of humanity in medicine. What are your chances of getting dumped by a hospital?

THE POLIO PIONEERS—Three decades ago Jonas Salk and Albert Sabin set off on different paths in the crusade against polio. Salk developed an injectable vaccine from a killed virus; Sabin created a vaccine based on a live but weakened virus that could be swallowed with a cube of sugar. Together they wiped out a plague on America's children, but they became bitter enemies. Today they are still arguing, Salk claiming that Sabin's live virus vaccine has accidentally crippled 99 people, Sabin staunchly defending the safety of his method, by far the more popular. In a rare dialogue, they air their philosophical and scientific differences.

WHAT'S WRONG IN FRIENDLY HILLS?—If, as some officials say, everything is fine in this small Colorado neighborhood, why have a dozen children died in the last two years of cancer, heart disease, and meningitis?

THE MAKING OF A BLOOD CLOT—For most hemophiliacs, factor VIII is the missing enzyme in a remarkable cascade of chemical events that normally clots the blood. But if hemophiliacs get their factor VIII from donated plasma, they run the risk of AIDS and hepatitis. Now two separate teams of genetic engineers say they can manufacture a substance that mimics the action of factor VIII, thanks to their own cascade of brilliant genetic tricks.

THE FIRST NINE MONTHS OF SCHOOL—Surprising lessons learned
by a fetus in the womb.

Clippings: Physician Charles Guest's musings in *The Lancet* on the Black Death
and the legend of the Pied Piper. A collection of the medical graffiti in the doctor's
lounge of Massachusetts General Hospital. From the book, Lisa H., the climax of
a grueling operation to restore the face of a young woman.

Business: Right next to the Kodachrome and the Ektachrome, you'll soon see
little yellow boxes labeled "Glucose test" and "Strep test." Why does Kodak want
to take a picture of your health?

Sportsmedicine: Exercise allergies—who gets them and why.

Special Report: LOW-TAR, HIGH-RADIATION—Cigarette tar contains
about 50 known cancer agents. But according to chemist Edward Martell, the real
danger in cigarette smoke comes from yet another ingredient: radioactive gas in
tobacco fertilizer. With every breath, he says, these radioactive materials become
trapped in smokers' bronchial tubes where they fire powerful alpha particles point
blank at sensitive lung cells. An analysis of Martell's claim—and of the Surgeon
General's cool reaction.

Challenge: Can you spot the 15 intentional errors in our detailed illustration of
the human skeleton? An engraved stethoscope to anyone who can.

Ethics: When doctors advertise.

Critic: A review of *The Doctor Stories* by William Carlos Williams: 13 stories,
six poems, and an excerpted chapter, all centered on this gifted writer's medical
career.

House Call: Our readers ask . . . Can you explain the differences between "Docs
in the Box," HMOs, and trauma centers? . . . Is there anything dangerous about
snoring? . . . I've heard about a new allergy medicine that doesn't use antihista-
mines and won't make you drowsy. How does it work?

Appendix
Additional Feature Ideas

THE TROUBLED SLEEP OF GENIUS—The nightmares of Robert Louis
Stevenson gave birth to *The Strange Case of Dr. Jekyll and Mr. Hyde;* the fright-
ening dreams of Mary Shelley spawned *Frankenstein.* It now appears, says a Tufts
University sleep researcher, that the same personality traits that cause lifelong
nightmares also endow a sufferer with creative genius—or with mental illness. Enter
the world of nightmares under the guidance of investigator Ernest Hartmann.

PATENTING THE PATIENT—In 1976 doctors at UCLA removed John
Moore's spleen as part of his treatment for leukemia. Last spring those doctors were
awarded a patent for a cell line derived from that spleen, which turned out to be a
productive source of interferon and other potentially useful biological substances.
Now Moore has sued the university, claiming that he never consented to the release
of his cells for possible commercial applications. A bizarre tale in its own right,
Moore's case raises larger questions about the doctors who use patients' cells, blood,
and organs for research and profit.

THE CHEMISTRY OF CRAVING—Addiction researchers have found that
patients trying to kick the habits of smoking, drinking, and drug use all experience
the same kind of chemical changes in their brains. What's more, by using a drug called
clonidine the scientists have temporarily blocked the craving that normally follows
withdrawal.

MIXED-UP MEDICATION—A 20-month-old Philadelphia boy came to the
National Institutes of Health for treatment. He died six days later when the hospital
workers mistakenly gave him an intravenous saline solution more than five times
stronger than the doctor ordered. Few hospital medication errors are fatal, but one
in ten patients does get the wrong drug or dose.

THE HEALING BRAIN—Norman Cousins preaches it, faith healers abuse
it, and now researchers are finding they can't deny it: The mind can cure the body.
A report on the even stronger evidence for the link between the brain and the immune
system.

SILICON SICKNESS—There may not be any burning rivers or smokestacks in Silicon Valley but it takes a lot of acid, xylene, and arsine gas to transform wafers of pure silicon into microchips. And it only takes a little of these chemicals to make workers sick. Just how clean is the Valley?

DR. HERETIC—Robert Mendelsohn, a physician with impeccable credentials and a grandfatherly demeanor, believes that ultrasound scans may cause leukemia, sees no reason for children to be immunized against diseases, and claims that American doctors made up the disease hypertension so they could sell pills. Through a nationally syndicated newspaper column, three books, and frequent radio and TV interviews, he has alienated most of the American medical establishment. Is Mendelsohn a publicity-seeking crackpot or a much needed gadfly?

MOLECULAR MAGNET—Researchers have dubbed it the magnet that pulls needles out of the genetic haystack. The DNA probe can be designed to signal the presence of defective genes, identify harmful bacteria and viruses, even chart unknown areas of human chromosomes. More than a few great leaps in basic medical understanding are expected from this remarkable tool.

SHOPPING FOR GENES—There's a new kind of seed catalog going around. It's published by Robert K. Graham, proprietor of the Repository for Germinal Choice, better known as the Nobel Prize sperm bank for the quality of its depositors. Can Graham really deliver a tall, blond kid with a flair for math or a brunette with virtuoso potential on the bass trombone? A pair of our writers, posing as prospective parents, visit Graham's bank and offer a consumer guide to the new sperm supermarkets.

PIECE OF MIND—Genetically infertile mice have given birth to healthy offspring after they received brain tissue transplants that restored a missing sex hormone. Now researchers' thoughts are turning to bigger brains.

THE 1985 HOSPITAL CHECK-UP—The hospitals in our 10-best list will treat you better and charge you less.

SEXAHOLICS ANONYMOUS—Some therapists say that one in 12 people are addicted to sex the same way that alcoholics are to drinking and compulsive gamblers are to betting. Profiles of four patients with this newly recognized problem and an analysis of the different approaches their doctors are taking.

The Premier Issue

You may want to compare the prospectus with the actual contents of *Hippocrates'* premier issue, May/June 1987:

This Issue: Editor's note

Vital Signs: Shocking Snakebites. Why Your Foot Has an Arch. Childish Analogies. Everybody Needs Calcium

The AIDS File: Do Condoms Protect?

Vital Statistics: How Many Women Would Choose Their Baby's Sex?

Postmortem: The Irish Giant and the Body Snatcher

Food: Spicy Food and Taste Bud Burnout

Drugs: The French Pill—Abortion or Retroactive Birth Control?

Stitches: The Good News Cover-up

Rounds: Case of the Vanishing Shadow

Features:

THE HELL IN MY HEAD: There are 40 million headache stories in the United States. This is one of them.

PART OF LIFE: The rock climber's artificial ligament, the piano player's electronic ear, and other healing parts.

THE OTHER SIDE OF BEEF: Ranchers are growing slimmer cattle. Butchers are trimming away more fat. But is light beef really better?

DELIVERY REFUSED: Fed up with malpractice suits, obstetricians in Brunswick, Georgia, decided to show the lawyers what the town would be like with nobody around to deliver their babies.

STRESS, SUCCESS, AND SAMOA: If you've ever wondered what personality has to do with stress, and what stress has to do with heart disease, you should have a talk with this Samoan chief. Especially if you think you don't have the time.

JUST TESTING: The results of your medical tests are correct: True or False?

Clippings: Dr. Science on Watermelons and People. To Kids, It Will Always Be Spinach. The History of Colds. Richard Selzer's Belle of Grand Rounds.

Sports: How High Can You Jump?

Mind: What Patients Hear Under the Knife

Family: The Personality Genes

Appendix: Sources and Additional Reading

Housecalls: What Causes Goose Bumps? Is There a Mouthwash That Prevents Cavities? Are More Babies Born During Full Moons?

Hippocrates' *Growth*

Charles Truehart wrote of that first issue in the *Washington Post:* "It's very good. . . . The writing in *Hippocrates* is informed and supple, despite heavy doses of first-person singular; the design and artwork are striking, with shades of *Science 86;* and the regular departments are all you might expect."

The first issue in 1987 offered a 300,000 rate base. It climbed to 350,000 that fall, 400,000 in 1988, and 500,000 in 1989. James S. Martay, the New York-based executive publisher responsible for ad sales and one of the initial fund-raisers, and his staff sold 108 ad pages during 1987, bringing in $535,000. In 1988, the numbers soared to 214 and $1,525,000, respectively. Its best prospects for ads were food and auto companies. Most disappointing were over-the-counter drug makers—leaving *Hippocrates* shy of budgeted ad goals.

Hippocrates delivered in-depth, well-crafted stories and was rated the No. 1 health magazine by *U.S. News & World Report.*[35]

Hippocrates celebrated its first anniversary with the National Magazine Award for general excellence for magazines with circulations of 100,000 to 400,000, praised for finding a niche between "high-brow medical magazines and popular health magazines." Advertising had more than doubled, and the magazine planned to become monthly in the next year, hoping to raise its 400,000 circulation to 800,000 readers in two years. About 90 percent of its subscribers in 1988 were college educated, and two-thirds were women.[36] It is now published seven times a year, and its circulation has continued to increase.

Schrier said *Hippocrates* has two missions: to show the impact of nutrition and medicine on people's lives and to give the reader information on which to act in his or her own best interest. "It's service journalism in the best sense," he said.[37]

Hippocrates continued to grow. In less than two years, circulation almost doubled, and advertising revenues almost tripled. In 1988, Time Inc. invested $9 million to acquire a 50 percent interest, with options for a full buyout in the early 1990s.

"We're still a young magazine," Schrier said in 1988, "spending more than we're making"—$1 million to $2 million, publishing executives estimated.

S. Christopher Meigher III, Time Inc. executive vice-president and group publisher, said the partnership provided an infusion of cash "to achieve the growth they were beginning to feel was inherent." He said, "*Hippocrates* is a superior magazine with the potential to be a leader in the health category, an area where we expect long-term growth."

Hippocrates' target is women. In 1988, about 75 percent of its readers were female. Its more sophisticated editorial content appealed to the more affluent (average household income, $48,600) and better educated (78.6 percent attended college).[38]

When Time made its investment in 1988, Elliott wrote that Time's expertise could make a difference on newsstand sales, then just 5 percent of total circulation (very low), and, in selling advertising, Time would share its considerable experience

HEALTH & MEDICINE FOR PHYSICIANS

HIPPOCRATES

THE SECRET

Everyone trusts him. He's also one of the thousands of doctors with the AIDS virus who are afraid to tell their patients. What would you do?

When Columbus Discovered Good Health

Bush and Clinton on Abortion, Insurance, and Family Health

Hippocrates for physicians is a spin-off of *Health* magazine, originally called *Hippocrates*, and uses a large amount of editorial copy from *Health*. (Courtesy *Hippocrates*.)

and resources. Advertisers could qualify for a package rate that combined ad pages in *Hippocrates* with similar pages in Time's *Cooking Light* and *People.* Spinoff potentials were considered—video, pamphlets distributed via doctors' offices, even other magazines. One newsletter was under way, and three more were to be tested in 1988.[39] *Consumer Magazine Rates and Data* in 1992 indicated that *Health* is sold in combination with *Cooking Light.*

Although the $9 million investment was a relatively small one for Time, the company said it would take an active role in the magazine's management and had ambitious plans for *Hippocrates'* expansion. Time would appoint half the members of the company's board, though operations would continue to be led by president and editor Eric Schrier.

Hippocrates was the third magazine in which Time acquired a half or nearly half stake. At that time, it also owned 49 percent of *Parenting* magazine and a half-interest in Working Woman/McCall's Inc., publisher of the two women's magazines.[40] *McCall's* since has become a property of The New York Times Company and *Working Woman* one of Lang Communications.

Hippocrates won the 1989 National Magazine Award for a single-topic issue.

The name was changed to *In Health* in January 1990, when *Hippocrates* became the name of a business publication for physicians. Schrier said the editors had found out that many copies of the original *Hippocrates* mailed to physicians' waiting rooms had never reached them because the physicians took them home and read them. Thus, beginning in 1990, *Hippocrates* was created for those physicians.

After Family Media ceased operations in 1991, *In Health* bought rights to the name *Health* and changed its magazine's name once again with the February 1992 issue.

Hippocrates, the Business Publication

When consumer magazine *Hippocrates'* name was changed to *In Health* in January 1990, the name *Hippocrates* was transferred to a business magazine created for physicians, made up 60 percent from editorial in *In Health* and 40 percent from editorial created for *Hippocrates.* Using controlled circulation, this new *Hippocrates* quickly reached its target of 120,000 physicians.

The publisher's editorial profile of *Hippocrates* as a business magazine looks a lot like the one for the consumer magazine (only this one carries pharmaceutical advertising):

Hippocrates focuses on information and important news relevant to the impact that health and medicine have on people's lives. Departments include: Vital Signs, Vital Statistics, Food, Healthy Cooking, Fitness, Family, Vanities, Drugs, Mind, Rounds, Stitches, Help Yourself, Housecalls, Clippings, Reflexes, At the FDA, Appendix.

Hippocrates' 1991 mid-year BPA audit confirmed a total circulation of 128,352—121,492 nonpaid and 6,860 paid. The business analysis of one issue's circulation showed the magazine's recipients were in internal medicine (43,707 [including osteopathic 834]); family practice (35,403 [0 osteopathic]); general practice (25,652 [8,983]); cardiovascular diseases (10,602 [239]); nephrology (3,707 [75]); endocrinology (2,784 [34]); diabetes (497 [0]); and other osteopathic physicians in other specialties (5,980). Total circulation for the analyzed issue was 128,332: 112,187 medical physicians and 16,145 osteopathic physicians.

As emphasized earlier in this chapter, there is no typical magazine launch. This is not a rags-to-riches lucky start. It is an example of how experienced, award-winning magazine editors started a new magazine and sold a major stake in it to the world's largest magazine publishing company. This is the same company that bought *Southern* magazine, suspended it, converted it to *Southpoint,* and killed it, all within less than one year. *Hippocrates/In Health/Health* is an example of knowledgeable people having to work very, very hard to launch and needing the infusion of *Time*'s cash to keep going and growing. There are few Cinderella stories in magazine publishing.

Air & Space Smithsonian

Spinning off *Air & Space* from *Smithsonian* illustrates another approach to testing a magazine. After two years of discussion of Walter Boyne's idea for a magazine that reflects the broad interests of the National Air and Space Museum, a sample of *Smithsonian* subscribers was surveyed about the proposed magazine in March 1985. The response by 62 percent was encouraging, as was the indication that 20.6 percent would subscribe to *Air & Space* and 8.6 percent would buy gift subscriptions.

A random sample of 412 visitors to the museum was surveyed in March 1985; 41 percent said they would subscribe for themselves or someone else and 41 percent said "maybe" they would subscribe. Almost equal numbers would subscribe at three suggested prices, $15, $18, and $20. The respondents were split evenly between first-time and repeat museum visitors.

A self-administered survey of 1,100 museum visitors from August through October 1984 had found that 88 percent would subscribe to a quarterly museum journal, that their primary interest was in new developments in aviation and space, and that 18 percent currently read an aviation, space, or science magazine.

Test mailings offering subscriptions to the proposed *Air & Space* went out in the summer of 1985 and were analyzed that September. A recommendation to proceed with the magazine was made to the secretary of the Smithsonian Institution and to the Smithsonian's Board of Regents. An editor, an art director, and an advertising director were hired, a circulation consultant was brought in, and they began to assemble their staffs. The publisher and general manager of *Smithsonian* added those same duties with the new magazine. The full mailing using the test package that had pulled best went out at year-end, and the first issue was published in the spring, dated April/May 1986.

The idea was informally considered for about two years, but the actual process of starting the magazine took about one year. A dummy was prepared for prospective advertisers, and the magazine's design was developed, with no intention of looking like *Smithsonian.* The magazine is published bimonthly and, for the first six months of 1992, had a circulation of 331,000. At the same time, *Smithsonian,* started in 1970, was circulating 2.18 million copies each month.

The first issue of *Air & Space,* dated April–May 1986, followed two years of discussions and one year of serious study of the magazine's feasability. It benefited from its association with already successful *Smithsonian.* (Courtesy *Air & Space.*)

Caribbean Travel & Life

O. Keith Hallam, Jr., who once owned a restaurant in the Caribbean but had no background in magazines, started *Caribbean Travel & Life* as a quarterly, then increased to bimonthly. Advertising was a major frustration, said Hallam. He expected the islands' tourist bureaus, Caribbean cruise lines, airlines, and other travel companies to view his magazine as an ideal advertising vehicle. However, he immediately found out that advertisers are highly skeptical of new magazines. The most common reply was, "Come back and see us in a year or so," he said.

The first issue had 12 pages of advertising, but only 5 were paid ads. The spring 1987 issue had 28 paid advertising pages for $75,000 in advertising revenue.

From island tourist surveys, Hallam had found that Caribbean visitors tend to come from 10 major American cities and earn at least $50,000. A demographic research firm compiled a list of names and addresses to target those households. Hallam used that list to select potential readers, who received a free copy and a subscription offer. It sold for $3.95 an issue or $12.95 a year. Hallam said he and others had invested $500,000.

The Hearst Corporation

The Hearst Corporation's approach to new magazines has been to start them as annuals and then, if they strike a chord, to increase their frequency. The method holds losses to a minimum. In 1975, Hearst introduced *Colonial Homes,* which was converted in 1979 to a bimonthly. In 1978, its *Country Living* appeared and caught readers' fancy so swiftly that it went bimonthly in February 1980.

One of Hearst's launches as an annual, *Colonial Homes* now appears bimonthly. (Courtesy of *Colonial Homes* Magazine / Hearst Corporation.)

Hearst Corporation's *Country Living* began as an annual in 1978 and moved to bimonthly publication in 1980. (Courtesy *Country Living*.)

A High-Risk Business

Even though hundreds of proposed new magazines each year never even make it past the drawing board to the first issue, entrepreneurs continue to attempt to launch their ideas. If their magazines survive, investors must often wait three to five years to see a profit, according to Richard L. LePere, a Washington-based magazine consultant.

The industry's average net profit is 10.65 percent, according to the Magazine Publishers of America. However, LePere emphasizes wide variations, from magazines losing money to those with more than 40 percent profit.

Behind most magazine start-ups is a young, energetic, never-say-die individual, who, if he or she weren't selling a magazine, might enthusiastically be selling something else; someone who would sell the house, sell the car, sell the home-heating oil, if need be, to make his or her magazine go. "It's like religion," one magazine consultant said. "The person eats, sleeps, and dreams his magazine."

Thomas O. Ryder, former president of American Express Publishing Company, warns that inexperienced magazine creators who are strapped for cash can fall into some serious traps, such as depending on free copies to get readers and boost circulation high enough to attract advertisers. "It cuts the costs at the beginning, but it cuts the potential at the end," Ryder said, adding that revenues ideally should come evenly from advertising and subscriptions.

Ryder also was skeptical that any consumer magazine could be launched for less than $1 million, particularly if the creators have no experience in magazine publishing. "The most inspired ideas might well come from people who have a dream. But the failure rate among those people is extraordinarily high," Ryder said. "There are a few people who are so determined and so talented" that they can make it work. Probably the most common reason magazines don't succeed is inexperienced management.

It's not impossible to start a new magazine if you are not already a major magazine publisher. However, in today's crowded media market, it is difficult. Magazine industry knowledge and experience, coupled with adequate financing, will help tip the balance toward the side of success.

Notes

1. Edmund Wilson, "The Literary Worker's Polonius," in *The Shores of Light* (New York: Farrar, Straus and Giroux, 1952), p. 593.
2. N. R. Kleinfield, "The Itch to Start a Magazine," *New York Times* (2 December 1979): 10F.
3. James Playsted Wood, *Magazines in the United States,* 3d ed. (New York: Ronald Press, 1971), p. 207.
4. W. A. Swanberg, *Luce and His Empire* (New York: Charles Scribner's Sons, 1972), pp. 59, 62–63, and 66; Theodore Peterson, *Magazines in the Twentieth Century,* 2d ed. (Urbana: University of Illinois Press, 1964), pp. 236–37.
5. Peterson, pp. 237–38.
6. Swanberg, p. 144.
7. John Mack Carter, "The Pros Said It Couldn't Be Done, but *People's* Making It," *Folio:* (February 1976): 58.
8. Ibid.
9. *Time* (4 March 1974): 42.
10. *Media Industry Newsletter* (13 June 1977): 1; (8 August 1977): 1.
11. Ibid.
12. *Time Incorporated 1980 Annual Report.*
13. *USA Today* (10 February 1983): 1D, 2D.
14. Ben H. Bagdikian, *The Media Monopoly,* 3d ed. (Boston: Beacon, 1992), p. 4.
15. Ibid., p. 240.
16. Time Warner 1991 Annual Report, p. 8.
17. "Lessons of Leadership: John H. Johnson of Ebony," *Nation's Business* (April 1974): 48.
18. Ibid., p. 46.
19. Peterson, p. 66.
20. *Nation's Business* (April 1974): 49.
21. Ibid., p. 48.
22. Peterson, p. 66.
23. *Nation's Business,* p. 50.

24. " 'Failure Is a Word I Don't Accept,' an Interview with John H. Johnson," *Harvard Business Review* (March–April 1976): 85.
25. *Nation's Business,* p. 49.
26. *Time* (4 May 1970): 79–80.
27. *Newsweek* (17 July 1972): 71.
28. *Media Industry Newsletter* (23 February 1973): 3.
29. Speech by publisher Edward Lewis to the ASME Editorial Luncheon, 14 September 1976.
30. Marjorie McManus, "The Essence Magazine Success Story," *Folio:* (December 1976): 28–29.
31. McManus, p. 28.
32. *Media Industry Newsletter* (9 January 1980): 6.
33. John Love, "Birth of a Notion," *TWA Ambassador* (October 1980): 47.
34. Stuart Elliott, "Profile: Vital Signs: Hippocrates Editor Eric Schrier Is Healthy, Wealthy, and Wise," *Continental Profiles* (January 1989): 41–42, 44.
35. Ibid., p. 44.
36. Katherine Bishop, "Magazine Finds a Niche in Medicine and Health," *The New York Times* (31 May 1988): [n.p.].
37. Ibid.
38. Elliott, pp. 24, 40–41.
39. Ibid., p. 45.
40. Laura Landro, "Time Inc. Buys 50% of Magazine Devoted to Health," *Wall Street Journal* (28 July 1988): [n.p.].

4

Editorial Concepts

A plan to serve women with information and features about parenting, health and medicine, beauty, fashion, self-improvement, food and nutrition, home decorating and design, personalities, and current events provides a basic concept for a magazine. A concept is a mental image that may be abstract or concrete. An editorial concept often begins as general and largely abstract and is refined and developed toward the specific and concrete. As this process takes place, the editorial concept is developed into an *editorial formula* from decisions made about the kinds of content the magazine will publish, the kinds of readers it will cater to, and the kinds of advertisers it will attempt to attract.

Redbook is edited for young working mothers and women juggling job and family. Its content includes parenting, health, sexuality, and fiction, divided into at least eight departments. (Courtesy *Redbook*.)

Editorial Formula

There is no universal definition of an editorial formula. Basically, it is the mixture of editorial material that makes up a magazine, the content that establishes the magazine's personality. Formula is the continuing or long-range editorial concept of the magazine expressed as specific kinds of content or topics. It can be broken into at least three major components: departments, articles within departments, and general types of content.

Departments

The most obvious component of a magazine's formula is its departments that continue from issue to issue. Readers are familiar with the departments in their favorite magazines, and that is one reason to departmentalize content. In *Better Homes and Gardens,* these inlcude On the Cover, Between Friends, The Family at Home, Family Matters, Good Food, and Shopping. Some of these are further subdivided. The Family at Home includes Gardening, Decorating, Building, and Crafts. Articles in Family Matters deal with Education, Parenting, Health, Environment, Travel, and Pets.

Redbook divides its content into Stars & Entertainment, Love & Sex, Health & Healing, Beauty & Fashion, News & Views, Short Story, Food & Nutrition, and You & Your Child. *Family Circle*'s departments include Food/Nutrition, Beauty/Fashion, Decorating/Crafts, Health/Fitness, Articles, How-To's, and Regular Features. *Southern Living*'s content groups include the current month's features, Travel, Gardens, Homes, Foods, Directories, and Southwords, several regular topics.

Articles in *Skin Diver* are grouped under Photography, Dive Equipment, Caribbean Diving, Pacific Diving, Live-Aboard Diving, Florida Diving, Miscellaneous, Columns, and Departments. Many consumer magazines list short items that appear in every issue as "Departments." *Popular Mechanics* features Automobiles, Boating, Home Improvement, Aviation, Science/Technology, Electronics, and Departments.

Columns, bylined or on specific topics, may function as departments. Books about the South and Southern Journal in *Southern Living* are examples. Circle This, Letter from the Editor, and Best Reader Tips appear regularly in *Family Circle*.

Articles Within Departments

Most departments are large enough to contain several articles, and some of these articles' topics may be repeated in nearly every issue. Money Facts (a registered service mark) by Jane Bryant Quinn is a regular feature in *Woman's Day*. Three examples from *Family Circle* are Women Who Make a Difference, What's for Dinner? and Beauty and Fashion Hotline. *Better Homes and Gardens* has Prize Tested Recipes, Family Network, and The Man Next Door. All three are registered service marks.

General Types of Content

In place of or in addition to departments and continuing articles within departments, magazines have more general types of content as part of their formulas. Fiction is an example. The fiction may not appeal to the same type of reader each issue and may be on vastly different subjects from issue to issue, but fiction itself is a continuing element of the formula. Another magazine may have a travel piece each issue. One time it may appeal to readers interested in inexpensively roughing it along the Atlantic seashore; another time it may tell about luxurious accommodations in Aruba. Although the appeals are different, travel is a component of the formula. Poetry, cartoons, jokes, news, editorials, and photo essays are forms of content that can be included under this heading.

Formula itself is a sterile term. It is obvious that a magazine's character or personality results from creative editing by an imaginative editor and editorial team. Beyond the subject matter discussed in the magazine are the angles, writing style, illustrations, graphic display—many, many nuances that cannot be reduced to formula.

In a sense, the editorial concept or objective is a basic plan agreed to by the publisher and editorial staff about what the magazine is to be. The formula itself deals with editorial content, both the subject matter and the mode of presentation necessary to carry out the concept.

The key to success is to attract people to buy the magazine, and then to keep their interest with content that is in tune with their thinking, issue after issue. The magazine must be reader-oriented and appeal to enough readers to keep circulation up and advertisers interested. On a sponsored or controlled circulation magazine, the trick is to get the intended audience to read the publication.

Some editors insist they never edit to a formula. They may be right, but any magazine edited with a degree of consistency has a formula, though it may be implicit in the editor's thinking rather than in the form of a written statement. Most of these editors certainly know where their magazines are headed and try to steer them on a clear course. Norman Cousins was one of these. In an editorial for *Saturday Review,* he wrote, "The one thing I learned about editing over the years is that you have to edit and publish out of your own tastes, enthusiasms, and concerns, and not out of notions or guesswork about what other people might like to read."[1]

As he was launching *World,* Cousins said,

There are two ways to produce a magazine. You can get a marketing organization to tell you what people want and then edit to meet their needs. Or you can edit to please yourself, as I do, and hope that enough people share your enthusiasm and concerns to make the magazine a success.[2]

Actually, Cousins had several continuing departments, features, and monthly supplements in his magazine—what could be called a formula. However, he was one of those editors whose ideas and tastes fit in with those of his readers well enough that he didn't have to consciously tell himself what his readers were interested in.

This suggests the ideal editor, one who is so close to his or her readers and their enthusiasms and tastes—in fact usually a step ahead—that the editor's interests dovetail with theirs well enough to maintain their loyalty while attracting new readers. Most great editors have had that characteristic: George Horace Lorimer of the *Saturday Evening Post,* Edward Bok of *Ladies' Home Journal,* and DeWitt

Wallace of *Reader's Digest*. For a few such geniuses, an editor's decision to edit a magazine to please oneself may work, but, for most editors, guidance by a formula is essential.

Publisher's Editorial Profile

The publisher's editorial profile of each magazine listed in Standard Rate and Data Service publications describes the magazine for advertisers and potential advertisers. The statements tend to be general and, in some magazine classifications, such as women's magazines, almost indistinguishable. Nonetheless, they are useful in giving a capsule description of the editorial formula or, in a few instances, the editorial concept.

TV Guide's entry starts with editorial concept and concludes with editorial formula:

TV Guide watches television; network—local, cable/pay—with an eye for how TV programming affects and reflects society. Its national editorial section looks at the shows, the stars and covers the medium's impact on news, sports, politics, literature, the arts, science and social issues through reports, profiles, features, commentaries and backgrounders. The local section contains network, local and pay/cable programming information for 106 local edition areas, that includes a Pay-TV Movie Guide, expanded grids, daily previews and close-ups on important programming.

The publisher's editorial profile of *Seventeen* briefly describes its formula:

Seventeen is a general service magazine for young women emphasizing Fashion, Beauty, and Lifestyle information, including health, food, careers, relationships, sports, and entertainment.

The Rotarian also describes its formula in its publisher's editorial profile:

The Rotarian addresses the personal and business interests of a selected audience involved in business or one of the professions. The chief purpose of *The Rotarian* is to report Rotary news and general subjects directed to the interests, loyalty and involvement of its member audience. Regular monthly departments feature Executive Health, Book Review, Trends, and Manager's Memo. General articles cover such topics as business, travel, health, education, environment, management and ethics, sciences, sports and adventure. Rotary's four avenues of service are stressed: (1) advancement of international understanding, goodwill and peace; (2) better vocational relationships; (3) better community life; (4) better human relationships.

Redbook's entry deals with the target audience and then goes into a general description of formula:

Redbook Magazine is edited for young, working mothers, women juggling husband, family, home and job. Editorial deals with fashion, beauty and health articles. Also covers food and nutrition, parenting, relationships, sexuality and fiction.

Southern Living's entry closely parallels the departmentalized content of its monthly issues:

Southern Living is edited for, and concerns, the tastes and interests of contemporary Southerners. The magazine regularly traces developments in the areas of travel and recreation, homes and building, gardening and landscaping, and food and entertaining.

According to Roland Wolseley, determining the formula requires consideration of several major factors:

1. Purpose of the magazine
2. Market for the magazine
3. Standard of living of the potential readers
4. Educational and cultural level of the potential readers
5. Competitors in the field and *their formulas*
6. Tested formulas—whether existing formulas have worked
7. Climate of opinion of the public generally, and how it might react to the proposed magazine
8. The financial horizon or limits set on the formula by the financial condition of the magazine's owners

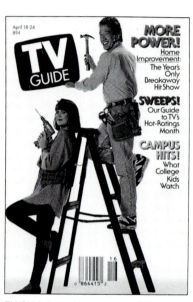

TV Guide has changed several times over the years, as the television industry it watches has developed from broadcasting into a complex field with cable and pay-per-view options. (Courtesy *TV Guide*.)

His last point suggests that the owners should be able to sustain the intended formula over a long period of time until the magazine becomes established, or the magazine may drastically change when portions of the formula are eliminated or modified for economic reasons. Such changes might involve dropping extensive four-color printing, eliminating articles by top-name writers, going to less-expensive paper stock, or sacrificing other content that is too costly.

Editorial Objectives

An objective is a desired goal or end that the magazine wants to achieve. An editorial objective could be to get a specific bill passed by Congress or to increase awareness of a communicable disease by a measurable amount among its readers. The magazine supports passage of the bill until it is passed or defeated, or it publishes information about the disease until surveys show that the goal of increased awareness has been achieved. If the bill is passed or the awareness goal is achieved, the magazine has achieved its objective.

Public Relations Magazine Objectives

Especially in a corporation's public relations program, objectives for employee, customer, and dealer magazines may be stated so all involved are re-reminded where the magazines are headed. In each instance, the readers' and the corporation's interests must be considered in developing reasonable objectives.

On an employee magazine, the editor often is in the middle between production employees and management. Employees want good wages that continually increase, while the company wants reliability and a high level of productivity. To be effective, an editor must make the employees aware of the company's expectations in terms of the employees' expectations and from their point of view.

Employee magazines may pursue objectives, such as increasing customer satisfaction, reducing waste in supplies or raw materials, improving the quality of the product, or improving on-time delivery. They may deal with more personal topics, such as reducing stress, personal finance, health and safety, alcohol and drug addiction programs, drug testing, and other issues that affect employee performance.

After examining both the employees' and the company's expectations, a list of objectives can be developed. Common objectives for *employee magazines* include

1. Informing employees of company news and policies
2. Explaining and interpreting company policies in terms of employees and their interests
3. Developing employees' pride in their jobs and their company
4. Developing loyalty to the company
5. Helping to improve the company's product quality, efficiency, and customer satisfaction

Sales magazines usually are edited to help salespeople operate more efficiently to maintain or increase their sales. To achieve this objective, they include articles about new products, improvements in existing products, new applications for existing products, and ways in which salespeople have made big sales. Other content typically includes company promotional activities; company policies regarding merchandising, returns, guarantees, sales contests, and discounts; competitors' activities and sales pitches; success stories of company salespeople; and techniques of selling. They often contain light and humorous material to win readership and in keeping with the tradition that conversation is a salesperson's stock in trade.

Dealer magazines generally are expected to build brand loyalty; therefore, they tell about the company's products, describe successful merchandising ideas, and try to increase cooperation between the merchandiser and the manufacturer by explaining and interpreting company policies.

Customer magazines attempt to contribute to the prestige and goodwill of the company and, in the long run, to build customer loyalty and repeat sales. The formula usually centers on interesting, useful information, ideas for using the product, and expert information on maintenance of the product, especially in the automotive field, along with some entertainment.

Shareholder or *corporate magazines* are some of the most colorful and elegantly designed magazines. Aimed at shareholders who are not active in the management of the company, they tend to deal with large issues that affect the company, international operations, changes in operations, and plans for the future. Environmental concerns and world markets are typical topics. A shareholder magazine generally has two major functions: (1) to inform readers about the company specifically and about the industry it is part of and (2) to win or hold readers' approval of management's activities and policies. Several shareholder magazines have broader scopes and are issued to customers and government and civic leaders as well. These often contain more articles not related directly to the company.

In planning how to meet the magazine's objectives, the editor of a public relations magazine must keep in mind that the magazine must earn and retain the acceptance and respect of readers, as well as skillfully present the management viewpoint.

Maytag Merchandiser is published for Maytag dealers and salespeople. (Courtesy *Maytag Merchandiser*.)

Editorial Plans to Meet Objectives

The formula and objectives imply long-range plans, which involve imaginatively determining what kinds of pieces in the formula to run in each of the next several issues. Depending on the type and frequency of the magazine, editors work several issues and several months ahead. *Better Homes and Gardens* provides its promotion department with editorial plans 11 months ahead of an issue's publication date. The editors of many monthly magazines work about six months ahead in their detailed planning. The astute editor plans ahead to have the right article at the right time—not just a timely article that fits the department or formula, but the article that will appeal to the mood of the public at the time it is published.

At any given time, the editor is planning several issues ahead, as well as closing the current one. He or she has to keep in mind how long it takes to get assigned articles from staff writers and free-lancers. A public opinion survey may take two or three months to plan and conduct before someone can even begin to write the article. Translating objectives into specific articles that will meet them is a major challenge of editing. The topic, the angle to interest readers, the length, and the illustrations all affect the ultimate decisions. To successfully meet this major editing challenge, editors must keep records of article ideas and assignments made for each issue to keep track of how things progress toward deadline.

Balancing Content

Part of editing is balancing content, both within one issue and over a long period of time, perhaps a year's issues, in fulfilling the formula and objectives. Readers like variety and quickly sense monotony in topics or content. The formula itself suggests balance of content. Some magazines even break their formulas into percentages.

A public relations magazine for employees may have a general formula and balance, such as 40 percent company news and features, 20 to 40 percent general (noncompany) features, 5 to 20 percent employee news, and 5 to 15 percent employee participation and opinion.

How content is balanced varies from editor to editor. Some do it all in their heads and come out beautifully. Others go as far as to store in computers the amount of each type of article so they can get printouts showing percentages for each issue and the year-to-date. In between, some keep lists or charts of the kinds of content in the formula; the article types, titles, and amounts for each issue; and cumulative figures for the year. Whichever system is used, the editor must make a conscious effort to balance content.

Balance involves (1) variety, (2) breadth of coverage, (3) consistency, and (4) purpose. Few readers can take a steady diet of heavy articles or light articles; a mixture must be provided to maintain interest and to let readers pace themselves through the issue.

Variety in types of content is essential, too, such as balancing human interest articles against serious articles, text against illustration, long pieces against short ones, sprightly or inspirational material against bland or routine subjects, or company news against general features. Good editors cover a broad range of topics of interest to readers, from recurring themes and routine material to new ideas and developments. Editors continually generate new ideas to go along with their blend of standard or traditional fare, such as the January and February income tax tips and the March and April gardening tips.

A final reminder on an issue's content comes from Herbert Mayes, former editor of *McCall's:* "Vital to a magazine are the regular columns intended to capture readers' issue-to-issue attention. . . . They are bread and butter on the editorial menu." He advised, "Never consider a magazine schedule ready to go unless it is at least as good as the last one, and when possible introduce an unexpected feature."[3]

Regional Editions

Nearly 200 magazines offer regional or demographic editions to capitalize on regional advertising revenue. This way, a business in a large metropolitan or sizable geographic area can reach prime prospects at reasonable rates while avoiding wasted circulation of its ad in copies of the magazine distributed in other parts of the country.

The number of regional editions a magazine publishes depends on its circulation and the location of that circulation. Demographic editions can be offered if the magazine has enough subscribers in a given occupation or income group.

Time magazine's circulation is divided into 11 regional editions, such as the Eastern edition of 1.4 million circulation. *Time* also offers 50 spot market editions on alternating weeks. Its demographic editions include the *Time* Business edition for 1.65 million business executives, *Time* Top Management edition (617,000), and *Time* Top Zips of 1.4 million subscribers in the highest income Zip code areas. State editions are available for all 50 states and the District of Columbia. That's 115 editions of *Time* in the United States.

TV Guide has 115 editions, *Family Circle* 72, and *Better Homes and Gardens* 95, and America's largest circulation magazine, *Modern Maturity,* has 13. *Newsweek* lists 105 editions, including *Newsweek* Woman, *Newsweek* Business, *Newsweek* Homeowner, and *Newsweek* 50 Plus. *National Geographic* has 30 editions, *Playboy* 14, and *Ski* and *Skiing* 3 each.[4]

Although advertisements in some of these editions, particularly for small circulation areas, are sold in only full-page units, many are not. The result is that many of these editions need editorial matter to fill the space left after regional or demographic ads have been dummied. How the editorial operation fits in with regional editions varies among magazines.

In a study limited to magazines with six or more regional or split-run editions, Carol Reuss found that about one-third of the magazines have no editorial involvement in regional editions, about one-third maintain a bank of material that the

Outdoor Life publishes its editorial content in four regional editions: South, Midwest, East, and West. About nine pages per issue are strictly regional editorial content, the rest national. In most magazines, only advertising is published regionally. (Courtesy *Outdoor Life*.)

makeup or production editor can use to fill the remaining space in regional editions, and about one-third generate at least some material for specific regions or demographic groups.[5] Only two magazines in the study, *Farm Journal* and *Outdoor Life,* regularly run special sections of editorial content in regional or demographic editions. *Farm Journal* has been issuing geographic editions since 1952, when it began with three. Advertisers requested even more editions, until there were 39. *Outdoor Life* published regional inserts, each an eight-page section on yellow stock, for its regional editions. The articles varied from short news items to multiple-page articles, with all copy oriented to the outdoor activities and life of the region involved. Magazines that reported creating special copy for regional or demographic editions included *McCall's, Successful Farming,* and *Nation's Business.*[6]

Knowing the Reader

Effective editing involves meeting objectives, balancing content, and, ultimately, appealing to the reader. Editors learn to know their own readers, but communication research tells us something about readers in general that can help us be more effective editors.

1. People tend to read, look at, and listen to material they already are interested in. People who are interested in a subject, even if they don't know much about that subject, welcome information about it. However, those who have no interest are a poor target for such information.
2. People tend to read and listen to material that they agree with and to avoid that with which they do not agree. If people are confronted with material they disagree with, they tend to interpret—or misinterpret—that material to make it conform to what they already believe. People see the world through a filter of attitude patterns, and they try to keep those patterns intact by screening out material that would disrupt them.
3. People tend to check their opinions with authorities. Through personal influence, these opinion leaders can be important in causing people to make up or change their minds. These authority points seem to be scattered throughout the population. People find these opinion leaders at their own level, although they may have different authorities for advice on different subjects. Opinion leaders are heavy users of mass media, but they also get opinions from their opinion leaders. It is an intricate network of personal influence and media.
4. People tend to check their opinions and attitudes against those of the groups to which they belong. Attitudes with anchors in the group are hard to change. When the media's content comes up against these attitudes, little headway is made in changing opinions, values, or behavior.

Magazine Influence

Some magazine editors believe they have great impact on large numbers of their readers. Other editors feel a close personal relationship with their readers, even if they have not met them. Many editors take almost any feedback from readers as evidence of great success, and a few even wonder if their readers are paying attention to what they are publishing. What is the influence of a magazine and its editor?

All mass media probably have their greatest influence over a long time span; a single magazine issue or television broadcast seldom has a noticeable effect. One article may trigger a newspaper editorial, a rash of letters to legislators, a congressional speech or bill, or an article or series in other publications. However, this is the exception rather than the rule, and magazine influence usually is more subtle.

Theodore Peterson suggests there is no good way to separate magazines from the culture in which they are a force and by which they are conditioned—no way to separate the effects of magazines from those of other forms of communication. He concludes, though, that the nature of the magazine suits it for introducing new ideas to a democratic society, for providing a forum for discussion, for sustaining campaigns over long periods, and for working toward cumulative effect rather than single impact. Like other print media, the magazine's appeal is more to the intellect than to the senses and emotions of its audience. "In short, the magazine by nature well met the requirements for a medium of instruction and interpretation for the leisurely, critical reader" in the first two-thirds of the twentieth century, he said.[7]

Peterson mentions several accomplishments of magazines in the 20th century. Magazines have helped foster social and political reforms; have interpreted issues and events and put them in national perspective; have been an inexpensive instructor in daily living; and have been an educator in our cultural heritage through their historical articles, biographical articles, and attention to art. The variety of magazines was noteworthy, arising from selectivity of audience. As Peterson wrote, "the typical magazine was not edited for just 'everybody'; it was edited for a following with some mutual activity or outlook. Because they sought out little publics within the population at large, magazines in the aggregate represented a wide range of tastes and opinions."[8]

A magazine is very much like a living organism and should not be overinstitutionalized in the editor's thinking. Magazine history suggests that an editorial concept can grow and mature after "birth" but that, as society changes, so must the concept and formula.

Notes

1. "Final Report to the Readers," *Saturday Review* (27 November 1971): 32.
2. Newspaper Enterprise Association interview, *Columbus* [Ohio] *Citizen-Journal* (11 April 1972): 12.
3. Herbert R. Mayes, *The Magazine Maze* (Garden City, N.Y.: Doubleday & Company, 1980), pp. 97, 119–20.
4. *Consumer Magazine and Agri-Media Rates and Data* (April 1992).
5. Carol Reuss, "Editorial Involvement in Regional/Split Run Editions," paper presented at the Association for Education in Journalism Convention, 1973; updated 1976.
6. Ibid., 1976 addendum.
7. Theodore Peterson, *Magazines in the Twentieth Century,* 2d ed. (Urbana: University of Illinois Press, 1964), p. 442.
8. Ibid., pp. 450–51.

5 Editorial Administration

ASPIRING editors often think almost exclusively in terms of working with words, photographs, and graphic materials to create an appealing editorial product, but, no matter how small the magazine, *administration* is also an important part of magazine editing. Magazines are businesses as well as literary creations, and they require the help of adequate capital, sound organization, and efficient administration to achieve success.

Types of Ownership

Magazines operate under a variety of ownerships. Three common structures are the multiple-magazine publishing company, the media conglomerate or diversified corporation, and the single-magazine publishing company. The multiple publisher issues several magazines and may operate each as a subsidiary, division, or profit center, or it may operate groups of magazines that way. If a single magazine or group loses money, corporation funds can be used to maintain operation until the magazine makes money again or is suspended.

The media conglomerate operates in several media fields, such as magazine publishing, cable television, television, radio, and possibly newspaper publishing. It also may have book clubs and direct-mail sales operations. There is no big difference between it and a multiple publisher except that, as we describe them, the conglomerate is more widely diversified, and magazine publishing may be actually only a small part of the operation.

Publisher

In virtually all magazine organizations, the publisher is the top executive, with final authority over all departments, both editorial and business.

The publisher, as owner or the owner's representative, is the ultimate policy maker for the magazine. In a multiple publishing house or conglomerate, he or she may be publisher of a group of magazines. Directing both editorial and business operations, the publisher usually is more inclined toward the business side because he or she has probably come up through the business ranks. The editor, then, must spend much time making the editorial staff's objectives, intentions, and positions known to the publisher and proposing policy that will benefit the total magazine in the long term.

The editor, too, realizes that, without adequate income and profits, the magazine is not likely to continue publication, and is primarily concerned for editorial excellence in the context of successful business. The necessity for business success on the single-magazine publishing operation is obvious. The magazine editor makes a profit or finds an angel to subsidize it—or it goes out of business.

Within the magazine organization, the editor is likely to be one of three persons who report to the publisher, perhaps through an assistant publisher. The other two are the advertising director and the circulation director. Editors try to remain apart from the advertising and circulation operations, but they assist with promotion and appreciate the interrelationship among editorial, advertising, and circulation that must be part of a successful magazine.

Editor

Titles of top editors vary—editor-in-chief, executive editor, editor. For simplicity and clarity, *editor* is used here. The top editor on most magazines of any size is an administrator who seldom puts pencil to copy or writes a piece unless he or she remains in seclusion at home or stays late at the office to get it done.

Most of the editor's time is spent in four major activities: (1) staff relations and communication, (2) editorial supervision, (3) planning, and (4) public relations. The editor, whose name is at the top of the masthead, is usually obsessed with shaping the magazine to his or her editorial plans and tastes and with keeping errors out of the book. He or she delegates as much work as possible, especially the routine, but dozens of undelegated concerns come to the editor daily and occupy much time.

Realizing that one person cannot put out a magazine alone, an editor spends a lot of time with the staff individually and in small groups to explain actions, ideas, and aspirations for the book. Personal contact and communication with the staff are essential for the staff's work and the book's content to be cohesive. This time spent in a combination of editorial supervision and staff relations may appear to be inconsequential to the casual observer, but it is essential to keeping a magazine on-target and on production schedule.

Walking through the office, chatting with staffers, suggesting changes or pointing to new directions, spotting errors or incorrect emphasis, may look like socializing or meddling. However, done with businesslike informality, it contributes to efficiency and effectiveness. The editor must determine the best way to use his or her unique attributes—personality and editorial judgment—to motivate and supervise the staff, giving it sufficient freedom to be creative, while at the same time firmly maintaining editorial standards.

The editor must be thinking ahead several issues while supervising the completion of the current one. One thinks in season (groups of three or four issues) or points of emphasis in the specialized field—trade shows, conventions, new model introduction. The editor may be concerned with appropriate content to get a consumer magazine through the usual summer slump in consumer magazine interest, and other content to capitalize on renewed interest in the book that fall. He or she may be planning a depth report or an analytical feature that can make an impact for the book when it covers the annual trade show or the annual introduction of new models in its fields. An editor (on a monthly) thinks, in general terms, six months to a year ahead, while jelling the next three or four issues in his or her mind. Typically, the April issue this year will suggest ideas for next April's issue, and some plans toward it may begin immediately.

Editors keep the advertising department advised of editorial plans, especially if doing so may mean selling a few more ads in a particular issue. Although no respected editor would promise a favorable article about a company or its product, it is legitimate and good business for the advertising sales personnel to know the subjects and themes of upcoming issues to help them sell space.

Planning often results in an *editorial calendar,* which can be used by the advertising department to sell ads related to the major emphases or features in each issue. Business publications, especially, plan their coverage around trade shows and individual areas of expertise within the industries they cover.

U.S. News & World Report listed an editorial calendar that included 17 special issues and reports:

Issue	Editorial Emphasis
February 10	Mutual Funds Special Report
February 24	Quarterly Business Report
March 9	Taxes Special Report
March 23	Best Graduate Schools Annual Guide
April 6	Home Annual Guide
May 4	Health Annual Guide
June 1	Retirement Special Report
June 15	Best Hospitals Annual Guide
June 22	Quarterly Business Report
August 10	Money Guide
Aug. 31/Sept. 7	Election Double Issue
September 21	Quarterly Business Report
September 28	Best Colleges Annual Guide
October 19	Careers Annual Guide
November 23	Home Technology Special Report
December 7	Quarterly Business Report
Dec. 28/Jan. 5	Outlook Double Issue

Promotional angles also are conceived and communicated to the promotion manager. Also, if newsstand sales are a significant part of total circulation, promotion may want tie-in material, such as point-of-purchase placards, cover stickers, newspaper ads, television spots, or other devices to boost circulation.

Editors tend to be strong-willed individuals who see the broad picture, working at fitting the pieces together, promoting their magazines, and seeking favorable relations with readers, constituent groups, and advertisers. They normally won't withdraw from the excitement of keeping everything moving, although they may need to keep in mind what they can do best and what other staffers do best. They know the magazine cannot exist without the editorial department, but they may have an internal sense of humility when reminding themselves that less than 10 percent of a magazine's income is spent on its editorial operation. The remainder goes to production, promotion, sales, and profit. Although continually fighting for a larger budget, the successful editor recognizes the importance of controlling expenses and carefully manages the budget.

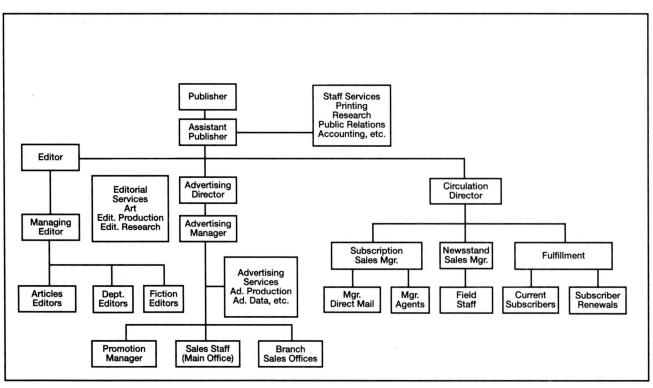

Magazine organization chart.

An important function within any organization is internal communication, and this supports the case for a small, efficient staff. The most effective communication usually is the give-and-take of interpersonal communication, or face-to-face conversation. Informal discussions about plans, articles, and editorial treatments are likely to be more productive than communication forced into a rigid structure. Some memos are inevitable (vacation policy, sick leave, fringe benefits), but personally checking with staff members to see that you are understood and that you understand their frustrations and emotional problems, as well as ideas, is imperative. If they get too far, the emotional problems of even one staff member can materially affect production of your book and throw it behind schedule.

The editor and publisher participate in basic decisions, Herbert Mayes, former editor of *McCall's,* observed. They determine circulation objectives, what advertisements will be accepted or rejected, the quality of paper to be used, the printer, and, with the circulation director, the size of each issue's print order. They join in determining the magazine's immediate and long-range goals.[1]

Public relations activities take a big chunk of an active editor's time. Public speaking opportunities are seized to advance ideas and promote the magazine's strength in its field. Publishers' groups, professional groups, civic groups, and groups of influential readers all want to hear a vigorous or thoughtful editor at times. Also, the editor wants the opportunity to speak and to get feedback, new ideas, and different angles from the members of these groups. The editor must get out and see what's going on in the field, as well as in the magazine office.

Although trying not to get tied down to the day-to-day operation, editors ensure a smooth work flow and efficient use of time and talent in the office. They may occasionally solve problems or establish new systems to increase efficiency, but they avoid routine mechanical functions.

Managing Editor

While the editor is involved in long-range planning, scheduling, and administration, the managing editor is concerned with the day-to-day and moment-to-moment chores of closing the current issue, taking care of the nitty-gritty of fitting all the pieces of a single issue into place and getting everything completed on time. One difference between an editor and a managing editor may be that the editor is looking further ahead and getting ready for the next three to six issues, while the managing editor is of necessity focusing on the current one.

For many journalists, the real action is in the managing editor's position. That's where decisions about whether to keep or discard a picture, how to phrase a title or blurb, or how to display an article are ultimately made. The managing editor works closely with writers, editors, art directors, and photographers to get the specifics right for the current issue.

Art Director

A well-staffed magazine is likely to have a full-time art director, who designs the magazine, selects typefaces for the title treatment or headlines, and plans display of pictures and of nonphotographic illustrations. He or she may or may not execute artwork for the magazine.

Art direction has been emphasized for years, since few editors are qualified to look simultaneously at the verbal and visual and to carry off a successful article display. This may be one reason the art director often is the number two person on the masthead, between editor and managing editor. In any case, the art director works closely with both of them to make the content as visually appealing as possible.

Quarterly and smaller magazines are more likely to have an outside art director from a design studio or an advertising agency do their issues.

News-oriented magazines often have less need for art direction, having established a formula or format that prescribes headline size and face, photo display, and departmental design, much like a newspaper's headline schedule and makeup plan. In this sense, *Time* and *Newsweek* are designed more like newspapers than magazines.

If the art director can also turn out finished art, so much the better, because art usually is ordered after the manuscript is in hand, and by that time the printing deadline is rapidly approaching. It's good to have a variety of art sources, but a good working relationship with one or two artists who understand your magazine, and who work rapidly, can yield excellent art almost by any deadline. Important maps may be produced in minutes; covers in a matter of hours. Artists who can do line drawings and turn out charts, graphs, and maps are relatively abundant throughout the country, and their services are relatively inexpensive.

Free-lance artists are readily available in most cities, as are writers and photographers. In New York, Chicago, and many large cities, they are listed in the telephone directory. In other cities, they can be found in ad agencies, creative printing and design studios, and sometimes in industrial design shops, from which they may moonlight for publications.

Smaller and less frequently published magazines that cannot support a full-time art director often find that their printers offer excellent art services at reasonable fees.

Computer-generated art, graphs, and graphic devices can be prepared by many people who cannot draw finished art. The movement to desktop publishing is leading toward having more and more graphics and art functions done in-house.

In a magazine, it is as important to maintain art quality as it is to maintain writing and photography quality. If some art you buy is not up to a publishable standard, do not hesitate to discard it. It is far better to pay for unpublished art than to ruin the quality of the magazine. Instead of thinking that you have paid for the art and, therefore, should use it, think of paying for overall magazine quality that may occasionally include the cost of discarded material that was carefully purchased.

Even when the art director is the number two person behind the editor, it is important to remember that a magazine editorial staff can have only one boss, one person in charge. Herbert Mayes advises and warns:

Art directors need to be pampered, praised, loved, especially in public. Now and then an art director could begin to feel he should be left to his own devices, his work not subject to the editor's veto. Permitted to get away with it, he becomes a burden. If I have said it before, it's worth saying again: There can be only one boss. It can't be the art director.[2]

Staff

Staff size is a function of the amount of work to be done and the level of efficiency desired. Editors often find that a small staff of 6 to 12 can work very efficiently without bumping into each other, duplicating effort, or having a clique on the fringe trying to be creative and becoming frustrated when their material is not used.

Magazines are highly individual enterprises, and the structure for one often will not work for another. However, generalizations are inevitable and give guidance to persons viewing the magazine scene or planning to work in it.

An entirely staff-written magazine is not typical of the industry. At the same time, free-lance writers find it relatively rough going if they don't also have a full-time job or, at least, a contract to do so many pieces a year for a magazine. Some material is staff generated—departments, continuing features, news sections, reader service features. Other material is commissioned out to columnists or regular writers who seldom come to the office.

Proper staffing is important to success. A magazine staff is not a machine or an organization chart into which editors and writers can be plugged like parts off a stockroom shelf. People who can work together, given sufficient freedom and a healthy amount of tension, can put together a lively magazine. An editor has to realize the tenuous balance between vigorous leadership (including decision-making ability) and staff freedom. The successful magazine is not a democracy but a product shaped, molded, and led by its editor.

In the office, a small monthly magazine may find it efficient to have 6 to 12 key staff members, including the following:

1. Editor or executive editor
2. Art director
3. Managing editor
4. Editorial secretary
5. Articles editor or senior editor
6. Copy editor
7. Production manager

Additional staff may include writers of staff-generated material, another copy editor or two, and a senior editor or two in addition to an articles editor. The staffing, titles, and structure must be designed for the individual magazine, not borrowed from someone's organization table or a textbook.

Major differences in staff size stem from frequency of publication (a weekly needs a larger staff than a monthly, a monthly a larger one than a quarterly) and the type of content (a news or home service magazine requires more staff writers than a think or opinion magazine that can commission much of its content).

The economics of magazine publishing prohibit employing unproductive staff members and encourage heavy use of commissioned articles that can be obtained at lower cost than staff-written material. Many of these articles are commissioned on the basis of queries received from free-lance writers, while others are commissioned to writers who have good track records and long association with a magazine. Some writers appear so frequently that readers tend to believe they are on the magazine's staff.

Larger magazines with heftier budgets contract with free-lance writers for a specified number of assignments each year. Under these arrangements, the contract writer covers the assignment and is paid whether the article is published or not.

Magazines that generate more content in-house may expand the number of persons in the basic positions that have been described, and they also staff departments of the magazine.

Among those with larger staffs, *Southern Living* lists 75 editorial staff members on its masthead, including 10 photographers and 4 staff artists but not including 16 editorial contributors. *Family Circle* has 56 editorial employees on its masthead, not counting 14 contributing editors and a 10-member health and medical advisory board, departmentalized like this:

1. Editor-in-chief
2. Creative director
3. Deputy editors (2)
4. Executive editor
5. Managing editor
6. Consulting editor
7. Articles (3 senior editors and assistant editor)
8. Health and Nutrition (senior editor, diet and fitness editor, and associate health editor)
9. Food (editor, associate editor, and home economist)
10. Home (director and decorating editor)
11. Fashion and Beauty (director, associate editor, and assistant editor)
12. Research (editor and researcher/reporter)
13. Copy (director, senior writer, and how-to's)
14. Art (2 associate creative directors, photo editor, assistant photo editor, 3 art associates, art production manager, and assistant)
15. Production (senior copy editor, copy editor, assistant managing editor, production editor, proofreader, and executive editorial administrator)
16. Editors at large (4)
17. Editorial associates (7)
18. Editorial assistants (3)

Family Circle, one of the largest women's service magazines, has a large and highly departmentalized editorial staff. (Reprinted from the December 22, 1992, issue of *Family Circle* magazine. Copyright © The Family Circle Inc.)

Country Home's masthead is more typical of moderate-sized magazines, with 14 editorial staff members listed:

1. Editor-in-chief
2. Executive editor
3. Art director
4. Senior editor
5. Copy chief/production editor
6. Interior design director
7. Interior designer
8. Building editor
9. Food and Tabletop editor
10. Antiques and Garden editor
11. Assistant art directors (2)
12. Administrative assistant
13. Art business clerk

In addition, *Country Home* lists 4 contributing editors, 16 regional editors, and 2 research, 1 test kitchen and 1 graphic reproduction employees.

One monthly that is largely staff written lists 46 editorial staffers. Another monthly with a smaller editorial well and more commissioned pieces lists 30. A magazine that uses book excerpts and outside contributions has 13 editorial staffers. Staff size is determined by the work load required by the editorial formula and the budget.

The one-person editorial staff performs the same functions as the large staffs, but on a smaller scale. The one-person staff has the added challenge of having to achieve sufficient self-discipline to get all the work done on time, from planning and scheduling through copyediting, title writing, layout, production, and proofreading.

Even one-person situations vary widely, from unpaid volunteer editors of association magazines that rely on members for manuscripts and photos to the well-financed corporation magazines whose editors can buy manuscripts, superb photos, and art direction by a studio. When budget permits adding a staff member, the first addition may be an art director-artist if the editor prefers to continue writing and editing copy or a writer-editor if the editor has expertise in graphics and layout. In some instances, a photographer would be added, but it takes a huge number of photo assignments to keep one photographer occupied full-time.

As a magazine gains financial strength, there is a temptation to add staff just because the money is available. However, some editors recognize that they are likely to sacrifice efficiency for size and keep as small a staff as can get the work done.

Encouraging Editorial Productivity

Editorial administration involves getting as much high-quality editorial work as is possible out of each editorial employee, including yourself. Varied approaches and procedures may be effective for different people. Howard S. Rauch of Gralla Publications has offered advice in the areas of hiring productivity, staff productivity, and personal productivity. Gralla has since become part of Miller Freeman, Inc.

Hiring Productivity

Spend less time in the screening process while selecting the best job candidate to increase hiring productivity. State a specific salary range in your ad to eliminate a lot of applicants who are far beyond the range. People who want more than the highest-stated salary will still apply. Cover that in the phone call arranging for the interview, making clear how negotiable you can be.

Toss aside any résumé not accompanied by a cover letter, and any résumé accompanied by a form letter with only a box number or the company name. This may eliminate up to 25 percent of the applicants, all who have not attempted to write a creative cover letter.

Classify all remaining résumés as A, B, or C. The A résumés most closely relate to the job needs. Interview and test the A candidates. Administer a one-hour exam on grammar, basic editing skills, headline writing, and news sense. (At Gralla, about

85 percent of the applicants failed.) Make no exceptions to testing. Advanced, experienced candidates should not be permitted to rely only on their clippings to prove their ability.

Conduct extensive interviews with all remaining candidates. Considerations in evaluating the candidate include punctuality for the interview, the introductory greeting, appearance, job history (including longevity), speaking and interviewing ability, enthusiasm for the job, travel experience, organization in approaching a new job, specific related skills and experience, ability to relate experience to your magazine's needs, professional samples, and productivity history—the ability to produce volume quickly.

Staff Productivity

Start with orientation and training. If you make a new assistant editor as knowledgeable as possible as quickly as possible, you will spend less time supervising that person. Both you and your employee become more productive as a result. One approach is to start with a 90-minute orientation on your magazine's policies the first day on the job, followed by an hour-a-day for two weeks to review facts of your field, editing techniques, your magazine's writing style, and other information the employee needs to function efficiently. Much of this training can be done by creating workshops on specific topics that can be repeated for other new employees later.

Recognition can increase productivity. List new editors on the masthead and give them business cards right away. Give them a good assignment and reward them with a byline as quickly as possible. For ardent journalists, nothing tops seeing their bylines in print.

Develop realistic standards of performance. Analyze routine work—how long it takes to write regular departments, lay out pages, read proof. Establish quantitative standards for how many new product items an assistant editor can write in 3 days or how many pages an associate editor can dummy in 2 days. If the standards are not achieved within 90 days, a conference with the employee is needed.

Specific quantitative standards are preferable to vague guidance, such as "the article is too long," "you haven't done enough work," or "this is dull." Use Gunning's Fog Index as one measure of writing. Give specific assignments, and be specific in critiques of those assignments.

Quantitative standards help you determine the size of the staff you need. Using a 20-day work month, make realistic estimates of how long it will take to make the assignments, write the material, edit the material, write the headlines or titles, design the pages, prepare the illustrations, proofread the type, and if necessary, paste up the pages. Assign these tasks to individuals in your analysis. One person may have 5 days of routine writing, 3 days of editing, 2 days of writing headlines, and 2 days of proofreading. This 12-day routine work month leaves 8 days for other assignments, such as attending a 3-day convention and writing two articles about it, or doing a major story that requires interviewing a dozen good sources.

With an analysis like this for each staff position, you can plan a reasonable and productive work schedule for every staff member, including yourself. Knowing how long it should take to write a single-source feature, or to edit the columns for one issue, helps everyone gauge productivity. If a staff member complains of having too much work, ask him or her to keep a record of how long it takes to do every task during a typical month, usually in days or half-days, and bring the results for discussion. A staff member may come up with 25 days of work for a 20-day month or only 15 days of work for the month and decide the job is not overwhelming after all.

The analysis of the amount of editorial content produced by all staff members can assist management. Calculate how much published material, in pages or column inches, is contributed by each staff member. Compare the results and analyze them. At Gralla, for example, staffers were expected to produce 200 to 250 column inches a month. One staffer who produced only 70 inches a month was found to be submitting inferior work that could not be published. Another had only 30 inches a month published, but that was because his editor was giving him poor assignments that could not result in publishable pieces. In one case, the employee needed to be replaced, and in the other the editor needed to make better assignments.

Personal Productivity

Magazines vary, and so do editors' jobs, but a checklist Rauch proposed can be helpful to most editors. The editor

1. Writes at least one important feature for every issue (of a monthly)
2. Has a timely and well-thought-out regular editorial column
3. Spends at least three working days each month in the field, meeting readers
4. Often seeks new contacts among readers, as opposed to relying on old friends all the time for story material
5. Takes personal interest in developing the skills of inexperienced staff members
6. Has created written, flexible job descriptions for all staff members
7. Provides errant staff members, when necessary, with written job objectives to be achieved within a specific time period
8. Supports the editorial chain of command, if one has been established
9. Introduces at least a half-dozen new, exciting, timely features every year
10. Secures speaking engagements on at least three or four industry programs every year
11. Spends company money as if it were his or her own and administers corporate policies as if they were personal policies
12. Reviews competing magazines consistently for strengths, as well as weaknesses
13. Reads his or her own magazine carefully on publication to become aware of all the mistakes the editor or someone else should have caught
14. Meets all publication deadlines, setting an example for the rest of the staff
15. Refuses to accept second-best performances from staff and self
16. Refuses to accept alibis, such as "not enough time" and "had to fill space," for running second-rate material in the magazine
17. Willingly does routine, nitty-gritty work in emergencies or when the work load is unusually heavy
18. Keeps personal business to a minimum while on office time[3]

Free-lance Manuscripts

The greatest amount of staff time and attention typically is expended on manuscripts, especially if the magazine accepts free-lance work. It is essential to establish and maintain a precise routine for handling manuscripts if chaos is not to overtake the operation.

The editorial secretary usually has a full-time job keeping track of manuscripts and queries. When a manuscript or query is received, the editorial secretary should immediately send a printed postcard acknowledging receipt and make a record with the author's name, basic information about the query or manuscript, the date received, and the person to whom routed.

Generally, junior editors review over-the-transom manuscripts and queries and have authority to reject the ones that obviously do not fit the magazine's formula. Because these should be handled within a matter of days, a writer who does not receive a rejection within two or three weeks should be buoyed with hope that the manuscript is at least receiving serious consideration.

Ideas and manuscripts of promise should then be routed to top editors, with the editorial secretary making proper notation on the author's record. If the editorial secretary has not received action on an idea or a manuscript within an established number of days, say 10, he or she should insist that the junior editors reach a decision so the rejection can be sent or the idea forwarded to senior editors.

The critical facet of a smooth-flowing operation is the fact that one person knows at all times where every query and manuscript is and has a record of rejections and acceptances sent out, including dates, deadlines, and prices offered. This may seem trivial or obvious, but it is neither—the load can be overwhelming. Small monthlies may receive as many as 40 manuscripts a day. Other monthlies report receiving 12,000 to 20,000 manuscripts a year.

Files are kept by authors' names so that the individual author's track record can be readily available (number of submissions, acceptances, rejections), and not by title, because titles often are not submitted with articles and submitted titles usually are changed.

If the manuscript or query goes to a senior editor, an articles editor, or an editorial committee, as in the case of scholarly and professional magazines, a decision still must be made within a reasonable amount of time and conveyed to the editorial secretary, who then issues the appropriate letter to the author.

Creating a series of form letters to authors is advisable to keep the work flowing and to minimize dictation time. Several letters may be kept at hand to deal with different situations. Four basic examples are

1. Frank rejection—a letter that simply states that the article or idea submitted is not suitable for publication in the particular magazine
2. Rejection with a warm paragraph—a rejection letter that indicates appreciation for having been able to see the manuscript or for the quality of its writing, perhaps with mild encouragement to the author for future submissions
3. Conditional acceptance—a letter that says the magazine would like to see the article the author queried about, but only if the author submits it on speculation. This gives the author the chance to follow through on his or her article idea, but does not guarantee acceptance when completed
4. Acceptance plus personal note—accepts the idea and includes a paragraph dictated by the editor including the desired slant or angle, the due date, the price to be paid, and anything else that is relevant to the assignment. If an article was submitted, the letter accepts it and specifies how much will be paid. Payment may accompany the letter or go out from the business office after publication of the piece.

Evaluation of queries and manuscripts more often than not is informally but carefully done. One junior editor may want to check with one or several others, both on especially good manuscripts and on borderline cases. An editor who likes a manuscript will want to share it with anyone who happens by. The same is true at the senior editor level, where the top editor may take a manuscript home overnight to see if it's as good as a glance or as another editor suggested.

Editorial boards make decisions on some magazines, but boards listed on mastheads more often are window dressing to impress readers that some well-known writers contribute to the magazine. Professional association and scholarly magazines are more likely to have a formal mechanism for reviewing and voting on manuscripts than consumer, business, or public relations magazines. On most magazines, the editors have a clear idea of what they want and exert leadership to see that they get it.

While a manuscript is being considered, everything about it—correspondence with the author, notes by other editors—goes along with it in a folder so that any editor reading it will have the full details available at all times. It saves the time otherwise required for going back to get files when letters or notes are wanted for reference.

Editors sometimes contact writers by telephone, especially if they have been published in the magazine before. After a telephone call, the editor must dictate a memo to the file to note specifics, such as due date, amount of payment offered, any expenses authorized, and suggestions to the writer for treatment of the subject.

Some magazines pay on acceptance, though many do not. Some buy well ahead of issue dates, and others work close to the next deadline. An adequate stockpile must be maintained so the magazine does not run short of copy, but not so large an amount that it becomes outdated and useless.

After publication, the magazine keeps a manuscript and all the material related to it—galley proofs, page proofs, relevant notes—for one year, in case objections, questions, or lawsuits arise.

Throughout all phases of contact, writers should be treated as cordially and politely as possible. Editors realize that these writers are an important part of their livelihood—without free-lance commissioned articles, most magazines would not be able to continue publishing.

Photography

As in the case of manuscripts, it is cheaper to use a free-lance photographer than to pay a photographer's salary and maintain a darkroom. Another reason outside photographers are used is based on the fear by some editors that an in-house photographer will see things the editor's way too easily, and they prefer someone who will think of different angles and be more creative. Telephone directories in most cities list photographers who can do good work, and photographers seek out magazines and offer to shoot assignments. Fellow editors can recommend free-lance photographers also.

Besides outside photographers, editors can call on picture services, both those that maintain files of pictures, any of which can be used quite inexpensively (such as Wide World), and those that have on call a network of free-lance photographers who can shoot assignments of excellent quality (such as Black Star or Magnum).

In-house photographers usually are prohibitively expensive for a monthly. Exceptions are obvious. *National Geographic* uses staff photographers in addition to free-lancers who do work of known quality. A multiple publisher such as McGraw-Hill or Chilton can amortize the cost of photography over several books and not saddle one with high overhead.

Some food and shelter books need photographers and a studio to provide photo illustrations for several of their departments. However, the typical magazine finds greater flexibility and availability in working with outside photographers who can work important assignments into their schedules relatively easily.

While providing the photographer with area for creativity, the editor must be thorough in making the assignment. Essential information the photographer must know includes the (1) subject matter; (2) specific people, activities, or scenes; (3) suggested emphasis or mood of the photos; (4) number of photos expected to be used; (5) deadline; and (6) amount of payment. A photography work order form often is used to formalize the details and keep track of them in written form.

When buying photos, the editor usually purchases only the rights for one-time publication in the magazine. The editor has complete rights to photography done by staff photographers, of course, and can sell the rights to those prints if they are marketable.

Photos can be used for public relations purposes in association, public relations, and other small magazines. After publishing a feature on officers, employees, local officials, or anyone else who might have some interest in the publicity, an editor routinely sends a set of the prints to the person or persons photographed, or otherwise involved, as a goodwill gesture. Some go as far as to have special folders imprinted: "Congratulations, you were recently featured in *Veeblefetzer World*." Inside are copies of the magazine or clippings plus the photo or set of photos. Of course, the folders must be made up and dispatched shortly after publication to make the maximum impact on the persons featured.

Production

Magazine production has traditionally been done outside the office, but the introduction of computers has brought much of the prepress phase in-house in many magazines. A production manager oversees a smooth flow of work from editorial and ad staff to the printer to assure that production schedules are met. Magazine presses usually are booked solid, and missing a deadline can both cost extra money and create a significant delay in printing and delivery.

The book has to close on time if it is to be printed and mailed on time. Editors are keenly aware of budgets and sometimes seem unreasonable in their demands to meet the schedule.

If desktop prepress is done in-house, the production manager supervises the employees who create the completed pages. If *mechanicals* (pasteups of pages ready to be photographed for printing) are used, the production manager must ensure that they are completed on time to meet printing deadlines.

A production manager also may be involved in mailing the magazine and filing the circulation audit statements, particularly on a smaller magazine.

Budget

No editor wants to be a slave to a budget, but none can ignore it. Wide variations in magazine sizes, overhead, salaries, type of content, income, and printing preclude the possibility of making firm statements about budgets. Most magazines do not own their own presses. They create an editorial product, try to get it printed and distributed at a reasonable price, and attempt to remain in business by making a profit. Operating one's own printing plant greatly decreases flexibility and ties up capital that cannot be afforded for that purpose. Several publishers operate subsidiary printing plants, but these usually must sell printing outside the company to generate sufficient work and income.

As with other aspects of magazine publishing, there is no typical budget. Insight into magazine finances is offered, though, by an analysis of 190 magazines, all members of the Magazine Publishers of America. Table 5.1 presents the data for 1991, when profit was 10.65 percent.

Budgeting

A budget is a plan for a business for a stated period, usually one year, and covers all income, expense, and profit items. A profit and loss budget, a balance sheet budget, and a cash flow budget are essential to the financial department. In addition, there are special budgets, such as advertising pages, subscription sales, and single-copy sales, and often payroll budgets and capital budgets.[4]

The process of budgeting, besides developing a plan for operations, gets people to think about their activities, allows them to examine alternatives, involves key people in decisions with each other, evaluates performance against the plan, guides control of the operation, and informs people of the total plan and their role in it.

Budget periods should coincide with accounting periods so that comparisons with actual figures can be made easily. This is by issue in the magazine business, except for weeklies, for which it is too time-consuming to be worthwhile.

TABLE 5.1
Magazine Revenues and Expenses, 1991

	Percentage of Total Revenues
Revenues	
Net advertising revenue (after all discounts and commissions)	47.14
Gross subscription revenue	39.00
Gross single copy revenue	13.86
Total magazine revenue	100.00
Expenses	
Advertising costs	9.59
Subscription fulfillment costs	2.27
Single copy sales costs	7.52
Subscription circulation costs	17.95
Editorial costs	9.47
Paper and printing costs	23.47
Distribution costs	8.29
Administrative costs	7.10
Other operational costs	3.69
Total magazine costs	89.35
Operating profit before taxes	10.65

MPA/Price Waterhouse Financial Survey of 190 magazines. Source: Magazine Publishers of America.

The most effective budgeting process involves everyone who is responsible for budgeting for their own areas; the overall budget results from coordinating and putting all these individual budgets together. A bureau chief in Miami budgets for his bureau. The director of the photo studio or photo editor budgets for the studio or photo department, and so on. Ultimately, the editor puts all the individual budgets together for the editorial budget that is submitted to top management.

This budgeting approach is effective because people are more likely to comply with a budget they helped formulate, it involves broad thinking and planning throughout the company, and many people become involved and feel that they are part of the team. By going into individual units and subunits—the lowest positions on the organization chart—detailed knowledge of the function and its costs go into the budget.[5]

The process usually begins several months before the end of the company's fiscal year, when the financial department issues background material to help plan the upcoming budget. These data vary but can include the current budget, actual figures to date and projections for the remainder of the year, anticipated inflation factors and price changes, economic conditions, status of the field covered, and the company's general approach to the upcoming year.

Department heads prepare their budgets and discuss them with the next person up the line. Sometimes other persons are consulted, and the department head reworks the budget. The process continues, with study of major and minor alternatives, until the overall budget is adopted.

As the year progresses, it is important to compare the actual figures distributed by the financial department against the budget to determine whether significant differences between budgeted and actual figures warrant action. If expenses are outrunning income or budget, controls or cuts may be necessary. If income is exceeding expectations, additional expenditures may be necessary to produce the additional editorial material and print the additional pages needed to go with the additional advertising pages being sold.

Major changes may necessitate rebudgeting. Some companies rebudget as a matter of practice every three to six months. When rebudgeting, it is advisable to keep the original budget and compare it, as well as the new one, with actual figures. Careful budgeting is time-consuming and should be done as needed but not so often that it overburdens the staff.[6]

An Actual Budget

Consider a 1989 budget for a trade association magazine listed in *Business Publication Rates and Data*. It has a seven-person editorial staff, salespersons in five regional offices, and a circulation of 70,000. The magazine's issues vary from 124 to 450 pages per issue. It printed 2,313 total pages in 1987 and 2,544 total pages in 1988. Basing the budget on the last couple years' experience and planned changes for the upcoming year leads to the new budget. In revenue items, the publisher budgets for a 3 percent increase in advertising, a 15 percent decrease in subscriptions, no change in mailing service (sending direct-mail advertising to the magazine's circulation list without releasing the list to advertisers), and a 30 percent decrease in reprint sales. The controlled circulation magazine will increase its circulation and press run, but it expects that circulation to be nonpaid. The revenue budget of $3,962,035 looks like this:

Revenue	
Advertising	$4,467,100
Subscriptions	100,000
Mailing service	20,000
Reprint sales	5,000
Production service	40,000
Total gross sales	4,632,100
Less agency commissions	670,065
Net revenue	$3,962,035

Some magazines would show only net advertising revenue by deducting commissions before stating the income figure. The production service item represents income from printing inserts and binding in preprints for advertisers.

Expenses are broken out in detail in seven broad areas: production, sales and promotion, salaries and benefits, operating, fixed, overhead, and administration. The production budget is straightforward, except that it includes the cost of editorial research (editorial survey and development), which more typically would be listed as an editorial expense:

Production
Paper (40 lb., no. 5 grade)	$500,000
Printing	475,000
Postage	365,000
Typesetting	11,000
Art/layout	46,000
Color separation	35,000
PMTs and film work	14,000
Editorial survey and development	14,000
Ad preparation	24,000
Mailing service	18,000
Inquiry card processing service	32,000
Freight	31,500
Production service	25,000
Total production expense	$1,590,500

A conservative estimate shows a profit of $2,000 (10 percent) on the mailing service and a profit of $15,000 (37.5 percent) on the production service.

The cost of sales and promotion comes to $888,000, as follows:

Sales and promotion
Sales salaries and commissions	$393,000
Sales office expense	67,500
Sales travel	50,500
Sales meals and entertainment	12,000
Monthly promotions	48,000
Special sections	8,000
Advertising	43,000
Seminars	35,000
Shows and exhibits	40,000
Circulation promotion	50,000
Editorial promotion	11,000
Other promotions	130,000
Total sales and promotion expense	$888,000

The sales costs are itemized as required by accounting conventions and the Internal Revenue Service requirement that meals and entertainment be broken out separately from travel. Monthly promotions consist of direct-mail advertising for the magazine. Special sections are occasionally produced through wholesalers in the industry. In this budget, no income was budgeted for the year, but $8,000 expense was to allow for any special section that may be developed and to keep the budget flexible. The $43,000 in advertising covers the magazine's monthly ads in Standard Rate and Data Service's *Business Publication Rates and Data.*

This magazine also promotes itself by conducting seven regional seminars for its industry each year. No selling is done at these seminars; the magazine disseminates its knowledge of the industry as a goodwill gesture to the seminar participants. The shows and exhibits item in the budget covers the magazine's participation in industry trade shows and conventions, including the cost of shipping its booth to the convention sites.

An aggressive editorial promotion program is conducted by sending reprints of key articles each month to industry leaders with notes, "We didn't want you to miss this important article" or "We thought you'd want to see this." The cost of house ads also comes under this item.

Other promotions include printing of the advertising rate card, an elaborate media kit, and the cost of premiums given to advertisers.

A new editorial employee and raises for others resulted in an increase of 34 percent in salaries and benefits for editorial employees:

Salaries and benefits
Salaries	$349,000
Hourly wages	80,000
Employer FICA	43,700
Pension	33,800
Group life insurance	5,400
Group health insurance	27,900
Workers compensation and miscellaneous	2,900
Total salaries and benefits	$542,700

Operating expenses were budgeted at $195,500 as follows:

Operating
Travel and entertainment, general	$55,000
Travel and entertainment, editorial	50,000
Office supplies	4,000
Bad debts and collections	40,000
Postage	3,500
Telephone and telecommunications	9,000
Dues and contributions	2,500
Miscellaneous	1,000
Professional services, including legal and audit	2,000
Personnel procurement	10,000
Temporary help	3,500
Relocation expense	15,000
Total operating expense	$195,500

This budget allowed increases in several categories: 72 percent increase in general travel and entertainment, 11 percent in editorial travel and entertainment, and 54 percent in office supplies because certain computer operations formerly provided by the parent association now were being billed. Decreases of 5 percent in bad debts and collections, 80 percent in postage, 65 percent in telephone and telecommunications, and 70 percent in miscellaneous were budgeted. Operating expenses were up 16 percent, to $195,000 from $168,600, partly because of recruiting and relocation expense for the new employee.

Fixed expenses looked like this:

Fixed
General insurance	$11,900
Depreciation	23,300
Total fixed expenses	$35,200

Deducting all of the expenses listed so far from the revenue of $3,962,035 leaves a balance of $710,135. This industry association bills each department for the space and general administrative costs based on the percentage of association square footage it occupies and its percentage of total association employees. The assessment for association overhead and administration for 1989 was $316,349, leaving a net operating income for this magazine of $393,786, or 10 percent (see table 5.2).

A City Magazine Example

Working up a budget involves summarizing records, then making projections and supporting them with a written statement about plans reflected in the budget. Information about previous years can be disseminated to department managers in the same form as their budget worksheets. In this example, table 5.3 gives information for the editorial department for the first six months of the current year. The previous year's actual figures also can be consulted, but, in this case, it was a bad year and the emphasis is on carefully planned improvement for the succeeding year. Table 5.4 shows the budget developed by the publisher. He was convinced that both circulation and advertising revenue could be increased and that some expenses that exceeded even the current budget could be controlled.

TABLE 5.2
Budget for a Monthly Trade Association Magazine 70,000 Circulation Averaging 212 Pages a Month

Revenue	
Net advertising revenue (after all discounts and commissions)	$3,797,035
Gross subscription revenue	100,000
Other revenue	65,000
Total revenue	$3,962,035
Expense	
Advertising	
Selling costs	$523,000
Research and promotion costs	304,000
Total advertising expenses	827,000
Circulation promotion costs	50,000
Editorial costs	668,200
Manufacturing and production costs	
Paper cost	$500,000
Printing and bindery cost	475,000
Other production costs	204,500
Total manufacturing and production expense	1,179,500
Distribution expense	365,000
Other operating expenses	162,200
Administrative costs	316,349
Total costs	$3,568,249
Operating profit	$393,786

TABLE 5.3
Editorial Department Information (Current Year)

	January	February	March	Total Through June (6 Months)
Pages				
Cover and contents	3			18
Listings	8			48
Reviews	6			36
Editorial, publisher's page	2			12
Puzzles	3			18
Columns	10			60
Short Stuff	5			30
Letters	3			18
Features	50			320
	90			560
B & W	36			216
2-color	20			120
4-color	34			224
	90			560
Expense				
Salaries				
Editor	$6,667			$40,000
Managing editor	5,000			30,000
Art director	5,000			30,000
Senior editor (2)	5,833			35,000
Assistant editor (2)	5,000			30,000
Copy editor	3,333			20,000
Editorial assistant	4,167			25,000
Editorial researchers (2)	3,333			20,000
	38,333			230,000
Columnists	4,500			27,000
Art and photo	18,000			112,000
Manuscripts	10,000			60,000
Travel, entertainment	3,000			18,000
Editorial research	—			—
Other	5,833			35,000
	$79,666			$482,000
Cost per edit page	$885			$893
% of total revenue	8.2%			7.5%

James B. Kobak, "Accounting for decision makers: budgeting," *Folio: The Magazine for Magazine Management*, March 1988, p. 126. Copyright 1988 *Folio: The Magazine for Magazine Management*. Reprinted by permission.

TABLE 5.4
Editorial Department Budget Worksheet (Succeeding Year)

	January	February, etc.	Total (12 Months)
Pages			
Cover and contents	3		36
Listings	8		96
Reviews	8		96
Editorial, publisher's page	2		24
Puzzles	3		36
Columns	10		120
Short Stuff	5		60
Letters	3		36
Features	50		640
	92		1,144
B & W	36		432
2-color	22		264
4-color	34		448
	92		1,144
Expense			
Salaries			
Editor			
Managing editor			$84,000
Art director			63,000
Senior editor (2)			63,000
Assistant editor (2)			73,500
Copy editor			63,000
Editorial assistant			42,000
Editorial			52,500
researchers (2)			42,000
	40,250		483,000
Columnists			56,000
Art and photo			235,000
Major story			85,000
Manuscripts			126,000
Travel, entertainment			72,000
Editorial research			—
Other			72,000
	$87,000		$1,129,000
Cost per edit page	$946		$987
% of total revenue	?		?

James B. Kobak, "Accounting for decision makers: budgeting," *Folio: The Magazine for Magazine Management*, March 1988, p. 132. Copyright 1988 *Folio: The Magazine for Magazine Management*. Reprinted by permission.

Meetings with department heads (editor, ad director, circulation director, production director, controller) in August and September reviewed figures, objectives for the succeeding year, and budget requests submitted by department heads. Key assumptions were made, such as a 5 percent increase in ad pages, a 5 percent increase in ad rates, and no increase in subscription or single-copy prices. Early drafts of the budget from the budget requests suggested that all of the publisher's objectives could not be met, which is usual. In arriving at the final budget, changes had to be made, such as a major reduction in editorial pages and costs, a 7 percent ad rate increase instead of 5 percent, a $2 increase in subscription price with no increase in the number of subscriptions, a reduction from 55-pound paper to 50-pound, and an added budget item of $20,000 for editorial and advertising research. The budget was approved at the November 1 budget meeting.

This budget was difficult for the editor, who faced a cutback of one-fourth of his editorial pages, the loss of two editorial employees (one assistant editor and one editorial researcher), and the cancellation of an added editorial assistant. The editorial budget as adopted is shown in table 5.5.

TABLE 5.5
Editorial Budget for Succeeding Year, as Approved

	Proposed	Approved
Pages		
Cover and contents	36	36
Listings	96	72
Reviews	96	72
Editorial, publisher's page (publisher's page eliminated)	24	12
Puzzles	36	24
Columns	120	96
Short Stuff	60	48
Letters	36	24
Features	640	456
	1,144	840
B & W	432	348
2-color	264	200
4-color	448	292
	1,144	840
Expense		
Salaries		
Editor	$84,000	$84,000
Managing editor	63,000	63,000
Art director	63,000	63,000
Senior editor (2)	73,500	73,500
Assistant editor (2) (1 eliminated)	63,000	31,500
Copy editor	42,000	42,000
Editorial assistant (2) (1 eliminated)	52,500	22,000
Editorial researchers (2) (1 eliminated)	42,000	21,000
	$483,000	$400,000
Columnists	56,000	48,000
Art and photo	235,000	170,000
Major story (eliminated)	85,000	0
Manuscripts	126,000	90,000
Travel, entertainment	72,000	54,000
Editorial research	0	20,000
Other	72,000	54,000
	$1,129,000	$836,000

James B. Kobak, "Accounting for decision makers: budgeting," *Folio: The Magazine for Magazine Management,* March 1988, p. 130. Copyright 1988 *Folio: The Magazine for Magazine Management.* Reprinted by permission.

Magazine executives are served by *Folio: The Magazine for Magazine Management.* Started as a controlled circulation bimonthly, it evolved into a paid circulation monthly. (Courtesy *Folio:,* Cowles Business Media.)

It is wise to make at least three budgets: high, low, and most likely. As the year progresses, monthly expenses that exceed the budget are reviewed with each department head to arrive at a mutual decision about where the needed cutbacks can be made. Should income fall below estimates of the most-likely budget, the low budget is invoked. If budgeted income exceeds the most-likely budget sufficiently, the magazine can move to the high budget. All operations of a magazine must be conducted so that budget adjustments can be made as necessary, and budget monitoring must be done at least monthly to avoid year-end surprises.

Magazines experiencing rapid growth or decline in circulation or advertising pages need to rebudget frequently or develop alternative budgets that can be invoked when needed.

Notes

1. Herbert R. Mayes, *The Magazine Maze* (Garden City, N.Y.: Doubleday & Company, Inc., 1980), p. 234.
2. Ibid., p. 99.
3. Howard S. Rauch, "Measuring Editorial Performance," *Folio:* (November 1984): 123–28.
4. James B. Kobak, "Budgeting for Fun & Profit," *Folio:* (June 1976): 46.
5. Ibid., pp. 46–47.
6. Ibid., p. 48.

6 Creative Editing

EDITING is a highly individual process. An editor's intellect and personality have great effect on the other staff members and the magazine, so generalizations about magazine editing have their exceptions because of the individualism and variety in the magazine field.

Editing is supervision of the whole range of editorial functions, from planning content to preparing for the press run. Long-range plans are made, article ideas considered, articles assigned, manuscripts scheduled into specific issues, and illustrations planned and ordered. Articles are edited, titles written, and layouts planned and approved. Copy is typeset, proofs are read and corrected, page proofs are checked and corrected. Finally, the issue goes to press.

Specific activities of an editor at any given time depend on the frequency of the magazine, the size of the staff, and the editor's mode of operation. A top editor may seldom touch a pencil to a piece of copy. He or she may be an executive who assigns articles, selects manuscripts, and gives direction to the rest of the staff. It is these executive activities that give a magazine its special character, that make it different from others in the field. Because they are so varied and often intangible, these activities are difficult to catalog. Some magazines succeed in maintaining reader appeal over long periods of time because of the creative talents of their editors, while others fail because their editors lack those talents. These special talents first show themselves in general planning.

Planning Is Crucial

Planning, the crucial step, is where the editor's expertise really shows. If the editor can plan the right editorial content for the readers, assign the right writers to the right topics or personalities, and get the right illustrations for each issue, the magazine can succeed. Looking ahead to future issues is important to the well-being of any magazine. An editor must have a clear idea of what is coming up and shape current issues to that concept.

To get ideas, evaluation, and occasional articles, any successful editor must have a large number of personal contacts. He or she must use good editorial judgment to keep them in balance, realizing that the people closest to an editor are not necessarily representative of people in general or of the magazine's readers. A wide range of contacts can open the way to significant manuscripts by important persons as well as insightful and entertaining pieces by free-lance writers. An all-staff-written magazine can benefit from occasional outside articles and photo features.

The small magazine often relies more heavily on over-the-transom pieces. Religious and association magazines particularly need material offered by free-lancers, plus articles requested from members and authorities.

Planning may be largely a one-person operation, a cooperative conference with an editorial board or staff, or a combination of the two. Except in some association and professional journals, most editors insist on decision-making power to avoid editing by committee.

Staying a Step Ahead of the Reader

Editorial imagination or creativity is learned rather than taught. It grows from the individual editor's background, interests, abilities, and contacts. How an editor thinks of devoting an entire issue of a magazine to a book like *Hiroshima* by John Hershey, as *The New Yorker* did, or to a week's American combat fatalities in Vietnam or a Hemingway novella, as *Life* did, is not easily pinpointed. Some editors' creative ideas work—and some don't.

Why one editor invites a respected psychologist to become a regular contributor to the magazine, perhaps just hours or days before another editor tries the same, is not easy to say. Sometimes it can be chalked up to inspiration, other times to serendipitous insight, digging, suggestions from colleagues, or a casual remark overheard at lunch. Too much time spent evaluating an idea may mean missing the opportunity; not enough may invite a blunder. It's not pure luck, although luck helps.

The great success of George Horace Lorimer as editor (1899–1936) of the *Saturday Evening Post* has been attributed to his ability to appeal to the businessman and his family, perhaps projecting him an income level or two beyond his status and showing him a life he might achieve if he persisted and gained economic success. Lorimer aimed at a middle-class readership and never strayed far from its tastes, although he did publish short stories by F. Scott Fitzgerald and William Faulkner. His magazine was a conservative, stabilizing influence, not an agent for social change.

Edward Bok, editor of *Ladies' Home Journal* (1889–1920) advised women how to rear babies and campaigned against French fashions. He moved the women's magazine from its preoccupation with moralizing and sentimentality to a service publication that appealed to women's interests and practical problems. He had architects prepare plans for houses and sold blueprints by the thousands. He campaigned against venereal disease in 1906. His campaign to clean up American communities stirred action from backyards to municipal projects. He succeeded in having a large billboard at Niagara Falls removed, and his mere threat to publish prevented the erection of a huge sign at the Grand Canyon. His crusades of national importance usually succeeded.

DeWitt Wallace had an idea he couldn't give to a publisher, so he and his bride sent a direct mail piece to prospective subscribers on their wedding day, and returned from their honeymoon to a mail box filled with 1,500 orders for *Reader's Digest*. Henry Luce originated a magazine concept that has been modified over the years, but *Time* remains preeminent in its field in circulation and advertising income.

Truly creative, imaginative editors are not plentiful, even in a country with thousands of magazines. The magazine with a predictable formula from issue to issue remains in the majority. Some magazines are so departmentalized and institutionalized that the reader can almost tell in advance which kind of tulip will be mentioned in the gardening article next month. This does not lessen the service rendered by that magazine. It may, however, challenge editors to put more effort into developing fresh treatments of service articles that readers are counting on. After all, April 15 is income tax deadline every year, and taxpayers need advice on how to complete the gauntlet with a minimum of pain. Solid, straightforward information simply presented often is the answer.

Magazines are edited with emotion, enthusiasm—creative passion. Magazine editing is a team activity, and every team needs a captain. The editor may be a strong, top-down authoritarian or more collegial, listening more to senior editors and department editors and giving them more authority in shaping each issue and the magazine.

Magazines reflect their editors. Changes may be subtle when a large-circulation consumer magazine gets a new editor, but more often than not readers will remark about the changes they see. Changes made by new editors frequently are publicized in the trade and consumer press and occasionally are advertised. Nearly every time you notice a major change in a magazine's design or content, you will find that the magazine's editor has been on the job only a few months, just long enough to effect the changes you have noticed.

An outstanding regional magazine that was brash, fresh, and creative from the beginning, *Texas Monthly* has won National Magazine Awards for general excellence (twice), reporting (twice), public service, specialized journalism, and photography. (Courtesy *Texas Monthly*.)

As we've observed, creative editing is not easy to pin down, and, once pinned down, it quickly becomes a dated example.

Three examples of creative editing, and National Magazine Award winners of 1988, were related to the October 1987 stock market crash. *Harper's* won the award for essays and criticism for "The Next Panic," an article by L. J. Davis that provided a "prescient analysis of the fragile state of the stock market published five months before the crash," the judges' citation said. *Atlantic* won the award for public interest for "The Morning After," an analysis of the American economy by former Secretary of Commerce Peter Peterson. *Money* won the personal service award for its December article "After the Crash: The Safest Place to Put Your Money Now." Timeliness can greatly contribute to editorial creativity.

Cooperation between two city magazines, *Washingtonian* and *Baltimore,* earned them the National Magazine Award for news reporting for their effort that reconstructed the Amtrak-Conrail collision of January 4, 1987.

Creativity includes publishing the right article at the right time, or publishing it at all. *Consumer Reports* published a series of three articles by Trudy Lieberman, "Life Insurance: How to Protect Your Family." Designed to help consumers save money and provide financial security for their families, the series covered term, whole life, and universal life insurance, leading the reader through an evaluation of personal insurance needs, how insurance is priced, a rating of 180 life insurance policies, and a hard look at how insurance is sold. In awarding the series the 1987 National Magazine Award for personal service, the judges wrote that the 73-page presentation "is a perfect example of how service journalism at its best can responsibly guide attitudes and actions."

Consumer Reports won the personal service award again in 1990. "Beyond Medicare" effectively untangled the mysteries of what Medicare does and doesn't cover and offered practical guidance and assistance on how to help fill in the gaps in "a comprehensive treatment of the Medicare muddle."

Farm Journal won the personal service award in 1986 for five articles of assistance to farmers in a particularly difficult time, "Your Call Can Be Heard," "There Is Life After Farming," "Bootstrap Plans to Beat Tough Times," "Rescue from Suicide," and "What Distressed Farmers Need Most."

Long classified as a "quality" magazine, *Harper's* dates from 1850 and tries each year to publish one or more articles or essays likely to have some effect on the national discourse. It received the 1988 National Magazine Award for essays and criticism. (Courtesy *Harper's*.)

Baltimore Magazine's cooperative effort with *Washingtonian* won them both the 1988 National Magazine Award for news reporting. Both magazines had the same publisher. (Courtesy *Baltimore Magazine*.)

Creativity and excellence usually originate from a magazine's main mission. *Consumer Reports'* three-article series on life insurance was recognized by the National Magazine Award for personal service. (Courtesy *Consumer Reports*.)

Farm Journal won the personal service award for a series of articles aimed at helping farmers cope with unusually difficult times. (Courtesy *Farm Journal*.)

Sensitivity to an important human topic and presenting that topic by reporting or describing real people's lives is another approach to magazine creativity. "The Liberation of Lolly and Gronky" by Anne Fadiman in the December 1986 *Life* was the longest article the magazine had ever published. In presenting it the 1987 National Magazine Award for reporting, the judges cited it as

a sensitive, straightforward presentation of an unsettling subject of growing importance— whether the terminally ill elderly have a right to cause their own deaths. The article is a skillful interweaving of personal, anecdotal, and objective material. It manages to cover the range of current religious, ethical, medical, political, and legal positions in the context of a compelling human case.

The article was described as contributing to the advancement of knowledge; showing enterprise, thoroughness, and reliability in the reportage; and exhibiting a very fine style of writing.

Rolling Stone received the same award the preceding year for "The Plague Years" by David Black, a "remarkably sensitive and comprehensive treatment of AIDS," in which "the reader is drawn into sharing the frustrations and excitements of the investigating scientists" while never losing sight of the victims and their suffering.

Veteran editors recommend a surprise in every issue, an article the reader is not expecting. One of these may have been *Money*'s "Inside the Billion-Dollar Business of Blood" in March 1986, which "documents the failure of the blood industry, including the American Red Cross, to heed evidence that AIDS can be transmitted by transfusion." In presenting the article the public interest award for 1987, the National Magazine Awards judges wrote,

The article, which specifies steps that can be taken to increase public safety, has already had an impact on the industry: tests proposed by *Money* are now being used by the Red Cross and other blood banks. In short, not only is the article's subject matter vitally important to anyone who has had or expects to have a transfusion, but it is noteworthy and creditable that a personal finance magazine like *Money* should have spotlighted this dramatic aspect of the AIDS blight.

Philadelphia won the 1977 public service award for an emotionally powerful article, "Forgotten Children," on the loneliness and despair in a state institution for the retarded. The specialized journalism award in 1977 was presented to *Architectural Record* for spurring international competition to find architectural solutions to slums.

Architectural Record received the National Magazine Award in specialized journalism for its support of international competition to find architectural solutions to slums. (Courtesy *Architectural Record*.)

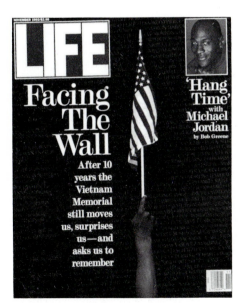

Life says its mission is to show the world through photojournalism. It also is known for its anniversary and follow-up pieces. (Courtesy Time Inc.)

Time Inc.'s *Money* has been recognized for its unusual article on the "Billion-Dollar Business of Blood" and its "After the [1987] Crash: The Safest Place to Put Your Money Now." (Courtesy Time Inc.)

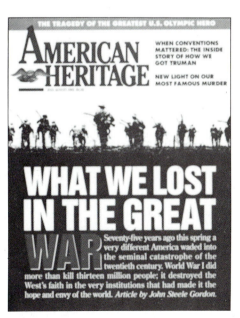

American Heritage received the National Magazine Award for its single-topic issue, a medical picture of the United States, and for general excellence in the same year. (Courtesy *American Heritage*.)

The cover story in this issue of *Business Week,* a survey of the changing role of women in top management, received the 1976 National Magazine Award for public service. (Courtesy *Business Week.*)

Extensive and imaginative coverage of a single important topic provides significant service to readers as *Business Week* did in this issue on The Quality Imperative. (Reprinted from the October 25, 1991, issue of *Business Week* by permission © 1991 by McGraw-Hill, Inc.)

The American Lawyer devoted 60 of its tabloid-size pages in March 1990 to America's drug problem and won the National Magazine Award for a single-topic issue. (Photograph by Alexandra Avakian / Woodfin Camp. This photograph is reprinted with permission from the March 1990 issue of *The American Lawyer.* © 1990 *The American Lawyer.*)

"The class of the opinion field," the citation for 1992 National Magazine Award for General Excellence under 100,000 circulation said, "*The New Republic* offers lucid analysis, sophisticated reporting, and the zest of a good argument." It also won the 1992 Reporting award and the 1991 General Excellence award. (Reprinted by permission of *The New Republic* © 1992, The New Republic, Inc.)

To organize and conduct the international design competition for a settlement to house an impoverished community in a developing country, *Architectural Record* established the nonprofit International Architectural Foundation and announced the competition in its April 1974 issue. Consultation and support were received from the United Nations Environment program, the Union Internationale des Architects, and the Philippine government. The foundation received 2,531 registrations from architect entrants in 68 countries and 476 submissions to be judged by a distinguished international jury. The winning designs were presented in the May 1976 "Human Settlements" issue.

Business Week's issue on "The Quality Imperative" received the 1992 National Magazine Award for single-topic issues. "*Business Week* does more than just describe the problems of quality facing American business; it offers practical and useful solutions. Everything about this issue communicates the essence of its subject: indepth reporting, intelligent writing, a clear and coherent graphic presentation. And . . . a richness and flair."

Its tough-minded look at the drug epidemic and the failure of the justice system to control it won the single-topic issue award for *The American Lawyer* in 1991. "From its opening page, the magazine forcefully grabs its readers and never lets go. With passion and compassion, case studies consistently drive the debate back to its human roots. The reporting is confident, the writing incisive; together they make a convincing case for rethinking our approach to the drug laws, their enforcement, and the treatment of the users themselves."

Distinctive reporting earned the 1992 reporting award for *The New Republic.* "In three brief, restrained yet explosive dispatches from the front, Michael Kelly got the [Persian Gulf] war story that colleagues missed," the award citation read.

"A haunting portrait of young Crow Indians, whose extraordinary success as basketball players has, for generations, led to their destruction as human beings" received the 1992 feature writing award for *Sports Illustrated.* The citation said "Shadow of a Nation" was "more than a sports story, it explores a cultural tragedy."

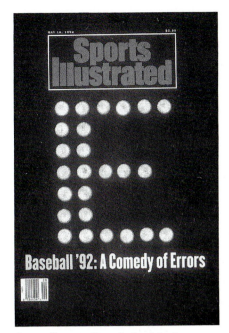

Sports Illustrated has distinguished itself with two General Excellence awards in the 1 million plus circulation category, the 1992 feature writing award, and a service to the individual award. (Courtesy Time Inc.)

Three articles on pregnancy and abortion in three issues over a 10-month period in *Glamour* were selected for the public service award. *Glamour* has published more articles on abortion over the last 20 years than any other women's magazine. (Courtesy *Glamour*. Copyright © 1991 by The Condé Nast Publications Inc.)

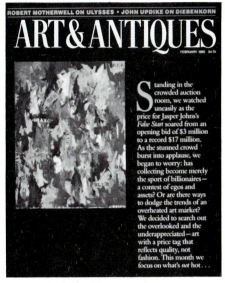

Serving readers with exceptional information about their special interests from 17 fields of art and antiques earned *Art & Antiques* the National Magazine Award. (Courtesy *Art & Antiques*.)

The public interest award in 1992 went to *Glamour* for three articles, "Teenage and Pregnant," "Where Are the Doctors Who Will Do Abortions?" and "A Town Held Hostage." The articles looked at how parental consent laws force teenage girls with divorced parents into painful court proceedings, how abortion foes discourage an increasing number of physicians and hospitals from performing abortions, and how an anti-abortion crusade can disrupt a community. The judges wrote that "*Glamour*'s well-reported real-life stories break new ground in an old debate and represent public interest journalism at its best."

The editors of *Art & Antiques* surveyed 17 fields of art and antiques and guided the reader to overlooked areas where a buyer with a discerning eye and the willingness to learn can uncover affordable treasures in "What's Not Hot." The article, which won the 1990 special interest award, included pertinent illustration, was studded with facts and anecdotes, and was written with insight and flashes of humor. The article was conceived on the subway by then editor-in-chief Jeff Schaire, who came up with the title and let the staff do the rest. "The cover lines were especially controversial and went through more re-writes than any comparable block of text in the magazine's history," wrote Schaire's successor, Rob Kenner.

Family Circle's full-scale investigative report on toxic contamination in Jacksonville, Arkansas, "Toxic Nightmare on Main Street," received the 1991 public interest award. The judges hailed this article as an example of how journalism can serve the public interest by exposing the calculated indifference of public servants.

A special editorial team investigated the effects of toxic waste in Jacksonville, Arkansas, as a follow-up to a previous report. *Family Circle* received the public interest award for the resulting article. (Reprinted from the August 14, 1990, issue of *Family Circle* magazine. Copyright © The Family Circle Inc.)

"From the heavily mortgaged chicken houses of the contract farmer in 'Don't Count Your Chickens' to the breakneck speeds of the production lines in 'Inside the Slaughterhouse' to the frustrations of slaughterhouse inspectors in 'The Fox Guarding the Henhouse,' *Southern Exposure* tells the very human story of an industry that feeds millions of Americans every week and reportedly makes far too many of its customers and workers sick. The articles attracted the attention of the media and of state and federal regulators, resulting in fines and legislative action designed to make the poultry industry safer for both its workers and its customers. This is the 'alternative' press at its finest," the citation for the 1990 public service award said.

Sports Afield married information and sensitive advice with illustration, type, graphics, and photographs in its award-winning preseason guide to deer hunting. (Courtesy *Sports Afield.*)

Washingtonian is a distinguished metropolitan magazine and has won five National Magazine Awards through 1992, including feature writing in 1990. (Courtesy *Washingtonian.*)

Almost legendary for its photographic excellence, *National Geographic* won four of the first eight National Magazine Awards in photography after the category was begun in 1985. It also has won a general excellence award and a single-topic issue award. (Courtesy National Geographic Society.)

Known for its long, thorough pieces, *The New Yorker* won the 1991 reporting award for its piece on the merger of Time Incorporated with Warner Communications. The reporter's "command of the facts enabled her to tease from her sources the interplay of personalities and personal styles that shaped the merger, an event that is redefining the economic foundations of the magazine business and other sectors of the communications industry," the judges wrote.

"Whether writing about a convicted murderer or a Supreme Court Justice, *Mirabella* brings to every page a sharp intelligence and a discerning eye for arresting images. This is a magazine that knows its readers take nothing for granted and rewards them by returning the compliment every month," the judges stated in their citation for the 1992 General Excellence Award in the 400,000 to 1 million circulation category.

Sports Afield's preseason guide to deer hunting started with a fold-out deer-locator map and continued through advice-laden sections that were sensitive to humane considerations, reminding readers that poor choices of equipment can result in unnecessary suffering for the deer. The judges for the 1992 National Magazine Award for special interests said, "Expert integration of type and graphics, photos and illustration, reporting and presentation made this an outstanding example of what magazines can do."

A free-lance profile of a black laboratory assistant who, without formal scientific training, became a pioneer in cardiovascular medicine and a legend in the world of heart surgery won the 1990 feature writing award for *Washingtonian.* Through painstaking research, author Katie McCabe created an inspirational portrait of Vivien Thomas, an unrecognized genius. The piece had been rejected by several other magazines.

New York won two awards in 1991. The personal service award for "Sparing the Child" on "the horrific subject of child abuse—shattering, but never sensationalized, it combines first-rate reporting with specific step-by-step advice and guidance through the city bureaucracies in search of help and, possibly, hope." The special interests award: "With wit, charm and intelligence, [David] Denby educates both novices and experienced enthusiasts about the complex array of expensive equipment for music reproduction. In raising the buyer's guide to a higher level, this

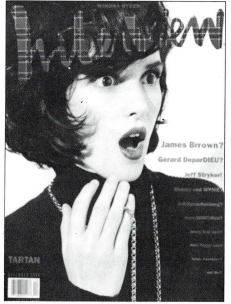

Interview varies its design and title logo. It won the National Magazine Award for General Excellence in the 100,000 to 400,000 circulation category in 1990. (Courtesy *Interview* Magazine, Brant Publications.)

three-part entry provides the consumer with information needed to make smart choices, while deflating the hype about recent technological developments. Although words are no substitute for sound, you almost hear the music."

Creativity in photography is important too. *National Geographic* is virtually a monthly textbook in photographic excellence, as attested to by its four National Magazine Awards in photography of the eight presented since the category was begun in 1985. *Geographic* won in 1987, 1989, 1991, and 1992. It also won the general excellence award for more than 1 million circulation in 1992 and the single-topic issue award in 1990 for its celebration of La Belle France's 200th birthday anniversary.

A free-lance article about a boy who was tortured to death by his mother and stepfather won the 1981 public service award for *Reader's Digest*. "The Murder of Robbie Wayne, Age Six" by Mary Jane Chambers "dramatically brought to millions of readers the too-often hidden problems of child abuse," the judges said. Mrs. Chambers had become interested in the trial of the mother and stepfather when it took place in Oklahoma in 1979.

A magazine must give readers a lot of what they want, but it must go beyond and give them what they want before they know they want it. Some of this material may have low readership, but a cumulative effect eventually will result in some gains. Talented editors are in touch with their areas of concern or subject matter well enough to be ahead of the reader. They sense when to add a new department or treat a new topic.

Forecasting Trends

Success comes to the editor who can see a trend developing and plan the magazine's approach to it, timing it to break just when the readers are most receptive to it. Trends usually develop slowly, even in today's fast-paced society, and so quietly that they often are missed until too late. Wide contacts with people "where the action is" is one key to forecasting trends.

As many of the National Magazine Awards–winning entries mentioned earlier in this chapter illustrate, the leading magazines publish early, long before the topic or issue has become a common subject of discussion: corporate women executives, published in 1975, whether the terminally ill have a right to take their own lives in 1986, AIDS in 1986. Also the public quickly forgets, so an article on child abuse published in 1980 must be followed with others, including another award winner published in 1990.

Fads fly by, and readers tire after several successive articles on some subjects, but the magazine editor must remain alert to leads and follow up those with promise.

Editorial leadership, though, can quickly transform into a fad and lose its impact, and the magazine its distinctiveness. The fad often is the method of treatment of a topic, rather than the topic itself. Sometimes the difference between following a fad and continuing a legitimate service is difficult to discern.

Movement leaders get space in numerous magazines, and popular movie and TV stars get coverage when they are hot. At various times, Christie Brinkley, Princess Diana, Brooke Shields, Elizabeth Taylor, Cher, Cindy Crawford, and Madonna have appeared on numerous covers in a short span of time. Perhaps it is editors who tire of the frequency of these people on covers more than the public, but editors who want covers to sell their magazines stick with the most popular people on them.

Striving to be the leader in a field, as if not difficult enough for the creative editor, is complicated by the need to work well ahead of publication dates. A consumer monthly may outline its ideas a year in advance and make assignments as the ideas jell. By three or four months in advance, most articles need to be in good shape, ready for copyreading and art direction. Now and then a piece may be polished and inserted on deadline, but an entire issue cannot be produced that way.

Completing some articles on schedule is comparatively easy in such fields as fashion, where the showings to buyers take place months in advance of retailing the merchandise. The whole process is scheduled so the fashion magazines can show what's new and whet appetites for the apparel soon to be in the stores. Many business publications, whether for housewares or durable goods, are in a position to follow similar courses. The tough decisions can be what the big social problem will be in six months, which best-seller or TV show will appeal to parents of teenage children, which actor will make a good story, what should be published on the domestic economy. Every editor seems to have about as many tough decisions as easy ones in keeping the book vibrant, well toned, and on the leading edge of reader interests.

Good editors have a knack for coming up with the apt topic and a twist in its treatment to make it different. They are idea people and they come in contact with numerous interesting people who also have ideas. They read voraciously and think about what they read. A person who doesn't have more ideas than he or she can develop and publish isn't likely to be a successful editor.

Besides planning ahead on seasonal and topical articles, editors buy an inventory of pieces that can be used as the months roll along. The inventory shouldn't be so large that some of it is likely to become out of date, but there should be a cushion of material so that the editors are not forced to rush headlong into their next issues at the last moment, with a bare minimum of usable material. Thorough acquaintance with the subject matter, the field, and the magazine's readers make planning ahead easier. Planning is work and takes conscious effort.

Working with Outside Sources

Staff writers, photographers, illustrators, and correspondents are sources for the bulk of the material in today's magazines. Outside sources account for a substantial amount, especially in the idea and opinion books.

Editors approach top-name talent for specific pieces. Occasionally, a bidding war among magazines takes place, but that's not common. The relationship may begin when free-lance pieces arrive at the office and the editor likes them so much he or she buys almost anything the writer can turn out. Eventually, the writer's quality may decline, and the editor needs to maintain high standards while appreciating the writer's past service.

Free-lance offerings arrive with regularity in most magazine offices, and those free-lancers want and deserve prompt responses. A writer has invested valuable time digging into a subject and putting it in writing. Presumably the writer is familiar enough with your magazine that he or she thinks the piece is the type you usually publish or should publish. What a typical serious writer wants most is your honest answer as soon as possible.

If you reject the piece, reject it promptly so it can be submitted elsewhere. If you think the writer has promise but needs editorial advice before starting a piece, suggest that he or she query you in the future before writing.

A piece that is good but needs revision should be returned with the specific suggestions for revision. Holding a manuscript for a month or more won't improve it and won't likely make your decision any easier. If others on your staff must be consulted, do that, but keep the paper moving. Don't let an advisory or associate editor halt the process by leaving it in his or her *in* basket. The American Society of Journalists and Authors Code of Ethics and Fair Practices formerly stated that a writer was entitled to an answer about a magazine's intentions with regard to purchase, revision, or rejection of a manuscript within 21 days of its submission. That has been deleted in a revision of the code, but it is a good guideline for an editor to follow. The code specifies:

A writer is not paid by money alone. Part of the writer's compensation is the intangible value of timely publication. Consequently, if after six months the publisher has not scheduled an article for publication, or within twelve months has not published an article, the manuscript and all rights therein should revert to the author without penalty or cost to the author.

A magazine's policy dictates how and when it pays. Professional writers obviously prefer to be paid on acceptance, and they're more likely to submit a good piece for that type of book in the future. The American Society of Journalists and Authors has a terse bit in its code on this:

The writer is entitled to payment for an accepted article within ten days of delivery. No article payment should ever be subject to publication.

Many editors do pay only on publication, and, although it never should happen, a writer occasionally has a piece accepted for payment on publication only to have that editor be succeeded by another who ships back the manuscript with no payment or kill fee.

Imitation as a Road to Success

The leader in the field may remain the leader, but there usually is opportunity for imitators to achieve commercial success. Confession magazines present a good example of imitation. *True Story* appeared in 1919 and was an obvious success by 1926. Magazine success cannot be hidden, so other publishers brought out similar magazines. Even Bernarr Macfadden, originator of *True Story,* started imitations of that magazine.

Imitation was the major factor in several other types, including the factual detective, fan, pulp, and men's magazines. *Playboy* was an imitation of *Esquire,* or what *Esquire* had been.

Reader's Digest was imitated by a number of digest magazines in the late 1920s, but most dropped by the wayside. Specialized topics are served by the digests that stayed around, such as *Catholic Digest* (1936), *Children's Digest, Baseball Digest* (1942), *Golf Digest* (1950), *Football Digest* (1971), *Hockey Digest* (1972), *Basketball Digest* (1973), *Soccer Digest* (1978), and *Bowling Digest* (1983). Six of these come from the same publisher.

Time (1923) was well established when two other major national magazines, *Newsweek*—founded by the first foreign news editor of *Time*—and *U.S. News* appeared in 1933. *Business Week* (1929), which resembled *Time* in its coverage of business news, was a conversion of McGraw-Hill's *Magazine of Business.*

Any successful editorial idea suggests possibilities for other magazines, often most successful when applied in a special interest area or toward a different audience. No box score of imitative successes and failures is available, but failures seem to have outnumbered the successes. Imitation in editorial formula, as well as article topics and treatments, will be tempting to editors and publishers for a long time to come.

Editors of popular magazines will continue to get leads on significant topics from magazines of opinion, professional and scholarly conventions, and news reports. The border between imitation and creativity or leadership isn't always clearly distinguishable.

Seasonal Content Recurs

At first you may wonder what it might be like to write something "new" for *American Funeral Director,* a magazine for funeral directors. However, most magazines in a special interest field have the same situation. Readers have a basic interest in the field or they wouldn't ask for the magazine, but how does an editor hook readers into this issue's articles and keep them there?

Lane Palmer, former editor of *Farm Journal,* discussed this at length with an agricultural journalism class at the University of Wisconsin and later in a bulletin issued by the Department of Agricultural Journalism. Farmers obviously are interested in farming, but how much will they read if it's something they already know? Three basic questions guide the editors of *Farm Journal* and relate to editors of other magazines:

1. What's on farmers' minds this month? (The surest way to get a reader's attention is to promise help with a problem that's on the reader's mind at the moment.
2. What is there new to say about it? (You have to promise something the reader doesn't already know.)
3. What does it mean to the farmer in Lincoln County? (It may be interesting as an example, but what does it mean? What can it do for the typical reader elsewhere?)[1]

Significance, or meaning, is what Palmer calls the "so-what" of an article. An article full of examples but no so-whats isn't helpful to readers; they want the so-whats, not just the examples. Palmer adds,

There is as great or a greater danger in writing with too much "so what" and too few examples. I suspect that this is the problem with many of the lectures in classrooms. It's what we mean when we say that a prof lectures almost entirely in theory. It's what students mean when they say they want teaching with more relevance—they want theory related in some form familiar to their every-day experience.[2]

Suppose the article has some solid information and some reader interest, but it just doesn't grip you enough as an editor to make you believe your readers will stay with it. Palmer's four-word description of the ideal *Farm Journal* story applies to most magazines:

NEW, YOU, NOW, and HOW. We want to write the NEW ideas which YOU, the average farmer, can use NOW and here's HOW. We seldom find a story strong on all four counts. If it is really a NEW idea, it is probably not ready for use NOW. Farms vary so much by enterprise and size that we probably can't tell farmers HOW to use the idea in a single article.[3]

News and continuing concerns are part of every field. Magazine editors know, too, that a big portion of their readers continually change, so a topic can be brought back occasionally if it does not become bothersome to the loyal reader.

Gardening magazines have similar subjects season after season—issue after issue, but different or unusual gardens can be found to show as examples; varied plantings of the same basic plants can be designed; issues can be themed around trees, then shrubs, then flowers; and content emphasis and approach can be varied in other ways. A home service or personal finance magazine may run a series of articles every winter on how to do your income tax. If the tax laws don't change, the tax forms do, and people forget about details of deductions, dividends, and the like from one year to the next.

The *new* may lead into repetition of continuing details that need to be repeated—such as what is deductible from income tax and under what conditions. *How* and *now* always have strong appeal when the topic is relevant to the reader. Late summer and early fall magazines occasionally carry a title like "What You Can Do Now to Cut Your Income Tax Next April." Magazines write lots of articles in the second person, talking with *you,* the reader, instead of in the impersonal third person, used by newspapers.

Later chapters will discuss editing manuscripts, and details of that need not be covered here. According to Palmer, after all the techniques, style, grammar, and other details are mastered,

Superior or great writing calls for something that you don't find in the rule books. The best an editor can do is to recognize it when he sees it and prints it. The nearest I can come to describing it is to say that the sort of informational writing I've been talking about speaks mainly *to the mind*—to the reader's *reasoning powers*. Great writing does this, too, but it speaks as well *to the heart*—to the reader's *emotions*.[4]

Visual Versus Verbal

Any photographer can tell you a picture is worth 10,000 words, but most editors come up through the writing and editing ranks and think verbally more than visually. Photojournalists recognize the importance of words as correctives for distortion, and for the two-dimensional representation of a three-dimensional scene. They know that words are needed to identify, explain, and complete the story begun by the picture.

There's no need for an either-or argument. Both pictures and words are needed, and the best editor is the one who most expertly considers how words and illustration, including graphics, can go together to present content effectively to the reader.

An editor may not be his or her own art director or photo editor, but it's obvious he or she must think as they do, as well as about manuscripts. Going back for pictures after a manuscript is completed may not be the most effective or most efficient way to do it.

Ideally, the planning of illustration should begin with the planning of the story. Before you sit down at the typewriter—in fact before you start interviewing—you should ask yourself: "What will be the most effective way of telling this story? Can I tell it mostly with photographs? With drawings? With charts? The word-oriented writer particularly should force himself to go through this thought process. Otherwise, he'll find himself going back to his sources for pictures after the writing is done. He will always be illustrating his manuscript rather than telling the story in the most effective form."[5]

Editing cannot be reduced to a formula or step-by-step process applicable to all magazines; an editor's creativity must always provide the dash of seasoning that is never measurable, but always vital.

Notes

1. Lane M. Palmer, *Publishing Magazines to Meet Reader Needs and Interests* (Madison: Department of Agricultural Journalism, University of Wisconsin, 1971), pp. 43, 45.
2. Ibid., p. 50.
3. Ibid., p. 45.
4. Ibid., p. 52.
5. Ibid., p. 66.

7 Article Editing

IN the previous chapter, the point was made that editorial decisions based on thorough planning often make the difference between quality magazines and run-of-the-mill magazines. In extreme cases, the creative decision making of top editors can actually determine the ultimate success or failure of their publications.

Month after month, or week after week, editorial activities such as article editing are carried out that bring these creative decisions to fruition or let them slip into oblivion. These activities are also important aspects of editing because they result in specific *verbal-visual* packages for readers. Here the editor takes up where the writer leaves off, and the key to success is represented by the combinations of those two words: verbal and visual.

Unlike the writer, the editor cannot think of words alone. In processing the article manuscript, the editor must visualize it in a final form. The graphic treatment given to the title, the space allocation, the spot used for it, the page layouts, the typographic treatment assigned to the text, and the illustrations to supplement the words all are interrelated and cannot be separated. Putting the article in perspective with the rest of the content in a magazine further complicates the work of the editor as he or she processes manuscripts.

Editor-Author Relationships

Much of the preliminary article editing is, of course, done by the authors. Good writers know their magazines well enough to step back from first drafts, consider the needs of their intended readers, and complete the necessary revisions to target their articles directly to those needs. Except for the lowest level of markets for magazine writing, a writer's work that is replete with errors of syntax and spelling is rejected out of hand or returned for further editing by the writer. If adequate care is exercised with revisions, authors can endear themselves to their editors by eliminating most, if not all, corrections or revisions by editors.

In discussing the author-editor relationship from his standpoint as editor of *Smithsonian,* Don Moser writes:

First of all, most of the writers who work for us frequently are doing so because they are good—they have an instinct for what is worth telling and what ought to be left out. They can etch in characters deftly. They can write compelling narrative, and smoothly shift gears between narrative and exposition. They understand change of pace, which is one of the most important skills a magazine writer can possess, and one that many, unfortunately, do not possess. They write prose that is stylish without being affected or overwrought. They avoid clichés both in writing and, importantly, in thinking. In short, they apply many of the skills of a novelist. With writers like these there's usually not much fuss and bother. Once they have reported the story, they generally have a better idea of how it ought to be shaped than the editors do. We might say add a dash of this or subtract a bit of that, or suggest an organizational change here and there, but we don't really get into heavy editing or rewriting. . . . Contrary to popular belief, editors don't really want to edit—they want to find the right story and the right writer, get in a terrific piece, run it without change and go home from the office early.[1]

Editor Moser goes on to say, however, that things aren't always as easy as he or other editors would prefer. "There are some stories," he says, "that have to be kicked back and forth a lot before they ever make it, others that get kicked back and forth a lot and still don't make it, and some that you know from the beginning are never going to make it."

Evaluating Manuscripts

The selection of content tests editors' mettle more than any other single task. As they apply their knowledge of reader interests to the evaluation of manuscripts, editors must also apply their professional and technical skills. These skills are needed for their visualization of the final product that might emerge from the raw material they are evaluating. In manuscript evaluation, the concept of visualization is all important. Weaknesses in the raw material can be corrected, and a good editor should be able to see through them. Prose can be sharpened. A weak title can be strengthened. Confusing, complicated data can be clarified with graphs, charts, or other visual aids. Organizational faults can be eliminated if the writer is guided carefully through meaningful revision.

As they use visualization as an aid to evaluation, editors must constantly remind themselves that they are serving as their readers' gatekeepers, determining what information will flow to the reader and what will get no farther than the editor's desk. Whether they open or close the gate should depend on the interest and needs of readers, not on their own biases or interests.

To be responsible gatekeepers, editors must know their readers intimately. They must know their interests, their strengths, and their weaknesses. An editor is both a follower and a leader, having to know and follow the interests of readers while providing the guidance and leadership they need. Magazine editors have always known that they must follow the interests of their readers if they are to succeed, and they have felt reasonably certain of their ability to measure reader interest. Their own experience, plus that of the editors who have gone before, provides an empirical set of rules for measuring reader interest. These guidelines can be reinforced with quantitative results of readership surveys.

There is no doubt that readership studies are a valuable tool for an editor in evaluating manuscripts. Good magazine editing demands periodic measurement of readership of all elements within a magazine. However, readership, even at its best, can be truly reliable only for guiding an editor in following readers' interests; it reveals what the reader was sufficiently interested in to read in a previous issue. Its value in pointing out new directions—in providing a base for leadership by a magazine—is limited.

Editorial leadership is important for all contemporary magazines, and, for the large number of specialized business publications and other similar magazines, this aspect of editing is exceptionally important. How is an editor to know what his or her readers *need* to know now, especially if readers have no strong feelings about the material? How can an editor know what his or her readers will need to know in a few months or a year, so he or she can present the needed material in advance? These are the demands of editorial leadership, and they are difficult to meet.

Editors, however, do have some advantages over their readers when it comes to determining present and future needs. They can attend conferences and brainstorming sessions with leaders in the field covered by their magazine. They have the opportunity to gather and analyze information on a much broader and more detailed basis than an individual can. Also, they probably have working for them a staff of field editors, department heads, and other specialists who can provide a breadth and depth of knowledge that no reader could be expected to have.

Editorial Teamwork Provides Leadership

Editorial teamwork shows in the high quality of articles in such leading magazines as *National Geographic*. Starting with photographer-writers in the field and working through several stages of evaluation and elimination, *National Geographic*'s team

(a)

(b)

(c)

(d)

(e)

Figure 7.1 The teamwork that results in top-quality articles by staff members begins in the field with the photographers and writers. (a) *National Geographic* photographer Lou Mazzatenta is dwarfed by his subject, the sphinx, then under repair. (b) Mazzatenta is joined at a picture editing machine by picture editor Elie Rogers, where they work together to edit out the best photographs. (c) Next, the photographs are boiled down to a select group and the editor determines if the coverage is acceptable for publication. (d) Constance Phelps, director of layout and design, is shown at a computer work station as she designs the pages for "Ramses the Great." (e) Last, the pages, complete with color prints, are "on the board" for a final check by the three staffers. (Courtesy *National Geographic*. Photo credits: (a) Elie Rogers, © *National Geographic;* (b–e) Maria Stenzel, *National Geographic*.)

produces memorable photo essays such as the one on "Ramses the Great" (figure 7.1). Senior Assistant Editor Lou Mazzatenta did the field work and was joined by Picture Editor Elie Rogers and Director of Layout and Design Constance Phelps in producing what turned out to be *Geographic*'s most popular picture story in 1991. Readership figures proved the editorial team was right, but only after the fact.

Thus, it is possible for editors to provide leadership by pooling their knowledge with that of their staffs and applying it to manuscript evaluation. This leadership must be exerted at an early stage of manuscript evaluation—when the subject, as contrasted with the manuscript as a literary package, is being evaluated. It is most important when the consequence (as contrasted with the interest) of a subject is being considered. Does the subject now have or will in the near future have some bearing on the well-being of a large number of readers? If so, it has consequence. Readers often have little or no initial interest in material that may eventually prove to be of considerable consequence to them. Editorial leadership is being exerted when subjects are covered that may not have shown up too well on readership reports but are of importance to readers nevertheless.

Once the consequence of a subject has been determined, potential verbal-visual treatments must be considered. Editor Lane Palmer of the *Farm Journal* once gave an excellent example of this aspect of evaluation.[2] The subject under consideration was zoning, which Palmer said "was as important to farmers as they were indifferent to it." The *Farm Journal* had run earlier articles on the subject and was "rewarded with a deafening silence." This time, Palmer said,

We decided to go all out with illustration. We settled on three of the worst things that can happen to a community as a result of having no zoning: a car junkyard, a roadhouse, and a highway cluttered with a jungle of roadside signs. With the help of three picture agencies, we ran down the best, or perhaps I should say the worst, photos of the three we could find. Then we tied the three together with a huge ink blot and carried it under the title "Want One of these Blotting Your Farm?" We were rewarded with reprint requests from all over the country, which taught me this lesson: If the subject really matters to your readers, you, the editor, are the only reason why it will not be read.

In this example, the *Farm Journal* combined the knowledge of what its readers needed with the ability to visualize and follow through with an approach that caught reader interest, thus providing true editorial leadership. Editor Palmer, like other editors who have made their magazines leaders in their fields, has given a lot of thought to bases for manuscript evaluation. He says:

The editor debating whether to use readership studies or his own judgment is in exactly the same position as a president or governor wondering whether to follow the polls or to attempt to lead them. In a democracy, the majority of voters (customers, readers) rules, and the politician or editor who ignores the fact does so at the peril of his own career. Yet at the same time the public wants to be led, wants to be taught, to be challenged. So indeed the editor walks a tight-rope between readership and leadership. Knowing what subjects will interest your readers—deciding what to print and what to leave out—it, by all odds, the greatest challenge in editing. . . . How you say something and how it looks to the readers are important, but the most important thing of all is what you choose to write about.[3]

Magazines of different types face somewhat different manuscript evaluation problems. A highly technical periodical, for example, may require the use of an advisory board during the selection process. Because no editor and no staff of such a periodical could be expected to be sufficiently knowledgeable in all aspects of the magazine's coverage, manuscripts may be circulated to outside experts for assistance in evaluation. Academic magazines often use a similar system.

Regardless of the evaluation system used, and regardless of the source of the manuscript (free-lance or staff writer), often the decision cannot be a simple yes or no. In fact, it probably is most common for the decision to be a no or a tentative yes, because it is typical for magazine manuscripts to go through some revision before being published.

Polishing and Shaping Up Manuscripts

Assuming that its subject gains approval, the manuscript is considered as a verbal-visual offering that must come up to certain literary and graphic standards. Bringing it to an acceptable level may require only minor change or extensive revision, token graphic treatment or a full-blown visual dressing up.

Polishing and shaping up require careful attention to an article's approach, direction, organization, completeness, literary style, and mechanics of style. An article's approach to a subject is a primary determinant of readership. Some changing and sharpening of the approach is perhaps the most common improvement an editor can produce as he or she works with a manuscript. Sometimes called the *slant* or the *angle,* the approach should be signaled by the title and carried forth quickly and vigorously in the article's beginning. If the purpose of the article is to provide assistance to the reader, the reader's potential benefits from that assistance should be alluded to immediately. If, on the other hand, the article's reason for existence is entertainment, its opening should set the stage for what is to follow.

Citing some of his reasons for rejecting articles for *Smithsonian,* editor Moser considers one of the main problems to be

Failure to recognize the difference between the subject and the story. Subjects are often broad landscapes, and decisions have to be made about what path the story is going to take. A question we sometimes ask is "What's the headline?"—which isn't as flippant as it sounds. (To put it in the language of English composition, what's the topic sentence?) If the writer can't answer that question, the piece is apt to ramble all over the place. This is a case where advance discussions between writer and editor can sometimes be quite useful.[4]

For editors of specialized vocational and technical magazines, working for a new approach to basic subjects is a constant problem. Some subjects must recur because they are basic to the industry being served, but the approach must be varied—new and different each time if readership is to be expected. Cooperation between writer and editor is needed if the best approach is to be found. In one instance, *Farm Journal* editor Lane Palmer worked with one of his new editors through four beginnings of an article on farm record-keeping before he was satisfied with the approach.[5] Two of the beginnings were roughed out by Palmer, the other two by the original writer. The final version was worth the effort, however, because it gave action and life to an oft-repeated subject.

Article beginnings are of special importance for any kind of magazine, and they often require an editor's special attention. *Smithsonian* editor Don Moser also listed as unacceptable articles with

a lead that does nothing to draw the reader in—usually some kind of rambling generalized paragraph that sounds like the beginning of a term paper. [Or] failure to set the story up properly, or at all. Somewhere high in the story the writer has to give the readers some idea of what the piece is about and why it's going to be worth reading. This failing is very common, but fortunately, it can usually be fixed by the writer or even by the editor.

Some revision is often required, too, because an author loses sight of the direction his or her article should take. Once the beginning sets the approach, a well-structured article follows a straight course to its conclusion. Side trips, though they may be interesting, cannot be permitted to let an article lose its direction. Although it is a more common fault among beginning writers, straying from the central subject also occurs in the product of seasoned professionals. The temptation to toss in a bit of interesting but extraneous information is just too tempting, especially if that bit of information was acquired only after some hard digging. It is the editor's job, however, to "blue pencil" the article back on course.

At *Smithsonian,* editor Moser finds that some writers fail to recognize what is important or interesting and, thus, don't give a key point the emphasis it deserves. "Often the most salient points get buried in a subordinate clause in the middle of a sentence in the middle of a paragraph in the middle of a story. This, too, can sometimes be fixed, although it does make you wonder what the writer may have left out totally." Moser cites an example of "one writer, a scholar with a head full of wonderful material, used to turn in unpublishable stuff. A couple of us would take him to a long lunch, ask him leading questions, get him telling stories—and frequently interrupt to say 'put that in'; the end product was usually pretty good."

Flaws of subject organization can be kept to a minimum through effective outlining, but restructuring at the editing stage often is necessary. Serious organizational faults usually require further work from the author, but skillful editing can do wonders with a minor rearrangement of facts, the addition of transitional devices, and similar structural aids.

The lack of some bits of pertinent or sometimes vital information is another common shortcoming that must be corrected before the publication of a manuscript. Depth of coverage is essential for any magazine article, and shallow treatments must be subjected to further work. Incomplete manuscripts must be bounced back to the author with sufficient comment to guide him or her in gathering the missing material and incorporating it into the piece.

So far, our discussion of the role of the editor in processing manuscripts has dealt with substantive matters: evaluating the subject in terms of reader needs and interest; checking the approach, direction, and depth of an article; and correcting flaws in organization. Editors must also be concerned with literary quality as they process manuscripts.

Magazines represent the broadest possible range of literary effort, from concise news presentation to the most creative and best of prose. The breadth of the subject makes a thorough discussion of literary style impossible; such a discussion would take volumes. In the last few years, however, there have been certain basic trends and points of emphasis in writing for all magazines to which we can give attention. These have included the demand for clarity and effective communication, as reflected in the work of many with readability research; the emphasis on humanizing even the most complex subjects to hold reader interest; and the emphasis on anecdotes, description, and narration in fact-article writing.

Beginning with the readability research of Rudolf Flesch in the 1940s, the attempts of several individuals to measure the effectiveness of writing have had a strong effect on magazines. Clarity of presentation is sought by virtually every magazine, and any method for measuring and improving writing on that score would naturally be welcomed. To exactly what degree the specific techniques of various systems are accepted and applied varies widely, but the effect of the principles enunciated by these "readability experts" has been almost universal.

The Chilton Company, a Philadelphia-based publisher of specialized business magazines, employed Robert Gunning (*The Technique of Clear Writing* [New York: McGraw-Hill, 1968]) as a consultant for several years and applied his measurement system to its magazines. Annually, three issues of each Chilton magazine were tested and the results shown on a graph that told the individual editors exactly where their scores placed their product in relation to a minimum standard. Gunning's system records a Fog Index, the score based on the average number of words per sentence and the number of "hard" words (three syllables or more). With a score of 13 as acceptable, Chilton officials were pleased to note a drop in score from their industrial publications from 14.4 to 12.9 in eight years. Merchandising magazines produced by Chilton also improved from 13.2 to 11.7. The company management was convinced that the improved scores reflected improvement in their editorial offerings.

Not all magazine publishers use readability measurement in the same fashion, nor do they all use the same systems or the same consultants. In general, however, the accepted conclusion has been that there are certain measurable aspects of writing that indicate the effectiveness of the writing sample in getting its message to readers. For those with an interest, some detailed study of readability systems will be helpful, but many editors concern themselves only with some general principles stemming from all the systems together. These include the following basic guidelines:

1. Short sentences are more effective than longer ones.
2. Shorter words are better than longer ones.
3. Common words are better than the uncommon.
4. Human interest, as measured by such things as personal references, adds to readability.

Although these guidelines tend to oversimplify the formulas of readability measurement, and the formulas themselves are imprecise yardsticks, there is merit in their use. In the unscientific world of written communication, even an imperfect base for judgment is welcome.

The first three readability guidelines are rather easy to apply. By reducing a words-per-sentence average from 50 to 18 or 20, an editor can be reasonably sure that he or she has improved the chances of reaching the receivers with the meaning of the message. If the editor can cut the syllables-per-word average from 2 to nearer to Flesch's suggested 1.5, he or she can also be relatively confident that reader comprehension will be better. If the ratio of common words to total words improves, it is a tangible bit of evidence indicating improved readability.

The fourth guideline, however, is perhaps most important and most in need of attention. Readability research is substantiating a long-standing empirical judgment of editors and writers: the reader's interest in the subject has a direct bearing on his or her ability to read and understand the written material. Given the subject, the editing job then is to maximize the reader's interest in it.

Humanizing for Maximum Interest

The dominant conclusion about getting and holding reader interest from which editors approach their work is that subjects need to be humanized whenever possible. To tell a story in terms of human beings instead of statistics—to show consequence in terms of one person or one family rather than a mass—is to get a jump on readability by maximizing interest.

For example, a writer may submit an article on a subject that is of consequence and interest to a magazine's readers. In this case, let's assume the article is for a business publication serving retail office supply outlets and the title is "Ten Ways to Improve Stapler Sales." You know the article is based on interviews with several merchants who have been successful in greatly increasing their sale of staplers. The article as written is concise and highly readable from the three rhetorical aspects of readability measurement; the sentences are short and the words are short and common. The advice the article offers seems sound, and there is a built-in interest because the subject offers assistance to readers. The effort to inject more human interest into the article might, however, call for some revision. The approach might be changed to fit a new title: "Six Dealers Tell: HOW WE BOOSTED OUR STAPLER SALES." Instead of straightforward preaching to readers, the article would relate, in the words of the successful dealers, their own success stories. Additional readership would be expected because of the introduction of people and their experiences. Editorial hunches and readability measurement agree: people like to read about people.

Anecdotes, Examples, and Description

The trend toward humanizing subjects when possible has been paralleled closely by an increased awareness of the need for adding color to writing. Competition for reader time has forced more effort in this direction. Also, the new generations brought up with a perpetual flow of entertainment coming from their television sets are forcing magazines to make even vital information take on some flavor of entertainment, if the magazines want them as readers. The result has been more and more emphasis on rhetorical devices traditionally rooted in fiction writing.

The anecdotal approach has become so pervasive that observers have complained about articles being big Dagwood sandwiches, with layer on layer of anecdotes, making it almost impossible to find the factual meat in between.

Be that as it may, skillful editors guide their writers into an approach that uses anecdotes, examples, and description to add color, action, life, and interest to articles of any subject. A good case in point is an article in *Medical Opinion,* a magazine written, to a large extent, by medical personnel. The article reached out for readers with the title "Dream On, Bureaucracy, Dream On" and led into the text with the subtitle "After you scrub with pHisoHex and relax with a cold Fresca, imagine that you're sitting in the FDA [Food and Drug Administration] and overhearing the discoverers of insulin, penicillin, and digitalis plead their cases for safety." Dr. Frank B. Nordstrom, the author, then began with an anecdote:

The ringing of the telephone dragged me away from Howard Cosell and the Monday night football game.
"This is the emergency room, Doctor. Mrs. Mortis has just brought her son in with a scalp laceration."
"Excellent. It's almost half time. I'll be down in a few minutes and sew him up."
Mrs. Crossman, our efficient ER nurse, had the area shaved and all the instruments laid out by the time I arrived. Donning gloves, I had started to clean the wound when Mrs. Mortis interrupted.

"You're not going to put the oily white poison on little Rigor's skin, are you?"

"Why, Mrs. Mortis, that isn't oily white poison. That's pHisoHex, an excellent germicide. It's more effective than . . ."

"Apparently you don't keep up, Doctor," she replied in a voice edged with steel. "No son of mine will ever be smeared with the likes of that by the likes of you. Come Rigor, let's find a more competent physician."

Stunned, I drove home to the glowing TV tube, but not even the corn-pone brandishments of Dandy Don could erase the image of that bizarre scene.

The doctor continued his article with some dialogue that led into another anecdote, this one relating to the Food and Drug Administration's banning of a cyclamate soft drink. He then used a dream device, with dialogue between a fictional FDA authority and the discoverers of insulin, penicillin, and digitalis, leading to the banning of their discoveries because of side effects. The result was a fast-moving satirical piece that made its point effectively and would produce a high score on any interest-measuring system.

Not all articles can get this type of treatment, and not all writers are able to carry it off, especially in highly technical fields. However, when the opportunity does present itself, most editors welcome the anecdotal approach, especially if such opportunities are not common.

The Mechanics of Style

Editors are expected to be experts in the mechanics of language. As they process manuscripts, one of their chores is to bring a meticulous correctness to the language being used. Although magazine audiences vary as to their sophistication and knowledge of language, it behooves every editor to strive for this correctness, because all audiences contain some self-styled grammarians who bitterly object to sloppy usage.

The primary problem for the editor, of course, stems from the fact that language changes, and there is no absolute agreement on some points in the first place. However, despite this truism, good editors arm themselves with the best dictionary they can find, plus a good manual of style and follow them as closely as they can and with consistency. By so doing, they can be reasonably assured that their usage passes muster with even the most discriminating readers. For editing changes made in the name of better usage, the final test must be, however, clarity of meaning.

Of special importance for any publication is uniformity in the mechanics of style. Clarity stems, to a great extent, from uniformity. For example, if comma usage is consistent throughout, variations in opinion on the use of commas at least do not interfere with intended meaning. Uniformity in capitalization, use of figures, and other variable aspects of mechanics (insofar as is possible) also contributes to an impression of careful editing and reliability.

Careful editing is essential to creation of a good editorial product, but care must be taken to prevent editing from interfering with an author's style. Authors often deliberately set aside some fine points of grammatical construction to achieve a special style dimension for their prose. This is their right, and editors should tolerate these variances, provided only that meaning is clear and the style peculiarity is, in fact, an effective device. Throughout all their work in processing manuscripts, editors must be sensitive to the rights of authors. Any change constituting meaningful revision should be referred back to the author for execution.

Creating Titles That Sell

Pound for pound, line for line, and word for word, titles that are both eye-catching and informative are the most effective sales tool an editor has for selling the content of a magazine. With only a few choice words, a title has more power to determine whether an article will be read than any other single element with which an editor has to work.

Along with photographs, titles are a primary tool for getting the reader's attention. Then, working with subtitles, they carry the basic responsibility for luring an audience into reading the articles they describe.

Therefore, regardless of what else might be said about titles, we must start with an appreciation of their goals: to capture readers, to grab their interest, and to persuade them to read an article.

Probably the best source for aid in writing and presenting effective titles is the work of the best professionals, who, weekly or monthly, create and publish titles that pass their tests in the marketplace.

Also, there are textbooks for magazine article writing that contain much useful information about creating effective titles because writers, too, are involved in their preparation. In some instances, writers phrase very effective titles that can be used as they are, or with only slight modification. Sometimes even a free-lancer, who has studied the market well, hits the bull's-eye with a title.

In the vast majority of instances, however, the final published titles show the fine hand of the editor. In developing titles, whether modifying an author's efforts or starting anew, editors work with better perspective because they have a complete verbal-visual package in mind. They don't restrict themselves to phrasing alone, or type display alone, or placement alone. They are also aware of their illustrations and the assistance that can come from a subtitle. They work as if all these elements are members of a team, each to be used for maximum effect in achieving readership. All along the way, they know they must work within certain space limits and that brevity and conciseness are mandated.

In many ways, titles are an editor's severest test of word skill and judgment; he or she must pick the exact few words that will most accurately describe their subject and, at the same time, appeal to the greatest possible number of readers. Titles can also represent the editor's toughest test of creativity as he or she tries to make them unique, or at least different enough to be appealing.

Writing Effective Titles

Title writing is creative because there are no limits to their form. Anything goes as far as literary devices are concerned. Form follows function, however, if titles are to be truly effective. Consequently, we shall first look at titles from the standpoint of content.

In content, titles usually fall into one of these two groupings: *descriptive* or *suspenseful,* those that tell and those that tease. A descriptive title is written primarily to give information about its article; it is assumed that interest will be aroused because the article's subject and approach are interesting. A suspenseful title is written to tease, to arouse curiosity by withholding some basic information for the article itself to reveal. Most editors, confident in their content, place greater reliance on descriptive titles.

Descriptive Titles

The preference for descriptive titles stems from a conviction that most readers look to a title for a quick answer to one basic question: "What is this article about?" Some editors are even convinced that readers are sometimes alienated when attempts to be cute or to build suspense delay the answer to this question beyond the title.

Descriptive titles can be dull and unimaginative, but they need not be. As we will see shortly, they can vary widely in form; the fact that they are intended to be straightforward answers to basic questions does not limit creativity in approach.

This demand for creativity of approach varies somewhat with the potential lack of latency or interest of readers. It also increases with the competition for reader attention from other media or other activities. The reader who has a built-in interest in a subject and picks up a specialized interest magazine looking for information can be enticed to read on without any special gimmicks. If the title tells readers in specific, accurate terms what the article is about, they'll probably read it. Even in these instances, however, it is not wise to accept an audience as "captive" and proceed to bore it with unimaginative titles; all audiences are subjected to competition for their time from other media or activities.

Nonetheless, what is perhaps the most common descriptive title is a simple label consisting of only a noun, or a noun with a modifier or two. Although there is nothing spectacular in its rhetorical form, this basic type is widely used in magazines of all descriptions, as these examples indicate:

> Farm and Ranch Vacations (*Family Circle*)
> Skier's Picnic (*Ford Times*)
> Newark's Street People Teachers (*American Education*)
> The Miraculous New Eye Exams (*Woman's Day*)
> The Tempting Siren Called Speed (*Reader's Digest*)
> Those Fantastic Planes of World War I (*Boys' Life*)

The following examples, although they are somewhat different because they begin with a verb form, are substantially the same from the standpoint of content:

> Learning to Like New Zealand (*Holiday*)
> Scouting in Denmark (*Boys' Life*)
> Decorating with Quilts (*House and Garden*)
> Stalking Wild Foods on a Desert Isle (*National Geographic*)

The titles in both these lists simply represent, in each instance, the attempt on the part of an editor to give a simple, direct answer to the reader's natural question: "What's this article about?" The same objective is present in these examples:

> Machiavelli: The Man and the Reputation (*Reader's Digest*)
> Health Care Politics: How the Game Is Played (*Medical Opinion*)
> Communications Update: Intercoms (*Modern Office Procedures*)
> Richie: My Son, My Enemy (*Reader's Digest*)
> A Dry Basement: The Myth That Becomes a Reality (*Good Housekeeping*)

In these five instances, the editors are shifting the word order of each so that the central subjects can be given primary display, with the modifiers being pushed into a secondary position. A variation of this form incorporates a question following the subject designation.

> Employee Loyalty: Where Is It? (*Journal of Organizational Communication*)
> Web Offset Air Pollution: Just How Serious Is It Today? (*Inland Printer and American Lithographer*)
> U.S. Military: Servant or Master? (*Reader's Digest*)
> Being a Working Wife: How Well Does It Work? (*Reader's Digest*)
> Paris High Society: Is It in Decline? (*Newsweek*)
> The Three-Year B.A.: Boon or Bust? (*AAUP Bulletin*)

Although the question portion of this title form may, in some instances, constitute an effort to arouse a reader's curiosity, it usually is designed to help the title be more specific. One of the basic tests of a good descriptive title is the degree of specificity it has. Any title that would fit, without alteration, more than one article, is probably in need of revision. It almost certainly is too general in scope. Articles take specific approaches to subjects, and titles should reveal that approach. Consider, for example, an article on hogs for a farm magazine. It might be titled with just that one word; however, that obviously is too general because readers have been exposed to scores of hog articles before. The title might be made more specific if it is given one modifier and becomes "Hog Care," but actually it still would not be sufficiently tailored to the writer's approach to the subject. Even "Tips on Hog Care" is still too general, as well as trite. In one such article for the *Farm Journal,* the author's approach was to show that farmers suffer losses on hogs that get bruised on their way to market. More specifically, his piece related examples of specific dollar losses resulting from bruised carcasses. The title as it appeared was "It Costs $5 to Kick a Hog," a statement that was specifically tied to the article's approach, or slant. It brought a high readership score for the article.

One way to show the approach of many articles is to start a title with *how, what,* or *why.* This title form is especially common among specialized magazines because the readers of these magazines are often looking to them for information about the hows, whys, and whats of their profession or avocation. However, their use is not restricted to any single magazine type, as these examples show:

How to Hang Anything on a Wall (*Family Circle*)
How to Care for Gift Plants (*Good Housekeeping*)
How to Make Schools Fit for Children (*Better Homes and Gardens*)
How to Talk to a Baby (*Reader's Digest*)
What It Takes to Keep a Big Rig Planting (*Successful Farming*)
What Revenue Sharing Means to Education (*American Education*)
Why the Vietnam War Drags On (*U.S. News & World Report*)
Why Father Zicarelli Is Now in Poughkeepsie (*New Yorker*)

In several of the examples already presented, the title writer obviously tried to inject some extra spice and variety by using special word tricks. Such rhetorical techniques for titles are unlimited. In fact, when it comes to form, the classifications of titles seemingly have no limit. Every gimmick a word artist can conceive is a potential title device, provided only that some caution and good sense are used. Gimmickry that stands out as gimmickry can be worse than a straightforward approach. However, the unique, the offbeat, the clever twist that gives a title something special is a source of pride for the editor and a joy to readers.

Some Special Title Gimmicks

Rhyme, alliteration, puns, figures of speech, coined words, deliberate repetition, and literary allusion are some of the devices that can be enlisted in the effort to get special appeal for titles. Here are a few examples from contemporary magazines:

Take a Gander at These Geese (*Better Living*)
The Guest Is Best at Saratoga (*Sports Illustrated*)
The Pill in Perspective (*Reader's Digest*)
The New Liberated Lingerie (*Woman's Day*)
Boy on a Barge (*Boys' Life*)
Age of Shovelry (*Reader's Digest*)
Rip-roarin' Rural Sport (*Country Living*)
Blazering Along the Gunflint Trail (*Chevy Camper*)
Bungalows for Bluebirds (*Ford Times*)

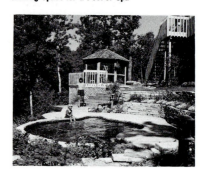

A play on words, alliteration, or other literary devices can add interest to titles. (Courtesy *Garden Ideas and Outdoor Living, USAir Magazine,* and *Elks Magazine.*)

Quotations also serve as a handy title device. Personal accounts naturally lend themselves to quotation titles that may, in their form or content, fit other categories. The mimicking brought on by a rash of such titles as "I Was a Spy for the FBI" has not deterred editors from using them, including the rhyming and alliteration that have subjected them to mimickry. Entertainment magazines (movies, radio-TV) make the most use of quotation titles, but so do some general and other special interest periodicals, as the following examples indicate:

> The Summer I Wrapped Cabbage Heads (*Reader's Digest*)
> How I Played Third Base (*Boys' Life*)
> I Thought We'd Take the Din Out of Dinner (*Reader's Digest*)
> Bill Cosby Reveals: "Why I Am Becoming a Teacher" (*Family Circle*)
> What I Learned from Three Cultures (*Redbook*)

Involving the Reader

The reader can be brought into the title through the use of direct address; readers are enticed into the article because the title is directed to them. As can be seen in some question titles, any literary form can be involved in direct address ("Do You Know How to Play with Your Child?" and "How to Impress Your Coach"). Here are other examples:

> If You Want Help on Your Income Tax Return (*Reader's Digest*)
> So You Think You Own Your Own Land! (*Farm Journal*)
> You, Too, Can Find Connubial Chaos (*Reader's Digest*)
> Take Your Pick of the World's Jazziest Hamburgers (*Family Circle*)
> How to Drive Your Children Sane (*Reader's Digest*)

Asking a Question

A common alternative to the basic label telling what an article is about is the question title. If an editor knows his or her readers well enough to select a subject that solves a common problem or answers a question on their minds—and then asks that same question or poses that problem in the title—he or she has a natural winner. The question form seems to rank second in popularity only to the basic label, perhaps because in many ways it is simply a disguise. Analyze these two question titles:

> Do You Know How to Play with Your Child? (*Woman's Day*)
> Raise Hogs in the Dark? (*Farm Journal*)

Both could have been presented as positive statements: "How to Play with Your Child" and "Raising Hogs in the Dark." Both would then have been typical descriptive titles. By putting them in the form of a question, the editor attempts to make them a little more thought-provoking and intriguing. Nevertheless, they answer the basic question "What is the article about?"

Suspense Titles

On the whole, however, the primary goal of the question form is to arouse interest and create suspense to carry the reader into the article. Note that these deliberately withheld information:

> What Chance for a United States of Europe? (*Reader's Digest*)
> Are Kids Psyching You Out? (*Learning*)
> Does More Time in School Make a Difference? (*Saturday Review*)
> Should You Own Property Together? (*Better Homes and Gardens*)
> Is the U.S. Going Broke? (*Reader's Digest*)

Readers have to go at least to a subtitle before they know the answer to these questions; it is hoped that their interest has been piqued sufficiently to get them to read beyond that.

Another form used to create suspense is the provocative statement, one that is so startling, so contrary to readers' knowledge or assumptions, or so general that it teases them to read on. With these titles, the goal is to arouse questions in the readers' minds that can be answered by the article. Each of the following titles raises such questions:

Dr. Land's "Impossible Dream" (*Popular Science*)
2,400 Miles by Hand Power (*Sports Illustrated*)
Convoy to Nowhere (*Aramco World*)
Fables, Foibles, and Fools (*Ohio Bell Voice*)
A Moment Can Last Forever (*Reader's Digest*)
Love, Marriage—and Crime (*Reader's Digest*)

All of the literary gimmicks can be used in suspenseful titles too. Alliteration, puns, and the like are not restricted to any particular category. As a matter of fact, our attempts to categorize titles does not mean that rigid classifications really exist; even a quick look at the examples presented reveals instances in which titles fit several categories. Neither do we mean to imply that editors do or should approach titles with categories in mind. Ever-present should be the image of the reader and the goals that a title should achieve. If a title appeals to readers sufficiently to "flag them down" and encourage them to read further, it is a good title.

So far, our discussion has been limited primarily to the main title. It is obvious that, in many cases, especially those that deliberately tease the reader by withholding information from the main title, subtitles will be needed. Although subtitles have a value as a visual transition from large type to small type, their more important function is to increase the reader interest that the title has spawned. They are vital bridges between title and text.

To cause reader interest to grow, subtitles are usually written to provide detail that wouldn't fit into the main section. Their goal can be related to the sales role of titles; any sale requires a clincher, something the customer can't resist, something to "close" the sale. The effective title sparks the interest, while the subtitle closes the sale.

Subtitles may follow the approach started by the main title, or they may shift the direction. For example, if the top title is a label, the subtitle may simply be an attempt to add some interesting facts; it carries forward the assumption that, if the article is accurately described in the title, readers will come to it, or the label title may be followed by a question or another device to suspend reader interest by creating curiosity. With suspended interest titles, the same options are open—follow with a subtitle that is in the same vein, or shift to one that is descriptive. All the literary techniques, from allusion to puns, are also appropriate for subtitles.

Let's look at some of the titles already cited as examples to see how various editors used subtitles. Following its title based on an allusion to the well-known advertising line, "When You're No. 2, You Try Harder," *Sports Illustrated* added specific facts and word tricks:

WHEN YOU'RE NO. 2, YOU DIET
When Jurgensen was hurt, Billy Killmer became the No. 1 Redskin quarterback. However, don't count Sonny out, he's counting calories

In another article, *Sports Illustrated* followed with facts that came in question form:

2,400 MILES BY HAND POWER
Or how else would you get a surfboard from Boston to Miami?

Following a catchy title, *Woman's Day* used a subtitle beginning with a question and ending with more specific facts:

THE NEW LIBERATED LINGERIE
What's going on? Nothing much!
That's what's great about the
new underthings. They're airy,
light, stretchy, comfortable. Just
like a second skin, only better

The preceding examples all show subtitles as independent units following a main title. Even this aspect of usage is subject to variation. Some titles are really dependent, either reading into the title or out of it and not standing independently, or, as the following example from *Popular Science* illustrates, it can combine both techniques:

Come for a ride on
BILL LEAR'S NEW STEAM BUS
A light steam turbine drives this converted bus.
Will it perform reliably?
Free of emissions?
And how does it compare with the diesel?

Here, also from *Popular Science,* is a short subtitle leading into the longer main title:

Now They're Building
AIRPORTS THAT TAKE THE HASSLE
OUT OF CATCHING YOUR PLANE

Fortune led into a moderately long title with a subtitle of about 30 words:

Beneath the ritual histrionics of the presidential campaign, deeply divisive forces are tearing at the U.S. political system. The Republicans will have trouble of their own, but a far graver threat is
THE TIME BOMB INSIDE
THE DEMOCRATIC PARTY

The editors of *Woman's Day* gave excellent graphic treatment to a main title (Pick Me Ups Under $10) that led into a routinely displayed subtitle:

Add a little magic to a familiar
sunny-day wardrobe—new snap,
new shine—to lift the spirits
without lightening the
purse too much

The Blurb Background as a Subtitle
A few words about the author or circumstances surrounding the preparation of an article are often used in much the same fashion as a subtitle. Called *blurbs,* these word groups are displayed just as subtitles are, and they often perform the same function. The stamp of authority can be put on an article through the use of a blurb that establishes the qualifications of the author; audience interest can be stimulated by promotional material contained in the blurb.

When in Doubt, Use Subtitles
The examples of subtitles given here are only a small sample of the potential variations; as with titles, there is really no limit on their manner of presentation. These examples do show, however, the importance and need of subtitles. As a general rule, titles need the extra, more specific information that comes from a subtitle to tell a reader what he or she wants to know before deciding to read an article. When in doubt, it is wise to assume that the reader needs a subtitle as the second part of a one-two combination.

So What Are Subheads?
Subtitles are sometimes called *subheads,* but, actually, the terms are not synonymous. Subheads are units of type display usually used between paragraphs as headings for the portion of the article immediately following. They have traditionally been used as a means for some typographical relief in a large mass of body type. They can be used in a wide variety of forms, however, and they can also serve a more useful function.

Rather than being used merely for visual relief, with little or no attention being given to their content, subheads can be useful "rechargers" of reader interest. If they are to be effective, care should be exercised in their writing so they do en-

Figure 7.2 Subheads, if given special treatment, can relieve monotony and create interest. (Courtesy *Journal of Organizational Communications, American Education, Tempo.*)

courage a reader to continue. Without meaningful content, subheads are often no better as visual aids than white space, which, when judiciously used, can break up type masses and provide optical reference points just as well as type.

Common forms for subheads include single boldface lines that are centered or placed either flush to the left or flush to the right. Capitalization and special boldness given to the first few words of a paragraph can also create the effect of a subhead. These are traditional newspaper forms, and they find their best usage in the magazine field among "newsy" magazines.

Other magazines, some of them not concerned with news material, have developed forms that give more responsibility to subheads. Meaningfully written and given special size, important position, and/or special graphic treatment, these subheads are, in reality, titles for the portions of articles they precede. Figure 7.2 shows how some editors have used subheads effectively.

Headlines in Magazines

Headlines, like the traditional subheads, are a product of the newspaper. As the name implies, headlines are standardized lines of type used to head a story and are placed at the top of the story. In selling news to readers, they are probably unbeatable. They have been perfected in newspaper offices with that goal in mind, and there is no reason they should not serve the same functions in magazines.

Figure 7.3 Newsmagazines such as *Editor & Publisher* often use standardized news headlines rather than distinctive titles. (Courtesy *Editor & Publisher*.)

Their use has served *Time, Newsweek,* and *U.S. News & World Report* well because of the content and general style of these newsmagazines. There are also many specialized newsmagazines, such as *Editor & Publisher, Chemical Week,* and scores of others, that also rely on newspaper-style headlines (see figure 7.3). Timeliness and a news orientation are usually the characteristics that point magazines toward headlines rather than individually designed titles.

The attributes of a good magazine headline are the same as those of a newspaper headline. They usually contain one to three lines of display type, all of the same size and style, and usually flush left. They may contain a second unit (deck) of one to three lines in a smaller type size. Each deck is a skeletonized sentence that tells, as concisely as possible, the gist of the news that follows, and each may include a short line above or below the main lines to create some white space. However, rarely is much extra white space used. Unlike magazine titles, headlines do not get a third, half, or full page of space for display; unlike magazine titles, they are often all from the same type family.

The following are helpful maxims for writing effective news headlines:

1. Headlines should be skeletonized sentences.
2. All headlines should include a verb, except when the verb would be a form of "to be" and is implied in the headline.
3. If possible, the verb should be in the first line to give action to that line.
4. Every line of a headline should be a complete thought unit; hence, an adjective and its noun should be on the same line, and a verb and its auxiliary should be on the same line.
5. It is possible, and sometimes preferable, to omit the subject in a headline (as in "Sues Partner for Contract Cancellation").
6. Headlines should be specific.
7. Headlines must be accurate; their condensation should not permit ambiguities or misleading implications.
8. Any abbreviations used should be well known to readers.

Correction and Verification

Editors have forever been faced with two truisms. One is that nothing does a publication more damage than errors, especially when they occur frequently enough to create an impression of carelessness. The other is that, no matter how great the effort, errors sneak into copy, sometimes in the most surprising places. There is scarcely an editor alive who has not experienced the dismay of finding a *typo* (typographical error) in a title line in huge type after every remote detail of the body copy was carefully checked and rechecked. Sometimes the obvious is overlooked, whereas minute detail is thoroughly scrutinized.

Despite the inevitability of errors (even *Time* and *Newsweek,* protected by armies of researchers and the most skilled of editors, must occasionally "eat" inaccuracies), the battle against them never ceases. Although absolute accuracy may be a Holy Grail always sought and never achieved, the continual effort to keep errors at a minimum has resulted in a high standard of accuracy among American magazines. Every procedure that can serve to ferret out errors, large or small, has been and continues to be a must for all magazines.

One of the best guardians against error is a knowledgeable editor. Editors who are well-read, who have stored away in their bank of knowledge great quantities of information, are able to detect errors that would go unnoticed by less capable guardians of a magazine's reputation. The broad educational background required of modern journalism students, if backed up by a continuing search for knowledge, provides an indispensable component of a good editor. In the editing of specialized magazines, this broad background must be complemented by detailed knowledge of the magazine's specialized area. The editor of a farm publication must know farming; the editor of an oil industry periodical must be an expert in that field; and so it goes for any subject. In highly technical fields, even the best-prepared editor may find it necessary to use the additional safeguard of an advisory board for the reading and evaluation of manuscripts.

Much more checking and rechecking with sources is required of the magazine journalist than the newspaper writer or editor, if for no other reason than that time permits it. It is much better to have sources verify the material they have provided before publication than it is to have them complain about inaccuracy after publication.

The Mechanics of Copyediting

The copy editor of a daily newspaper no doubt envies the time between issues available to the editors of weekly, biweekly, and monthly magazines. Magazine editors appreciate their time advantage; they realize that it represents the opportunity to give their copy the added dimension it must have to compete with other media. However, this time advantage must be, and is, taken up with providing the additional depth and quality expected from magazines. It does not provide any opportunity for less efficient handling of copy.

Traditional Copyediting

Consequently, as magazine editors work with a manuscript, they use every shortcut and efficient procedure available to them. Primary among these is a set of symbols for marking corrections of grammar, punctuation, spelling, and mechanics of style. These copyediting symbols, although they may vary slightly in their use from one office to another, are essentially standardized among all print media. As one can see in figure 7.4, they are based on common sense and the desire to be quick and efficient in relating changes to a printer. The beginner should be certain to avoid confusing these symbols with those used to mark corrections after copy has been set in type. Proofreading symbols are used for that purpose. The essential characteristics of copyediting symbols is that changes are marked at the point errors occur and not in the margin. All copy for typesetting should be typed double- or triple-spaced to permit the use of these marks in the line and at the spot they occur. Figure 7.5 shows an article that has been corrected using copyediting symbols.

Computerized Copy Processing

As each day goes by, more and more copyediting is being handled via computerized devices. Word processing software varies among computers; the procedures vary according to the brand of the device being used.

Desired Correction   Symbol to Use

1. Change small letter to capital ....   a̲
2. Change capital to small letter ....   A̸
3. Change form in numerals or abbreviations:
    3 to three ....   ③
    three to 3 ....   (three)
    Street to St. ....   (Street)
    St. to Street ....   (St.)
4. To start a new paragraph ....   ⌊Now is the
5. To put space between words ....   Now⌷is
6. To close up (remove space) ....   home town
7. To delete a letter and close up ....   judgement
8. To delete words or two or more letters ....   to fully receive
9. To delete one letter and substitute another ....   believe
10. To delete two or more letters and close up ....   accommododate
11. To insert letters or words ....   not well
12. To transpose letters or words if adjacent ....   recieve
13. To insert punctuation:

    comma⌄   colon⁚   apostrophe˅
    period.   exclamation⌡   opening quote˅˅
    question mark?   hyphen=   closing quote ("
    semicolon;   dash —   parentheses ( )
14. To center material ....   ⌋News Notes⌊
15. To indent material ....   ⌐All the lines⌐
                                      are indented⌐
16. Set in boldface type ....   The news today
17. Set in italic type ....   The news today
18. To delete several lines or paragraphs, box in the material and X it out ....   ⊠

Figure 7.4 Copyediting symbols.

Hamilton

New Open Records Law

COLUMBUS, OH—⌊A major step in Ohio's efforts to provide the fullest possible freedom of public information for the citizens of the state was taken when the new "open records⌣" law became effective this week.

⌊Passed by a near-unanimous vote in this year's Ohio General Assembly, the law provides that records on all levels of local and state government, with certain exceptions, shall be open to the public. The exceptions are records pertaining to physical or psychiatric examinations, adoption, probation, and parole procedings, and records prohibited by state or federal law Penalty for noncompliance with the new law is a $100 fine per offense.

⌊Full text of the law states:

⌊"Sec. 149.43. As used in this section, 'public record' means any record required to be kept by any governmental unit, including, but not limted to, state, county, city, village, township, and

more

Figure 7.5 A page of a manuscript after copyediting. Note that all corrections are made at the point of error, not in the margin.

Proprietary systems, designed by vendors offering their specialized wares to print media publishers, are highly sophisticated and have been geared to permit complex correcting and copy manipulation with very few key strokes. Some multipurpose personal computers have more complex and less sophisticated provisions for basic copyediting, but there are principles that prevail for most systems.

As one can learn from experience with traditional copyediting, the corrections and changes made by editors range from minor, single-character changes to the total rewriting of certain passages. Computerized systems have compressed these into five basic maneuvers: (1) delete, (2) add, (3) replace, (4) transpose, and (5) move.

To permit these maneuvers, copy is displayed either in quantity on a video screen comparable to that of a small TV or in just a few words or a line on a very small screen. Access to the point of the change to be made is usually by way of a cursor (a light that can be moved from place to place by keys or other devices such as a mouse).

Production-related aspects of copyediting also show the advantages of computerized editing. Fitting of copy to space and specifying printers' instructions are routinely handled by computerized systems, especially those that form complete front-end systems, from keyboard to type proofs. The fact that all parts of the system have been designed to work together makes communication among the parts simple and easy. Working with human printers is sometimes more difficult.

The need to prepare raw materials so printers can produce magazines efficiently points up the dual nature of magazine editing. As they attempt to make content match readers' needs, editors must also edit the material to meet the needs of their production partners, the printers.

Many of the production aspects of editing are looked on as techniques, skills, or chores because they relate directly to the manufacturing of the magazine. It is true that there are techniques and skills to be learned, but there is creativity involved also.

Two other points should also be made: (1) not all editing decisions can be based entirely on creative urges—cost of production is always a factor and (2) research must be used to keep editors in tune with their readers. The next chapter shows how research can provide basic guidelines for creative decisions.

Notes

1. Letter dated 29 August 1988 to Russell N. Baird from the editor of *Smithsonian* Magazine, Don Moser.
2. Lane M. Palmer, *Publishing Magazines to Meet Reader Needs and Interests* (Madison: Department of Agricultural Journalism, University of Wisconsin, 1971), p. 71.
3. Ibid., p. 20.
4. Moser.
5. Palmer, p. 26.

Magazine Research

8

R ESEARCH has not been embraced by most magazine editors. Magazine editing is and should be creative. Research often is viewed as limiting creativity. Research can be helpful, however, by telling an editor what kind of people the readers are, their reading preferences, their interests, and their goals. It can give editors a clear picture of their target audience and the depth of their interest in the magazine.

Research can provide important information and help editors make decisions, but the results seldom are so clear that they make a decision for an editor. Research is based in the past, telling you how readers responded to material that has been published, and it is limited by the respondents' experience. Research findings cannot tell you what future results will be, but concept testing can reduce the likelihood of failure of a proposed new department or feature. Research always has to be viewed in context, against benchmarks, in comparison with other findings. The inconclusive nature of most research irritates editors who prefer yes-no answers. Whatever the research findings, a human must make the subsequent decisions.

Journalists believe in knowing everything possible before making decisions, so it is natural that they use available research data and foster additional research. A full-scale research bureau or department isn't necessary, nor is a continuing effort that always looks at the same situations or aspects of publishing. Public opinion and market research organizations can be retained to do occasional research projects, which may be more helpful than continuous research by a big, established research department within the publishing company. Results of other people's research can suggest approaches to editing, as well as additional research studies to undertake.

Editors can use research: (1) to make decisions about the mechanics of editing, (2) for guidance in choosing content, and (3) to put their jobs and goals into perspective by gaining insight into communication behavior generally.

Mechanics of Editing

Numerous studies have provided a wealth of information about how material presented one way is more effective than that presented another way. Titles, captions, illustration size, type size and leading, and subtitles have been studied. In many instances, custom or common belief has been confirmed by research; in fewer instances, it has been found erroneous.

Article Titles

Saturday Evening Post, Wallaces Farmer, Wisconsin Agriculturalist, Farm Journal, and other magazines have researched the effect of titles on readers. The overall finding has been that readers do not like cryptic or unclear titles; they don't like being tricked into reading something in which they may not be interested. Readers tend to react more favorably to dramatic words and titles they can identify with, including words such as *I, how-to,* and *you.*

Subtitles had been viewed by some editors as giving away too much of the article, thereby reducing readership. Research, though, found the opposite. Using subtitles increases readership, and the best location is beneath the title. This supports the finding that people read what they are interested in; therefore, telling them more about the article makes the title more recognizable and sharpens their interest. Subtitles can be placed above the title for variety—*Saturday Evening Post* found it most effective for them to read directly into the title, rather than be a separate unit of thought.

Captions

Photographers occasionally insist that a photo is too good to be ruined by a caption. Captions are needed, however, to complete the story that a photo begins—to set the location, the time, the sequence of events, the significance or outcome, and the identity of the persons involved. Research has supported the case for captions, indicating that readers prefer full, informative captions placed near the pictures they explain. An individual caption for each picture is preferred to a single block of captions describing several photos.

Wilson Hicks, the first picture editor of *Life* and later its executive editor, so firmly believed that words and pictures have to combine into a single idea when neither is complete without the other that he titled a major address "One Word Is Worth 10,000 Pictures." Words provide the corrective for camera distortion, translating a three-dimensional scene into a two-dimensional picture or selecting only one representation of a sequence of events. The camera lies, often unintentionally, and words are needed to put the scene in its proper context.

Layout

Most layout studies have confirmed existing practices or beliefs, at least in essentially mechanical areas—for example:

- Large illustrations generally draw more readers than small ones.
- Unusually shaped halftones—tilted, football-shaped, jagged, silhouetted—tend to irritate readers. They prefer square finish halftones.
- Photographs are more effective than sketches in illustrating articles. The most effective sketches are clear, realistic ones.
- Four-color photos increase readership but black halftones are second, not duotones or black halftones printed on colored tint blocks.
- Readers prefer, about two to one, conventional layouts in this order: picture, headline or title, deck or subtitle, body type. Placing the title beneath the body type seems disordered or unnatural.
- People are reluctant to read more than two or three lines of italic body type. Research does not clearly indicate that it is more difficult to read italics but simply that readers don't stick with it.
- The standing head in the department or column should not overwhelm the head or title about the issue's specific topic. Regular readers will seek the standing head, but the fresh head can bring in readers who might skip that department or column.
- Readers usually see the lead picture and read its caption before reading the lead of the article, so the article lead should not repeat the caption.
- Pictures grouped together have greater reader interest than pictures scattered throughout an article. A group of pictures tends to function as one large illustration instead of several small ones.
- A small amount of text and large picture on the opening page seems to increase readership—for example, about 20 percent text and 80 percent illustration.
- Pictures should not be so small they are difficult to see. Something not worth showing large enough to see is not worth showing. (Editors who feel compelled to use pictures because they have them or have paid for them should develop the art of discarding anything marginal or questionable. Every time you add a picture to a layout, you increase the competition among the pictures for the reader's attention and decrease the potential readership of each picture.)
- For titles, readers seem to prefer simple type faces that are familiar to them from a variety of publications.

Other studies have been unable to detect significant differences between readers' preferences for ordinary type design and design considered superior by a jury of graphic design experts. Such findings are disconcerting to art directors and designers who try to match the mood of the face to the content or emotion of the article. One operational principle is to avoid the monotony of using all simple, widely used faces for titles, while avoiding faces so ornate they are difficult to read or attract too much attention to themselves. Research confirms that Roman type can be read faster than other faces.

In planning the break-of-the-book, editors may want to consider that one-fourth of their readers start at the back and move to the front. Features at the back in one- and two-page units can capture attention and create something of an opening section for readers who begin at the back. Reader research also suggests it is wise to open the editorial section at the front of the book with the article that is expected to appeal to the largest number of readers.

Even reasonably clear research findings such as these are not something to be slavishly followed. Magazines would become dreadfully monotonous if every spread looked almost like every other one because research suggested that a certain treatment was more effective. Obviously, for one type of layout to be more effective than others, it must be compared with others. Monotony of design might decrease effectiveness throughout.

Some well-designed magazines, however, use the same type face, type size, line length, and number of lines for every article title. Often called "bookish" layout, it is used in think and opinion magazines and some newsmagazines, in which readers actively seek out the content they want to read. Readers of *New Republic* are accustomed to their magazine and know how to read it. They would be startled by dazzling graphics. Editors should be selective in choosing which research results to use in their books. If the research results are not compatible with the personality or editorial purpose, they should not be used.

Choosing Content

Choice of content is an editorial decision, even when research results are available. A major finding is that articles of expected low readership combined with several of high readership can reach a larger total audience than an issue of all higher readership items. A study of 47 issues of *Saturday Evening Post* found that aiming one-half to two-thirds of the editorial content to majority readership and using the remaining space for special or unusual articles of low interest resulted in higher total readership because people who normally would not buy the magazine were attracted to an article that did not appeal to the majority of *Post* readers. Cover lines promoting these articles can help sell these issues.

Farm Journal editors check with their readers periodically. By nature, the dairy editor goes to dairy country and finds high readership of dairy articles. The hog editor goes to hog farming areas, with like results. They also report back to headquarters that general articles on schools and health are low in readership. The overall picture is, however, that the general articles that departmental editors find low in readership are consistently read across all farming specialties, which adds up to relatively higher readership. The hog farmers are not reading dairy articles, and the dairy farmers are not reading hog articles; consequently, the readership of these articles may not be as high as the more general material.

An editor may find it useful to visualize a core of the magazine, one-half to two-thirds, as being aimed at the general or overall readership and the remainder as an opportunity to serve the special interests of both existing and potential readers. A portion of each issue should be available for low-interest material that the readers are not expecting.

Related to this is the reader's intensity of interest, which often is difficult to gauge. Only 5 percent of the readers of an employee magazine may read an article on an employee speakers bureau, but those who do may be intensely interested in it, perhaps because they are part of the speakers bureau. The same holds for promotions and other personal items in some magazines. No one advocates giving the entire magazine to this type of content, but intense reader interest among a small number can contribute to greater overall readership of the issue.

An occasional survey can identify topics that deserve further or different treatment. When transferability of milk quotas was a complex issue in Wisconsin, *Wisconsin Agriculturalist* found that 72 percent of the farmers had not heard of the issue. More discussion of the issue was needed so farmers could vote on it intelligently.

Understanding of readers also helps temper judgments that otherwise would be based on folklore. *Business Week* once ran pictures of bathing beauties to illustrate an article on the Jantzen company. Everyone knows that some readers like pictures of pretty girls. Although the pictures were too large to be ignored, they were outscored in readership by four charts on the state of the economy, a picture of a new Cadillac, a picture of an old Rolls Royce, and two of "the worst pictures of a tunnel" the editor had ever seen. Business people read *BW* for business information rather than photos of models in swimsuits.

An executive at *Life* already knew that pretty girls, babies, and animals on covers don't help sell magazines. Analyzing newsstand sales by cover illustration, he had found that pictures of children actually decreased sales and that one cover featuring a sexy pose of a motion picture star had the lowest single-copy sales of the year. More inquiry into why people buy a specific magazine and what content interests them can help identify illustrations and covers that are more relevant to their interests and more likely to increase readership and sales. Some stars and public figures have noticeably increased newsstand sales of other consumer magazines.

Audience Research

Magazines find out about their audiences in varied ways. Commissioned research for individual magazines or publishing companies, industry-sponsored research, and syndicated research by one research firm for a number of magazine publishers all add to the data available to an editor. The bulk of magazine research is done to increase the sale of advertising, but some is done for the editorial department.

Readership surveys are made by going to readers' homes with copies of the magazine to find out which articles they read. Usually, readership is gauged as "read all," "read most," or "read some." Over a period of time, an editor can determine the types of articles that score best and consider whether to use more of those types. He or she can find out what scored low and, if the survey is cross-tabulated, can find whether low-interest items were read by people who read little else in the issue.

An editor must consider whether readers get the magazine by action on their part—paying for a subscription—or as the result of a condition—such as being an employee of a company. Readership tends to be lower in the latter instance, and editors work hard to make such magazines more appealing. A study of employee magazines can combine an attitude or opinion survey with the readership survey to gain further insight into readership. One study found that about one-third of the employees' attitudes were "highly favorable," one-third "favorable," and one-third "unfavorable." Readership among the unfavorable group predictably was lower than among the other two groups. The president's letter on page 3 scored 59 percent among the highly favorable and 16 percent among the unfavorable. However, an article on new machinery that would change production methods and possibly displace some workers was read by as many unfavorable as highly favorable and favorable, 32 percent.

If the magazine is part of the public relations or the personnel department, the survey may be tabulated by readership classifications for comparison—by job title or department, by length of service with the company, or by plant, if several plants are involved. Results can furnish an insight into existing problems, potential problems, and areas with few or no problems—and give the editor information about how effectively the magazine is reaching its readers.

Mail surveys can be used to gauge readership of general content areas, departments, and some specific articles. A self-administered survey should contain background questions to help the editor evaluate readership results: how regularly the respondent reads the magazine, how he or she rates the magazine overall, and which items or departments he or she reads regularly, occasionally, seldom, or never. Intensity questions yield valuable data here too.

READER RESPONSE

Each issue of NB Eye will carry a Reader Response Card.
We'd like to know what you think of our magazine. Please let us know by answering the questions below, detaching the card and sending it to us either by interoffice or U.S. Mail.

Please rate the articles in this issue.	Great	OK	Dull	Didn't Read
Puttin' on the Ritz for 50 Years Now	—	—	—	—
The Merry Month of the Peanut	—	—	—	—
By Appointment to Her Majesty the Queen	—	—	—	—
New Products: Variety Is Spice of Recent Introductions	—	—	—	—
Profile: Calvin D. Ferber	—	—	—	—
Hail to the Chefs!	—	—	—	—
Recipes: The Peanut, More Than a Snack	—	—	—	—
INFO	—	—	—	—

Comments

Subjects I'd like to see covered in future issues.

Fill in below *only* if you wish to be contacted about your ideas for NB Eye.

NAME   DEPARTMENT

PLANT/OFFICE   SUPERVISOR'S NAME

WORK TELEPHONE (   )   HOME TELEPHONE (   )

Reader survey cards bound into magazines solicit readership information and opinion. Each article is listed with Likert rating scale responses of "Great," "OK," "Dull," and "Didn't Read." If the reader does not return it by interoffice mail, a postage stamp is required. That modest investment may skew results by decreasing response. Postage-paid cards yield better results. (Courtesy NB Eye, *Nabisco Brands, Inc.*)

Plant Engineering Courtesy of Technical Publishing, a company of the Dun & Bradstreet Corporation.

EDITORIAL QUALITY AUDIT RATING FORM

For article titled:_____
(Please write in article title)

Nine desirable article characteristics are listed below. Please evaluate this article by circling the number that best rates each characteristic, USING THE SCALE BELOW:

	Deficient	Fair	Good	Excellent
1. The article provides information promised in the title.	1	2	3	4
2. The article presents useful technical data or original ideas.	1	2	3	4
3. Text is organized in logical sequence.	1	2	3	4
4. The article "reads" easily (considering relative complexity of subject).	1	2	3	4
5. The article length is appropriate to subject matter. (Should be: Longer ☐ / Shorter ☐)	1	2	3	4
6. Technical points are explained clearly and are easy to comprehend.	1	2	3	4
7. Illustrations, tables and charts help explain text and add to article value.	1	2	3	4
8. Technical details in illustrations are easily understood.	1	2	3	4
9. The article is useful to me in the performance of my plant engineering duties and responsibilities.	1	2	3	4

(If you circled (1) or (2): Is the subject of the article:

☐ Outside your job responsibility?
☐ No present problems on this subject?
☐ Not pertinent to your plant situation?
☐ Just a poor article?

NOTE: PLEASE USE REVERSE SIDE FOR COMMENTS ON ANY ASPECTS OF THE ARTICLE NOT COVERED IN THE ABOVE RATING-- (Optional But Valuable To The Editors).

Your Name:_____

Figure 8.1 Articles can be evaluated by a reader panel using a Likert scale on an instrument like this one from *Plant Engineering*. (Courtesy of Technical Publishing, a company of the Dun & Bradstreet Corporation.)

Mail readership surveys are more economical than personal interview ones and can be helpful to the editor. These usually involve sending a copy of the magazine to a subscriber soon after the regular copy was mailed, along with instructions about how to mark the survey copy. For example, readers may mark an article they noticed with a check mark, one they read some of with a single line, and one they read most of with a double line.

Other surveys send a copy of the issue with a questionnaire or cards on which the reader checks his or her level of readership. One mails a miniature facsimile copy of the issue with a 12-page questionnaire booklet in which respondents can check boxes beneath each facsimile.

Samples are systematic or random and their sizes vary widely, roughly from 250 to 500, with readership results often based on the first 100 returns. Because of differing methodologies, results from different services cannot be directly compared. Even results from different magazines using the same service cannot be directly compared.

Readership scores are not an absolute measurement of editorial effectiveness. The procedures in the mail surveys are especially prone to large error allowances, so an item read by 72 percent of the readers may not be significantly better read than an article read by 64 percent. Scores for a large number of articles over a period of time should cluster around certain types of content and give the editor an overall indication of what material is most popular and least popular as of the time of publication. Because they take place after publication and require time to complete, readership surveys cannot give the editor immediate information.

The **reader panel** is another approach, one that *Plant Engineering* has taken. To obtain reader reaction at modest cost, the magazine uses the panel to measure readership of all feature articles and to monitor editorial performance. Based on a pilot study, the size of each panel was set at 25, and nine panels are used on a rotating basis for the biweekly magazine.

For each article, a panelist is given a form on which to rate on a four-point Likert scale whether the article was deficient, fair, good, or excellent on nine items (figure 8.1). These include whether the article provides the information promised in the title; the article presents useful technical data or original ideas; the text is in logical sequence; the article reads easily; the length is appropriate; technical points are explained clearly and are easy to comprehend; illustrations, tables, and charts help explain text and add value to the article; technical details in illustrations are easily understood; and the article is useful to the rater in fulfilling plant engineering duties and responsibilities.

Panelists are asked each year if they are willing to serve one year and are told they will be sent six articles four times a year. Articles are enclosed with the letter of invitation so the person can perform an audit before accepting.

The first 15 completed forms to arrive are used to compute the final score, because the pilot study showed that results from 15 to 60 persons were within a few percentage points of each other. The guidelines for interpreting scores are based on the percentage of a perfect "excellent" score on all nine items. Below 65 percent is poor, 65 to 75 percent is fair, 75 to 85 percent is good, and 85 percent or higher is excellent. Fewer than six articles a year attain 85 percent or higher, and editors who write or edit an article that reaches this height are given a plaque and a check.

Articles that score under 65 percent are analyzed to learn why they were rated so low, and articles over 85 percent are studied with care to determine why they did so well. One finding was that subjects of limited interest routinely score lower than articles with broad scope. One example of a decision made from this research is that product case histories as feature stories were eliminated after they consistently scored low.

Panelists are not offered payment; the appeal is "help us do a better job for you." At the end of the year, token gifts such as framed prints and books of broad interest are sent to the panelists.

On occasion, an item has been tested before publication. One was a new department that had a successful tryout with the panel before appearing in the magazine. The program also has made everyone on the staff more conscious of elements that contribute to high article readership.

Computer models can be useful in assessing an overall situation or a portion of it. *Playboy* used data from 52 issues to gain insight into factors that had greatest impact on magazine sales. For each issue, the number of copies sold, number of competitors' copies sold, cover price, unemployment statistics, dollars spent on promotion, number of subscriptions serviced that month, number of copies distributed, number of full-cover displays, number of days on sale, and a score of several editors' estimates of the effectiveness of the cover, cover blurbs, and content of the issue were entered into the computer for a stepwise regression analysis that pointed to the variables that combine best to produce the equation that equals total sales. The variables influential in estimating sales were the number of subscriptions, number of copies distributed, unemployment, competitors' sales, number of days on sale, and qualitative index of appeal of the cover, cover blurbs, and content. One of the least influential items was the amount of money spent on promotion. The analysis also pointed to February and October as months when sales were somewhat lower than expected rather than the conventionally held July and August, and it showed that seasonal variations were almost negligible, cover price changes only temporarily affected sales in an inflationary period, and the number of editorial pages in an issue had no correlation with newsstand sales or subscription sales. The most controllable factors, then, were the subscription list, the editorial content, and the cover.

Opinion or **attitude surveys** can develop a profile of a magazine and its readers. Several questions should be asked about each major concept or point, because a single, straightforward question will not yield a reliable result. Statistical analysis with principal components analysis or multiple regression groups the related responses and identifies whether their results are significant. The research also should delve into various parts or departments of the magazine to identify strengths and problems.

Likert-type questions give the respondent a choice of four or five responses of varying intensity. The respondent is asked to check the one that most closely represents his or her opinion about the item. A mean score for an item can be used to compare it with the same item asked about another magazine and, in some cases, can be cross-tabulated with related items to give a more sophisticated analysis of audience opinion of the magazine. Respondents could be asked to rate an article as very interesting, interesting, uninteresting, or very uninteresting; greatly important, moderately important, somewhat important, or unimportant; or very useful, moderately useful, slightly useful, or not useful. A reader could be asked to give a magazine an overall rating in broader terms, such as excellent, very good, good, fair, or poor. The scores for several magazines rated this way could give a general idea of how each magazine ranks within its competitive field.

The conceptualization and planning of research is the key to its validity and reliability. If questions are not prepared to make distinctions needed to obtain useful data, the research effort is wasted. While editor of *McCall's,* Herbert Mayes underwrote the cost of a study of six issues of six consumer magazines to find out which covers were most successful at selling copies on newsstands. The successful issues, the research firm reported, had covers with one large illustration, with red the dominant color, and three blurbs or cover lines. The unsuccessful issues had covers with one large illustration, with red the dominant color, and three blurbs or cover lines.

Also remember that, for research about your magazine to be useful, its results must be compared with those for another magazine or with generally accepted benchmarks. Otherwise, you have only a descriptive study that gives you a profile but no context or means of interpretation.

Focus groups can be used to test concepts for new magazines, proposed design changes, and changes in content. Small groups of 6 to 12 persons are assembled to discuss the topic and often also to evaluate competitors. Groups usually are selected in several cities to keep the results from being too narrowly tied to one city or geographic area. Time Inc. filmed focus groups in preparing *TV-Cable Week* for publication and used some of that film of people criticizing competing TV magazines in a promotional film.

Market testing is the ultimate test in introducing new magazines. Test issues are published and placed on sale in selected markets, often a dozen or so. If sales of the test issues, usually at least two, reach targeted goals, the magazine is fully launched. Even then, some successfully test-marketed magazines fail.

Content Studies

Content analysis tells an editor how much of each type of material has been published in a given period of time. The results can be matched with content objectives, if they have been quantified.

A formula book that has set rigid content goals for the year may plan meticulously to keep very near those projected goals throughout the year. Allowing for seasonal variation, by the end of March one-fourth of the goal should have been achieved.

Other editors check only periodically to make sure they are balancing the content close to the way they intend. Occasionally, the analysis reveals a mistaken memory or an erroneous hunch by showing overcovered and undercovered areas.

Better Homes and Gardens used these categories:

1. Building
    Architecture
    Materials, modernization, maintenance, repairs
    Financing and insurance
2. Children
3. Gardening and flowers
4. Food and nutrition
5. Home furnishing and management
    Appliances, equipment, housewares
    Tableware
    Decorating and home furnishings
    Homemaking and home management
6. Travel and transportation
    Travel
    Transportation
        Automobile, trailer (including highways)

7. Business and industry
8. Health and medical science
9. Sports, recreations and hobbies
10. Cultural interests
11. General interest
    Insurance and savings
12. Miscellaneous
13. National affairs
14. Foreign and international affairs
15. Amusements
16. Beauty, grooming, toiletries
17. Wearing apparel and accessories
18. Fiction and stories

TABLE 8.1
Editorial Content of 74 U.S. Magazines, 1991

Type of Editorial	Percentage
Culture and humanities	15.9
Food and nutrition	8.8
Sports, hobbies	8.6
National affairs	7.7
General interest	7.2
Health and medical science	7.2
Home furnishing and management	5.7
Amusements	5.6
Wearing apparel	5.3
Travel and transportation	4.4
Miscellaneous	4.3
Beauty and grooming	4.0
Foreign affairs	3.8
Business and industry	3.3
Children	2.6
Building	2.5
Gardening and farming	1.8
Fiction and stories	1.3
Total editorial	**100.0**

Editorial pages for the 74 magazines in the study were multiplied by the circulation of the magazine for total editorial pages distributed to weight results according to each magazine's circulation.

Source: *The Magazine Handbook, 1992-1993* (*MPA Newsletter of Research* No. 64), p. 35; R. Russell Hall Company. Reprinted by permission.

Editors' and readers' impressions of content emphasis usually are incorrect. Content studies correct those impressions. Comparative studies of content coverage among several or all magazines can be useful. Some researchers have tallied the mentions of a topic in *Reader's Guide to Periodical Literature* and other indexes to find out how many articles have been published on a given subject. In some cases, the results can be used to promote the editorial product of one's magazine.

Probably the most controversial topic over the last 20 years has been abortion. If someone were to ask which of the 12 largest women's magazines had published the most articles on abortion, how would you answer? *Columbia Journalism Review* in March/April 1992 reported that *Glamour* had published the most articles (37) between 1972 and 1991, followed by *Mademoiselle* (28), *Vogue* (19), *McCall's* (12), *Good Housekeeping* (10), *Cosmopolitan* (9), *Redbook* (9), *Family Circle* (5), *Self* (4), *Ladies' Home Journal* (3), *Woman's Day* (1), and *Better Homes and Gardens* (0). *Self* wasn't started until 1979, and two editors interviewed for the piece said advertisers had not complained about the controversial content.

Similar studies on other subjects, especially the heart of the magazine's mission, can be done to demonstrate how well the magazine is performing in basic content areas. The R. Russell Hall Company measures and reports the content of 74 American magazines. It weights the findings according to circulation by multiplying the number of editorial pages in a given magazine by that magazine's circulation. The result is an indication of the magazines' editorial impact on the reading public. Using this method, culture and humanities accounted for 31.2 billion magazine editorial pages of a total 196.9 billion editorial pages in 1991, or 15.9 percent. Table 8.1 reports the percentages of total editorial content in these 74 magazines from the Hall data.

Advertising Research

Demographic studies are used primarily to sell advertising, but their results show attributes of the audience that are worth examining (see table 8.2). They may confirm some editorial hunches and correct others.

The statistics may be dizzying at first. After some reflection and realization that a number isn't as precise as it first seems, a general idea of the audience may emerge. For example, a skiing magazine found, through an independent research firm's study, that 47 percent of its readers considered themselves expert or advanced, and 38 percent considered themselves intermediate skiers. Only 11 percent were novices. These figures confirm the obvious, that readers of a special interest magazine have serious interest in the subject. Readers had skied an average of 21 days during the preceding season; 46 percent had taken a skiing vacation. After examining the ski equipment market in detail, the study delved into credit card ownership, private club membership, travel to Europe apart from skiing, beverages served when entertaining, camera ownership, TV and stereo ownership, auto ownership, motorcycle and motorscooter ownership, boat ownership, investments, age, education, and income.

TABLE 8.2
Categories Typically Used in Demographic Studies

Age	Household Income	Education	Occupation
18–24	Under $10,000	Grade school or less	Managerial professional
25–34	$10,000–$14,999	Some high school	Technical
35–44	$15,000–$19,999	Graduated high	Administrative support
45–49	$20,000–$24,999	school	(including clerical)
50–54	$25,000–$29,999	Some college (at	Sales
55–64	$30,000–$39,999	least one year)	Operative, Nonfarm laborers,
65–74	$40,000–$49,999	Graduated college	service workers, private
75 or older	$50,000–$74,999		household workers
	$75,000–$99,999		Farmers, farm managers, farm
	$100,000 and over		laborers
			Craftsmen
			Other
			Self-employed
			Unemployed—looking for work
			Retired
			Student (full-time)
			Homemaker (not employed
			outside home)
			Disabled
			Temporarily unemployed

Advertisers and researchers use only those items that help identify specific prospects for their products.
Source: American Association of Advertising Agencies.

Demographic data standing alone are vague, but, compared with those of similar magazines or national averages and viewed over a number of successive surveys, they can show where the magazine stands in relation to other magazines and how the audience is changing.

It is not uncommon for a magazine to begin with a relatively young readership, say nearly all in the 18–24 range, and 20 years later find that a big portion of the readership, perhaps one-third, is in the 35–49 age group. Numbers by themselves say little. They have to be compared with other numbers.

You may edit to an intended audience and use demographic data to see how well the audience fits the objectives, or the other way around.

Demographic studies have been part of the advertising scene so long that they are almost unquestioned. However, John O'Toole, when president of Foote, Cone & Belding, asked if Grace Slick, the rock singer, and Tricia Nixon Cox, the former president's daughter, are one and the same person. Advertising researchers, he said, would classify both as white women in the same age group, as college graduates, people who work and have a family income in the same category, residents of an urban area in a household of two to three members, and probably people from an "upper-income family with [a] professional or executive father who belongs to the Republican party." He said that the type of thinking that concludes that two so dissimilar persons are statistically equal is the type of thinking that has led to an erosion of public confidence in advertising. There's a message there for editors too. If you can't see the people behind the numbers, it may be better to ignore the numbers.

Psychographic Research

Demographic variables do not identify or describe all aspects of consumer behavior. In recent years, attempts have been made to measure other types of variables that predict consumer behavior.

Life-style segmentation assumes that people live in a way similar to their neighbors, so marketers will want to target clusters of these people. Life-style clusters are more accurate characterizations of consumers than any single variable, and especially demographic variables.

SRI International developed a widely used system called VALS (Values and Lifestyles System), which classifies people according to their values and life-styles, and has updated it to VALS 2, which puts more emphasis on the unchanging psychological underpinnings of behavior. VALS 2 segments effectively link consumers to buying patterns for products, such as automobiles, that engage the consumers' ego. The two key elements in VALS 2 are the consumers' resources and their self-orientation.

Consumer resources in VALS 2 include income, education, position, self-confidence, health, eagerness to buy, intelligence, inventiveness, interpersonal skills, and energy level. These are material and acquired attributes and psychological qualities. Resources tend to increase from youth to middle age, then diminish with old age. The oldest segment is the one on the bottom, strugglers, with a median age of 61.

In self-orientation, principle-oriented consumers are guided by their views of how the world should be, status-oriented consumers by the actions and opinions of others, and action-oriented consumers by a desire for social or physical activity, variety, and risk taking.

The VALS 2 group are

- *Actualizers,* who have the highest incomes and such high self-esteem and abundant resources that they can indulge in any self-orientation. Image is important to them as an expression of their taste, independence, and character. Their consumer choices are directed toward the finer things in life. They constitute 7.2 percent of the U.S. adult population.
- *Fulfilleds,* who have ample resources and are principle-oriented, mature, responsible, well-educated professionals and are 10.4 percent of the U.S. population.
- *Believers,* who possess scant resources and are principle-oriented, conservative, and predictable consumers who favor American products and established brands. They are 18.0 percent of the population.
- *Achievers,* who have ample resources and are status-oriented, successful, work-oriented people who get their satisfaction from their jobs and families. They constitute 13.3 percent of the population.
- *Strivers,* who possess scant resources and are status oriented; style is extremely important to them as they strive to emulate the people they wish they were. They are 13.9 percent of the population.
- *Experiencers,* who have ample resources and are action oriented. They are the youngest of all segments (median age 25), have a lot of energy they exert into physical and social activities, and are avid consumers and heavy spenders on clothing, fast food, music, and other youthful favorites, with emphasis on the new. They compose 13.5 percent of the population.
- *Makers,* who possess scant resources and are action-oriented, practical people who value self-sufficiency. They are focused on their families, work, and physical recreation, and they have little interest in the broader

world. As consumers, they are unimpressed by material possessions other than those with a practical or functional purpose. They are 12.0 percent of the population.

- *Strugglers,* who have minimal resources—too few to be included in any category of self-orientation. Within their limited means, they tend to be brand-loyal consumers. They represent 11.8 percent of the population.

The extent to which each of these groups uses the four major media is shown in table 8.3. Raw data have been converted to an "index" number based on the figure 100 representing the U.S. average. In this table, one can see that actualizers are 1.43 times their average proportion, or 43 percent above average, in their use of magazines and 14 percent below average in use of television. Three demographic categories that typify prime target adults are shown in table 8.4. Of all U.S. adults who attended or graduated from college, actualizers compose 2.4 times their average in the overall population (index 240, 2.4 times or 140 percent above average).

TABLE 8.3
Media Exposure by VALS 2 Typologies

Typology	Magazines	Mean Levels of Exposure*		
		Television	Radio	Newspapers
Actualizer	143	86	98	140
Fulfilled	124	96	98	125
Experiencer	112	101	104	90
Achiever	116	87	106	120
Maker	103	90	116	120
Striver	92	95	104	92
Believer	82	112	93	99
Struggler	55	123	81	71

* 100 = U.S. average

Magazine reading is most heavily concentrated among actualizers, fulfilleds, experiencers, and achievers. These individuals are characterized as successful, motivated, and well educated. Television viewers are concentrated among the strivers, believers, and strugglers. These people are poorly educated, with limited social, economic, and emotional resources.

Source: 1988 SMRB/VALS 2 in *The Magazine Handbook* 1990–1991, Magazine Publishers of America Research Newsletter No. 59, p. 44. Reprinted by permission.

TABLE 8.4
Target Demographics by VALS 2 Typologies

Typology	% U.S. Adults	Att./Grad. College		$40,000+ Household Income		Professional Managerial	
		%	Index*	%	Index*	%	Index*
Actualizer	7.2%	17.2	240	18.3	255	20.7	288
Fulfilled	10.4	21.8	210	14.5	140	24.5	236
Experiencer	13.4	12.6	94	11.6	86	9.7	72
Achiever	13.3	29.1	219	32.4	244	28.8	217
Maker	12.0	6.7	56	6.4	53	4.5	37
Striver	13.9	9.3	67	7.9	57	7.2	52
Believer	18.0	2.4	14	8.8	49	3.8	21
Struggler	11.8	0.8	7	0.0	0	0.8	7
Total U.S.	100%	100%		100%		100%	

* 100 = U.S. average

By VALS 2 typologies, the prime target adults are concentrated among achievers, actualizers, and fulfilleds. Achievers are those successful, career-oriented individuals who are deeply committed to work and family. Actualizers are those successful, "take-charge" people with high self-esteem and abundant resources. Fulfilleds are mature, reflective people who value order, knowledge, and responsibility.

Source: 1988 SMRB/VALS 2 in *The Magazine Handbook* 1990–1991, Magazine Publishers of America Research Newsletter No. 59, p. 43. Reprinted by permission.

Changing Nature of a Magazine's Audience

The editor must realize that the audience is not the same from one issue to the next. The types of people interested in the magazine's content may not change drastically, but it does change.

The magazine formula also may change, by necessity or desire, fostering a change in audience. However, only a segment of the audience—a majority for most magazines—is stable; even those people are changing as they grow older, more or less affluent, and more interested or bored with the magazine's material. A very large minority do not renew their subscriptions on expiration. Thus, a magazine is appealing to a constantly changing overall audience that is homogeneous but is made of subaudiences with a variety of interests.

Demographic and psychographic data can be helpful in showing audience shifts. Reader surveys add to the depth of knowledge about readers and their changing interests.

Perspective from Communication Behavior

Understanding how people use mass media in their daily lives can place the editor's work in context and contribute to greater effectiveness. "Knowing the Reader" in chapter 4 summarized the broad background of media use. People use a complex web of media to varying degrees, and no one medium can claim to be the cause of a given effect.

Comparing only two media, the 1989 Simmons "Study of Media Imperatives" for the Magazine Publishers of America found that 34 percent of U.S. adults were heavy users of magazines and light users of television and 31 percent were light users of magazines and heavy users of television. The target audience usually differs from the total population, however. In the demographic classification of professionals and managers, 48 percent were heavy users of magazines and light users of television and only 17 percent were light users of magazines and heavy users of television. In this study, 20 percent of all the adults were heavy users of both magazines and television and 15 percent were light users of both.

As table 8.5 shows, Americans also cite magazines as the main source of knowledge and usable ideas in seven fields of interest important in their daily lives, as compared with television, radio, and newspapers.

Because readers seek material they are interested in, the editor might as well make the appeal direct, though not trite or dull. At the same time, the editor must recognize that it is tremendously difficult to change established beliefs. Once the reader forms an opinion, its holder searches the media for material that agrees with it. The editor's best chance at persuading a reader is to find an issue about which he or she has not formed an opinion. Given a strong factual basis for a recommended opinion, the reader may accept it.

TABLE 8.5
The Medium That Contributes the Most Knowledge and Usable Ideas

Interest Area	Percent of U.S. Adults Using			
	Magazines	Television	Newspapers	Radio
Automobiles—buying, operating, and maintaining automobiles and other passenger vehicles	39%	17%	23%	3%
Beauty and grooming	56	20	7	1
Clothing and fashions	56	18	18	*
Food planning, buying, preparing, and saving	41	15	26	1
Mental and physical health	41	29	12	4
Personal and family money matters	39	14	25	3
Personal and business travel	39	17	27	2

*Less than 0.5 percent

Source: *Study of Media Involvement*, Audits & Surveys, MPA and Publishers Clearing House, April 1991, pp. 10, 12, 14, 16, 18, 20, and 22.

Research Sources and Status

Opinion research firms that can do reliable, valid studies are readily available. An increasing number of magazines appear to be doing their research in-house, even if they have no research department. Large numbers of college graduates have sufficient backgrounds in public opinion and attitude measurement to help design and conduct such studies. Also, editors untrained in research who want to try a do-it-yourself survey can call on university journalism schools and psychology departments for expert assistance.

A study by McGraw-Hill Research for *Folio:* found that 65 percent of the 583 magazines responding conduct research. Of those conducting research, 57 percent conduct market studies, 55 percent do demographic surveys or reader profiles, 54 percent conduct surveys for editorial articles and features, and 44 percent perform studies to determine the editorial effectiveness of their magazines. Only 2 percent reported they are involved in syndicated readership studies, such as Simmons Market Research Bureau, and only 5 percent are involved in reader traffic studies, such as Starch and Readex, which gauge readership of advertisements in issues of magazines being studied. Simmons figures project total audiences for magazines in its studies, time spent with the magazine, and extensive marketing data by product category and magazine. The Simmons report requires about 40 volumes to contain its data.

In the McGraw-Hill Research study, three-quarters of the respondents believed research is "very important" or "important" to the sales staff, and 58 percent said that studies determining the effectiveness of editorial content are "very important" or "important" to the editorial staff. Cost, time, and staff limitations were the three most mentioned problems with research. The cost problem was reflected in the techniques used to complete survey interviews, with 72 percent being conducted by mail. The other techniques were 7 percent telephone, 6 percent in person, 5 percent by a selected panel, 5 percent by a focus group, and 5 percent by other methods. About one-third (31 percent) of the magazines doing research had a research department within the company, but 48 percent were conducting their editorial research in-house.

Although academics and professionals alike have espoused the importance of research for years, research is not as widely accepted and not as effectively used as it could be. A study of research conducted at the Medill School of Journalism at Northwestern University involving 535 professionals in both MPA and ABP member magazines reported that research potentials and limitations are not clearly understood.

Pierce Hollingsworth, Jr., wrote in *Folio:* that a sales executive responded, "You need to look beyond the numbers to trends." Gil Maurer, president of Hearst's magazine division, responded, "Editors by and large are terribly naive about research. They mistrust it." Richard Stolley at Time Inc. says, "Research tells you what's going on, not what's going to happen." He also says that, in a start-up situation, cooperation among all departments is essential in planning, conducting, and using research. Hollingsworth writes, "The sales department wants clean, clear, attractive, simple, and favorable tools. The editorial department wants predigested directions that look ahead. The circulation department wants detail, consistency, and verification. The researcher, on the other hand, often doesn't even have a publishing background and has a tough time wrestling with this communication problem." Maurer says, "The problem in using research is that it takes a great deal of sophistication to use it well—and I have found that quantitative research is misused more than it's well used."

Research No Substitute for Editorial Imagination

Research is not used more widely by editors partly because they quickly learn that it has limitations and cannot make decisions for them. Most research is based on the past, what has been published or what readers have experienced. Most readers cannot visualize and evaluate something they have not seen or read, and they cannot suggest bold new approaches, new subject matter, or new issues that should be probed.

Behind the statistical tests and mountains of data, people who understand research know it is only as good as the thinking, intellectual conceptualization, and rigor that went into it. A statistic stands for something that has been conceptualized by a person, and, if that concept is inadequate, the statistic is meaningless. The research design is as important as the execution, and usually more demanding. Improper sampling, question wording, interviewing, coding, or tabulation can throw the results off enough to make them unreliable, but you have nothing if the design is faulty.

Research can be helpful in the ways that have been discussed: to find gaps in the reader's knowledge, to find how readers feel about the magazine, to find what they are reading and how intensely they are interested in it, and to find the most effective ways of presenting material. Research can cut down the risks, but it should not be used to avoid boldness or as an excuse to take the safe course.

The editor still must be the leader. Editors occasionally make misjudgments; however, the great editors have been willing to gamble when they were sure they were right, and the great publishers have backed them.

Break-of-the-Book: Editorial Planning

9

ALLOCATING space within an issue of a magazine is called *breaking the book;* during this process, generalities must be translated into specifics. Broad concepts or formulas must materialize in the form of specific articles and departments; these in turn must then be converted into specific pages or spreads located logically among the other material being offered to readers. The nitty-gritty of putting an issue together is usually the responsibility of managing editors, although they may be operating under a different title. For the purposes of this discussion, we simply call them editors.

As they break the book, editors are concerned with such decisions as which articles merit two pages or more and which get only one, which article is the "lede" or cover article, which departments will be placed up front and which must go back, and what material will be produced in color. Careful, detailed planning and efficient procedures are required if these decisions are to result in the production of an issue that interests a maximum number of readers.

Although these are editorial decisions, they are complicated by factors stemming from advertising and production requirements. For example, except for some public relations and association magazines supported by sponsors, the sale of advertising dictates the size of an issue. The sale of ads to be printed in color also directly affects the potential use of color on editorial pages. Also, printers and their equipment sometimes seem to be total dictators of planning because they must work within precise mechanical limitations.

Editorial decisions relating to break-of-the-book cannot be totally separated from advertising and production requirements. To clarify our discussion here, however, these aspects of issue planning are held over for the next chapter. It suffices here to know that those ramifications must ultimately be considered.

Editorial issue planning starts long before detailed work begins on an issue. One of the astonishing things to a newcomer in the magazine field is the amount of preliminary time that must be allowed for each issue. Except in the case of weekly newsmagazines, issues must be completely planned several months, or at least several weeks, in advance of publication. Some smaller magazines and newspaper Sunday supplements may require only five or six weeks, but six months is typical for most standard magazines. In the magazine field, editors must be accustomed to planning Christmas issues after rushing in from early morning rounds of golf in mid-July. When the halls are decked with holly, they must think of their readers' midsummer interests.

As the most preliminary planning for one issue gets under way, another issue is rolling off the presses, still another is in the typesetting stage, one is ready for layout, assignments may have just been made for another, and one or two more issues may be at a different stage of preparation. Sound complicated? It is. To put together well-balanced, interesting issues regularly under such circumstances, an editor must establish efficient procedures for every step.

Each issue of a magazine starts with planning. Here, senior editors at *Architectural Record,* a McGraw-Hill magazine, confer with editor Walter F. Wagner, Jr., AIA (extreme left).

The First Step: Preliminary Planning Session

Planning and scheduling are, for a magazine editor, like the proverbial hen and the egg; both must be started at once. Planning starts with a schedule, but the schedule has to start with planning. For the moment, let's look at necessary planning procedures, then turn our attention to scheduling.

The first step in the creation of an issue is preliminary planning. At this stage, an issue is discussed in only the most general terms. As a matter of fact, several consecutive issues may be discussed at the same time to build continuity from one to another. Sometimes more than one issue is needed to explore a subject adequately, and these issues must be coordinated. This coordination is established in preliminary planning sessions. The main goal of such sessions is to set a pattern for each issue that directly relates to the magazine's basic formula, character, or concept. The sessions serve as a bridge, linking the subject matter of each issue to the long-range approach of the magazine.

As pointed out in chapter 5, preliminary planning goes on continually on an informal basis. For magazines with fairly large staffs, these planning sessions may be somewhat formalized, and they should involve all staff members with executive positions. The advertising director can receive valuable guidance from these sessions, and he or she can contribute substantially to them. Cooperative ventures in which the advertising and editorial departments coordinate their activities should get their start at these early planning sessions.

Sometimes the central theme for an issue can originate in the advertising department, and sometimes considerable space can be sold when space salespersons know of pending editorial approaches that relate to their clients. Input from the research department is vital; readership and readability study results can guide editorial staffs to an improved product. Other departmental executives, including the circulation director, can provide valuable input as ideas are sought for subjects that will be on readers' minds half a year in the future. An art director can join the brainstorming by offering suggestions for potential visual approaches for subjects that come up for discussion.

Editors who must work alone or have only one or two assistants can proceed much more informally with their planning, but they cannot do without it. Neglect of long-range planning on even the smallest publication breeds disorder; unless a long-range course is charted, a magazine is almost certain to drift away from its basic goals.

Building a Theme

If preliminary planning is successful, whether it occurs in a formalized session or in an editor's mind as he or she meditates over a cup of coffee, it produces a general thrust for an issue. This may be in the form of a single theme, or it may be only agreement on the subject for a lede feature, backed up by one or two major article ideas.

The use of a single theme for an issue (or perhaps even two or three consecutive issues) has become widely accepted practice. A theme provides a handy organizing device for an editor; when all articles relate to the same subject matter, an issue automatically emerges as an organized unit. The demand on magazines for increasingly thorough treatment of subjects can best be answered with a thematic approach too. Circulation and advertising departments find it advantageous for their promotional campaigns when they can point to themes that have been thoroughly presented in the past or are on the drawing board for future issues.

Any theme that is selected must, of course, be of direct interest to a majority of readers. It must be general enough to get interest from a broad range of readers, but not so general that it lacks unity or destroys potential future themes on related subjects. An editor of a company publication who chooses employee fringe benefits as a theme for an issue may regret the choice later as he or she realizes that retirement benefits alone would make a good theme. He or she is then faced with the prospect that, even though the treatment of retirement was skimpy, devoting a full issue to that subject in the near future would appear repetitious. In the case of a consumer magazine, an editor who has started with American education as a theme may discover that it is too general a subject and that a focus on American universities would produce a much better issue.

Generating Ideas

The accent at all early planning sessions is on ideas, and, the greater the input, the greater the potential for stimulating issues. The idea for a theme or an article can come from anyone or anyplace. Any of the departments whose representatives attend planning sessions can be a source. So can letters from readers; whether complimentary or critical, letters often provide a good gauge of the subjects that readers have on their minds. So can an idea file. A wise editor carefully follows the content of other periodicals and clips and files articles or issues that might relate to his or her own magazine. Every day's newspaper is a potential source of editorial ideas. General magazines explore subjects that the editors of specialized magazines might later find can be tailored to their specialized interests, and vice versa. A loaded idea file can start more action at an issue planning session than any other source, and a good editor is never without one.

The Second Step: Converting Ideas into Articles

With the theme or general direction of an issue already established, it is time for the editor and the staff to plan again, but this time the goal is to get going on specific publishable articles. What were general subjects in the preliminary planning session must now jell into tangible features that will occupy prescribed pages in the issue.

At this stage of planning, it is important for the editor to work with the editorial assistants, such as artists and photographers. If the issue under consideration is to follow a theme, the theme must be broken into component parts, which are then assigned to appropriate personnel for completion. The artist, with preliminary sketches, can help develop the slant or angle for each item. As work progresses, the issue begins to take shape. An issue intended to focus on the elderly in American society begins to shake down into articles on financial problems, health problems, psychological difficulties, institutions serving the elderly, and other elements within the general theme. The health program piece begins to take on a still more specific direction: the government medical program. As the editor, artist, and other staffers try to pin down the subject still more specifically, the artist may suggest an angle emphasizing difficulties with red tape. Unwarranted delays in government payment for medical care, difficulties in qualifying for assistance, and other procedural problems appear to be at the heart of the problem. The suggestion for artwork showing elderly citizens in hospital beds and bound up in red tape as a title illustration is approved, and the writer and photographer are ready to develop the feature. Bit by bit, the other subjects gain specificity, and a full list of specific articles and assignments is completed.

The primary goal at this step is to narrow down a subject to its most precise point. Should any photos be used? Should photos be the primary means of telling the story, or should they be secondary to text? Should an article rest basically on an opinion poll, or should it be translated in terms of one person or one family as a case example? Should the writer concentrate in an interview on what the source says, or should he or she prepare to do a personality sketch of the interviewee? How long should the article be? Will it probably get four pages, or is it more likely to be forced to fit into only two? These and other similar questions must be answered if assignments are going to materialize as an editor hopes they will.

Checking the Stockpile

At this stage of breaking the book, or earlier, the magazine's stockpile of manuscripts must be checked for any usable material. Themes and approaches don't just materialize suddenly; they usually result from an accumulation of attention to several aspects of a problem. This accumulation often continues over an extended time period. During that time, staffers may have completed specific features or just done general spadework on articles that now fit a selected theme. Free-lance writers also may have provided some pieces that can be used as submitted or with moderate revision. Consequently, a magazine usually has a substantial backlog of manuscripts on file. This backlog should be carefully checked before final assignments are made for each issue, and a continuing effort should be made to maintain an adequate supply of material on hand.

Developing Continuing Features or Departments

A primary strength for many magazines is their standing features, such as a column, a special-interest department, or even cartoons. *New Yorker*'s cartoons, *Newsweek*'s columns, *Time*'s book review section, *Family Circle*'s money management, Burton Hillis' "The Man Next Door" page in *Better Homes and Gardens,* and *Playboy*'s centerfold are well-known examples of hundreds of successful offerings of this nature. In the public relations magazine field, such departments or standing features as job promotions or letter from the president have been mainstays for some magazines, whose purposes can be furthered through these continuing offerings. Efforts to discover and promote standing features are worthwhile for any magazine, and they should be constantly under way.

However, the decision to create a topical department or to drop one must be recognized as having sufficient importance to require careful thought and research. The fact that any item is to run steadily in issue after issue is enough to force considerable attention to such an editorial decision. Once a decision is made to grant continuity to a feature or department, issue planning must take into account the readers who are accustomed to finding it in every issue. Some readers get strong feelings of attachment to particular offerings, and this should be considered when decisions are made as to the way in which such offerings are to be handled. Sometimes popular features can be used to bolster readership in a particular section of a book—the back, for example.

Reviewing the Complete Issue

The planning for an issue begins in very general terms and then becomes very specific. Before the planning stage is complete, an issue should be subjected to another general overview. As part of this overview, the actual breaking of the book occurs.

Use of a Miniature Dummy

To visualize the complete issue, most editors create a miniature dummy containing the number of pages set for the issue. An 8½ × 11-inch sheet of paper folded three times at right angles and then trimmed forms a handy 16-page section. The small 2¾ × 4¼-inch pages thus formed are easy to work with, and as many sections as are required can be put together to form a complete issue in miniature. Pages can then be numbered and brief notations made on each page as content is assigned to the page.

By thumbing through the miniature dummy, editors can begin to get a feeling for how the issue is shaping up. Keeping both production and content requirements in mind, they now can make definite space allocations. As they do, they mentally check out several requirements of a good issue.

Checking for Completeness

The first check is for completeness, or comprehensiveness. Does the issue, as a whole, deal with its theme or subjects in adequate depth? Sometimes, as articles pick up their angles, they leave some aspects of the subject uncovered or inadequately treated. Weak spots or complete omissions can be detected in an overall analysis of an issue, while they are easily overlooked when an issue is viewed in its individual parts.

Checking for Variety and Balance

Are there sufficient variety and balance in the issue to provide something worthwhile for every type of reader being served? There is a tendency for editors to prepare whole issues directed entirely toward the largest segment of their audiences, while neglecting smaller segments. Research has shown that a diversity of articles can result in greater overall readership than an issue full of features to please the majority. The old *Saturday Evening Post* discovered that it got peak readership if it directed about 8 of its usual 12 to 15 articles per issue to the majority and used the remaining 4 to 7 to lure smaller groups.

One of the failings of some research, as well as editorial intuition, has been the tendency to neglect the *intensity* of reader interest in some subjects. If, for example, only 10 percent of an audience are interested in a subject, yet that interest is so intense that failure to include it loses that particular audience segment, it is obvious that the subject merits careful editorial scrutiny, to say the least. Besides, sometimes new readers for the "majority" content can be picked up through the use of editorial matter that appeals directly to their strong "minority" interests, thus providing an overall gain in readership and/or circulation.

A good issue contains adequate variety to appeal to the special interests of all readers, but it maintains a reasonable balance of material with broad appeal. In addition, the material should be distributed throughout the issue so that the variety is apparent. An occasional change of pace is essential, or an issue can seem to be monotonous. Longer articles should be interspersed with shorter pieces. Subjects that are serious should be broken up by an occasional light treatment. Picture stories get more impact if they are separated by interspersed presentations where the emphasis is on text. Pages that are framed with margins make those that use bleed photographs pick up added impact. For the person who flips the pages of a magazine, checking the content, the impression should be one of variety and liveliness.

For some magazines with a specialized role to perform, the matter of content distribution is unusually important. For example, the editor of a company magazine for circulation to employees in a number of plants throughout the country may be forced to exercise special caution to avoid letting any one plant dominate the content. A feeling that "it never has anything in it from our plant" cannot be permitted to gain foothold among readers. *Republic Reports,* a magazine serving employees of many Republic Steel installations, has used a system of a definite percentage allocation of space to each plant in each issue to solve just such a problem. A fairly complex record-keeping system was devised to guarantee the desired space distribution. An engineering magazine might also find that care is needed to prevent

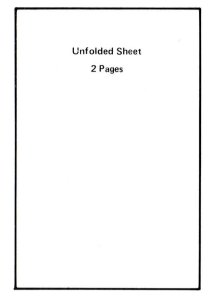

Unfolded Sheet
2 Pages

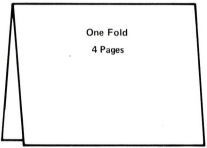

One Fold
4 Pages

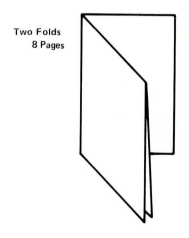

Two Folds
8 Pages

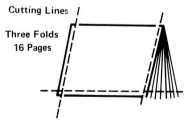

Cutting Lines

Three Folds
16 Pages

Folding a miniature dummy: unfolded sheet, 2 pages; one fold, 4 pages; two folds, 8 pages; three folds, 16 pages. A folded sheet must be trimmed along all outside edges.

content from becoming overloaded with material of interest to only one kind of engineer to the detriment of those with different special interests. In all such cases, it is wise to set distribution goals and then establish a control method that helps achieve those goals.

Catering to the Backward Reader

All magazines have what can be called backward readers—those who do their flipping of pages from the back to the front. *Newsweek,* some years ago, explored the habits of its readers in this regard and discovered that almost as many scanned each issue from back to front as did from front to back. Quick observation in any periodical reading room will verify that finding; in some college classes, the back-to-front viewers are in the majority.

The traditional approach to allocation of space in an issue was to present all the editorial strength up front or in the middle and let the back of the book be a dumping ground for continuations that could be buried among fractional-page ads. Readership tests subsequently showed a substantial loss of audience for the material that was near the back.

Most magazine issues are now given two openings: one in front and the other in the back. The back opening, unlike the front, is usually restricted to a single page; we have not yet accepted the idea that pages should go in sequence from back to middle. However, it is now common to use a strong, single-page feature on the left page facing the inside back cover to lure backward viewers into starting their reading quickly. For example, *Modern Maturity* uses "Last Look," and *Mother Earth News* has "Last Laugh" as complete opening features at the back of the book. *Newsweek* and others turn over a left-hand back page to opinion writers, and some magazines display "letters to the editor" or other high-interest features in that spot. All of them represent efforts to accommodate the reader who starts from the back.

While checking over the miniature dummy for comprehensiveness, variety, and balance, the editor should also see if the back of the book has been given adequate strength.

Avoid Pitfalls in Planning

With the planning steps completed, the editor is ready to proceed with the other steps involved in getting an issue together. If planning has been careful and complete, the likelihood of major crises occurring is reduced but not eliminated. Nature has a way of interfering with even the best laid plans. Interview subjects die or otherwise make themselves no longer appropriate subjects for planned articles. (A famous movie star was featured in a personal interview story regarding her "fantastically successful" marriage; before the ill-fated magazine hit the stands, newspapers were carrying a sensational story on her impending divorce.) Late developments bring on changes in reader moods, and what looked like good subjects in June might have to be scrapped just before an August copy deadline. Pitfalls emerge even with the most careful planning.

To keep pitfalls to a minimum, editors take on the roles of bookkeeper and expediter. They need adequate records to maintain a constant check on the state of affairs for each issue, and they must organize the staff's efforts so each necessary chore is completed in proper sequence on time. Obviously, the exact nature of the records an editor must keep varies considerably among the types of magazines, but in most instances they involve at least two functions: (1) scheduling and (2) maintaining and recording copy flow.

Scheduling

A schedule is as important to the publication of a magazine as it is to the operation of a railroad. Each issue has a final publication date, its "end of the line." To reach its final destination on schedule, an issue must pass all way stations, and it must pass them on time. A schedule that can reasonably be met by everyone involved, and that is complete enough to provide checkpoints for all important stages (plus some allowance for unavoidable pitfalls), is an essential element of magazine editorial bookkeeping.

As indicated earlier, every good schedule begins with planning. Unless it is scheduled, essential planning is likely to be neglected in the rush to meet other deadlines. Even the most preliminary discussions should be scheduled, with sufficient lead time provided to allow for reasonable completion dates for all other steps. A skeletonized schedule for the December (Christmas) issue of a monthly magazine might look something like this:

1. Preliminary planning session: June 15
2. Specific planning session: July 15
3. Assignments made: July 18
4. Copy deadline: September 1
5. Manuscripts edited and illustrations scaled and sent to printer: September 10
6. Galley proofs from printer: October 1
7. Galley proofs corrected and returned: October 8
8. Page proofs from printer: October 23
9. Page proofs approved and returned to printer: October 27
10. Issue completed: November 10

This schedule has been labeled "skeletonized" because it would have to be much more detailed for the actual operation of many magazines. In most cases, sectional deadlines are scheduled, permitting some parts of the magazine to be held for completion close to the issue date, while other sections have earlier deadlines.

To be effective, a schedule obviously must be individualized. An example of a deadline schedule for a magazine with many pages and many color illustrations is shown in figure 9.1. This *Woman's Day* special interest magazine, *101 Craft Ideas,* eventually emerged as 100 pages, including ads, almost exactly six months and 23 deadlines later.

In figure 9.2, we see an adaptation of a schedule for the external public relations magazine for E. I. du Pont that includes a step necessary for most organizational magazines: approval by executives. Whether the organization being served is an industrial concern or a trade association, its basic public relations nature usually requires that content be approved by members of the administrative hierarchy. If that approval isn't scheduled, the schedule is unworkable; approvals can take up as much issue-preparation time as any other production step (and sometimes more). We can note in this illustration also that the du Pont schedule is established for four issues; in many situations, multi-issue scheduling of this type can be extremely helpful for long-term planning.

In sum, a written, precise schedule is required for the efficient completion of each issue of a magazine. These schedules can be as different from all others as their circumstances dictate because a good schedule is tailored directly to an individual situation. They must, however, be complete; every step that involves time must be included on a schedule.

Keeping Track of Manuscripts and Illustrations

Manuscripts and photographs flow into most magazine offices continually, with the tide ebbing at times, perhaps, but always leaving enough material to create confusion unless it is handled efficiently. A record must be maintained of all editorial material from the time it is received until it has been published or otherwise disposed of.

One of the first questions asked at issue planning sessions is, What's on hand? Unless a stockpile inventory is kept, an accurate answer may be difficult to get. Also, good relationships with free-lance writers requires an ability to respond fully and accurately to their queries about articles submitted at a prior time. As deadlines approach, the stage to which all copy has progressed must be quickly ascertainable.

Record-keeping, consequently, should ordinarily consist of the following:

1. A form recording all editorial material that comes from outside sources
2. An inventory form showing all manuscripts and illustrations in the stockpile
3. A copy control form for the current issue, showing the status of all assigned manuscripts or illustrations
4. A production record noting the completion of production milestones

FROM: Nancy Kay   DATE _____

TO: F. Bowers   F. Klein   L. Dugbee   B. Besten
        K. Bienstock (3)   G. Allen   E. Reed   B. Bowen
        S. Lembo (2)   G. Disch   B. Gift   E. Friedhof (25)
        T. Marvel   M. Choma   R. Toner   S. Miller
        C. Lake   D. Mandolfo   J. Costa
        C. Friedlund   F. Devlin   B. Preye
        R. Mattison   H. Samuel   J. Rubessa
        H. Price (2)   E. Frieden   B. Holman
        B. Matela (5)   J. Curcio   S. Ber

NUMBER____2_____   TITLE ___WOMAN'S DAY 101 CRAFT IDEAS___

SUBJECT _____WORKING PRODUCTION SCHEDULE_____

COVER TO ART DEPT.	SEPT. 27
COVER ART TO ENGRAVER	OCT. 11 1st
COVER PROOF OK	NOV. 8
COVER FILM TO PRINTER	NOV. 15
COVERS 2, 3, 4 TO PRINTER	NOV. 15
4-COLOR ART DEADLINE	OCT. 11 1st
4-COLOR PROOFS OK	NOV. 8
4-COLOR FILM TO PRINTER	NOV. 15
FIRST COPY OUT	SEPT. 22
50% COPY OUT	OCT. 4
FINAL COPY OUT	OCT. 18
FIRST ART TO PRINTER	OCT. 18
50% ART TO PRINTER	NOV. 1
FINAL ART TO PRINTER	NOV. 15 FINAL
SHOP SECTION CLOSING	OCT. 18
SHOP SECTION DUMMY TO PRINTER	NOV. 8
SHOP SECTION ART & EDIT. MATERIAL DEADLINE	NOV. 8
AD CLOSING	OCT. 4
AD MATERIAL DEADLINE	NOV. 8
AD DUMMY TO EDITOR	NOV. 3
AD DUMMY TO PRINTER	NOV. 8
FINAL OK OF BLUES	NOV. 22
FIRST SHIPPING DATE	DEC. 15
ON SALE DATE	JAN. 9

Specifications to follow

Figure 9.1 A schedule as distributed to appropriate personnel for one of the special interest magazines of Fawcett Publications. (Courtesy Fawcett Publications.)

A manuscript receipt record should provide for appropriate notations of all material received from outside sources. A centrally located record of the disposition of such material is essential; there is no purpose in maintaining a record of articles that can't be found when an article gets lost. If a record form must travel throughout the office with the manuscript, it should be a supplement to a central record.

An inventory record is also needed for most magazines. This record should provide all the information needed to enable an editor to assess quickly what material he or she has on file by subject and, perhaps, proposed issue date. Thus, when the question What do we have on hand? pops up, an answer can be obtained quickly, whether the question relates to a particular subject, staff member, or issue date. What do we have on traffic safety? What do we have for a September issue? What picture stories done by Johnson and Murray do we have on file? The search for backlog material usually begins with one of these types of questions.

Another handy record is what might be called a copy control sheet. It is designed to give an editor information quickly about the status of every article or other piece of editorial material that is scheduled for inclusion in an issue. Has the as-

DUPONT CONTEXT			
	AUG	NOV	FEB	MAY
Copy (approved by story source) complete	Mon Jun 26	Tue Sep 26	Tue Dec 26	Tue Mar 27
Copy to editors	Tue Jun 27	Wed Sep 27	Wed Dec 27	Wed Mar 28
Copy out for departmental approval	Fri Jun 30	Mon Oct 2	Tue Jan 2	Mon Apr 2
Layouts, cropping complete	Fri Jun 30	Mon Oct 2	Tue Jan 2	Mon Apr 2
Color copy to printer	Mon Jul 3	Tue Oct 3	Wed Jan 3	Tue Apr 3
Copy approved by departments	Fri Jul 7	Mon Oct 9	Tue Jan 9	Mon Apr 9
B&W photos to printer	Mon Jul 10	Tue Oct 10	Wed Jan 10	Tue Apr 10
Copy to typesetter	Tue Jul 11	Wed Oct 11	Fri Jan 12	Wed Apr 11
Type galleys in hand	Thu Jul 13	Fri Oct 13	Tue Jan 16	Fri Apr 13
Corrected repros in hand	Mon Jul 17	Tue Oct 17	Thu Jan 18	Tue Apr 17
Random proofs in Wilmington	Wed Jul 19	Thu Oct 19	Mon Jan 22	Thu Apr 19
Dummy in Wilmington	Thu Jul 20	Fri Oct 20	Tue Jan 23	Fri Apr 20
Mechanicals in Wilmington	Mon Jul 24	Wed Oct 25	Thu Jan 25	Tue Apr 24
Dummy approved by company executive	Tue Jul 25	Thu Oct 26	Fri Jan 26	Wed Apr 25
Mechanicals to printer	Wed Jul 26	Fri Oct 27	Mon Jan 29	Thu Apr 26
Form proofs in Wilmington	Fri Aug 4	Mon Nov 6	Tue Feb 6	Fri May 4
On press	Wed Aug 9	Thu Nov 9	Fri Feb 9	Wed May 9
Advance copies in Wilmington	Mon Aug 14	Tue Nov 14	Wed Feb 14	Mon May 14
Ship to Eden Park	Tue Aug 15	Wed Nov 15	Thu Feb 15	Tue May 15
Distribution complete	Fri Aug 18	Mon Nov 20	Tue Feb 20	Fri May 18

Figure 9.2 Many magazines set editorial schedules for more than one issue at a time. This one, which establishes basic deadlines for four issues of an external company magazine, also introduces a new element as an essential item on the schedule: approval of various company executives. To be effective, schedules must be tailored to the local situation and incorporate all time-consuming steps involved with an issue. (Courtesy Dupont *Context*.)

signment been made? Who has the assignment? Are photos involved? Are the text and/or photos complete? Has the material been copyedited? How much space is it going to occupy? A form set up so that a mark or a word or two is all that is needed to record this kind of information prevents costly miscues or misunderstandings. A quick glance can reveal problem areas and provide a base for follow-up action as needed.

A record also is needed to provide a checklist of all the steps involved in getting material ready for a printer. The schedule for an issue outlines these steps, and a production checklist provides a means for ensuring the completion of all production steps on schedule. Because this information is of interest to the entire staff, it is often maintained in a form that is available for all to see. Many magazines have a tradition of putting an issue *on the board,* a term used to describe the practice of displaying all pages (blanks) on a display board, on a bulletin board, or around the walls of the office. As each production step is completed for a page or spread, it is entered or checked off. When check marks have been placed after steps, beginning with assignment made and going through assignment completed, articles edited, galley proofs read, page proofs approved, and finally to form closed, the job for that issue is completed. The posting of new page sheets signals the beginning of the day-to-day chores of another issue.

Two Dictators of Issue Planning: Publication Date and Printer

All the work in planning an issue must fall within the confines dictated by a magazine's publication date and its printer. There may be some elasticity possible in other aspects of issue planning, but the publication date *must* be met, and the needs of the printer *must* be met. Good magazines meet their publication dates regularly; not to do so results in almost certain reader disaffection, trouble with postal authorities, and disaster in terms of advertisers. Every step in putting together an issue is related in time to the publication date; schedules start with that date and work backwards.

If a printer is to produce the magazine as expected, the schedule must also be adhered to and the limitations of the equipment considered in all phases of issue planning. A printer can do no more than the equipment makes possible; a press that has a maximum speed of 10,000 sheets an hour cannot be speeded up to 20,000 to make up for time lost by a magazine staff. If the press accommodates a form large enough for 16 pages, the editorial staff must plan for forms that fit that press. So it goes with all aspects of getting material into type, on the press, and into the hands of readers.

Good printers are cooperative, and they adjust to emergencies as well as they can, but there is a point beyond which they cannot go. The following chapters deal with the procedures necessary to get a magazine issue through its production stages, starting with issue planning.

Break-of-the-Book: Production Planning

10

AS editors allocate space in each issue to articles and departments, they must work within some unyielding restraints that stem from factors relating to the financing and production of magazines. The number of pages in an issue, for example, cannot be freely set to accommodate editorial needs; budget and mechanical restraints exert an influence in this instance and also seem to cast their shadows on editorial decision making at every step.

If a magazine is supported by advertising, the total number of pages available for an issue is determined on the basis of a ratio of advertising pages to editorial pages. Space rates and production costs usually require that more than half the pages be sold, and it is common to operate with a six to four ratio: income from six pages of ads are required to support four pages of editorial matter.

Some editors, especially those of specialized business magazines, feel the influence of advertising in another way: their front covers have been sold. Like it or not, this premium space has been set aside to provide income, with little or no space allocated on the cover to lure the reader to the magazine with editorial matter.

It is also common for an editor to find "position" sold; advertisers have purchased a particular place in the magazine, as well as a certain amount of space. Front of the book, back of the book, inside front or back cover, "next to editorial matter" are all common position requirements that editors may have to accept as they allocate space to editorial matter. Ads are placed first, before editorial, in most magazines.

Along with being told that an issue will contain "X number" of pages, of which certain ones already contain ads, editors are often limited as to the use of editorial color from the sale of ads. That is, ads may have been sold to be printed in black plus one or more additional colors, and, for efficiency in printing, these same colors on prescribed pages (those that fall within the same form) will be all that the budget will allow.

Another advertising-related problem that often presents itself at break-of-the-book time is a preprinted insert. Often consisting of four pages, with only two pages (one side of the sheet) already printed with the ads, the other two pages must be "backed up" by the editor. Often these inserts are printed on special paper, so that working them into the binding can cause problems of appearance, as well as complicate the pagination process.

Mechanical requirements also have an obvious effect on issue planning; novices who haven't yet given the mechanics of printing a thought quickly become aware of the fact that no printing system yields an uneven number of pages. True, we might print on only one side of a page, but the back of the page is always there, even if it is blank. Magazines are not printed one page at a time, however. They are either printed on large sheets that contain several pages or on a *web* (roll) of paper that also contains several pages after being printed and cut into sheets. Figure 10.1 shows a sheet emerging from a typical sheet-fed press, and figure 10.2 shows a web-fed press in operation. Both kinds of presses are in common use; the sheet-fed is for smaller circulation magazines; the web-fed is for those with large circulations.

Basic Press Operation

Printing presses, whether web-fed or sheet-fed, put an image on paper by way of a system for separating the image area from the nonimage area so only the image areas carry ink to the paper. In the most common printing system, *photo offset lithography,* the image area is receptive to the greasy ink, and the nonimage area repels the greasy ink. Another common system for magazine printing, *rotogravure,*

Figure 10.1 These sheets are coming off a typical sheet-fed magazine press, which is printing eight pages at one time on one side of the sheet.

Figure 10.2 A multiunit web offset press.

relies on depressed areas holding ink to form an image area, while the flat part of the plate carries no image. Regardless of the printing method, the printing presses are designed to print on common sizes of sheets, or webs, of paper.

A press's capacity can, therefore, be stated in terms of the size of sheet it can print, as well as the number of impressions per hour it can deliver. The size of the printing area corresponds to the size of the sheet and can be translated in terms of the number of pages that can be printed at one time. Most magazine presses have image-carrying areas big enough to print either 8 or 16 pages "up." A sheet containing 16 pages is usually printed 8-up (on one side of the sheet), and then the stack of sheets is turned over to have the other 8 pages printed on the other side.

The page capacity of presses is of extreme importance to editors because the number of pages up (in one form or on one plate) is the basic unit of production planning. More is explained about these planning units later.

Another fairly obvious point must be made here. Each impression of plate to paper carries an image in one ink, ordinarily black. Every additional color requires an additional impression. Multicolor presses essentially are nothing more than individual presses hooked together so one can print black, the next an additional color, and so on, up to four or more presses or units in line.

Presses also can be *perfecting,* meaning that they print on both sides of the paper at one time. In essence, a perfecting press is the same as a two-color press; one unit prints a form on one side and the additional unit prints another form on the other side.

It must be kept in mind, however, that presses printing more than one color, or with the ability of perfecting the sheet, cost more than presses of the same size that are limited to one form. Even with multicolor presses, the basic goal of production planning is always to keep the number of required impressions to a minimum. Planning that wastefully requires a second press run, or a two-color press instead of a one-color, is wasteful and unacceptable.

Magazines at any level of circulation, from the smallest to the largest, must be planned with production efficiency in mind. To see how editorial planning must take production requirements into account, let's look at the basic production steps, relating them first to the smaller magazines using sheet-fed presses.

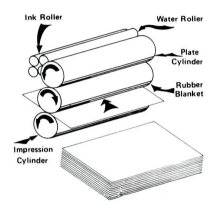

Diagram of an offset press.

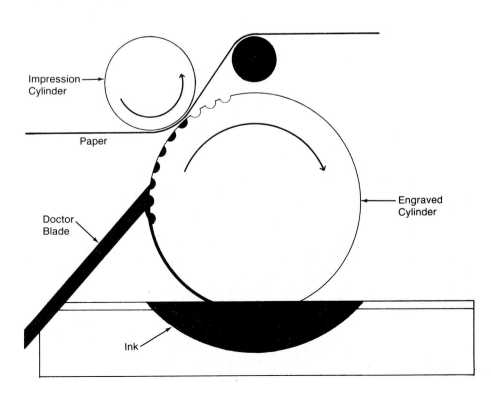

Diagram of a rotogravure press.

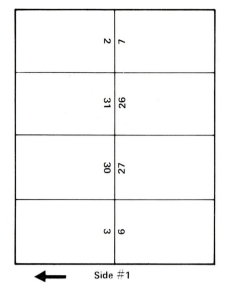

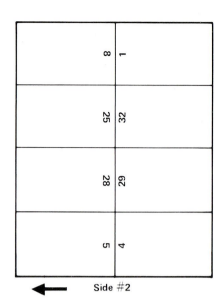

Side #1

Side #2

Figure 10.3 A sheetwise imposition for the outside 16-page signature of a 32-page self-cover magazine.

How Signatures Affect Editorial Planning

Signatures are the large sheets that, when printed and folded, are bound together to form a magazine or another publication. All aspects of issue planning are affected by the facts that (1) magazines are made up of signatures and (2) the size of the signatures is determined by the size of the printing press. Signature sizes vary, but the number of pages that are included in a signature must contain multiples of 4 pages. For magazine production, signatures usually contain at least 8 and, more commonly, 16 pages. Because it is most common for small magazines, the 16-page signature is used here to show that such planning is necessary and that it may involve half-signatures.

A typical flat-bed cylinder press for magazine production handles a sheet big enough for 16 pages, 8 on each side. That is, it prints 8-up. The plate carrying the image to paper, therefore, accommodates 8 pages, and the printer must arrange those pages on the plate so that (1) the correct pages print on each side, and (2) all pages are in proper sequence and right side up when the sheets are folded into signatures and bound into a magazine.

The arranging of pages on the printing plate so pages in the magazine end up in proper order is called *imposition,* and it is a matter of prime importance for printers. Figure 10.3 shows the typical imposition of a 16-page signature, with 8 pages on each side of the sheet. This kind of imposition is called *sheetwise* or *work-and-back,* and it represents the preferred way to handle a signature. The required number of sheets is first printed with an 8-page plate on one side, then the press is cleaned, a second plate is put on, and the other 8 pages are printed. Suppose a signature of only 8 pages is needed, and the same press is to be used. With proper positioning of pages, the printer can put all 8 pages on the plate and print half the number of sheets needed. The sheets can then be backed up with the same 8 pages, and then cut in half to form twin 8-page signatures, as shown in figure 10.4. This imposition is called *work-and-turn* because the sheet is first *worked* (printed) on one side and then turned over and printed with the same plate on the other side.

A 24-page magazine, for example, would probably be printed with one 16-page sheetwise signature and one 8-page work-and-turn signature. Most small magazines are what are called *self-cover,* meaning that the cover pages are part of a basic signature, not a separate 4 pages wrapped around larger signatures.

How Imposition Affects Issue Planning

Imposition affects issue planning because it has a direct effect on potential deadlines and the cost of color. Editors and printers both usually prefer to print magazines in pieces, or sections. In order for printing to take place, all pages on a plate must be completed. Therefore, in figure 10.3, for example, pages 1, 4, 5, 8, 9, 12, 13, and

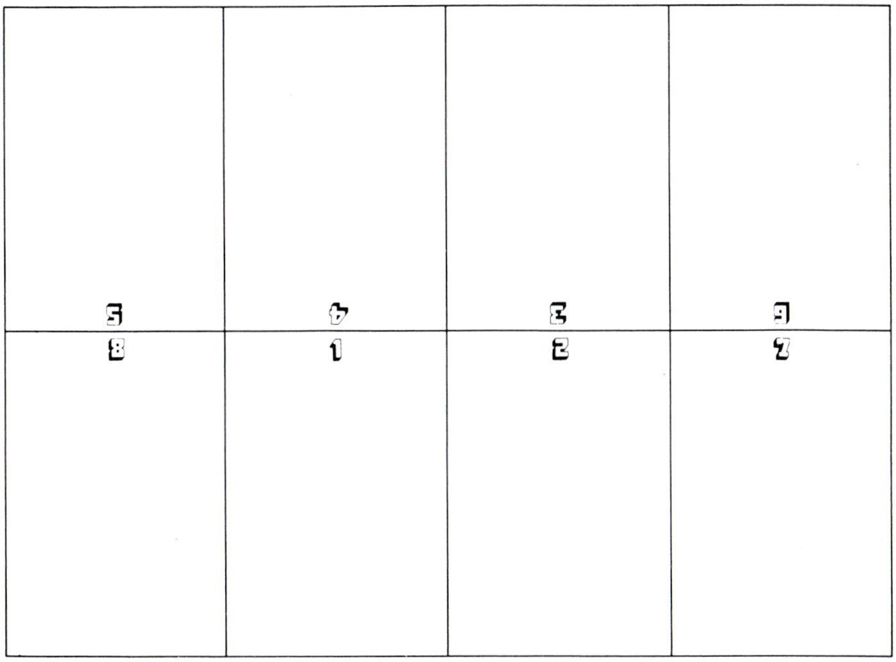

Figure 10.4 An eight-page work-and-turn imposition. After the sheet is printed, it is cut into twin eight-page signatures.

16 would comprise one printing unit, and pages 2, 3, 6, 7, 10, 11, 14, and 15 would be on the other plate (would print on the other side of the sheet). In figure 10.4, all pages from 1 through 8 would be on one plate.

Planning for deadlines and the use of color must be geared directly to imposition. As shown in figure 10.3, the 8 pages on one side of the sheet could be completed, sent to the printer, and actually be printed while work was being completed on the remaining 8. Conceivably, however, 14 pages could be completed and printing would still be impossible because, for example, pages 1 and 2 were incomplete. With regard to color, compare the difference in cost of printing all the pages on one side of the sheet in one additional color with printing only 2 pages (such as 1 and 2) in the additional color when those 2 pages are in different forms. Twice the press time is required for the latter. More about planning by printing units is presented later.

The location of each page on the sheet is determined by the imposition and folding of the sheet. In only one specialized printing technique (see *split roller* later in this chapter) is it necessary for editors to know these specific locations. However, editors do need to know which pages are in each signature and, in sheetwise imposition, which pages fall on each side of the sheet. To have this information, they must also know how sheets will be folded and which binding system is being used because they directly affect the pagination within signatures.

Folding and Binding

Magazine signatures are usually created with standard right angle folds; the first fold of the longest dimension produces a 4-page signature; a right angle fold in the newly created longest dimension produces an 8-page signature; the next fold a 16-page one; and the fourth fold creates a 32-page unit.

Binding starts with the signatures folded but untrimmed. When bindery operations are concluded, the complete magazine is trimmed on the top, right, and bottom edges.

Bindery operations may be carried out by the printer, or by a firm engaged only in binding. Most magazine binding today is either *perfect* or *saddle-wire*, although a few magazines are still *side-wire* bound (see figures 10.5, 10.6, and 10.7). Most magazines that are thicker than a quarter of an inch (and such things as mail-order catalogs, mass-market paperbound books, and telephone books) use perfect binding. With this method, signatures are stacked and clamped. The binding edge of the stack is then roughed up, and a coating of highly flexible glue is applied; a separate cover is wrapped around the stack and held in place by the glued edge, called the *backbone*. If staples are used to form the hinge function in this kind of binding (instead of the elastic glue), it is called side-wire binding. The staples are applied through the top of the stack to the bottom, about an eighth of an inch from the backbone.

In saddle-wire binding, the signatures are not stacked atop each other; instead, they are inserted within one another, as if each were a saddle. Staples are then driven from the outside to the inside of the centerfold. Most magazines are saddle-wire bound, unless they are too bulky.

Selection of the binding system is important. Generally speaking, saddle-wire binding is efficient only for the thinner magazines, which reach only about ¼-inch thickness. Leading magazines such as *Time, Newsweek,* and *Modern Maturity* are bound by this method. As one can imagine seeing figure 10.7, the problem with the use of saddle-wiring for thick magazines is the effect that trimming the open edge has on page size and margins. The center pages, because they jut out more, lose more in trimming. Consequently, the thicker magazines such as *Popular Science, McCall's,* and great numbers of specialized business publications are bound by either of the other methods. The real importance of binding to the magazine production chief is, however, not related to selecting the right system of binding. Instead, the effect of binding on signatures and imposition is of prime importance.

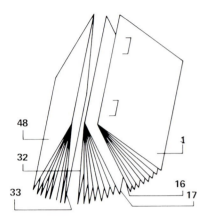

Figure 10.5 When three 16-page signatures are stacked before binding, as shown, all pages in each signature are numbered consecutively. If staples are driven into the stack from the top through the bottom, the binding is called *side-wire.*

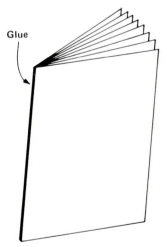

Figure 10.6 When glue is applied to the backbone of a magazine to bind the sections together, the binding is called *perfect.*

Figure 10.7 In saddle-wire binding, signatures are inserted rather than stacked, and, for all but the center signatures, pages are not numbered consecutively—half are from the front of the magazine and half from the back. In this example, the outside signature contains pages 1–8 and 41–48.

Putting Them All Together: Signatures, Folding, Imposition, and Binding

Most small magazines are put together with the sheetwise imposition of 16-page signatures with standard right angle folds. Under these standard circumstances, it is quite easy to determine which pages go on each side of the sheet and, consequently, in each printing form.

The most common small magazine is composed of 32 pages, so let's use that as our first example. First, draw a horizontal line. On the top of the line at its extreme left, write the number of the first page in the signature. In this instance, the number is 1. Then, working from the left, add numbers in pairs, alternating between the bottom and top of the line until you have added half the pages in the signature.

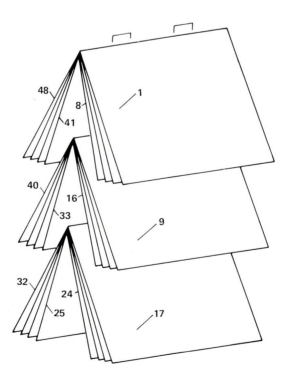

Then work from the right in the same manner, starting with the number of the last page in the signature (page 32 in this case) and continue until the other half of the pages in the signature have been listed. This is the result:

1	4,5	8,25		28,29	32
	2,3	6,7	26,27		30,31

In this same example, how would the pages fall on each side of the sheet that forms the center signature? The first page is 9, and the last is 24, so, following the same procedure, we get this result:

9	12,13	16,17	20,21	24
	10,11	14,15	18,19	22,23

In each case, the numbers above the line are on one side of the sheet, and those below the line are on the other side.

Commonsense planning in this case would provide for four deadlines—one for each set of eight pages in a printing form, and the same four units for color planning.

A 24-page magazine with the same equipment would be completed with three press forms—one for an 8-page work-and-turn signature, and the other two for the 16-page, sheetwise-imposed signature. Assuming that the 16-page signature is on the outside, the page forms would be as follows:

1	4,5	8,17	20,21	24
	2,3	6,7	18,19	22,23

9,10,11,12,13,14,15,16

Working with a Miniature Dummy

As suggested in the previous chapter, a miniature dummy can be very handy in planning an issue. There is no better way for checking the break-of-the-book to see that content is as it should be *and* to make certain that no costly production errors are being made. For the novice, miniature dummies are also an effective method for learning the practical aspects of signatures, imposition, and binding.

To create a miniature dummy for the 32-page magazine diagrammed in the previous section, use two sheets of ordinary typing paper. Fold each as the printer would fold the large sheet: break the 11-inch depth in half (makes 4 pages); then break the 8½-inch dimension (makes 8 pages); then make the last fold by breaking the longer remaining dimension (5½-inch) to form the 16-page signature. Repeat the process for the second 16-page signature. Then, assuming that saddle-wire binding will be used, insert one signature into the other. Label the front of your miniature magazine with "page 1" and the back with "page 32." Numbering the remaining pages is somewhat difficult, but it can be done by opening the folds just enough to write the page numbers.

Now you can unfold the sheets to know which pages are on each side of the sheet, and they will conform to the diagram. To be able to turn the pages of your dummy, the top (or bottom, depending on your fold) must be trimmed along with the outside edge. By keeping two miniatures, one with the folds trimmed and the other without trimming, you can have one with "turnable" pages to check content and the other with untrimmed sheets to check for deadlines and color usage.

Miniature dummies for any number of pages and any folding or binding can be made in similar fashion, but variations in folding can present complications. Printing from a web rather than sheets makes all of production planning more difficult and complicated.

Web Offset Printing

Many magazines are printed on multiunit web offset presses, as was shown in figure 10.2. As circulation and color requirements increase, the probability of moving from sheet-fed to web presses increases. There are so many alternatives for collecting and folding pages as they are cut from the web that only the printers themselves and skilled production managers can work out efficient impositions for these presses.

For one thing, web presses are perfecting; there is no way to print one side and then bring the paper back to the front of the press to "back it up" as we did in earlier examples. They are also composed of several units, can use varying widths of webs, and can use more than one web, making it possible to get a wide range of other possibilities. Only the cut-off point is unchangeable.

Web presses of a size suitable for magazines commonly print 16-page or 32-page signatures. To get a basic idea of the versatility of web printing, look first at figure 10.8, with one web of paper receiving eight magazine pages in black on both sides of the web. This is the simplest use of the web. Figure 10.9 shows one web of paper going through two units, producing black plus a second color for the eight pages on each side of the web. Note that the colors can differ on the top and bottom.

In figure 10.10, a four-unit press is receiving two webs, the top web being printed in black on both sides, plus red on the top and blue on the bottom. The bottom web is being printed in black on both sides, plus yellow on the top and green on the bottom, before merging into one 32-page signature.

One of the most common problems of a magazine is providing process color for several advertisers, but only black plus one color for many others. Figure 10.11 shows a six-unit press with two webs: one printing process colors on both sides, and the other using the remaining two units to get black plus one color on each side.

Computerized Imposition

These examples illustrate only a few of the complexities of imposition planning for web offset. Computerization of this process is now possible and should grow rapidly because of these complexities. Programs such as *Impoze* of Production Graphics Interchange can take into account production requirements, advertiser requests, and editorial goals while putting an issue together (figure 10.12).

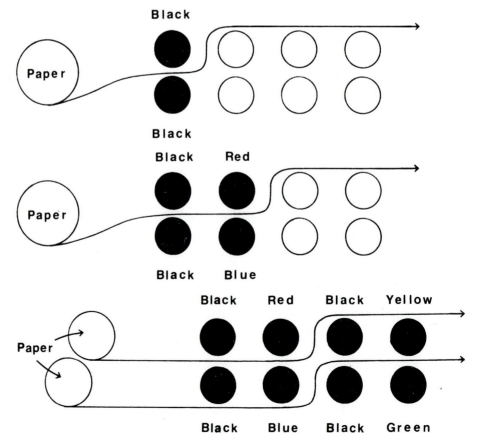

Figure 10.8 The simplest use of a web for magazine printing, eight pages in black being printed on the top and another on the bottom. A basic difference in web press operation is illustrated here; if the back side is to be printed, it must be done as the web goes through. Webs are not rewound and returned to the feeding end of the press, as sheets would be for a sheet-fed press.

Figure 10.9 With the addition of a second unit, a second color can be printed on both sides of the web, and the color being added to the top can be different from the color being added to the bottom.

Figure 10.10 In this drawing, a four-unit press is receiving two webs, the top being printed in black on both sides, red on the top, and blue on the bottom. The bottom web is being printed in black on both sides and yellow on the top and green on the bottom before merging into one 32-page signature. Each of the four units applies ink to eight pages on each side of the web.

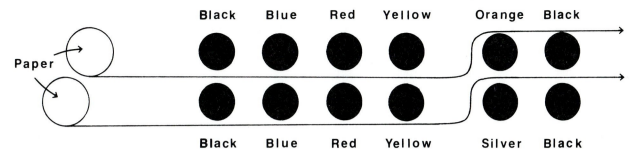

Black   Blue   Red   Yellow   Orange   Black

Paper

Black   Blue   Red   Yellow   Silver   Black

Figure 10.11 A six-unit press with two webs, one being used to get process color on both sides of one 16-page unit and the other printing black plus an additional color on both sides of the other 16 pages. The two sheets are folded together as a 32-page signature.

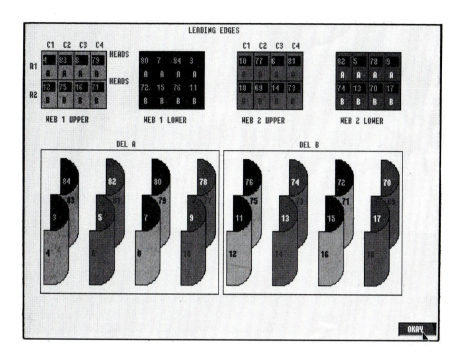

Figure 10.12 Using the *Impoze* program, a production specialist can do most of the time-consuming work of imposition by computer. By clicking Query Imposition, he or she can see, on the screen, the full issue as put together by the computer. (Courtesy *Magazine Design and Production* and Jeff Parnau.)

Whether imposition is computerized or not, imposition problems illustrate the need for channeling all production decisions through one person, usually the editor in a small sheet-fed situation or a specialized production manager in a web-fed situation.

Efficiency of production is essential to avoid waste and increasing cost, and efficiency starts with the coordination of all aspects of production planning under one person. The title of that person is inconsequential—it may be managing editor, art director, or something else—but ultimate authority in production matters must rest with that person.

The mere fact that more than one person works directly with a printer is enough to create a widening variety of production problems, including unnecessary cost. Advertising, editorial, and circulation departments are all involved with production, but an efficient operation is not possible if each department head works independently with the printer. If printers have the choice of blaming late delivery and overtime on the ad director for accepting an ad after deadline, or the editor for failure to provide illustrations on time, or the circulation manager for not being ready with address stencils, they have magazine staffs at their mercy. However, if printers deal directly with only one person, and that person has the power to force staff compliance with deadlines, as well as the power to negotiate printing contracts, the printers live up to their obligations or lose the contract. Normally, they live up to their obligations in this situation because the staff's compliance with deadlines, thanks to the production chief's insistence, makes it easier for them to do so.

Although persons responsible for supervising production can come from any department, they must first of all be knowledgeable in all aspects of printing that relate to the magazine. They must also be able to see the complete, overall production picture so they can put the needs of all departments in proper perspective. They cannot be so imbued with the income-producing role of the advertising department that they fail to see the consequences of failure to meet production schedules in order to permit a special late closing for an advertiser. Neither can they be so involved with the editorial department that they permit that department any indiscretions that get in the way of production efficiency. In the final analysis, they are in charge of the manufacture of a product that several departments have contributed to, and they must have the authority to coordinate all their efforts once the manufacturing stage is reached.

Production supervisors should start this coordination at the earliest stage of production planning. The printing process used and the printer hired to do the job should require their approval. Paper choice and paper buying should be under their control. They should constantly check the quality and delivery performance of their printers and correct any shortcomings through prompt negotiation with the printer.

Perhaps the most important of the contributions of production supervisors are in the planning and scheduling area. They should determine and enforce the production deadlines for all departments, basing their decisions on the contract requirements with the printer. It is essential to have an air-tight schedule of closing dates for all editorial and advertising sections that guarantees delivery to subscribers on time. The most tempting reason for breaking a closing date, especially with the smaller, specialized magazine, is the large, late-arriving ad that would give a nice boost to an issue's advertising space total. As enticing as an extra few hundred dollars may be, the delay of a closing for this reason is usually a long-run liability. Printers whose schedules are thus disrupted cannot be expected to adhere as strictly to their future delivery commitments as they should. Also, once advertisers discover that a magazine will break its schedule to get a late ad, they are all inclined to expect the same treatment. The result is a delay in publication, a delay in collecting from all advertisers, and the creation of reader resentment that eventually makes the magazine a less effective advertising medium. All this for a few extra dollars, which, in most instances, are forthcoming from the following issue anyway because, when pressed, the advertiser will usually accept the later publication. In most instances, especially when the ad's net revenue (after agency commission and other deductions) is considered, the added income wouldn't justify breaking the schedule under any circumstances.

Editing to Meet Production Requirements

Editorial departments like to stretch schedules, too, and reasons for doing so seem ever-present. However, rarely can the benefits outweigh the cost of schedule breaking. Cost is forever the handmaiden of content, and any decision to delay an issue for a late-breaking event must weigh the cost as well as the improved reader service. As a matter of fact, if a magazine's production is to be efficiently handled, all editorial decisions must be related to production procedures. Nowhere is this cooperation of editorial and production so obvious as in situations where a technique called *split-roller* printing is used.

Split-Roller Printing

Many contemporary magazines exploit split-roller (split-fountain) printing to keep color costs down. The technique is especially common among specialized business magazines with relatively low circulations but complicated color requirements. These complicated color requirements stem from the fact that specialized business publications are usually loaded with advertising, and the advertisers specify and pay for one or more colors to be added to black for their advertisements.

In split-roller printing, the ink roller and the ink fountain on the press are divided so more than one color can be fed into the press for each impression.

To use a split roller effectively, an editor must know the location of each page in its printing form in addition to knowing merely which pages are in the form. Each segment of the roller carries the ink from its segment of the fountain over the pages that are in a channel covered by the roller section as it moves across the form.

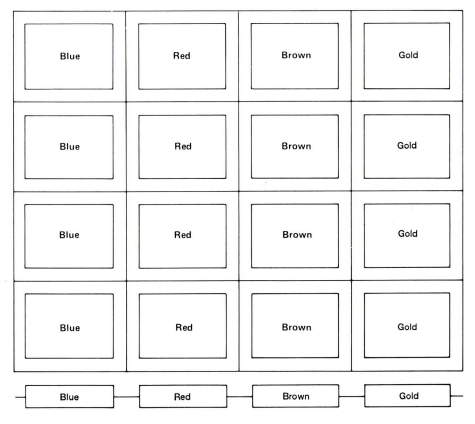

Figure 10.13 By splitting the ink roller and fountain, four different colors might be applied to one printing form with only one additional press run.

Figure 10.13 has been drawn to show how, with a 16-page work-and-turn imposition, a complicated color run necessitated by advertisers could be used to gain extra color for readers without added press time. When each of four advertisers stipulated that their ads be printed in one color besides black, and each one wanted a different color, the ad manager and editor cooperated with the production manager with this result. The red ad was assigned to page 2, the blue to page 6, the gold to page 8, and the brown to page 4, so that each would be in a separate channel. Pages 9 through 16 were to contain editorial matter, so the editor used the color from each channel to add reader appeal to those pages. Hence, with only two press runs, the first for black and the second with split sections of the roller, the editorial pages received four colors in addition to black.

The possibilities for wasting money in this situation are endless. The editor insisting on a color not available from an ad, the ad manager insisting on a special position for an ad that would take it from the appropriate color channel—each would require wasted cost for color. With split rollers, color *bleeds* (extending off the outside edge of a page) are restricted because, for offset printing, a 4½-inch gap is needed between the split sections. A bleed color page, because it reduces the gap area, cancels out the possibility of using the adjoining channel for another color.

Although it would seem that splitting the rollers and ink fountains would make the technique costly, printers who specialize in magazine printing are prepared to offer split fountain printing at a very reasonable cost when compared with the cost of added runs or added units.

Wraps, Inserts, and Tip-ins

In spite of the most careful planning, there are cases in magazine production that call for printing and binding sections that are smaller than the usual signature. These may be only a single sheet (two pages) called a *tip-in;* a four-page section wrapped around a signature before the signature is bound in place (a *wrap*); or a four-page section placed inside a signature for binding (an *insert*).

As a general rule, the smaller the number of pages being printed at a time, the higher the printing price per unit. Consequently, wraps, inserts, and tip-ins are avoided in favor of 8- or 16-page signatures. A decrease in binding strength when using inserts and tip-ins represents a disadvantage.

The most common reason for using the smaller page units is the demand from advertisers that their product be shown on a special paper stock or with another special treatment. Occasionally, an editorial section, such as a "late news" department, is reproduced on a special stock and inserted to create an impression of unusual timeliness for the section.

As mentioned previously, advertisers often print two pages of a four-page insert and leave the other two to be printed (backed up) with editorial matter. These instances, and the other uses of small page units, require careful planning to meet standard closing dates and to keep pagination in order.

Cost and Quality Go Hand-in-Hand

Much of the emphasis in this chapter has been on controlling cost—avoiding unnecessary expenses. That does not mean that the concern for quality expressed in the previous chapter is abandoned when one shifts attention from editorial content to production requirements. As a matter of fact, the two are interdependent.

The magazine graveyard is filled with the corpses of scores of magazines whose cause of death is simply listed as cost. Like the proverbial housewife who explained her monthly checkbook deficit by saying simply that she ran out of money before she ran out of month, magazine autopsies often trace the cause of death only to the point of ascertaining that the victim ran out of income before running out of cost. Obviously, this kind of verdict is oversimplified and much too general.

Setting aside the failures that might better be traced to editorial inadequacies, there are enough examples of success in fighting the cost battle to suggest that, in many instances, there are ways of controlling or overcoming the cost problem. An increase in the mailing cost, for example, can be fatal to one magazine while another, serving the same audience and facing the same new burden, can absorb the cost and remain alive.

The truth is that identical magazines, even though produced in the same plant, can show totally different cost pictures. These differences—and they can be substantial enough to be a "life or death" level—stem from the ability or inability of a publishing venture to control its costs through efficiency of operation.

The importance of production efficiency becomes apparent in such life or death situations. The efficient magazine survives, and the inefficient one dies.

In many instances, inefficiency doesn't show itself so readily. In some situations, for example, favorable competitive advantages or special income potential permits a periodical to survive in spite of inefficiencies. There is a loss in such a situation, however, either by unnecessary profit reduction or, more probably, by a lower level of service to readers. Every unnecessary cost eliminates the possibility of adding pages, more color, or another benefit for the reader. In the long run, perhaps these are the more critical situations, because the magazine industry as a whole is the loser. Magazines that die because of inefficient production usually deserve their fate and are no longer around to plague the industry. However, those that stay alive and hobble along, providing only minimal reader services, tend to reduce the status of all magazines in the competitive mass communication industry.

As we will see in later chapters, technological developments have placed the control of production cost and efficiency more and more directly in the hands of magazine editorial staffs. Much of what formerly was production is now editorial, and the blending of the two presents the opportunity for better years ahead.

Steps of Production

W HEN Benjamin Franklin and Andrew Bradford started the first American magazines in 1741, there was no separation between their editorial and production operations. Both men were printers as well as writers and editors, and the thought of sending their material to outside printers probably never occurred to them.

Instead, it was the custom of the day for typesetting and even printing press operation to be in-house—that is, performed at the same place and by the same people who prepared the editorial content. Editors often put their thoughts into words as they stood at a printer's type case, picking up each metal casting of a letter or other character and lining it up in a printer's composing stick until their article was completed.

Such simultaneous writing and typesetting continued well into the 19th century, finally giving way to a separation of these functions when technology produced more complex machines and methods for printing production. Skilled machine operators were then called on to produce, in type, the words of writers and editors.

Although much magazine production work is still done by contract printers totally separate from editorial staffs, an unusual cycle is now being completed that is bringing printing chores in-house once again. In a classical example of the cyclical nature of history, many magazine writers and editors of today are simultaneously writing and typesetting their wares, just as Franklin and Bradford did.

Obviously, they are not using the handset metal type and the stone makeup tables of Franklin's era. Instead, they have at their command marvelous new machines that eliminate the need for separate human typesetters and page makeup persons. As they keyboard their words and instructions at a machine, today's writers and editors are also putting their words into type and perhaps even positioning their material on pages.

Without attempting to assign the production functions to either outside printers or in-house staff activity, let's first sketch the basic steps involved in magazine production. Some of these already have been shown to have a direct bearing on issue planning. The basic steps are

1. Copy processing: getting words into type
2. Illustration processing: converting illustrations from the original image to an image on a printing plate that can carry ink to paper
3. Combining words and illustrations into pages: preparation of a mechanical, the camera-ready pasteup of type and illustrations. A separate mechanical is needed for each color to be printed.
4. Photographing the mechanicals to create negatives to be exposed on a printing plate
5. Fastening the negatives (stripping) into opaque masks so material is in correct page position when exposed on a printing plate
6. Imposition: the positioning of pages in the mask so that, when they are exposed on a large printing plate and then printed on large sheets and folded, they are in proper sequence

7. Preparing a press plate by beaming light through the mask containing the page negatives

8. Printing signatures, the large sheets that, when folded, become sections of the magazine. For each color, the paper goes through a press or press unit one time (two colors, two impressions). Separate plates are needed for each color to be printed.

9. Folding: folding the large sheets into the desired shape and size (*format*)

10. Binding: putting the folded sections (signatures) together with glue, wire, or string

These production steps are shown in figures 11.1 through 11.10.

Figure 11.1 Copy processing starts at a keyboard, such as the one being used at this video display terminal. If copy is first created at a typewriter, it may have to be rekeyboarded for type to be produced.

Figure 11.2 Continuous tone illustrations, such as photographs, must be photographed through a screen in a process camera. They may be enlarged or reduced at this step. Here, the cameraman adjusts the lens. The camera extends into another room on the right and contains a vacuum frame holding a film screen tightly in place over the unexposed film. Exposures from lights (in center, behind cameraman's forearm) create a dot pattern on the film as the light passes through the screen.

Figure 11.3 All line copy, such as type and line drawings, must be accurately positioned and fastened down on a mechanical, which is then photographed with the process camera.

Figure 11.4 A vacuum copy board such as this one holds mechanicals or individual line drawings that must be photographed in the process camera. Here, some line copy, which had to be reduced separately, is on the board.

Figure 11.5 Separate masks for line work on pasteups and individual illustrations to be double burned in position must be prepared. Page negatives on the left have blank spaces for the illustrations; the mask folded back on the right contains the illustration negatives that are to fill the blank spaces. Each mask is exposed (burned) in position on a plate. Negatives have been carefully positioned (registered) so the illustrations appear exactly where they should.

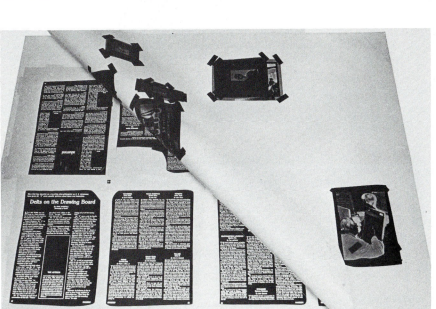

Figure 11.6 Imposition of pages in a mask. Eight-page negatives are in position in the mask shown partially here. The halftone negatives in the upper mask (folded to the right) must also be placed to fit the imposition of the pages.

Figure 11.7 After the printer has painted (opaqued) out blemishes on any of the negatives (a) the plate (b) is burned. This plate contains 8 pages to be printed on one side of a sheet, which, when folded, forms a 16-page signature.

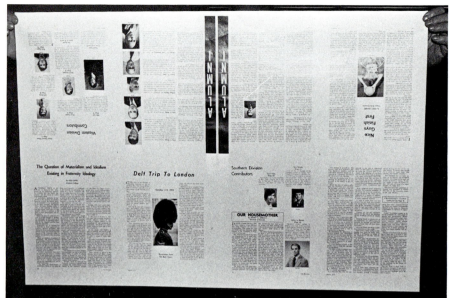

(b)

(a)

Figure 11.8 The printed sheet. Here, the result of one impression from the press onto paper is checked. Note that the sheet contains several pages; it is turned over and printed on the other side to form a signature.

Figure 11.9 A folder folds the large sheet three times to form a 16-page section of a magazine.

Figure 11.10 This saddle binder drives staples from the back to the center of the signature, which have been stacked like saddles and are now ready to be trimmed as they emerge from the binder.

Selecting a Process and Printer

The steps described and shown in the illustrations in this chapter show the production of a magazine by *photo offset lithography;* the vast majority of magazines are produced in that fashion. Except for final platemaking, these steps are the same for other processes as well.

Magazines with larger circulation and extensive color requirements are printed on web presses containing several units, as described in the previous chapter. Magazines with primary emphasis on picture reproduction and multimillion circulations may be produced by *rotogravure,* a process that carries ink to paper from depressed areas in copper cylinders. Roto does an exceptional job of reproducing photographs, but the mechanics of the process make type reproduction less sharp than with offset.

Letterpress, the traditional process of printing from raised metal type and metal photoengravings of pictures, has virtually been eliminated from magazine production. In cases where letterpress is still used, it is likely that new platemaking methods have been adopted that make its production steps the same as those for offset or rotogravure.

Circulation, size, and basic production requirements virtually dictate the selection of one of the three processes for a magazine, but selection of a printer is a different matter.

Selecting a Production Partner: The Printer

For all magazines, including those with fairly complete in-house production facilities, the selection of a printer is an important decision. Even for magazines that go all the way to page pasteups in the office, the printer is a vital part of a magazine production team. He or she is the manufacturer of the final product. Printers often can cause more disappointment, create more confusion, destroy the budget more efficiently, and generate more frustration than anyone else with which a staff must deal. On the other hand, they can be the fountain of all wisdom, the reliable right arm, the savior of the budget, and the meticulous craftspersons that all magazine production people so desperately need. If only editors could have some extra-sensory means for perceiving how capable and compatible a printer might be, they could improve their odds considerably. However, with no such magic method available, magazine editors and publishers must choose printers with only the available facts plus good judgment as their guides. Good judgment requires a consideration of quality and service, as well as cost.

Checking Quality

The time to determine whether a printer can produce high-quality work is before a contract is signed, not after. A reasonable evaluation of a printer's capability can be made by carefully analyzing the work he or she is doing for others. Printers will provide samples of their output, and, the more similar these samples are to your magazine, the better the analysis can be. Check carefully the three basic elements of a piece of printing: type composition, illustration reproduction, and page appearance.

One of the important factors of type composition is the availability of desired typefaces. The printer's type catalog tells you whether he or she has both body and display faces that are adequate for your needs. If you want a type style that one does not have, he or she may order it for you but usually only at a cost beyond what you ordinarily would pay for typesetting. For offset magazines, it is important to know what kind of machine will be used for composition because of the difference in quality and capability among the many strike-on and photo-setting systems that are available. The system the printer will use should be capable of the quality and speed you need.

In any case, check the printer's samples to see if the equipment and its operators have produced composition that shows good spacing and correct hyphenation. Sloppy operators or unsophisticated machines can produce a disturbing variation in word spacing as they justify lines to make them flush on the right; and sometimes neither the machine nor the operator seems to know what a syllable is.

Where specialized typesetting companies are available, it may be wise to contract with one of them for your composition. In the larger cities, especially, there are type composition houses that offer the finest quality and service because they are specialists in this one phase of printing production. Their quality and service may more than compensate for the inconvenience of dealing with another supplier, and the possible additional cost.

The reproduction quality of photographs and other illustrations is controlled by the printer only in part. The original artwork may or may not have been good; but such things as inking and impression are indications of a printer's presswork and make-ready skill. Whatever the cause, any evidence of poor reproduction of photographs in any printer's samples should be looked into. Especially among offset printers, the skill with which halftone negatives are made can vary considerably. Any inadequacy in this department can be a primary source of frustration for the editor, art director, and entire production staff as they try to produce a high-quality publication.

General page appearance can reveal a lot about a printer's quality, especially in offset lithography. Such things as slight deviation in the placement (registration) of colors, some little specks of ink where they shouldn't be, and slight imperfections of alignment here and there can reveal a lack of care with the opaquing or stripping of negatives. A "washed-out" appearance in any or all of the printing area may indicate a failure to control the ink and water balance on an offset press as carefully as a first-rate printer would control them.

For assistance in evaluating a printer's quality, a consultation with one of the users may be in order and produce good results. Another editor who is working under contract with a printer can give insights into the printer's capabilities that an evaluation of samples may not disclose.

Checking Service

Consultation with another customer, plus a visit to the printer's shop, provides the best opportunities to check on the service you can expect from a printer. From one, you can get a view as to how well a printer delivers on promises; from the other, you can get an idea as to his or her capability to render good service. Generally speaking, it is wise to get a printer whose equipment obviously is capable of handling a magazine of the size in question. The printer who seeks your business on the grounds that your magazine will be the biggest thing he or she handles, hence it will get top attention, should be checked out thoroughly. Such printers may not be able to deliver when breakdowns or other emergencies arise in their shops. It is usually safer to be one of several similar jobs that a printer turns out as a matter of routine because he or she is geared to handle a good volume of magazines of your size.

By checking with an editor of another magazine the printer produces, you might discover something about how well that printer keeps to a promised schedule. It is also important to know if the strippers or make-up persons follow your dummy specifications absolutely. Also, if the first proofs contain very few errors (are "clean"), there is less possibility of errors getting into print. An attempt should be made to be satisfied on all these points before signing a contract.

Ironically, the service performance of a printer may be the most difficult factor to determine in advance, while, in many cases, it can be the most important aspect of a satisfactory relationship between a printer and a magazine staff. A few missed deadlines can destroy quality because of the rush they may cause, and production delays can cause all kinds of problems with distribution. Any advance checking that reveals anything of a printer's level of service is well worth the effort.

Checking Cost

Although one might get the impression that printing costs are so standardized that shopping before buying is wasted effort, this is not the case. It is true that unionization tends to standardize wage levels in geographic regions, but there are other factors that produce some rather wide variations in pricing among printers. For example, the installation of a new piece of equipment may give one printer a decided price advantage over others who are using older equipment or doing a job by hand, or the need to keep expensive equipment busy may cause a printer to price work low for jobs especially suited to that equipment. The pricing of printing is essential, therefore, when a magazine is first introduced and periodically thereafter.

The difficulty with checking printing costs is that there are so many variables that it may seem almost impossible to make accurate comparisons. The only way to get a realistic basis for comparison is to provide a complete, detailed set of specifications on which prices can be obtained. These specifications should be based on common printing trade practices and expressed in terms and measurements used in the industry. Sizes of type, for example, should be expressed in points, with *body* types being those of the smaller sizes (under 14 points) and *display* types those of 14 points or larger. A point is considered to be 1/72d of an inch.

The use of additional white space between lines (called leading) has an obvious effect on the total amount of typesetting in any printing, so it should be among the specifications for type. Other dimensions of printing are based on picas (12 points, 1/6th of an inch). Printers use picas to express column widths, margins, and the white space breaks between columns.

Printing specifications should include at least the following items: trim page size, type page size, number of pages, number of copies, type composition, preparation of mechanicals, paper, color and cover requirements, illustrations, binding, proofs, production schedule, and distribution.

1. *Trim page size.* These are the dimensions of the magazine page after trimming—for example, 8½″ × 11″.

2. *Type page size.* These dimensions represent the type area after the margins have been deducted. The columnar structure of pages usually should be included here. The type area specification for an 8½″ × 11″ trim size might be type page size 45 picas by 58 picas, apportioned in three columns, each 14 picas wide and separated by 1½ picas, with a bottom margin of 4½ picas, top and outside margins of 3½ picas, and inside margin of 2½ picas. The reasoning behind the variation in margins is discussed in chapter 15. The important point here is to realize that type page size is a determinant of cost and should be part of the specifications.

3. *Number of pages.* For production efficiency, the number of pages should be a multiple of 4, or preferably 8 or 16. Also be sure that there is no confusion by stating whether the number given here includes the cover. A typical page specification would be 48 pages, self-cover, if the cover is to be part of a regular section printed on the same paper as inside pages, or 48 pages, plus cover, if the cover is to be printed separately in addition to the 48 basic pages.

4. *Number of copies.* The normal press run should be stated, with a request for the amount involved for adding or reducing that total by a hundred or a thousand copies. When setting the basic number, you must take into account the printing trade practice that permits a printer some leeway for unexpected waste. He or she may be permitted as much as a 10 percent underrun.

It is also important to get an understanding of the amount that will be involved for adding or deleting a 4-, 8-, or 16-page section of the magazine. This is one of the variables that can cause difficulty; the low bidder may turn out to be the higher bidder when you turn out an unusually large or small issue, unless you consider this cost at the outset.

5. *Type composition.* Every detail should be specified, including the size of the body type, whether leading (extra white space) is to be used, type designs, and the methods of composition that are acceptable. Wherever special sizes or styles are to be used, as in the case of photo captions and blurbs, these should be specified. In dealing with offset printers, especially, the stipulation of the composition method is important because it might be desirable to rule out some methods of strike-on composition in the interest of quality. It is best to specify the faces desired, because the choice of typefaces can affect cost, as mentioned earlier. It is possible, however, to stipulate only that type design will be selected from among those stocked by any bidder. Ordinarily, this is not wise unless the printers' catalogs of typefaces have been checked before inviting them to quote prices.

It should be noted again here that a magazine staff may compose its own type for offset production; if such is the case, the printer should be informed of the details of such an arrangement as they affect the printer. If you are using the services of a specialized firm for typesetting, this information should be given to potential printers.

6. *Preparation of mechanicals.* If pasting up mechanicals is going to be done by the staff, this fact must be relayed via the list of specifications. All production chores done in-house have an affect on printing costs and should be included (if titles are going to be hand drawn or prepared with paste-down letters, for example).

7. *Paper.* Here again, the specification must be detailed. Paper is an important determinant of both quality and cost for a magazine. Its quality importance is perhaps reflected in a simplistic definition of the difference between a magazine and a newspaper that was once given by a student: a newspaper is printed on poor paper and a magazine is printed on good paper. There are other differences, but there is no doubt that most magazines use a high-quality paper stock. Paper buying in the graphic arts is a highly technical science beyond the scope of this presentation, but there are some principles of which editors should be aware. They must realize, for example, that several factors enter into paper selection: technical requirements, the aesthetic "feel" or impression that is desired, and cost, including the effect of weight on distribution costs.

Technical requirements for paper vary with the process being used, and, obviously, the selection must take the method of printing into account. There are special papers for offset and special papers for gravure, for example, and the relationship of paper to quality of reproduction makes paper selection especially important. The smoothness of enamel-coated or supercalendered papers is often desired. Supercalendered papers are so-called because they are extensively calendered (squeezed between rollers sufficiently to get a smooth surface).

In addition to the degree of smoothness, paper surfaces can vary according to a desire for special textures. Paper can be made to look like leather, linen, or textured material. The texture may be applied before or after printing; in letterpress printing, it is ordinarily necessary for the printer or a special "pebbling" subcontractor to run the paper through textured rollers after printing to get this effect. Offset lithographers may simply print on paper already textured before they acquired it. Although most magazines wisely use a basic paper finish selected with legibility in mind and leave special textures to other media, occasionally a "mood" paper may be desired. Any other special technical requirements, such as being suitable for special inks, gumming, varnishing, and the like must also be specified to the printer.

Papers also vary according to weight, and weight has a direct and an indirect bearing on cost. It has a direct bearing because paper is priced by the pound or ton. Thus, by ordering heavier sheets than are really needed, an editor can waste money because total poundage per issue will be higher. However, the indirect effect of paper weight on postal charges is of even greater consequence. It is difficult for a beginner to comprehend the sums involved for postage in some magazine operations; some magazines have annual postal costs in millions of dollars. In fact, increases in postal rates have been a primary factor in the death of some magazines. Therefore, a specification that calls for paper that is any heavier than practicality demands can be extremely costly. Such waste could probably never occur with consumer magazines staffed with specialists in paper buying; nor would it be likely to happen in the publishing firms that produce several specialized magazines. They, too, have production specialists who are skilled enough to appreciate all aspects of paper buying. However, with the company magazines produced by public relations departments, postal bills and paper bills are often permitted to get out of bounds because unneeded weight has been specified for paper.

The specification of paper weight is complicated by the fact that the method for describing weight is in terms of the pounds per ream of a standard-size sheet. Thus, for the *book* paper usually used for magazines, a standard sheet is 25″ × 38″, and, if a ream of these sheets weighs 70 pounds, it is classified as 70-pound paper. If the sheets being used are half that size (25″ × 19″), obviously, a ream weighs only 35 pounds, but it is still classified as a 70-pound paper.

8. *Color requirements.* Most modern magazines make liberal use of color, either to bring full-life color to photos or to emphasize titles or other parts of a page design. Your specifications to a printer should indicate your normal color usage and request price quotations for the addition of one or more colors to a printed sheet, one or both sides. With all printing processes, the addition of color is a cost variable of considerable consequence. Other chapters provide additional guidance in keeping color costs down while getting maximum utility with color.

9. *Cover requirements.* As the magazine's showcase, the cover is entitled to special treatment. Any such special treatment—added color, stiffer paper, a slightly larger size—should be described.

10. *Illustrations.* This specification, for an offset magazine, indicates whether the use of screened photoprints on mechanicals is acceptable, which screen is to be used, and an approximation of the amount of space in each issue that will be occupied by halftones. Common screens used for magazines range from 100-line to 150-line for good quality of reproduction.

11. *Binding.* Unless a magazine's bulk prohibits it, saddle-wire binding is usually preferred.

12. *Proofs.* Mutual understanding about the number and kinds of proofs to be provided by the printer is essential at the outset of any editor-printer relationship. Both cost and efficiency are involved.

Ordinarily, galley proofs of all type that is set, revised galley proofs made after errors have been corrected, and final page proofs should be required. Reproduction and press proofs may or may not be required, depending on circumstances.

Revised galley proofs provide protection for printers and editors by permitting the detection of errors made during corrections before the material has been put into page form. It is more costly to make corrections after pages have been put together. Throughout the proofing process, printers bear the cost of their errors, but editors are billed for those they create or cause, or for the revisions made in the proofed material.

Page proofs should be used to check for any switching of captions and pictures or titles and articles, as well as such layout matters as alignment of elements. In offset, these proofs take the form of *bluelines* or *brownlines,* so-named because of their color. They are replicas, in blue or brown, of all the pages in a section. Corrections involving the placement of elements are not too difficult to make at this point; negatives can be pulled loose from their position in a mask and moved rather easily. However, type corrections require resetting and/or the making of a new negative as well as reinsertion into a mask. Hence, this is no time to be making type corrections; they should be caught in galleys or at least before pasteups are photographed.

Not to be overlooked in any process are proofs of illustrations. Photoengravers provide letterpress users with proofs of their plates so that quality of reproduction can be checked. Brownline or blueline proofs in offset should be used for checking the quality of illustration reproduction.

Reproduction proofs or their equivalent are needed for offset lithography in many instances. Type proofs that are "camera ready" are needed for pasting into page position, unless type is being provided in film form, ready for stripping into a mask.

Press proofs, though they offer the only possibility for absolute checking of all potential errors, are usually not required because of cost problems. Once a form or plate is on press, charges for time on the press begin. Unless an editor or production manager can be on hand immediately as the first copy comes off press, time charges can rise to unacceptable levels very quickly because, in this instance, the charges are completely nonproductive.

13. *Production schedule.* The number of working days needed to get to galley proof stage and then on to final delivery should be indicated by printers as they price a magazine job. A printer's ability to provide faster service should be considered along with price.

14. *Distribution.* The printer's responsibility for any part of the distribution of finished copies must be specified. Are wrappers to be used? Must the printer do the

addressing? Is delivery of copies to the magazine's office included? All such questions should be answered when a price is given, or the price can vary considerably according to the degree of responsibility for distribution a printer may assume is expected.

New Production Technology

Magazines have been facing stronger and stronger competition as each year goes by. Cut-throat competition from the other media, plus the competition among themselves, will continue to keep some magazines teetering on the brink of financial disaster. To survive, all magazines—large, small, general, and specialized—will have to take advantage of everything modern technology offers for their production.

The cost of production and the quality of content are obviously interrelated and directly tied to the technology used to put words and illustrations into print. The selection of the printing process to be used and the printer with whom a partnership is to be formed are preliminary planning decisions that have long-lasting effects. If these decisions are made knowledgeably, the day-to-day production decisions are easier to make and are much more likely to be made wisely. The degree to which production is brought in-house is also of importance and interest.

Many magazines still mark the separation of editorial work and production with the completion of words and illustrations on paper and edited with copy pencil and grease pencil. The raw materials are delivered, along with a layout plan, to a commercial printer, who takes over with the setting of type, the halftoning of pictures, and so on through binding and distribution.

Because in-house typesetting and page makeup have so many advantages, many magazines—especially small and specialized titles—are incorporating these activities into their editorial operations at an extremely rapid pace. Cost advantages, improved deadlines, and more total control over quality can result from what is only a reasonable expenditure of capital, even if only a portion of the preliminary work is moved in-house. With a small but versatile typesetter, an entry device or devices, and basic layout tools such as drawing boards and T-squares, many of these improvements can result.

A typical example of such a system is in use by *DIY Retailing,* formerly *Hardware Retailing,* a magazine published by the National Retail Hardware Association for those operating hardware, home center, and lumber yard retail centers. Like most such specialized publications, *DIY Retailing* is bulky and full of ads, and each issue is a major production effort.

As can be seen in the series of pictures in figure 11.11, production starts with typewriter copy from the editors and is edited for production in that form. A staff member then composes the type, both body and display sizes, on a computerized typesetter. At her screen and from her keyboard, she can use a wide variety of type designs very efficiently and while occupying very little space. Anyone who has worked in traditional systems with printers across town or in another city can appreciate the advantages of the proximity of in-house type composers. Correction of errors is much easier; after editors at *DIY Retailing* carefully read photocopies of proofs of set type, changes can be made quickly at the terminal keyboard. After proofs are corrected, the staff person with graphics responsibilities follows editorial dummies to paste proofs in page position. The advertising production manager plans the ad and editorial positions in the book and provides the staff with forms and imposition sheets. When the pages are complete, they are delivered to the printer, who completes the production of the issue.

Current Production Developments

In the current state of change that we see in magazine production, there is one thing certain. The evolution of in-house production systems will maintain a steady progression, with some magazines taking the first step by moving some basic typesetting chores into the office. Others with in-house typesetting will move from that stage to more versatile systems. Still others will be entering the "total pagination" group.

(a)

(b)

(c)

(d)

(e)

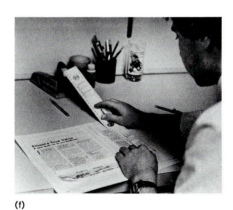

(f)

Figure 11.11 *DIY Retailing,* a magazine for stores catering to do-it-yourselfers, does much of its production itself. (a) Step one is the editing of typewritten copy. (b) Next, type is composed at a video display terminal, and output comes from the compact but versatile typesetter just to the right of the staff member at the VDT. (c) Careful proofreading, with one staffer reading and the other checking the proof, can be done immediately. (d) Meanwhile, ads are placed and imposition sheets are prepared. (e and f) Page mechanicals can then also be done by the staff, leaving only final production steps for a printer. (Courtesy *DIY Retailing.*)

The old-line methods, with the printer taking over typewritten copy and photos and doing all the production chores, are surely on the way out, but they are not yet a thing of the past. The factors of economics and editorial quality will continue to exert pressure on these methods, however.

As Robert Vereen, former editor of *Hardware Retailing* and now senior vice-president at *DIY Retailing,* put it:

In much of the same way as the pocket calculator has broadened its market by constant and drastic price reductions, so too has electronic typesetting come into the pocketbook and budget range of an increasing number of publications due to sharp price decreases and improved (really meaning simplified) technology.

Today any publication, even one that spends as little as $500 a month, can afford in-house typesetting.

Equipment for direct-entry typesetting (all that's needed for a great many smaller trade publications) costs as little as $7,500 to $10,000. Chemicals, supplies, etc., are minor: maintenance negligible.

Vereen also points out that in-house production facilities provide much more than an economic benefit:

For trade publications particularly it affords a time benefit of immeasurable value. In-house typesetting permits the extension of closing deadlines by as much as a week or more . . . [And] in-house typesetting, in-house pasteup and in-house production are far simpler than dealing with outside sources who can misplace your copy, miss your deadline, fail to properly proofread your material, etc. Control is easy; production is simplified; accuracy is improved—and most importantly, speed is assured.

This kind of a system, without multiple computer terminals and large-capacity computers, can be the most cost effective for many magazines and is especially common among specialized business, public relations, and association magazines. In many cases, however, the investment in computerized production systems has been cost effective, even for small magazines. More and more of all kinds of magazines are using electronic production technology, as described in the next chapter.

Electronic (Desktop) Production

MAGAZINE publishers for years have been looking forward to a totally computerized production system that would, in essence, cut the 10 printing production steps listed in chapter 11 to a mere one or two. Gone would be pasteup tables, photocomposing machines, film processing darkrooms, and even the traditional printing presses. In their place would be the computer; words and pictures would be entered into the computer, manipulated by keyboard or mouse into pages, and transferred directly to paper by computer-generated droplets or heat-fused powder.

The technology for totally electronic printing is at hand, and magazines of all types and sizes are on their way to electronic production. Customized (proprietary) systems designed for large circulation magazines such as *U.S. News & World Report* and *Time* magazine have now been matched by and blended with personal computer systems with equipment (hardware) so small and efficient that a total system can fit on a desk top.

For magazine journalism students, the result is a maze of technical adaptations that seem to be almost as diverse as the individual magazines themselves. Anyone entering magazine journalism now must have at least a basic understanding of these systems in order to move from one to another with ease.

Understanding Electronic Publishing

The first step in understanding electronic publishing is to know the terminology. The second is to understand the production steps when digital terminology is applied.

Proprietary systems use equipment programmed specifically for production chores. Their equipment tends to be much more expensive and larger than that of desktop systems. Their strength is their ability to produce the finest quality of printing available.

Desktop (DTP) systems often include hardware limited in quality potential, but the quality of desktop systems is rapidly approaching that of the proprietary equipment. Networking of personal computers with specialized equipment also is resulting in high quality levels for production.

Electronic Production Steps

Virtually all of the production steps listed at the beginning of chapter 11 can now be done electronically.

Step 1. Copy Processing: Getting Words into Type

For proprietary systems, specialized computer terminals (usually called video display terminals, or VDTs) are programmed for super-efficient word processing and conversion of words into limited typefaces and typesizes (figure 12.1). Editing tasks have been streamlined for fast keyboarding and easy type selection. Characters are displayed on the screen as they are created at the keyboard in the same manner that a typewriter shows them on paper.

Figure 12.1 Video display terminals in proprietary systems are efficient typesetting input devices, but they do not display the type and graphics as they will be in print. (Photo by Ralph Kliesch.)

Desktop and other systems based primarily on personal computers, such as Apple's Macintosh (figure 12.2) and IBM's PCs, use a variety of programs offered by a large number of software venders. With programs such as *Microsoft Word* for word processing and typesetting, desktop systems allow users to see, on the screen, exactly what the finished typesetting will be like.

Author-generated type can now be as sophisticated as that from professional shops. Software is readily available to permit such niceties as *kerning* (snuggling one letter under an extended stroke of another to improve spacing), adjustable letter and word spacing, precise line spacing (adding and subtracting white space between lines), and the running of text around graphics.

The use of drop capitals and the control of widows and orphans (short paragraph endings) are also available. In some systems, selected text can be displayed as underlined, outlined, or shadowed, as well as the usual medium, bold, and italic versions. Combinations, such as bold italic, can also be selected and viewed. These choices and size changes can be accomplished with a click of the mouse.

Much improved hyphenation and justification and an almost limitless selection of type fonts have helped eliminate some of the earlier shortcomings of computerized type composition. Users may even design their own typefaces, as well as alter letter proportions or posture.

The improvement of scanners (figure 12.3) and the accompanying software, which enabled scanners to read typewritten or typeset text in virtually any font, including display type, has been a major new efficiency. Earlier scanners (Optical Character Readers) were limited to a standard typewriter face and single-column messages. Now full pages of printed text can be scanned and stored in a publishing system for resetting under new specifications.

Copyfitting and editing benefits have been especially important too. The WYSIWYG (What You See Is What You Get) presentation of typeset material eliminates the need to compute space requirements and facilitates editing to space with an exactness not possible with manual computations.

Most important is the fact that only one keyboarding of type is needed; once type matter is stored in digital form, it can be changed, corrected, and/or incorporated with artwork into pages or moved from place to place electronically.

Step 2. Illustration Processing: Getting Photos and Artwork into Print

Personal computer advantages are most obvious in getting photos and artwork into print. Computers with graphic applications eliminate virtually all of the tedious work formerly required to get photos and drawings into print.

Graphic images can be created, altered, and revised on the computer screen through *Paint* or *bit mapped* images (figure 12.4). With both paint and draw programs, the computer screen serves as an artist's canvas, with the only limits on creation being those of the operator.

Figure 12.2 Screens on Macintosh and other graphics computer terminals show type and artwork as they will appear. (Photo by Ralph Kliesch.)

Photos can be scanned into a system and reduced or enlarged for reproduction, with quality depending on the capacity of the system. The higher the number of dots per inch (dpi) the more faithful the reproduction. Clip art services also provide users with drawings that can be scanned into a system (figure 12.5).

Step 3. Combining Words and Illustrations into Pages

The basic method for putting words and pictures into pages, as described in chapter 11, involved the preparation of mechanicals (pasteups). Although computer pagination for magazines was possible earlier with some complex proprietary systems, developments in 1984 and 1985 made this function commonplace for personal computers and made desktop publishing a common term.

What is known as desktop publishing became possible in 1985 with the introduction of the Macintosh by Apple Computers, the *PageMaker* program by Aldus Corporation, and a page description language, called *PostScript,* by Adobe Systems, Inc. With *PostScript,* a laser printer is guided into the conversion of page elements into *pixels* (dots). The page output of the printers varies in quality according to the printer's dpi.

Coining of the term *desktop publishing* is attributed to Paul Brainerd, president of Aldus, who conceived *PageMaker* (figure 12.6), the program that made it possible to select type and to lay out page design by computer.

Figure 12.3 Scanners convert artwork and type into digital form in a computer system, thus eliminating the time ordinarily needed for typesetting and image creation.

Figure 12.4 Paint and draw programs enable computers to store drawings and other artwork in dot (pixel) form or as images that can be enlarged, reduced, or otherwise manipulated. The student's drawing shown here was made using Aldus Freehand and will reproduce with sharp, uninterrupted lines. Bit-mapped images in pixel form are characterized by ''jaggy'' lines. (Photo by Ralph Kliesch.)

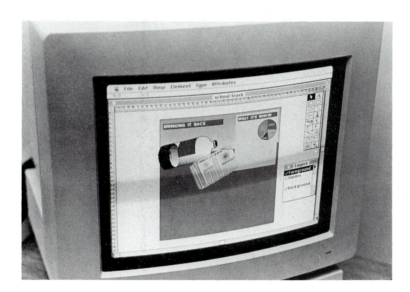

Figure 12.5 Printed publications traditionally subscribed to clip services, which provided catalogs of stock drawings that could be cut and pasted in position for reproduction in ads or other pages. Computer graphics firms now provide the service in disk form, with the important additional advantage that the images, such as these from the catalog of DeskTop Art®, can be combined or manipulated to form endless variations. (© Dynamic Graphics, Inc.)

Figure 12.6 *PageMaker* and other software enable the creation of full pages, with type and illustrations in position in a personal computer, thus eliminating the need for pasteups. (Photo by Ralph Kliesch.)

Figure 12.7 The use of icons, such as these in the toolbox for *Macpublisher III,* has made the use of desktop publishing seem possible for anyone by eliminating the fear of complicated computer coding. (Courtesy of Apple Computer, Inc.)

PageMaker has been improved and updated several times since its introduction; from the outset, it was intended to bring a graphic designer's pasteup board to the computer screen. *PageMaker* allowed text and graphic elements to be moved around and modified as if they had been backed with wax adhesive, cut, and positioned on mounting board. As the text for pages was input from word processors, it could be positioned column by column and page by page, just as typeset galleys were.

In updated versions, *PageMaker* users can automatically flow text from column to column and page to page, thus eliminating even the notion of typeset galleys. Also added were the abilities to set text around irregular drawings and other graphics, to alter tones of graphics and see the results immediately on the screen, and to carry out spot-color functions. In the last case, all elements including text and graphics or segments of graphics, can be defined for color, and the system produces the equivalent of overlays, complete with register marks.

Use of the mouse for the selection and placement of the activity being viewed on the screen has been an important foundation for the ease of operation and popularity of desktop publishing. Its efficient, codeless ability to move information from the user's mind into a computer eliminated most of the fear common among beginning computer users. Users like the availability of a "toolbox" (figure 12.7) containing friendly visual images (icons), such as the *hand* for moving elements and pointing to other tools, *scissors* for cutting unwanted material, a *paste jar* for affixing material cut or copied, an *arrow* for inserting new material, and a *camera* to copy material that can then be moved by using the paste jar. The mouse, using a rubber ball for rolling into position and a button to click for action, was invented in 1964 by Douglas Engelhart at the Stanford Research Institute as a result of research into several possible means for easy interfacing between humans and computers. Although the mouse control has not been universally used and has some limitations, it was a major factor in the quick popularity of the Apple Macintosh desktop publishing system.

Page design by computer has been enhanced by the capability of such programs as *PageMaker* and its competitors to include multiple "windows" on the screen. These rectangular areas can each be a display area for a different program, with the operator able to switch easily from one program to the other.

Expansion of Systems

Desktop publishing systems have proliferated with exceptional speed. Additional software for word processing and typesetting, for the creation of graphic images, and for page layout has been generated for the whole range of IBM-related MS-DOS competitors, as well as the Apple group. Quark's *Xpress* was the most used program by magazines in the early 1990s, followed by *PageMaker* and Xerox's *Ventura Publisher,* according to a *Folio:* magazine survey. Other common systems include Ashton-Tate's *Byline,* Digital Research's *GEM Desktop Publisher,* Gold Disk's

Professional Page, IMSI's *PagePerfect,* Laser Friendly's *Office Publisher,* Microsearch's *City Desk,* Software Publishing Corporation's *PFS: First Publisher,* Timework's *Publish It!,* and Springboard Software's *Springboard Publisher.* Some word processing programs, such as *WordPerfect,* have been modified to incorporate other publishing functions.

As pagination systems have proliferated and expanded, editors and art directors have expanded and extended their use of the capabilities offered. For example, some designers have made excellent use of *templates,* page patterns established in the system. These patterns set basic design characteristics that provide continuity and flexibility in page appearance (figure 12.8).

Other Production Steps

With computer pagination and laser printer output, the tedious preparation of pasteup is not needed, but commercial printers take over with the imposition of pages into signatures, the creation of negatives, and the platemaking. The computerization of these steps, however, is also underway. Programs are now available that permit editors and production managers to impose an issue in seconds instead of hours. The efficient placement of color, regional page changes, ad positioning, and the scores of other complications affecting the total number of pages and placement of pages are computerized.

Even folding and binding have been revolutionized. The computer customization of binding enables subscribers to have issues tailored to their desires. Some departments can be added and some subtracted during the binding process, with each copy addressed by computerized jet printing according to the content appropriate for each reader. Thus, the precise targeting of audiences for advertisers is possible.

Some Typical Applications

Magazines of all kinds and sizes are tailoring electronic technology to their needs.

Chesapeake Bay Magazine is a monthly special interest magazine published in Annapolis, Maryland, for an audience of recreational boaters and others interested in the heritage, life-style, and environment of the Chesapeake Bay region. Its 32,000 readers live in the metropolitan areas of Philadelphia; Baltimore; Washington, DC; and Norfolk, Virginia, and throughout the eastern and western shores of the Chesapeake.

For the past two decades, its audience and issue size have been growing. Its inhouse typesetting and pasteup production (such as those described in the previous chapter) have served it well. By 1991, however, the typesetter was wearing out and falling behind in its ability to meet the production needs of a magazine now ranging in size between 68 and 140 pages.

Publisher Richard J. Royer and his editor, Jean Waller, solved *Chesapeake Bay Magazine*'s problem by joining the scores of other magazines moving to totally electronic desktop systems (figure 12.9). As a privately published magazine, it had to have a system that was reasonable in cost but efficient over the long run. Writing in *Magazine Design & Production,* editor Waller described the problems associated with the change and the benefits derived from it. The system, using Macintosh computers, *QuarkXpress, DataClub,* and *Adobe Illustrator* software and a 1200 dpi laser printer lets a four-person production staff produce, with camera-ready quality, full editorial pages and much of the advertising. A commercial printer does the imposition, platemaking, printing, and binding.

For magazines with even smaller staffs and circulation than *Chesapeake Bay Magazine,* desktop publishing has been the ultimate solution as well. For example, Chuck and Sally Wright are the complete editorial and business staff of *Christmas Trees,* a magazine for Christmas tree growers. They are husband and wife; he is editor and publisher and she is the advertising and circulation director. All of their publishing activities are centered in a basement office of their home in Lecompton, Kansas.

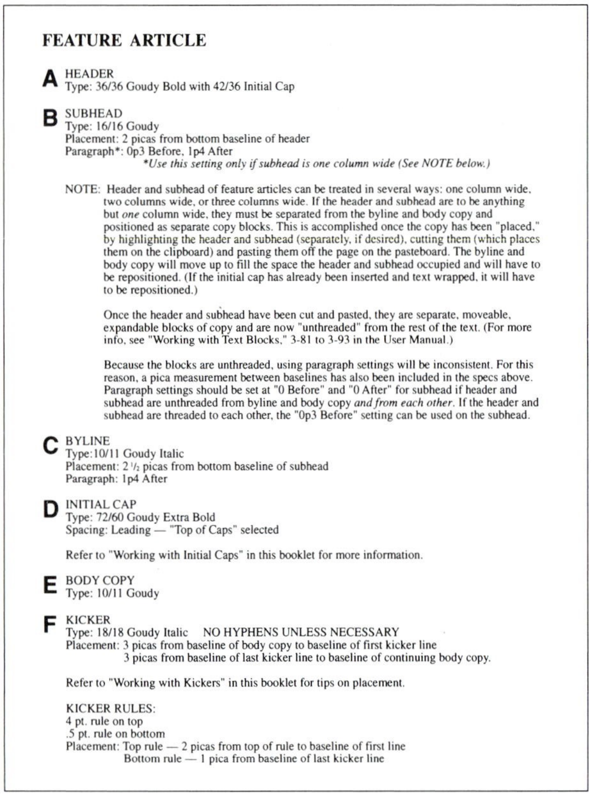

FEATURE ARTICLE

A HEADER
Type: 36/36 Goudy Bold with 42/36 Initial Cap

B SUBHEAD
Type: 16/16 Goudy
Placement: 2 picas from bottom baseline of header
Paragraph*: 0p3 Before, 1p4 After
**Use this setting only if subhead is one column wide (See NOTE below.)*

NOTE: Header and subhead of feature articles can be treated in several ways: one column wide, two columns wide, or three columns wide. If the header and subhead are to be anything but *one* column wide, they must be separated from the byline and body copy and positioned as separate copy blocks. This is accomplished once the copy has been "placed," by highlighting the header and subhead (separately, if desired), cutting them (which places them on the clipboard) and pasting them off the page on the pasteboard. The byline and body copy will move up to fill the space the header and subhead occupied and will have to be repositioned. (If the initial cap has already been inserted and text wrapped, it will have to be repositioned.)

Once the header and subhead have been cut and pasted, they are separate, moveable, expandable blocks of copy and are now "unthreaded" from the rest of the text. (For more info, see "Working with Text Blocks," 3-81 to 3-93 in the User Manual.)

Because the blocks are unthreaded, using paragraph settings will be inconsistent. For this reason, a pica measurement between baselines has also been included in the specs above. Paragraph settings should be set at "0 Before" and "0 After" for subhead if header and subhead are unthreaded from byline and body copy *and from each other*. If the header and subhead are threaded to each other, the "0p3 Before" setting can be used on the subhead.

C BYLINE
Type:10/11 Goudy Italic
Placement: 2 1/2 picas from bottom baseline of subhead
Paragraph: 1p4 After

D INITIAL CAP
Type: 72/60 Goudy Extra Bold
Spacing: Leading — "Top of Caps" selected

Refer to "Working with Initial Caps" in this booklet for more information.

E BODY COPY
Type: 10/11 Goudy

F KICKER
Type: 18/18 Goudy Italic NO HYPHENS UNLESS NECESSARY
Placement: 3 picas from baseline of body copy to baseline of first kicker line
3 picas from baseline of last kicker line to baseline of continuing body copy.

Refer to "Working with Kickers" in this booklet for tips on placement.

KICKER RULES:
4 pt. rule on top
.5 pt. rule on bottom
Placement: Top rule — 2 picas from top of rule to baseline of first line
Bottom rule — 1 pica from baseline of last kicker line

(a)

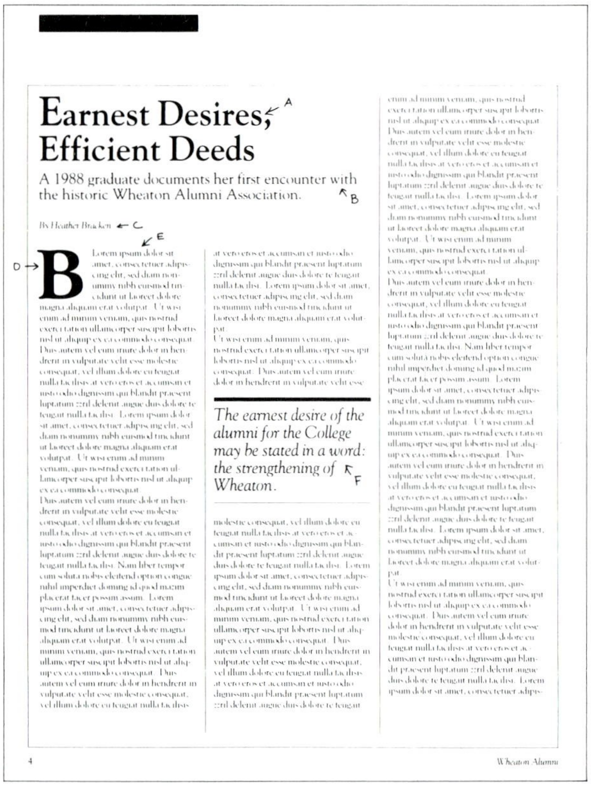

(b)

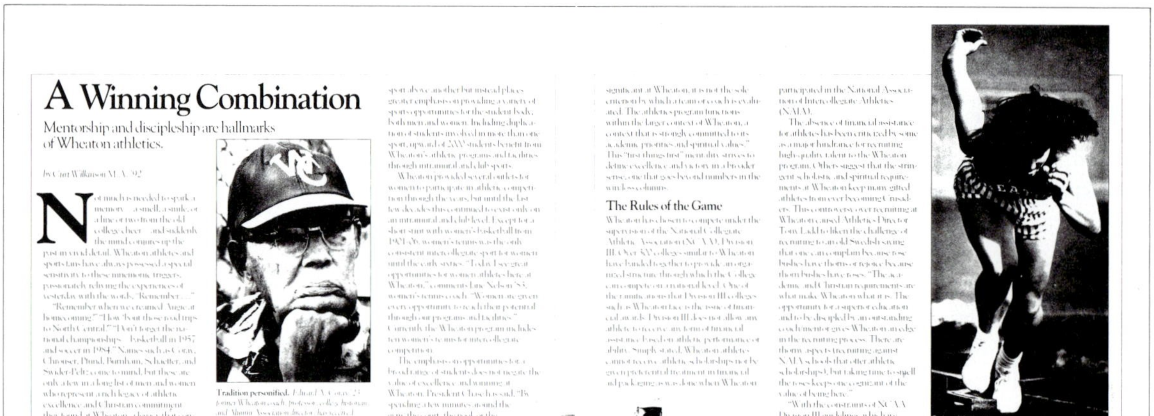

(c)

Figure 12.8 Templates are page layout patterns. When skillfully designed, they allow editorial staffers with no design talents to create pages that consistently adhere to the principles of good design. Shown here is (a) a sheet of specifications for the feature article pages of the *Wheaton Alumni* of Wheaton (Ill.) College, (b) the sample page illustrating those instructions, and (c) two facing pages of an article. Note that differences can and should exist as templates are followed, but the basic character of the design is retained. (Courtesy *Wheaton Alumni.* Template designer: ABS Graphics, Addison, Ill.—Susan Lauer.)

(a)

(b)

(c)

Figure 12.9 (a) Art director Christine Gill of *Chesapeake Bay Monthly* designs a page at her computer. (b, c) Examples of the excellent design produced with the desktop system. (Courtesy *Chesapeake Bay Monthly.*)

Obviously, the Wrights have a great interest in Christmas trees; they couldn't be in tune with their readers if they didn't. In fact, they have been growing and selling Christmas trees for years, and they have had an interest in the magazine publishing business since buying *Christmas Trees* magazine.

When the Wrights purchased *Christmas Trees* from the founding editor and publisher, the magazine had a circulation of 1,100 and was produced in a traditional manner. The Wrights gathered the editorial material, sold and designed their ads, and laboriously prepared address labels from a card file that never seemed to be up-to-date. Maintaining the card file of subscriber addresses was one of the tedious and undesirable tasks that never seemed to be quite caught up. Another dreary task was pasteup, and Chuck Wright especially remembers working with the little page numbers and trying to keep the correct running page lines on left and right pages. The magazine name always went with the page number on the left pages; the date was included with the odd-numbered, right pages.

Also, at that time, working with the printer was quite tedious. First came the typing of the copy, then trips to the printer to deliver copy and pick up the galley proofs for checking. Then came the page proofs, which often revealed the necessity for carrying material to the back of the magazine because articles didn't quite fit the intended space.

As the magazine grew in size and circulation (about 36 pages plus cover and more than 6,000 readers), the need for additional help was obvious. The Wrights turned to technology for assistance, and the payoff was immediate. The equipment they chose was the personal computer (Mac II) portion of a desktop publishing system (figure 12.10). In cost, their investment was minimal, but it provided solutions for all their problems. Type, including titles and display type for ads, is composed at the computer keyboard; pages and ads are laid out with the computer's *PageMaker* program and a graphics tablet mouse; all material is stored on a disk. The Wrights did not consider it cost-effective to purchase a computer-driven laser printer that turns out full pages. For less than $1 a page, a college computer center in Topeka provides them with full-page laser proofs, ready for the printing forms. Chuck Wright just takes his computer's floppy disk, containing the digitized pages for an issue, to the computer center and gets his 40 page proofs for about $40. In minutes, the pages can be pasted in position for delivery to the printer in Topeka. Consequently, the Wrights' investment has been unusually cost-effective.

Gone is the tedious pasteup—those little page numbers are automatically placed by the computer—and the trips to the printer for typesetting and proofs. The Wrights' use of another personal computer has also eliminated those subscriber information cards that never seemed to be current. The computerization of their most tiresome functions has changed magazine editing for the Wrights. Although he is fully aware of the cost advantages and the increased efficiency the computer has brought to *Christmas Trees* magazine, Chuck Wright is most impressed by another result: the improvement in quality. Not only is the computer page layout free of pasteup flaws, but he also has additional time now for getting to know his readers and fulfilling their needs. Time formerly spent over the layout table can now be spent at state tree grower meetings, trade shows, or with other endeavors that strengthen the essential bonds between the Wrights and their readers.

Figure 12.10 Working in his home office at his computer, Chuck Wright, editor of *Christmas Trees* magazine, can do all prepress publishing steps except the preparation of halftone photo reproductions. (Photo courtesy Tree Publisher, Inc.)

Although, in many respects, a small cottage industry operation, as represented by the Wrights, brings out the most obvious advantages for computerized editing and production facilities, medium- and large-size magazine operations of all varieties also have found such technology to be advantageous.

Systems for Large Magazines

One of the earliest totally electronic proprietary publishing systems was installed by *U.S. News & World Report* in 1974 (figure 12.11). *U.S. News* pioneered systems that could handle complete pagination, including continuous tone photographs. Modified since its installation, the system is also typical of sophisticated systems in that it incorporates the telecommunication transmission of pages to printing plants. As the pictures in figure 12.11 show, copy can originate from writers at any remote or on-site terminal, can be blended with photos to form pages in the computer, and can be transmitted in page form via Western Union's Westar satellite to printers at various locations.

(a)

(b)

(c)

(d)

Figure 12.11 (a) The writer-editor at the video display terminal is the central figure in the *U.S. News & World Report* electronic production system. Original stories are fed into the computer from these stations and can be called from storage for editing on the same video screen. All typesetting and page layouts are done at the terminals. (b) An illustration scanner electronically converts photographs to digital halftones in desired sizes and stores the information on magnetic tape and in the computer. From the computer, the halftones and page placement information go directly to a CRT typesetter, which produces full pages at the editorial location. (c) Typesetter output in the form of completed pages with all body type, display type, and illustrations in place is developed on photo paper in this processor. These page proofs can be read and corrected at the editorial office. Because all page components come from the computer in digital form, the pages can easily be transmitted by wire or other means to printers anywhere. (d) From this control center at *U.S. News & World Report,* completed pages in digital form are sent by satellite to three printing plants. At the printing plants, the pages are received on magnetic tape and then fed into typesetters. The typesetters produce full pages ready for platemaking. (Courtesy *U.S. News & World Report.*)

Typesetters in such systems are digital CRT (cathode ray tube) typesetters whose output is complete pages. They are digital in that they are computer-driven and CRT in that the computer-generated images are projected onto paper by a television tube. Phototypesetters, on the other hand, expose copy letter-by-letter in line position. Page output from CRT typesetters is virtually instantaneous.

The advantages of such systems are relatively obvious. Much later deadlines are possible. Quality control is totally within the editorial department. Copy can be edited exactly to space requirements, hyphenation and justification can be controlled by experts as well as the computer, and extensive verification and correction are feasible. At the same time, computer-generated graphics have made the illustration of complicated material much easier and more sophisticated.

Electronic Production Meets Customized Needs

There is an amazing array of system configurations now being used, each with an emphasis deemed especially valuable by the user. For example, in Columbus, Ohio, the electronic information service *CompuServe* provides about half a million subscribers with *Online Today,* a monthly computer communication magazine. This magazine averages 56 pages plus cover and is loaded with full color.

At *Online Today,* electronic transmission from computer to computer is its sponsor's lifeblood, and the magazine uses the electronic mail aspect of technology effectively for editorial administration, as well as production chores. Writers from all parts of the country transmit their articles via modem and telephone line to computers in the Columbus editorial offices. There, writers and editors use the WYSIWYG aspect of personal computers to be able to view their output on screen as it would look in type. The production department uses an electronic publishing system called *Xyvision* (figure 12.12) for prepress activities, including pagination, but typesetting is done by a local composition house, which provides laser printer proofs for corrections. Printing is done by R. R. Donnelley & Sons Co., a large printing firm headquartered in Chicago.

For weekly newsmagazines, the ability of electronic publishing to make possible the extremely late closing of pages has been a major factor, but design has also benefited. For instance, the highly publicized design change by *Time* magazine in 1992 blended desktop capabilities with its Atex proprietary system. Top editors joined designers, who used *QuarkXpress* programs and Macintosh computers to come up with the new design. The flexibility of the desktop system enabled the redesign team

Figure 12.12 Design and production staffs at CompuServe's *Online Today* magazine use their large *Xyvision* terminal screen to view typesetting and page design before pages are composed. (Courtesy *Online Today* and CompuServe.)

to experiment with various page grids, working and reworking pages until they came up with what seemed to be their best alternative. By producing pages on a laser copier, the group could submit its ideas to editors, who could make and see the results of their suggestions instantly.

Since its redesign, *Time* has been blending Macintosh and Atex systems and has been testing new programs that have even more reliance on the Macintosh hardware. *Time* also uses facsimile transmission of pages in negative form for platemaking to 8 domestic and 11 international printing sites. Thus, the issue that readers get on Monday is closed at 3:00 A.M. on Sunday, with printing starting at 7:00 A.M. and the shipping of copies beginning at 1:00 P.M. In some areas, readers can pick up a copy on Sunday.

Group publishers, such as Times Mirror Magazines (*Golf Magazine, Field & Stream, Outdoor Life, Popular Science, Home Mechanix, Ski, Skiing, Skiing Trade News, Salt Water Sportsman,* and *Yachting*), have made extensive investments in equipment and training to publish their magazines electronically. At Times Mirror, Macintosh and IBM computers and *PageMaker* and *QuarkXpress* have been used to bring prepress production functions in-house.

Penton Press, a printer as well as publisher of a group of specialized business magazines, has moved from a proprietary system to one based on desktop hardware and software. After buying an imagesetter for output, the company provided a network of Macintoshes for editors and artists. The company cited better response time, improved quality, and ease of redesigning as the major benefits derived by its magazines and its printing customers.

This ease of designing pages or redesigning complete magazines is often mentioned as a primary cause for a move to desktop capabilities. Some of the effects stemming from this advantage are outlined in chapter 15.

For R. R. Donnelley and Sons Co., a leading printer of magazines, a customized software program automating all production steps has met its needs best. Called *Magmaster,* the program permits a magazine production manager to prepare the layout of a complete issue on a personal computer, generate the necessary printing instructions, and send those instructions by phone. Only Donnelley customers have the program available to them.

Such examples of the great variety of electronic adaptations could go on and on, virtually without end. New uses, new software, and new equipment are coming into place for all kinds of magazines. No magazine is too large or too small, too general or too specialized, for finding advantages to move to an electronic system.

What's in Store

For students planning magazine careers, a knowledge of electronic production is essential and some hands-on experience is extremely helpful, if not required.

The trend toward desktop technology, either in combination with proprietary systems or on its own, makes familiarity with personal computers especially important. Some work with graphics software, especially the page design programs such as *PageMaker, Ventura Publisher,* and *QuarkXpress,* can also be especially valuable.

13 The Editor and Typography

T YPOGRAPHY can be defined as the use and arrangement of type. It can be an art, but for editors it is more than that. It is an essential part of their communication role, a tool for getting words into the minds of their readers.

Type has many faces, and it can be said that it speaks with many voices. Type can speak boldly, delicately, quickly, or slowly. It can be high-pitched or well modulated and deep. It can be old-fashioned or modern, active or passive. The many moods of type make typography a fascinating part of the magazine editor's role. It has its own technical language, too, that has developed through the centuries since Johann Gutenberg devised movable type. Some of its language, though seemingly outmoded by new technology, nevertheless holds on and must be learned by any users of type.

What Is Type?

Type, itself, once easily defined as raised alphanumeric symbols on a metal body whose faces were transferred in ink onto paper by pressure, now requires a much more general definition. Type now is any alphanumeric symbols used for duplication in any printing process. It includes the old-fashioned *hot type* cast in metal but also embraces a wide variety of *cold type* (any type not cast in molten metal). For example, typewriterlike machines place an image on paper by striking an ink-covered key against the paper (*strike-on* type). Adhesive-backed letters and numbers can be cut from sheets and placed into position for printing (*paste-down* type), or letters can be transferred to paper by rubbing the backs of sheets of what is called *transfer* type. Most common of the newer physical forms for type is *phototype,* letter images exposed in position on photo paper. A sophisticated variation of phototype is created via computer and cathode ray tube, with the letters being stored in a computer and exposed in great quantity instantaneously when the image on the tube is exposed on paper.

A type's *face* is the image it leaves when printed on paper. Its *body* is the carrier of the face and must be large enough to carry every part of the face, from the *ascender,* which rises to the top, to the *descender,* which drops to the bottom. Most of its letters are lined up to use only the center of the body and are called *center body* letters. The body can be artificially fattened without changing the face, thus separating the faces from each other by between-line spacing called *leading* (pronounced *ledding*).

Now, thanks to modern typesetting technology, the body can even be made smaller than the face through a technique called *reverse leading* or *back leading.* More about this later as we discuss type sizes.

Letters within a line of type can be squeezed together or spread apart; the first technique is called *minus letterspacing* and the second is called *plus letterspacing. Normal letterspacing* gives each letter its usual space. Spacing for letters is *proportional* to the width of the letter and not uniform, as it is on an ordinary typewriter.

Type Measurement

Type is measured in *points,* a unit of measure that is 1/72d of an inch. To understand type sizing, however, editors must do much more than commit to memory that there are 72 points in an inch. One of the thorny problems connected with type size stems from the fact that the *body* of the type determines the size, and not the *face* of any letter. Note in figure 13.1 that the body must allow for letters that go below a *base* line and rise above the *center body* area. Therefore, NO SINGLE LETTER OR CHARACTER IS EVER MEASURABLE TO DETERMINE TYPE SIZE. To put it another way, when ordering type size in an effort to have it be equal to some hand lettering, one cannot measure any of the letters created by hand to determine the point size to order.

Various letter forms also can be in identical sizes but appear to be quite different in size, as shown in figure 13.2. When the center body letters (a, c, o, e, etc.) use up a large portion of the body, the type appears to be larger than when the center body letters are small. The size of the center body letters is often referred to as the *x-height,* meaning the height of the small x of the typeface.

Type measurement is further complicated by leading, the addition of extra white space between lines by expanding the type body without increasing the size of the letter faces. When type was cast in metal, the addition of a point or two of additional lead above and/or below a line of type in the casting process provided a helpful benefit for readers by forcing lines apart, thus adding white space between them. In cold type systems, although no metal is used, the term *leading* still prevails. Eight-point type put on a 10-point body then provides 2 points of white space between lines, and it may also be referred to as "8-point leaded 2 points," or "8 on 10."

Computer Typefaces and Type Sizes

The most recent complication in type measurement has come from the programming for personal computers that permits the manipulation of typeface sizes and shapes not previously available. Some desktop publishing programs offer size capabilities in fractions of points as well as the ability to design individualized faces and to distort existing faces. As long as magazines continue to rely on commercial typesetting for the final product, however, it is wise to continue using traditional units and faces. Until a digital typesetting system is used, what is created and seen on a PC screen must be translated into those traditional units and faces.

Body Type and Display Type

Type that is in the smaller sizes typically used for the body of messages is called *body type;* type in the larger sizes typical of headlines is called *display type.* The exact point of separation is at 14 points; type 14 points or larger is display. The

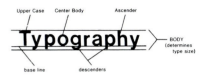

Figure 13.1 Type size is based on the normal body of a typeface. That body must include room for ascenders and descenders, as well as center body letters.

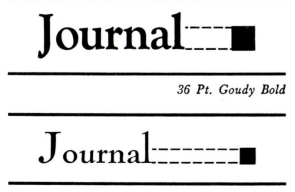

36 Pt. Goudy Bold

36 Pt. Nicolas Cochin

Figure 13.2 Although both of these are 36-point typefaces, the difference in their design makes one appear smaller. The black square represents the x-height (portion of body used for center body letters).

REVERSE LEADING

Figure 13.3 Reverse leading can pull all-cap lines together

Take stock in America.

Figure 13.4 Using some of the blank space on the body reserved for ascenders or descenders can tighten up lines in capitals and lowercase, sometimes with interesting results, including better visual spacing.

Figure 13.5 This paragraph has been set with three different kinds of word and letterspacing: normal, plus one unit, and minus one unit.

Figure 13.6 A portion of a line gauge, the printer's ruler used to measure type size and other dimensions of printing. The top line is in inches and fractions; the bottom line is in picas, subdivided into nonpareils (6 points).

newcomer should keep the point of separation in mind because procedures for handling body type differs from those for display type. These differences are pointed out as they arise in later discussions.

One must also be aware of a couple of tricks now available in typography and mentioned earlier: *reverse leading* and *plus or minus letterspacing.* Many photocomposition machines provide the opportunity for overlapping lines of type by exposing a line of type, then backing up and exposing another line in part of the space used for the first line, as in figure 13.3.

In many situations, reverse leading can provide better visual spacing for lines of display type (figure 13.4). For body type sizes, the area being occupied by type can be enlarged or reduced somewhat by having type characters crowded closer together or moved slightly apart. This *plus or minus word and letterspacing* often can be done without being apparent to readers. Various examples of this technique are shown in figure 13.5. At this writing, there is no research to indicate what effect the technique has on reading ease.

The Pica and the Em

The length of lines of type is expressed in *picas,* a unit equal to 1/6th inch, or 12 points. Printers' rulers, called *line gauges,* are a must for editors because they are marked off in picas, which are also used for expressing all other measurements used in printing: margins, column width, page size, and so on. A portion of a line gauge is shown in figure 13.6. Note that inches are shown on one edge and picas on the other; the smaller division within the pica represents 6 points.

Plus or minus word and letter spacing are alternatives to normal spacing. This paragraph has been set in normal, plus one, and minus one to illustrate the different results. Spacing variations also available include plus or minus one-half unit. Units are based on the em and are usually one-eighteenth of an em. Note the effect of plus or minus letterspacing on total space in this example. In large amounts of body copy, spacing variation can be responsible for enlarging or reducing space demand about 5 percent in each direction.

Plus or minus word and letter spacing are alternatives to normal spacing. This paragraph has been set in normal, plus one, and minus one to illustrate the different results. Spacing variations also available include plus or minus one-half unit. Units are based on the em and are usually one-eighteenth of an em. Note the effect of plus or minus letterspacing on total space in this example. In large amounts of body copy, spacing variation can be responsible for enlarging or reducing space demand about 5 percent in each direction.

Plus or minus word and letter spacing are alternatives to normal spacing. This paragraph has been set in normal, plus one, and minus one to illustrate the different results. Spacing variations also available include plus or minus one-half unit. Units are based on the em and are usually one-eighteenth of an em. Note the effect of plus or minus letterspacing on total space in this example. In large amounts of body copy, spacing variation can be responsible for enlarging or reducing space demand about 5 percent in each direction.

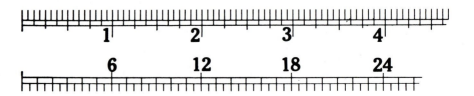

An *em* is a unit of measure that varies with the type size being used, because it is a square in the type size. That is, an em in 9-point type is 9 points wide, an em in 10-point type is 10 points wide, and so on. For magazine editors, the main exposure to the term is in line spacing (the standard paragraph indention is an em) and when it is used imprecisely as a synonym for a pica (a 12-point square).

The Many Faces of Type

Type has many faces, many personalities. Letter forms range from simple to highly ornate, with thousands of variations available. Many basic type designs came into existence because they were copies of the work of calligraphers of a particular time and place. Others have been designed in modern times to achieve a mood or accomplish a specialized objective.

To bring a feeling of order to the study and use of type, these variations are classified first in broad *groups,* then *subgroups, families, family variations,* and *fonts.* A quick look at basic letterforms will bring these divisions into perspective.

Recall that typefaces rest on a body, which determines their size. Looking again at figure 13.1, we can see that letters rest on a base line, with letters with *ascenders* (such as b, d, f) and capital letters (upper case) rising to the top of the body. Letters with *descenders* (such as g and y) reach to the bottom of the body. Basic letters (such as a, c, e) use only the center portion of the body. Noncapitals are called *lower case* to contrast them with capitals.

The Gothic Group

To form all letters of our alphabet in uppercase and lowercase, only basic, uniform strokes are needed (figure 13.7). Such letters are *monotonal,* meaning no variation in tone that could be created by changes in thickness of strokes, and *skeletal,* meaning there are no unessential strokes. Faces of this type are usually called *Gothic* or *sans serif.* The latter designation means "without serif"; a serif is a short stroke running counter to the main stroke of a letter. By adding monotonal serif (figure 13.8) we can create a type design usually called *square serif Gothic.* These two subgroups form a basic group with many variations, but all with a simple, strong character that makes them suitable for many uses.

The Roman Group

Letters designed with variations in the thickness of the strokes and distinct serifs (figure 13.9) form a group called *Roman,* using a letterform first used in the calligraphy of ancient Rome. The earlier Roman types, now called *Oldstyle,* were created with more angular strokes and less variation in thickness of strokes than those used for *modern Roman* faces (figure 13.10). Great variations in thickness of strokes, as well as thin, right-angle serifs are the hallmarks of modern Romans.

abcdefghijklmnopqrstuvwx
yz&?! ABCDEFGHIJKLMN
OPQRSTUVWXYZ $12345

Figure 13.7 The lack of unessential strokes and any substantial variation in thickness of strokes are characteristics of sans serif Gothic faces. Shown here is 30-point Futura Medium.

abcdefghijklmnopqrstuvw
ABCDEFGHIJKLMNOPQR
STUVWXYZ $1234567890

Figure 13.8 This is 24-point Karnak, a square serif Gothic.

Script and Cursive

The flowing letters common to handwriting are produced in type through many script and cursive faces (figure 13.11). Script types generally resemble the precise, formal handwriting typical of a former era. Their letters are designed to join. Cursives, as a rule, are more informal, resembling hand lettering more than handwriting. Their letters do not join.

Text (Black Letter or Old English)

The rather specialized types forming a group called Text, Black Letter, or Old English are ornate and patterned after the calligraphy of German monks (figure 13.12). This group provided the pattern for typefaces manufactured by the inventor of movable type, Johann Gutenberg. Unnecessary and duplicate strokes, totally unessential for letter formation, are the primary characteristics of this group of typefaces.

Figure 13.9 The Roman group is characterized by serifs and variations in stroke thickness. This 30-point Weiss Roman has moderate changes in stroke thickness, angular stroke thickness, angular stroke endings, and serifs that round into the stroke. These are common with Oldstyle Romans.

Figure 13.10 The stroke variation in this 30-point Bodoni, a modern Roman, is much greater than those of the Weiss. Note the hairline quality of some strokes. Serifs are thin and straight, not bracketed into the main stroke.

Figure 13.11 This 30-point Commercial Script (a) differs from the 24-point Mayfair Cursive (b) in that the letters join in the Script. The Script is also somewhat more formal.

Figure 13.12 This Engraver's Old English is typical of the Text group, used primarily for religious and related materials.

abcdefghijklmnopqrst ABC
DEFHIJKLMNO $1234567

abcdefghijklmnopqr ABCDE
FGHIJKLMNOPQ $1234567

abcdefghijklmnopqrstuvwxyz
ABCDEFGHIJKLMNO
PQRSTUVWXYZ&?!
(a)

abcdefghijklmnopqrstuvwxyz $1234567890
ABCDEFGHIJKLMNOPQ!?
(b)

abcdefghijklmnopqrstuvwxyz
ABCDEFGHIJKLMNOP
QRSTUVWXYZ $12345678

Novelty

The preceding four groups came into existence as reflections of the handwork that antedated typography. Many other faces have been created to perform a special task or create a novel impression. These faces are without limit, as figure 13.13 should suggest; each year, new faces are added to what appears to be an endless list. Types to suggest age, circus posters, the gay-nineties era, computers, Broadway, and the like provide special designs for virtually every mood or purpose.

Type Families

Within each group, there are smaller groups of type that so closely resemble each other that, if they were humans, they would likely come from the same family. These types are given a familial name and are said to be from the same family. Their names often are those of a designer, such as Bodoni, Garamond, and Zapf; they may also show the intended purpose, such as Commercial Script, News Gothic, or Dom Casual.

Just as with human families, type families have different personalities within them. Human families have members that are tall and short, fat and thin, upright and bent-over. Typefaces present a parallel in that they can vary in size, posture,

Figure 13.13 A few Novelty faces from a Zipatone, Inc., catalog illustrate the wide range of specialty types available from printers and suppliers.

Futura Light

Futura Light Italic

Futura Medium

Futura Medium Italic

Futura Medium Condensed

Futura Medium Condensed Italic

Futura Demibold

Futura Demibold Italic

Futura Bold

Futura Bold Italic

Futura Bold Condensed

Futura Bold Condensed Italic

Futura Extrabold

Futura Extrabold Italic

Futura Extrabold Condensed

Futura Extrabold Condensed Italic

FUTURA INLINE

Futura Display

Figure 13.14 These variations in the Futura family are typical of those usually available. Missing from this assortment are the extended variations that are often offered in a family.

weight, and width. Unlimited sizes and letter variations for type families are available if cathode ray tube typesetters are being used. Slanting, expanding, and constricting of letter forms are easily achieved with such typesetters. However, ordinarily, the family variations are limited to four, and the normally available sizes are 5½-, 6-, 7-, 8-, 9-, 10-, 11-, and 12-point for body types and 14-, 18-, 24-, 30-, 36-, 42-, 48-, 60-, and 72-point for display sizes.

For the Roman and Gothic groups, a standard family variation is posture, with the normal upright posture labeled as *roman* (note the absence of a capital) and the sloping posture called *italic* (figure 13.14).

The thickness of stroke—the resultant weight or darkness of a letter—can vary while other familial characteristics are present. Light, medium, and bold are basic for most faces, and extra bold variations are common also.

When the stroke and serif characteristics of a typeface remain constant, but the relationship of height to width is changed, the type is still in the same family. Common variations range from condensed (narrow width) to expanded (more than normal width).

Letters in *outline* are also available in some families or as special designs.

Type Fonts

A *font* of type is one size of one branch of one family, such as 8-point Bodoni Italic. Therefore, type selection eventually must come down to the font, for only when they know what specific size, branch, and family are desired can printers set type to a customer's satisfaction. The selection of the type font, plus other factors associated with type choice, is an important editorial function.

Type Selection and Use

"Types are meant for reading," and the selection and use of type should always be carried out with that maxim in mind. There are, however, substantial differences between what is expected of type in body sizes and large quantities and what is expected of display type in small quantities.

Hints on the Use of Body Type

Type legibility—its reading ease—is the primary factor in the selection and use of body types. For the body of articles throughout any magazine, the use of a typeface that is in any way difficult to read would be an unpardonable sin. Presenting what would be a good typeface in such a way that reading ease is impaired is equally deplorable. Research into body type selection has been ample enough to give us some general maxims that are useful:

1. Roman typefaces, either modern or Oldstyle, have the edge over all other type styles when it comes to reading ease. The only competitor is the Gothic group and some specialty types that have been designed to be read easily. Some faces with variation in stroke width but without serifs are reasonable choices.
2. Upright (roman) posture is better than italic. Italic is an excellent contrast choice for small quantities but should be avoided when the basic body type is being selected.
3. Medium weight and width are usually the more efficient selections. Designers place primary emphasis on their mediums; the extremes are then designed for special purposes. Bold types are useful for contrast but also are effective for older and younger readers. Condensed widths provide benefits in space use.

The factors involved in the use of type can influence the ease of reading as much as the actual selection. Some accepted principles involving type use include

1. White space is so important that most typefaces can be improved with a point or two of leading between lines. Margins and white space between columns must also be adequate to provide contrast to type. Nonwhite backgrounds should be used with care so that they provide adequate contrast.

2. Type size must be correlated with line length, but larger sizes are of benefit for older and younger readers. For magazines, 9- and 10-point sizes provide a happy compromise between the desire to make material as legible as possible and the necessity to put as much material as possible into restricted spaces. They also correlate well with common line lengths. A common rule of thumb for legible maximums of line lengths places the shortest line length at the length of one lowercase alphabet and the longest at two alphabets. The alphabet of 10-point Bodoni Book type in figure 13.15 measures 10 picas; therefore, line lengths should be no less than 10 picas and no more than 20 picas. This rule of thumb is especially good because it takes into account the setting characteristics of the individual typeface. Another guide suggests that the minimum line length should be, in picas, the same number as the point size (8-point type minimum length would be 8 picas, the 10-point type minimum line length would be 10 picas), and the maximum should be double that figure. In both cases, the midpoint represents the optimum line length. Also, the maximum in both cases can be enlarged a pica for each point of leading. Line length importance should not be underestimated when considering type legibility; anyone can see enough bad examples in print to see how difficult reading is when lines are extremely long or extremely short. The selection of type size also must be related directly to its design. If one were to analyze the various typefaces, it would be noted that there is a wide variety of perceived size impressions that can be gotten from different types that are all actually of the same size. This fact stems from the differences in design relative to the x-height. Compare the letter x in one 10-point face (Century, for example) with another (Baskerville) and you will detect quite a size difference (figure 13.16). Century looks much larger than Baskerville because the ascenders and descenders in Baskerville are so long, leaving less vertical space for the x-height. One must view a sample consisting of at least a paragraph or two before being able to logically settle on size and style. Better yet, seeing potential types in use in other magazines gives one a better sample. Viewing a sample containing a reasonable amount of type also permits one to detect any tone or feeling the type may seem to create when it is used in quantity. Such words as *coarse, fine,* and *rough* often come into the minds of designers as they look at a type area, because the overall pattern created by a typeface can form an impression. This impression should be considered as the type design is selected.

3. The setting of type in *justified* columns (each line flush to the left and flush to the right) seems to have no legibility benefit over setting *ragged right* (figure 13.17). Cost may help make the decision between the two; some computerized systems can produce type that is hyphenated and justified (h&j) more efficiently than ragged right because they are programmed to do so; in other instances, the elimination of h&j may be more efficient.

4. Capitals and lowercase obviously are more legible than all capitals; consequently, one doesn't see magazines with body type in all capitals.

Hints on the Use of Display Type

Although reading ease is an important factor in the selection and use of display type, the *suitability* of the type to its subject and audience is perhaps even more important. The fact that display type is often used as an attention-getter also makes a face's ability to carry out that function an important factor. Both of these points— suitability of the typeface to its subject and its capability to attract attention—are always in editors' minds as they use display type to create strong titles.

The first step in creating an effective visual presentation for titles is to allow sufficient space for them. Titles demand large amounts of white space, and the allowance of a third to a full page of space for a title is routine (see figure 13.18); anything less permits only a prosaic headline treatment.

The second step is to give type adequate size for attracting attention. Whereas a news headline as large as 72 points is rare, the type in magazine titles routinely exceeds that size. Especially in situations in which one or two key words with abundant white space are given primary responsibility for luring readers, those key words should get heavy display (see figure 13.19).

abcdefghijklmnopqrstuvwxyz

Figure 13.15 This lowercase alphabet in 10-point Bodoni Book represents a minimum line length for that size and face; double this length would be the maximum unless leading is used.

This is 10-point Century type. It has a relatively large x-height and, consequently, tends to need some leading between lines. The ascenders and descenders of letters in Century tend to be shorter than in many other types.

This is 10-point Baskerville type. It is designed to have a smaller x-height and longer ascenders and descenders. It looks smaller because of its design and seems to have adequate white space between lines.

Figure 13.16 Ten-point Century and 10-point Baskerville.

Volenikowa, a 39-year-old mill operator, fled with her family from their native Czechoslovakia during the Soviet invasion of Prague in the Spring of 1969. "We fled because we did not want to live like slaves," says Volenikowa. She went to work in the factory rather than continuing her career as a nurse because she felt that an error on her part resulting from language problems would be less serious in the shop than in a hospital.

Having never been in a factory before, Volenikowa had a lot of adjusting to do.

It is not only space, but time which dramatizes Iowa: In open prairie landscape, in its wooded valleys along its many streams, in its pure air (which can still burn you in summer and blast you in winter), its quiet small towns, its belief in hard work and in decency to your neighbor, its willingness to be taxed for top-level education, its cheerful conviction (in spite of some evidence to the contrary) that work and honesty will always produce the good life, Iowa keeps the good qualities of the 19th century. In excellence of its industries, which are,

Figure 13.17 Justified type (top) and ragged right (bottom).

Figure 13.18 Titles should be given ample white space for contrast. (Courtesy *Sun Magazine,* Sun Company Inc., and *The Quill.*)

The third step is to dress titles typographically so they fit the occasion and create the desired impression. Type can speak, not only through the words it conveys, but also through its form.

It is worth reemphasizing that typefaces can reflect moods and motifs. Some types are delicate; some are strong. Some are modern; others are old-fashioned. Some have class and tone; others are brash and bold. Some are formal, others informal. Some are masculine; some are feminine. If a typeface doesn't exist to match a purpose, designers can create such a face. For complete collections of these faces, see a good type specimen catalog from a large type composition company, or look at catalogs of graphics products suppliers, such as Zipatone, Chartpak, Formatt, and Prestype (figure 13.13 showed a few of these faces).

When used most skillfully, type form can speak in harmony with its message, reiterating or reinforcing its verbal message. Particularly when assisted by artwork, the typography of a magazine article title can be as much a part of the message as the words themselves. Figure 13.20 shows this principle in practice; in each case, a graphic aspect of the title has been designed to say visually what the words are saying verbally.

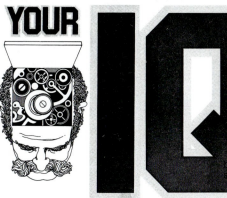

Figure 13.19 Large sizes of display type—much larger than those used by newspapers—are often used in magazine titles. (Courtesy *Sojourners* Magazine, and *Measure*, Hewlett-Packard Company.)

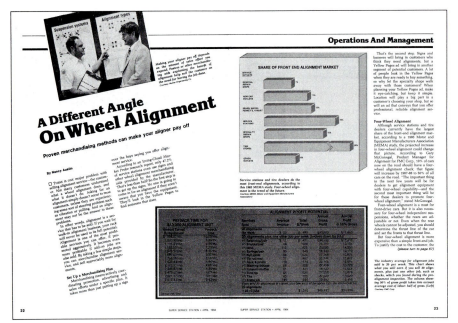

Figure 13.20 Type can be made to portray graphically the words of a title. (Courtesy *Aramco World* and *Super Service Station*.)

Variations in size and style of display type can also create necessary emphasis for certain portions of titles. For example, one word can be made to stand out if it is given italic posture and a size that is greater than that used for other words. Readers only pause for a few seconds as they view magazine pages, and emphasis for a key noun or gerund in a phrase or sentence in a title can make the difference in capturing greater interest. Irregular patterns of display type, visually interesting because of the shapes they form, can also stimulate interest. Figures 13.21 and 13.22 show these principles in practice.

The final question to be answered when selecting and using display type for article titles is, Where should the title be placed? The answer is simple: *anywhere*. Whether it is for a page, a two-page spread, or a fraction of a page, the placement of a title should be permitted to follow the dictates of attractive and efficient design, as discussed later in chapter 16.

Figure 13.21 Variations in size and style of display type can create necessary emphasis for certain portions of titles. (Courtesy *America Magazine*, reprinted with permission from the Fall 1982 *America*, © 1982 by 13–30 Corporation, 505 Market St., Knoxville, TN 37902, and *American Film Magazine*.)

Some Final Hints

Regarding the design and placement of titles, a final word of caution is in order. Remember that titles, by their nature, are way stations for the reader, not destination points. Hence, a basic guideline dictates that title type selection and placement cannot confuse the reader on the way to the next way station. It would be foolish to get a reader's attention only to lose it because he or she does not know where to proceed after reading the title or is not encouraged to continue because of poor type selection. In all aspects of creating titles, from rhetoric to typography, success is finally measured in how high a percentage of readers are stopped, and then encouraged to read on. Attempts to be "different" with type can create bizarre and undesirable results. The suitability of a typeface for a particular purpose should suggest itself and not be forced. Straining for special effects can be worse than monotonous type dress. Therefore, caution should be used when selecting types for mood and character. Don't create a hodge-podge of faces; chaos results.

Figure 13.22 Words grouped to form irregular shapes and patterns are a characteristic of the use of display type in magazines. (Courtesy *Aide Magazine* and *The Elks Magazine*.)

A reiteration of the maxim that "type was made for reading" is also in order. Graphic designers rarely use type upside down, because that obviously creates a problem for a reader. Many will, however, use type on its side or in other abnormal patterns that are also difficult to read. Readers read from left to right, and type should be displayed in that fashion. Also, avoid using delicate faces on textured papers; hairlines are lost on rough papers.

Readers are also accustomed to the contrast of black on white for type on paper, and variations should be used with care. Type can be reversed to be white on black or dark gray; it can also be used in color on gray or in black on color. Such uses can be effective, but care must always be exercised, lest the reader find the presentation too difficult to read and move on to other things. All type decisions should be made with the reader in mind.

Images: A Visual Typography

MODERN magazines exist in a visual age. With television in the forefront, the mass media have been converting Americans from *readers* to *viewers* who rely on images for their receipt of information and entertainment. This reliance on images seems destined to increase.

Image communication seems to be everywhere, not just bouncing across the television tube. Highway signs, once almost totally verbal, have been revised to become almost entirely pictographic. Textbooks at all levels have changed from sparsely illustrated word collections to visual delights, loaded with helpful illustrations, and magazines have come to rely more and more on illustrations to get their particular communication jobs done.

As a matter of fact, one might even go as far as to paraphrase Marshall McLuhan and say that for magazine editors "the image is the message." Magazine editors of the present and the future must be expert in the art of communicating by means of pictures or other images, because readership and understanding often depend on the visual aspects of a presentation. The skillful wedding of words with illustrations for effective communication has long been admired and sought; now the increased passivity of the recipients of communications simply makes the expert use of illustrations even more important.

Types of Illustrations

The photograph is undoubtedly the leading image form for magazines, but the term *images* was deliberately introduced here to make the point that all forms of illustrations have a place on magazine pages. Therefore, in this chapter, we are concerned with all types of artists' drawings—from the simplest line drawing in pencil or ink to the most beautiful watercolors or oil paintings. We also include all kinds of photographic illustrations, from black and white, through duotones and process color, to the elaborate line conversions or other gimmicks involving the photograph. Charts, bar graphs, maps, or any other illustrative devices are also included.

The Editor and the Illustrator

Although editors may have had some direct experience with photography or other illustrations, they are usually not as skilled or talented in these areas as the professionals who work for them. For that reason, the successful relationship begins with a feeling of mutual respect between the editor and the illustrators that gives the illustrators maximum creative freedom. Editors, with their knowledge of reader interest and their grasp of a magazine's direction, can and should make assignments and evaluate the work of their photographers and artists. However, once editors have established the guidelines for the work they want done, they should let the talent of their illustrators take over for the execution of an assignment. Otherwise, the true potential of the artist cannot be realized; all editors certainly want their photographers and illustrators to produce something better than what they, themselves, could produce. They want something that demonstrates the special talents for which they are paying.

Toward that end, an editor should provide adequate support in time and money. For example, it is unwise to seriously limit a photographer's film and supplies budget, especially if salary or travel expenses for an assignment are substantial. The same is true of drawing variations; the wider the selection from which to choose, the better the final quality. Ideally, the illustrator should provide full input during the selection process, also. Final selection must rest with the editor, but cooperative effort from the illustrator and the art director should enter the selection process.

Functions of Illustrations

Illustrations should be evaluated according to their functions. The photograph or other illustration is usually expected to accomplish one or more of these five purposes: (1) attract attention, (2) illustrate a point made in text, (3) tell a story itself with the aid of only a caption, (4) tell a story in sequence with other illustrations, and (5) give visual relief to a design.

Attracting Attention

The great picture magazines of the 1930s through the 1960s set the style for the use of a dominant picture as the key element on a page or on a two-page spread, and designers and editors have been adapting that idea ever since. In trying to tell stories with pictures, these magazines needed key or *lede* pictures, just as text articles needed strong beginnings. These pictures were selected to symbolize an article's theme and were given prominent position and size. Their role was to stop the readers' eyes in the hope that they would continue to read into the caption, title, and text (figure 14.1). A quick glance at a stack of contemporary magazines also provides examples of how large photos are used to attract attention to a magazine's cover.

Photos are not alone in working to attract attention. Other kinds of illustrations are used for the same purpose. In the preceding chapter, the point was made that titles should be treated as illustrations. Illustrations can also be treated as titles (as in figures 14.2 through 14.4). Actually, the term *title illustration* is the most accurate description of the lede photos mentioned earlier. Usually working in combination with a few words, illustrations frequently play the title role in magazines.

Any photo or drawing assigned this top billing should be given adequate display to perform its attention-getting task by means of greater magnitude, added color, or a special finish (such as outlining).

Illustrating a Point

The simplest role of the illustration is typified by the head-and-shoulder portrait, the "mug shot" as it is called. An article is about a person or perhaps just mentions a name, and the illustration shows readers what the person looks like, an assignment for which words alone seem inadequate. In the case of travel articles, the photographs or drawings may show what a place looks like, again filling in where words lack capability.

Illustrations take on increased importance when they are used to explain a textual point involving action; an illustration that shows a wood carver's technique with a cutting instrument, as well as how the carver looks, naturally carries a greater responsibility.

Charts, diagrams, bar graphs, maps, and other visual devices are especially effective in explanation situations (see figure 14.5). Figures are confusing, and reinforcement with iconistic devices is often needed by readers trying to grasp statistical material.

The familiar pie chart, however, has become trite because it has been so effective in such explanation situations. Editors of company magazines, trying to give meaning to budgets and annual reports, have used pie charts to the point of indigestion.

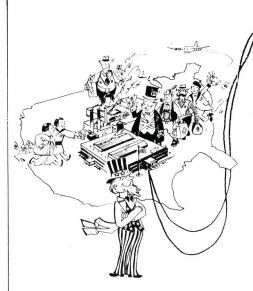

Figure 14.1 A photo or another illustration can actually be the lede of a magazine article. Here, editors used reproductions, in color, of colorful paints and quilts to perform the lede role in admirable fashion. (Courtesy *Sun Magazine,* Sun Company, Inc., and *Country Home,* © Meredith Corporation, 1983, all rights reserved.)

Figure 14.2 Illustrations can serve as the major element of titles. (Courtesy *BFG Tempo.*)

COAL?

DO AMERICANS USE COAL ?

Yes, slowly but surely, coal is inching its way up as a source of energy in the United States

FOR CENTURIES, coal and energy were virtually synonymous words. Prior to World War II, when you wanted to heat a building, boil water for steam, or smelt metals from ores, you used coal as fuel.

Even after the advent of petroleum in 1859 and the discovery of such large oil fields as Spindletop in 1901, coal continued to serve as America's basic fuel. In 1920, for example, two-thirds of the nation's energy came from coal.

But by 1945, coal's share of energy production had slumped to less than half of the total. By 1960, it had fallen to less than half of that. Today, coal supplies a mere fifth of the energy that America consumes. And even that seems to surprise many citizens.

"Coal?" they ask. "Do modern Americans actually use coal?"

You bet they do. Depending on where you live and work, you may consume a bit of coal every time you flip on a light. Your factory or office may have switched to coal without your knowing it. In some regions, you may even have a neighbor or friend who has switched to coal to heat his home.

It is a tradition almost as old as civilization. Before the birth of Christ, the people of China heated with coal. A thousand years ago the Hopis and other American Indians mined coal for parching corn and firing pottery. European coal mining dates to A.D. 1200. In the American Colonies coal mainly gained importance as a source of coke essential in casting cannons and manufacturing munitions.

Soon, however, the country's burgeoning rail network triggered a massive change from wood to coal for fuel. Coal-fired locomotives could travel farther on a load of coal; the best-quality coal generated four times as much heat as the same weight of top-grade wood. Trees were naturally scarce in the vast plains and deserts of the West, and many railroads found coal deposits near their tracks.

Steelmaking affirmed coal's ascendancy in the 1850s. America's population doubled between 1880 and 1918. The effect was a quadrupling of energy demand. Coal reigned as the darling of the industrial revolution, but the romance began to wane as trucking challenged railroads' preeminence in transportation in the 1920s. In the 1930s, the railroads themselves started switching to diesel locomotives. Utilities turned increasingly to hydroelectric or petroleum-fueled generating plants to meet growth in demand for electricity. Long-distance pipelines made natural gas more widely available, and its convenience cut sharply into demand for coal for home heating and other uses. Even in Appalachian coal country, the basement coal bin became as obsolete as the backyard woodshed.

By the end of World War II, coal had been replaced as the country's dominant source of energy by petroleum — oil and gas. Coal's problems were compounded in 1954 when federal controls were applied to wellhead prices of natural gas. This distortion of the free market eroded the cost advantage that coal still enjoyed in some uses and in some geographic areas.

Then came the Arab oil embargo in 1973-1974, accelerating petroleum costs, declining domestic reserves of oil and gas, and energy shortages. Suddenly, coal began to look good again to a nation seeking alternative energy sources.

And coal offers a plentiful alternative. By good fortune, coal constitutes America's most abundant fossil fuel. About 85 percent of the world's known coal deposits are found in only three countries: China, Russia, and the United States. More than one-fourth of all the reserves lie within the borders of the U.S., the "Middle East" of coal. At the present rate of use, this country has enough coal to last several centuries.

Yet, despite coal's many advantages — abundance, wide distribution, and versatility — few natural resources over the years have borne so many public relations woes. Senior Americans may remember how it was in earlier days when coal was the principal home fuel . . . the creaky coal wagon and later the dump truck . . . the billow of dust as the coal thundered down the chute . . . Dad banking the furnace at midnight . . . the kids hauling out the ashes . . . Mom fetching a scuttle for her kitchen stove. An early edition of Fannie Farmer's cookbook devoted much of a chapter to the intricacies of adjusting grates and dampers: "If these rules are not followed, ashes will fly all over the room," she admonished.

Middle-aged Americans likewise recall newsreel scenes of miners protesting working conditions and pay scales, of feisty union boss John L. Lewis fighting for their cause, and of political leaders threatening to seize the mines.

Some uncomplimentary and controversial public perceptions of the coal industry persist today. Certain environmentalists depict coal as a polluter of air and water and ravager of soil. Anticoal demonstrators climb smokestacks, picket plants, grab headlines, and file lawsuits. Concerns range from human health to the survival of the Earth as we know it. In the extreme, a few even advocate that Americans abstain from using coal altogether.

Given coal's blemished past, is this a valid modern view?

Consider More than half of U.S. coal today is recovered by surface mining. Draglines and power shovels remove overburden to extract coal, after which the

23

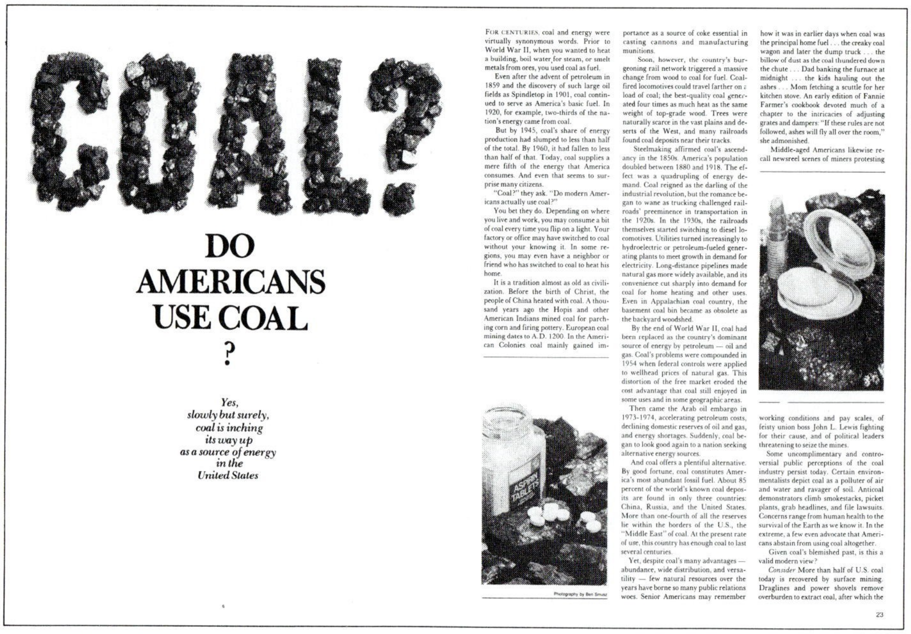

Figure 14.3 An illustration is the major element of this title. (Courtesy *Exxon USA.*)

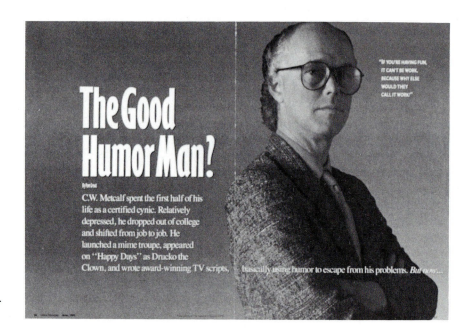

Figure 14.4 Two-page spreads displaying only a large photograph with a title and subtitle, no text, are becoming common because of their attention-getting power. (Courtesy *USAir Magazine.*)

Sometimes simple bar graphs can do a job well. However, most effective in many situations is the use of a pictorial symbol to represent large quantities, such as one apple to represent each thousand bushels of production in a specific area. With such self-explanatory symbols, an illustration can get meaning across more quickly and with fewer words of explanation than might be needed with a chart or bar graph. Four apples in a row contrasted to one apple, for instance, drives home a four to one ratio of apple production better than a 4-inch bar next to a 1-inch bar. A state map showing apple production by counties with such a pictograph is probably as concise and effective a device as one can find for explaining the pertinent figures.

For pictographs, the variation in the size of an object is less effective and more confusing than a variation in the number of objects. One can readily see difficulties that could arise from using an apple four times as large as another apple to show production differences. Does the bigger apple mean that better or bigger apples are being produced? Is it four or five times as large as the smaller one? Also, care should be taken to avoid trying to show too much in a single pictograph; a single comparison can be made quickly and accurately, but a pictograph becomes confusing when it is used in more complex situations.

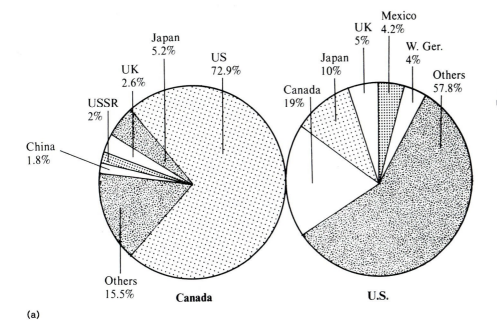

(a)

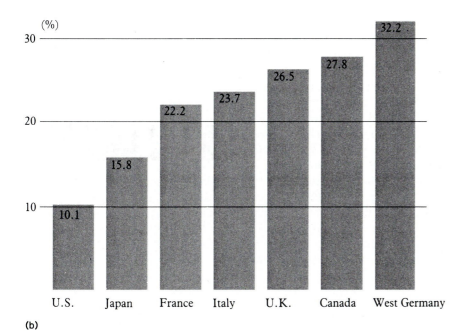

(b)

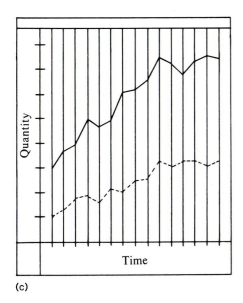

(c)

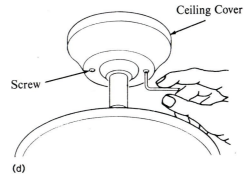

(d)

Figure 14.5 Charts and diagrams can serve useful explanatory roles: (a) pie charts show relative sizes of portions of a whole; (b) bar charts and pictographs show comparative amounts; (c) line graphs show trends over time; and (d) schematic diagrams can show how to carry out complex tasks.

Skillful editing requires thorough analysis of the illustrative needs of any article. What points call for an image to explain them? What type of illustration will make the point most effectively? What kind of production treatment, such as added color, will an illustration need for clarity? These questions should be carefully considered while all verbal material is being processed.

Telling a Story with Only a Caption

Magazine readers have been well trained by way of heavy exposure to cartoons to get a message from a single illustration with only a minimum of verbal explanation. One drawing or one photograph (witness the photo of a child with a disability and a caption, "Buy Easter Seals") can effectively tell a story or arouse a reader's emotions. A wise editor recognizes these single-image situations and resists any impulse to add unnecessary text or superfluous illustrations that can actually detract from the impact that one illustration can give.

However, the possibility of a single photograph telling a story or making a point without the aid of any words is so rare as to merit elimination from the list of possibilities. If for no other reason, a few words in a caption are needed to reinforce what the readers are convinced that the image is telling them. Readers translate a graphic image into a verbal one, and they need reassurance that their translation is accurate. The caption gives them this reassurance.

Telling a Story in Sequence

The use of a series of pictures to tell a story, aided only by a minimum of words, has been a common and effective magazine technique since the birth of the picture magazines in the 1930s.

Life and *Look,* the two giant general picture magazines, made the picture story a dominant form, as their spectacular successes created a new approach, called photojournalism, and a new breed of glamorous photojournalists. Then came the death of both the giants in the early seventies and some resultant speculation that perhaps the picture story was also dead, another casualty of the television invasion. Such speculation would appear to be short-sighted, however. As the discussion in earlier chapters of this text indicates, the overall decline of general magazines was based primarily on economic factors. Although the moving images of television must certainly have some ultimate influence on the uses of still photography, the picture story is alive and well.

One of the obvious uses of the picture story is in the "how to" area. One cannot imagine a more effective way of telling how to redecorate a room, remodel a home, or build a dune buggy than through a series of pictures. Neither is there a better way to take readers with you on a tour of a scenic attraction or to show the customer readers of a company magazine how a product is made. Regardless of the subject area of a magazine, whether it is a house and home, travel, customer relations, science and mechanics, or a specialized business interest, the picture story remains a viable form of effective communication. When the primary goal is to show readers something, rather than tell them, the illustration's role is dominant, and words are secondary. In all cases, however, success comes through a skillful merging of both.

The potential for telling a story through a series of drawings should not be overlooked. Long before the existence of picture magazines, Americans were avidly following their favorite comic strips, which are nothing more than stories told with a series of panels (drawings). In some instances, drawings can even be more effective than photographs; some "how to" instructions just don't lend themselves well to the eye of a camera, but they present little problem to the artist.

Perhaps the best example of the effectiveness of drawings in this sense is the "Wordless Workshop" of *Popular Science*. This feature has entertained and enlightened *Popular Science* readers by successfully showing how to complete a home workshop project without a single word of explanation.

Using Illustrations as Decoration

The weakest reason for using illustrations is for decoration, but there are instances when this motive alone provides adequate justification. Mention has already been made of the fact that we live in a visual age—that we have become passive receivers of communication. Reading does take effort, and editors must accept the idea that many readers have a low threshold of tolerance for masses of words. Consequently, situations do arise in which it is wise to relieve a verbal message with illustration, or perhaps provide an illustration only to decorate a page. In the first instance, the illustration is aimed to refresh the readers and help them continue reading. In the second instance, it is hoped that the attractiveness of the presentation will create a favorable impression. Just as Americans hang paintings and photos on their walls for aesthetic reasons only, so can editors use illustrations on their pages.

Obtaining Good Illustrations

Potential sources of good artwork and photographs are rather obvious: (1) a staff specialist, (2) a free-lancer, (3) a syndicate, (4) a public relations outlet, and (5) the editor. For most situations, these sources have been listed in the order of their desirability, but the wide range of magazine staffing capabilities makes it necessary to mention all of them. Some staffs are large and loaded with talent; others consist of an editor alone. Editors who can call on an art director and staff are fortunate; they can get skilled advice on the use of artwork, as well as on the preparation of finished illustrations. If they are assisted by one or more skilled photographers, they can assign the picture coverage they need and get professional results. In the foregoing situations, they can concentrate on sharpening their judgment of visual needs while using the supervisory qualities necessary for getting the most from talented members of their teams. They usually also have the option of buying the offerings of free-lancers in situations that are beyond staff capabilities or that present some financial advantages.

Many editors of smaller magazines must operate without full-time staff photographers or artists. They then prefer the output of skilled free-lancers whose services are contracted for as needs arise. Sometimes (as is the case with editors of some organizational publications), they must settle for the submission of amateurs and readers who might produce material meeting minimal publication standards.

Syndicates can provide photos and artwork that are technically of the highest quality. Material from these sources (often called canned material) usually has the disadvantage of not being tailored to a publication's need. Such stock material might turn up simultaneously in other periodicals, but there are situations in which even the prestigious newsmagazines, *Time* and *Newsweek,* rely on the output of the good photo syndicates.

Magazines of all sizes get photographs and, occasionally, other artwork from public relations outlets. Skillful public relations directors or agencies know the value of illustrations and provide media with technically excellent material. The problem of editorial judgment relating to the wise use of publicity material applies to illustrations as well as to verbal copy. Often, however, in small-staff, low-budget operations, good illustration becomes an "in" for the use of copy from public relations sources because the editor has few other illustrations available.

The last source of illustration is the editor. Although even Norman Cousins was known to use some of his own pictures while he was editing *Saturday Review,* editors usually lack the talent or experience to produce illustrations on a par with those of professionals. Editors are more inclined to recognize their shortcomings when it comes to drawings; they turn quickly to a free-lancer or a syndicate because the amateurishness of their work is instantly recognizable. Too often, however, they are willing to settle for their own photographs (everyone gets an occasional masterpiece), and the results are not at the quality level they should be. Unless they have come up from the photographers' ranks, editors should be as hesitant to use their own photos as they would their own etchings.

Selecting Illustrations

Whether they are selecting drawings or photographs, editors usually work with rough miniatures, usually produced in rough and miniature form so that large numbers can be made available with an economical expenditure of time and money. Free-lancers, when not operating on assignment, often produce finished work for selection, for obvious reasons.

The selection of drawings is somewhat easier than the selection of photographs because of the ability of the artist to modify miniatures to meet any desire of the editor. If none of the drawing miniatures represents exactly what is desired, the one that is closest to the desired image can be altered precisely to meet the need.

Photos can, of course, be modified to an extent. As editors view their proof sheets of scores of views, they can select a portion of any view for emphasis. In some instances, they may even be able to ask for further shootings to get exactly what they want. Usually, however, they are working within the limitation of what the photographer's skills brought through a camera's lens and onto film.

What Makes a Good Photograph?

Magazine editors, scanning their contact proofs with the aid of a magnifying glass, are searching for the photograph (or photographs) that will do a particular job for them. Consequently, they base their selection primarily on whether a photo performs its particular function. They also want a photo that is artistically pleasant, technically correct, and void of any unnecessary distraction.

Function

Photos are called on to do different things, from attracting attention to a magazine's cover to illustrating a particular point in a "how to" article. The essential basis for selection, therefore, is the ability of a photo to perform its function.

The photo that is to be pulled from a group and given the responsibility that goes with cover position must have some special qualities. It needs an instantaneous impact, an impact that carries with it some arousal of curiosity. It must have more communication ability than most photos; there may be a caption with it, but the photo must stand on its own sufficiently to cause a reader to direct attention to the magazine. It should be somewhat symbolic of the issue's best content. It ordinarily is large, so it should be especially good technically.

A photo that is to serve as the lede illustration of a major article needs many of the same qualities as a cover photo. It must get instant attention and be representative of the article's subject.

A photo that is to illustrate a point must clearly make its point. If it is to show how to apply a canvas canoe cover, its beauty is secondary to its clarity in showing how to hold the canvas and where to apply it first. The photo that is to stand alone with only a caption and title line must be selected with that function in mind; others with more impact but lacking storytelling completeness would have to be set aside.

In other words, content is king. It is the meaning that counts. Form and technical considerations, though important, cannot substitute for content.

Research and instinct have combined to give us some general guidelines for the kinds of content that have reader appeal: people, emotion, and action, with the emphasis on people. One need only think for a moment about favorite magazine photos, especially covers, to come up with examples of each of such appeals: babies, women, old men, famous, familiar, or unknown; tear-streaked faces, bright smiles, or a flag-draped coffin; sports action, crashes, animals in flight, and the much overdone use of glamour girls, bathing beauties, and other sex images.

Pictures without people, emotion, or action are rare because editors make a conscious effort to include one of the three elements in any photo; in most instances, the function of the photograph is accomplished more efficiently because of that effort.

Magazine photographers are artists in their own right. Consequently, they should be given the freedom and encouragement necessary to produce artistic photographs. An editor's primary responsibility to a photographer is to make it clearly known what functions a set of photos is to accomplish. Operating within the limit of function only, the photographer can proceed to turn out pictures that are artistically composed.

Good photographers see to it that their prints contain aesthetic beauty; then the role of the editor is simply to select those that best perform their editorial function. They must also, of course, be given the display they need for proper impact to avoid destroying their artistic quality through editing.

Technical Qualities

Photos for magazine publication must be suited for reproduction by the printing process a magazine uses. Some photos that would make excellent salon exhibits might be inadequate for magazine reproduction.

In general, photo prints intended for printing reproduction should contain a wide range of tones from very dark (but not black) to very light (but not white). Some salon prints are too dark and, after being screened and reduced to a smaller size, lose significant detail. Prints that tend to be contrasty, but with a full range of middle tones, provide the best copy for reproduction.

Engravers and lithographers also usually prefer glossy over matte finish, and they would rather reduce than enlarge from the original copy. Good craftspeople can work wonders even with small snapshots, but it pays to provide large (8″ × 10″ or 5″ × 7″), glossy prints when possible.

Improving Photographs

As they prepare photos for inclusion in a magazine, editors have two techniques at their disposal for improving them. One of these is *cropping;* the other is *retouching.*

Cropping is the figurative cutting away of portions of a photograph. Rather than use scissors or a razor blade to cut off a piece of the photo that contains disturbing background, the editor uses little marks to set off new dimensions (see figure 14.6).

The elimination of undesirable background is the most apparent improvement of photos through cropping, but not the only one. The placing of emphasis on the center of interest that results from effective cropping can improve a photograph immensely. Note, in figure 14.7, how tight cropping has added impact and "telling power" to the photo. By such cropping, the editor is doing the same thing for a photograph that good word editing does for a story—eliminating the nonessential, concentrating on the central theme, and adding to its impact by dramatic presentation.

Figure 14.6 Marks made with a grease pencil delineate the borders of the portion of a photo that is to be reproduced. These crop marks are placed to eliminate unnecessary detail and improve a photo.

Retouching, too, can improve photos by eliminating undesirable background; it can also contribute to an emphasis on a center of interest, though not so dramatically as cropping. Retouching is best left to the artist or engraver, but an editor should be aware of its potential (figure 14.8). Skillful airbrushing can change a harsh, disturbing background to a pleasing, neutral backdrop that highlights the central subject. Isolated blemishes can be removed, as in the case where the letters of a sign behind a portrait's subject seem to be coming out of the ears; the letters can be subdued or eliminated through retouching.

Some additional storytelling power can be added by retouching. The addition of dotted lines, arrows, or other identifying or directional marks often clarifies the point a photo is intended to make. In all retouching, however, the work should be done by a skilled artist, one who knows the capabilities of the reproduction process being used. Amateurish retouching is usually infinitely worse than none.

Color and Images

One of the most amazing things about printing is the fact that, using only black ink on white paper, images that are in full color around us can be communicated to readers. We look at pictures of blue skies and red roses and instantly recognize the sky and the roses for what they are. However, anyone viewing the status of the mass media today must be impressed with the increasing use of color for images. Newspapers such as *USA Today* and magazines of all kinds are loaded with more and more color. Television also has jumped from two-dimensional black-and-white to full, lifelike color. Along with the increased color has come the increased use of visuals called *graphics,* themselves in multicolors. The generation of such graphics via computer has helped increase their use and will continue to promote the use of more and better visual images.

Figure 14.7 After cropping, the photo in figure 14.6 does a much better job of emphasizing the central subject.

Figure 14.8 Airbrushing can make a reproduction better than the original photo by eliminating disturbing background elements and focusing attention on the central subject.

Functions of Color in Magazines

In magazines, color has many of the functions of illustrations, whether it is being used to form the illustration or is operating independently. At the beginning of this chapter, we pointed out the role of photos and other illustrations in attracting attention; color is at a par with photos in that regard.

Color in photos enhances their attention-getting value, of course, but color can also do the job alone. Color can assist in clarifying the message of a drawing; it can develop associations and psychological moods; and it can simply provide decoration.

Potential Use of Color

Virtually anything that can be put on a magazine page can be provided in color, including the body type. However, color for the sake of color alone often is worse than no color, so the successful use of color requires correlating the use with the objective. Body type in color, for example, is rarely as good as it is in black on white. Contrast is the source of reading and identification of images, and most colors pale in contrast to black for small type. The lighter the color, the less potential it has for use, and, in this case, a light color such as yellow is totally unusable. Brown on buff sometimes can be effective, as can blue or green on some shades of off-white, but, essentially, the use of color for body type is limited to occasional captions or other small areas that require special contrast with surrounding black-and-white areas.

Display type in color can be especially effective. Giving contrast to certain words in titles by using them in color can add to the attention value and communication value of the words.

Rules and borders in color can separate and draw attention to panels of text, such as staff listings on contents pages or author blurbs with or near title type.

Typographical *dingbats,* such as initial letters, stars, and bullets, can get special attention through color. Singling out items in a listing of a magazine's contents by placing a color check mark in front of them is an example of such usage.

Overprinting of type in color over illustrations provides a means of getting necessary contrast when black would not be suitable in many such situations.

The conversion of black-and-white photos into two-color reproductions, called *duotones,* sometimes can help set a mood for the illustration. Blue-and-black outside snow scenes, brown-and-black desert scenes, and green-and-black forest scenes are common uses for duotones. The effect is achieved simply by making two negative reproductions of the original photo, then putting one of them on the plate that applies black to paper, and the other on the plate carrying another color to paper.

The reproduction of original photographs or paintings in full color is perhaps the ultimate use of color in printing, but it is also very expensive. Original prints, paintings, and slides are reproduced in amazing fidelity in print. Called *process color* because it requires the process of separating colors out of the original before making separate plates to blend the primary colors again for full-color reproduction,

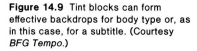

Figure 14.9 Tint blocks can form effective backdrops for body type or, as in this case, for a subtitle. (Courtesy *BFG Tempo.*)

Figure 14.10 Uniform tonal areas in 10 variations of tone can be obtained for little or no cost. The first block is 10 percent of full tone and the last is 100 percent (solid).

full color does more to enhance the presentation of pictorial images than anything else. When budgets permit, magazines use abundant amounts of process color because of its ability to show scenes exactly as we view them.

Color enhancement of graphs and charts can be especially helpful. Added dimensions can emerge from bar graphs and line charts when colors are added to black-and-white presentations.

Tint or tone blocks are also available for use in colors as well as black-and-white. As panels underlaying type (figure 14.9) or on their own, they can draw attention to what might otherwise be weaker areas of a page. Also effective in only black-and-white for some situations, tone blocks can be solid (meaning that they carry 100 percent of the tone to paper), or in any other percentage from 90 down to 10 percent, as shown in figure 14.10. Tone blocks have a singular advantage in that they are available at virtually no cost. Printers maintain a supply of film sheets that will yield the various percentages, and, unless the sheets must be specially cut, they can be used repeatedly.

Summary

All images, especially those in color, require special care in production and, in the case of process color, they can be a major budget item. Therefore, they should be used in a cost-effective and functional manner. Editors should be well grounded in the production aspects of image use presented in chapter 18.

15 Designing a Visual Personality

AS pointed out in earlier chapters, much of a magazine's success is determined by its ability to find its audience and to direct its objectives and content to that audience. It obviously follows that the design (the appearance) of a magazine must correlate closely with this editorial planning.

A magazine planned for an audience of doctors must be different in appearance from one planned for homemakers. One whose editorial thrust is to relate technical information would seek a different visual personality from one whose goal is to attract and hold the interest of professional and amateur bowlers from across the country. Scores of other examples could be cited, but the point is rather obvious that magazine design must be appropriate for its audience and objectives.

Some primary audience factors that must be considered are such basic reader characteristics as age, sex, occupation, and education level, plus an intangible—the probable intensity of interest. Although there has not been much research that is helpful in correlating magazine design with these audience factors, what has been done generally reinforces the intuitive practices developed by magazine designers over the years. The conservatism that comes with age is usually catered to with a layout approach that emphasizes stability and order. On the other hand, a periodical for teens suggests a design with action and "splash" loudly selling its wares. A magazine that caters to an audience of high educational level can take a classical approach to its basic design, and a women's fashion magazine that isn't visually fashionable itself certainly would be out of synchronization with its audience.

Intensity of interest is, perhaps, of most importance in layout planning. In this case, the importance of visual elements in a layout varies in inverse proportion to interest level. A physician or scholar seeking out vital information, thus having a maximum interest level, would find decorative visual elements unnecessary and perhaps even distracting. Periodical design in this instance is extremely low-key. However, for the magazine at the other extreme, such as one a company might distribute to its customers, a dynamic physical appearance might be essential to get reader attention, to keep readers interested in the material, and to create an impression of company dynamism.

Hence, the audience and objectives of a magazine tend to direct magazine managers toward decisions that set up a continuing visual personality for each magazine. The factors contributing to this visual personality are many. How much color and in what manner color should be used are two such contributors. So are the amount and type of illustration; an all-type scholarly journal has a different character from that of a sports pictorial weekly magazine. Even the type of paper selected (although production factors are important, too) is based on personality considerations. Magazines are sometimes even classed (as "pulps" or "slicks") according to paper stock because even so technical a decision helps set up a personality.

The layout personality of a magazine is a management decision because it is an element that must remain constant. To change from a picture magazine to one with a primary emphasis on text, from conservative layout practices to the bizarre, or from pulp paper to glossy stock are all changes that cannot be made from issue to issue. To change these and other basic elements of design is to change personality; changes in personality tend to destroy a magazine's identity with its readers and to reduce the readers' feelings of identification with *their* magazine. Such personality change decisions are primarily made by management; basic design elements are changed only after a careful analysis of the changes that might have occurred in the periodical's audience, or in the magazine's basic objectives.

Redesign: Same Face with New Makeup or a New Face?

As pointed out in previous chapters, audiences do change, and magazines must also change if they are to maintain their close relationship with their readers. Just as with humans, the age of its audience and the age of a magazine can dictate some changes in makeup for a magazine. Sometimes the changes are only minor and are made to keep up with the older readers, but sometimes bold changes to try to lure new readers are also needed. A little more rouge (color) may not be enough to cover the marks of age.

As the 1980s came to a close, several magazines underwent facelifts (figure 15.1), including *Esquire, Fortune, Glamour, Good Housekeeping, H. G., Mademoiselle, Ms.,* and *Self.* Writing in the *New York Times,* Debora Toth of *Graphic*

Figure 15.1 Changes in audience, editorial goals, or ownership prompt changes in visual personality, starting with covers, as these 1986 and 1988 covers of *Ms.* indicate. *Outdoor Life*'s redesign in 1991 was to give it "a distinctive new image," according to editor Vin Sparano. (Courtesy *Ms.* magazine and *Outdoor Life.*)

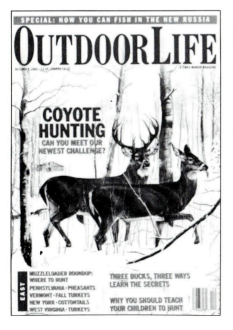

Arts Monthly described these changes and noted that, "while a redesign is almost always aimed at attracting new readers, a magazine must be careful not to alienate its old loyal readers and advertisers. There is a thin line between a redesign that works and one that goes too far and alienates readers. The magazine's editorial staff must know whom the magazine appeals to, who the audience is, and design the magazine accordingly." She also reported, however, that magazine industry experts say magazines should redesign at least every five years to stay current. The assumption must be, however, that the audiences will change significantly in that period.

The redesign of *Self* came about as it was reaching its 10th birthday and as it acquired a new editor, Anthea Disney. Since its founding, *Self*'s readers' median age had risen five years (from 24 to 29) and changes in content were in order as well as changes in design. Content changes included an expansion of coverage from health and fitness to include beauty and fashion and a short-story section. A slight change in the cover logo and an emphasis on soft, pastel colors were among the changes in appearance.

The *Ms.* redesign in 1988 also came under a new editor, as well as a new owner, Matilda Publications of Australia. At that time, *Ms.* was given a new size, a new logo, a more orderly design, and new editorial content designed to expand its audience. The new design (see figure 15.1) was short-lived, however, with continued losses forcing other changes by the end of the decade. A new owner, Lang Communications, closed it down in 1989 when slight circulation gains did not bring sufficient advertising support, but restarted it in 1990. With a return to its original feminist activist slant, a new bimonthly frequency, and the elimination of advertising, *Ms.* seemed to find its niche again in July of 1990, after a successful subscription campaign was followed by a sell-out of two press runs. Except for its logo, the *Ms.* for the 1990s had a different look, to a large degree resembling an opinion magazine. Excellent renewal rates for subscriptions and newsstand sales at a price large enough to keep the magazine in the black without advertising seemed to justify an optimistic outlook for success.

While the redesigns of the late 1980s seemed to be rooted in basic editorial changes, an increased emphasis on appearance alone signaled some changes in attitude toward design changes in the 1990s.

Trend Toward Redesign

The decade of the nineties has seemed to introduce an acceleration of emphasis on design and the trend toward redesign. With the increased emphasis on visual media—the move toward viewing rather than reading—even newsmagazines such as *Time* have redesigned to give more graphic power to their pages.

When *Time* introduced its new look in 1992 (figure 15.2), there seemed to be two forces at work enacting the change. One of these was the need to package its news and interpretation more dramatically to keep pace with the up-to-the-minute pictorial coverage of CNN and other broadcast outlets. The other was the new graphic and speed capabilities of desktop and electronic publishing as outlined in chapter 11.

In redefining the newsmagazine format, *Time*'s art director, Arthur Hochstein, along with other staff members and former art director, Walter Bernard, and his partner, Milton Glaser, used the capabilities of graphics computers to produce scores of test designs before making their ultimate decision.

As with all good design changes, the *Time* effort encompassed editorial structure as well as physical appearance. A well-organized table of contents page set the tone for new departmental divisions: "This Week," "Nation," "World," and others (figure 15.2). Overall, presentation was made stronger and organization became clearer.

Although *Time*'s change in appearance attracted much attention from the magazine industry, scores of other smaller magazines of every type also have been reporting design changes recently. Public relations magazines such as the *EMG Revue* and *The Edisonian,* both sponsored by Edison Menswear group, received new faces via Macintosh, *PageMaker,* and *Freehand* in 1990. The *MCI World* was changed the year before through the use of desktop technology. *Money* moved to what it

Figure 15.2 The new look for *Time* included a larger nameplate on the cover, new departments, and bolder visual treatments for inside pages. (Courtesy *Time*, The Weekly Newsmagazine.)

called a "fresh, elegant look" in 1990 to make it easier for readers to get information from its pages. Others include *Common Ground, The Journal of the Community Associations Institute; Electronics* of Penton Publishing; *Food & Wine; Seventeen; Re-Discover; Restaurant Hospitality; Redbook; McCall's; Texas Monthly; YM; Outdoor Life;* and *Harper's Bazaar.* No matter what the classification or the subject of their books, magazine publishers seem to be placing increased emphasis on design and visual personality.

It is important to reemphasize, however, that emphasis on design and on editorial quality go hand in hand. The winners of National Magazine Awards for design (*Vanity Fair,* 1992; *Condé Nast Traveler,* 1991; and *Esquire,* 1990) have been known for editorial leadership as well.

The reverse is also true. Although their awards were for content, other NMA winners obviously gave much attention to design. Note the strong type display, excellent page design, and effective use of a table in *Glamour's* 1992 prize-winning series on abortion and the visual power of *The American Lawyer's* winning series on enforcing drug laws.

Although the increased emphasis on design has resulted in the more frequent redesign of leading magazines, any "new look" should stay in place long enough to be viewed as a *constant* factor of a magazine's personality. Other factors, however, can be counted on to help maintain a recognizable personality from issue to issue.

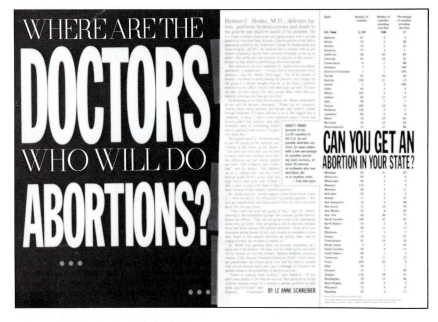

This article was originally published in *Glamour.*

(Courtesy *The American Lawyer.*)

Format

Another constant in magazine layout is the *format,* or basic size and shape of the magazine. Although the term is often more broadly used to include other continuing makeup characteristics, format is more precisely used here to describe only size and shape.

Magazines, though they come in all sizes and shapes, rarely *change* format. When a change is made, it, too, is a management decision based on the same factors that usually enter into the original decision.

Factors influencing this decision are usually functional. One of the first matters of concern, for example, is that the format can be produced with little or no waste in paper or press capacity. Consequently, formats tend to be somewhat standardized to fit common paper sheet sizes and printing presses.

In addition to production efficiency, ease of handling is also considered, as well as other pragmatic factors. Is it essential that the magazine fit into a standard filing cabinet? Must it fit into a standard bookshelf? Should it be small enough to fit into a pocket? The answer to one or more of these questions may direct the choice of format.

However, other factors related to the content and goals of the magazine are important too. For example, if one of the magazine's goals dictates that a primary part of content be comprised of large, dramatic photographs, one of the larger formats may be mandatory.

The following are the most common formats, although their exact dimensions vary considerably.

Miniature: 4½″ × 6″
Books: 6″ × 9″
Basic: 8½″ × 11″
Picture: 10½″ × 13″
Sunday supplement: 11″ × 13″

The most common of these formats is the 8½″ × 11″. It is most common, perhaps, because it can be cut without waste from standard paper sheets, and, as far as layout is concerned, it represents a compromise. It is easy to handle, it permits fairly dramatic sizing of photos and other layout elements, and it has the plus of being the same size as standard typing paper. Hence, it fits nicely into files or piles of paper, whichever is its final destination.

Perhaps least common is the miniature, which has experienced some popularity for consumer magazines relying on newsstand sales, but it creates many design problems because of its extremely small pages. The book size has been popular for digest magazines (perhaps because they give the impression of condensing much into a small package) and for academic and professional quarterlies. The fact that this format's dimensions are also common for textbooks might explain the latter use.

The two larger formats (10½″ × 13″ and 11″ × 13″) owed their original popularity to their ability to exploit the impact of photos and other illustrations. Pictorial magazines, home magazines, and fashion magazines used these formats, but most of these have bowed to economic factors and have reduced to the basic 8½″ × 11″ format. Mailing cost was one of the important factors in the decline of these larger formats.

The relationship of number of pages to page size also merits discussion. For magazines without advertising support, the number of pages can be a semipermanent management decision, just as format is. In such cases, the two decisions are closely related. For magazines relying on advertising, the number of pages usually is based on the ratio of advertising pages to editorial pages that provides a profitable operation. In such instances, the number of pages in an issue varies directly with the number of ad pages sold. For the nonadvertising magazine, the decision to be made may be between 16 pages, 8½″ × 11″ and 32-page pocket size. In this case, the flimsiness of 16 pages in the larger size might be justification to go to the greater heft of the smaller dimensions.

The Cover

A magazine's front cover is its most important page. It is the magazine's face; it creates the all-important first impression. Like a person's face, it is the primary indicator of a personality. Consequently, it should remain relatively constant in appearance. Human beings can smile, frown, or otherwise make faces that slightly change their facial features from minute to minute or day to day. However, only disease, serious injury, or malformation would ever force a person to undergo extensive plastic surgery for transformation of facial features. Similarly, a magazine cover, although it can tolerate minor changes, is not subject to major layout surgery unless equally serious layout problems demand it. In that case, a complete reshaping of the editorial personality usually takes place.

The basic design of the front cover, therefore, is of great importance, although it is usually created only once or twice in a magazine's lifetime. Before the artist or editor even begins design work, however, some basic decisions relating to the cover must be made.

Self-cover Versus Separate Cover

An editor's first cover decision is whether a *self-cover* or a *separate cover* is to be used. As explained in chapter 10, magazines are printed on large sheets folded into signatures (sections) that are usually 8, 16, or 32 pages in size. A self-cover is part of one of these signatures. It is printed in the same press run as a part of the large sheet.

A self-cover, being printed on the same paper as the inside of the magazine, possesses what may be an inherent disadvantage. If the basic paper stock is pulpy or especially thin, this disadvantage, reflected in the cover, may be of considerable detrimental consequence. If, on the other hand, the interior stock is high quality and has reasonable weight, the self-cover can be an advantage. In either case, however, printing on the large sheet rather than on a separate four-page cover sheet can be a production economy. Also, if only the cover is to be printed in more than one color, a self-cover can provide the extra color for all other pages on the form at virtually no cost.

Advertising Versus Editorial

For magazines with advertising, there may be strong competition from the advertising department for use of the cover, especially on specialized business publications. The premium price that can be commanded for the front cover is an attraction that is difficult to combat. The intangible benefits of a strong editorial cover—one that brings the readership, which, in turn, brings in the advertising revenue—must be weighed against the quick return from sale of the space. The other cover pages (inside front, inside back, and outside back) can provide an adequate amount of premium space for advertisers.

Laying Out the Cover

A good magazine cover has several jobs to do. In the first place, there is no other page that has as much responsibility for setting the tone, or personality, of the magazine. Second, the cover must be dynamic enough in appearance to draw readers to the magazine. Third, it must provide some continuing characteristics that identify it from issue to issue. However, it must also be flexible enough so that each issue can be readily identified as a different issue—to let the reader know instantly which issue he or she is viewing. Finally, it should lure the reader into the magazine.

Primary factors in setting the tone of a cover are the nameplate's type dress, the use or lack of illustration, and the overall design. Aside from the fact that it must be large enough and clear enough to quickly identify the publication, the nameplate has no typographic restriction. It usually is designed and created by an artist so it can be tailored to suit the tone of the magazine. Flowing scripts, bold sans serifs, ornate texts, common Romans, and any novelty types might be used, depending on the appearance desired. The nameplate design may call for the type to be printed in black or one or more colors, or the type may be reversed to be white against a black or colored background. Even if the front cover carries advertising, the nameplate has its role to play.

Most magazines use a combination of illustration and type on the front cover, but some use type only (figure 15.3). The fact that type only is used, in and of itself, helps set a tone for the magazine. For a newsmagazine, or perhaps what one might call a "newsy" magazine because it deals in short, timely items of information, the all-type cover can be appropriate. However, if photographs are a primary, basic, or important part of the content, this fact virtually dictates that one or more photographs be included on the cover. Otherwise, the cover doesn't accurately portray the character of the contents.

A look at the accompanying illustrations should also reveal that the overall design of the cover contributes to the impression it creates. By jamming a lot of elements on a cover, a feeling of life and action may be obtained. By concentrating on a minimum of elements, and perhaps placing those elements so that absolute balance results, the feeling of restraint, dignity, or conservatism may prevail. A design that calls for a single, large photograph has a different impact from the design that uses a number of smaller illustrations.

To draw attention to the magazine, most designers rely on photographs. If there is such a thing as a basic cover design, it is one that employs a single, striking photo to catch the eye. Color and/or type can also do the job, but only if adroitly used. Type blurbs are most effective in drawing readers inside the magazine, and, in the final analysis, perhaps this is the most vital function of a cover. Consequently, a cover that carries only a nameplate, photo, and date can fail to fulfill one of its primary missions. One of the cover trends in the seventies was toward the use of more type—more blurbs to sell the content to the reader. Note in the accompanying illustrations how some of the covers direct readers to the issue's most important features by way of type messages.

Because it has to stand the test of continued use, the cover design must be flexible enough to take care of the specifics of individual issues without losing its continuing identification. A design created to include a photo, but requiring that the photo must always be vertical in shape, is too restrictive. A design that provides for a distinctive nameplate to serve as the constant for the continuing identification and a spot for issue identification, plus a large open area for the use of a photo with blurb, can be both effective and flexible.

Design of Continuing Pages

In addition to the cover, most magazines have at least one other page that remains relatively constant in design from issue to issue—for example, a table of contents page. Many also have letters pages, editorial pages, or other continuing features. These pages should get the same design attention that a cover does.

The table of contents page, for example, should be professionally designed so that it has a constant form—a form that is different from the usual monotonous list of titles that is the curse of many magazines. It is generally wise to beef up the contents page by adding at least one other feature with substantial reader interest. Letters, a publisher's message, a column of interesting anecdotes, and the like can be used to prevent the page from becoming an interest graveyard. A design that deliberately calls for the use of one or more pictures to illustrate the contents listing can add some life to the page. Further help can come from the adoption of a device for drawing attention to the leading features in the listing: using a photo for each, varying the type size, or using a check mark, arrow, or other type of ornament.

Mailing information often is placed on the contents page; postal regulations call for its use up front in the book, and the contents page is the likely page for it. Masthead information also often finds its way to this page. All such information should be subordinated (buried might be a better term) in favor of more interesting material. Such material should be placed so that it can be found by those who seek it, yet without getting in the way of material that might interest most readers scanning the page.

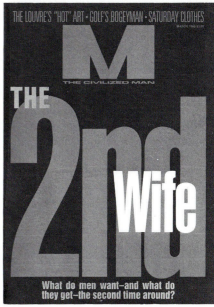

Figure 15.3 Although virtually all these magazines are computer magazines, their covers vary considerably. Some have all-type covers, and some contain advertising, but most of them rely on a strong photograph and heavy type display for their nameplate to attract attention. Almost all have some type devoted to a sales pitch for material contained inside. Note how the dynamic design without a photo is the strength of the cover for *M*. (Courtesy of *M—the civilized man*.)

Establishing a Page Grid: Traditional Approach

The establishment of a page pattern, a *grid*, is another important policy step in magazine design. The traditional approach to a grid is simply to determine margins, column widths, and any other typographical limitations set in advance to establish a consistency of appearance from page to page. The result is an appearance resembling traditional books.

Grids may also break the page into modules, setting a geometric pattern for page design that is asymmetrical and nontraditional. The horizontal and vertical lines that establish the modules provide a great variety of options that can reflect the tastes of the designer and objectives of the periodical.

Layout sheets containing all the grid lines are printed and serve as guides for page layouts. Working with grid sheets assures a magazine of page designs that are consistent with the personality set by design policy, whether it be traditional or contemporary. First, let's look at the traditional approach to developing a page grid.

Type Page Size, Margins, and Columns

A traditional grid establishes standard margins and a vertical division of space into two or three columns; there are no other modules formed by horizontal lines. The space inside the margins is referred to as the *type page size.*

Although there are no absolute rules to guide magazine editors and designers as they prescribe margins and column widths, there are some general principles relating to design and type legibility that can be helpful.

Margins are important to the design of a page because they constitute the frame that holds the page together as a unit. Consequently, margins should be large enough to overpower any normal internal lines of white space that might otherwise divide the page into undesired segments. For books, it is not uncommon for margins to comprise 50 percent of the page area, but for magazines 20 to 30 percent is more common. For example, an 8½ by 11-inch magazine with margins of 1 inch at the bottom, 1/2 inch on the outside and top, and 1/3 inch on the inside is devoting 20 of its 93.5 square inches of space to margins.

In the foregoing example, note that all margins are not equal, and such is usually the case. The inequality of margins stems from the fact that the optical center of a design is somewhat above the geometric center. You can affirm this principle very quickly by drawing intersecting lines from each of two adjoining corners of a page to their opposite corners, as shown in figure 15.4. A mark at the point of intersection (the geometric center) appears to be below center. By raising the mark slightly above the intersection, you achieve the appearance of having it at the center. The type page area, therefore, must be located somewhat above a centered position if it is to avoid the appearance of sliding down the page. Consequently, the bottom margin is always the largest.

Location of the type page within its margins is further complicated by the fact that readers always view two pages at a time when a magazine is opened before them. This means that the two inner (gutter) margins are side by side, thus forming a single gutter of white that is twice the inner margin's dimension. To keep this gutter of white under control—to avoid separating the two pages so completely that they cannot be tied together—the inside margin is made smaller than the others (see figure 15.5).

In traditional book margins (called *progressive* margins), the outside and top margins are not the same, either. The outside is larger than the top. The margins progressively grow smaller from the bottom to the inside, working in a clockwise manner on the left pages and a counterclockwise manner on the right pages. Many magazines, however, use identical margins for the outside and top edges of both facing pages.

Before applying these principles to the selection of exact dimensions for margins, it is necessary to consider the amount of white space needed to separate columns of type. Although a few magazines have used black lines as column separators when that seemed to be the fad, white space consistently serves as the more efficient means for separating columns. These column dividers must be of adequate size to give the reader a pronounced starting and stopping point. On the other hand, they

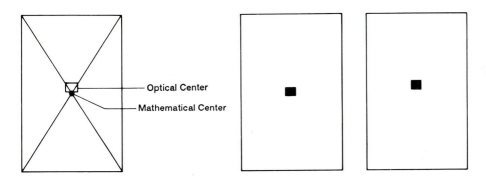

Figure 15.4 The optical center of a page is slightly above the geometric center. A spot located at the geometric center visually appears to be a little low; consequently, the optical center is usually used as the center for a type page, thus making the bottom margin larger than others.

In the figure: Optical Center / Mathematical Center

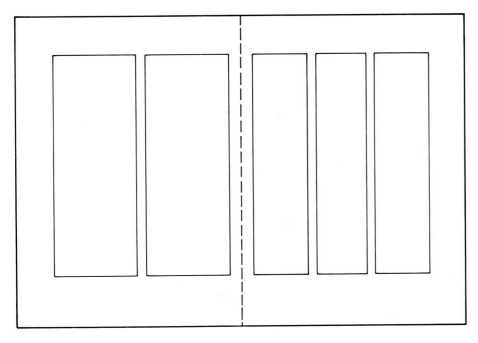

Figure 15.5 The establishment of margins and column widths and the amount of space to use as column breaks are the basic considerations in setting up a traditional grid.

cannot be so large that they break the page into design segments. Once again, only a commonsense principle is available to serve as a guidepost: these column dividers cannot be as large as even the smallest margin.

By applying our principles, we can come up with a usable set of margins and column dividers, if we start with either the smallest or the largest of the white space areas. As an example, let's assume that the minimum amount of white space that serves as a column break is one pica, and the maximum for that purpose should be two picas. Our smallest margin might then be set at three picas. If the gutter margin is three picas, the top might be four, the outside five, and the bottom six if we wanted progressive margins, or we could make the top and side both four and the bottom only five picas.

After making these decisions, the only remaining one would be with regard to the number of columns on a page. The decision as to column width actually is an important one because it has a direct relationship to the ease of reading. Type style and size, as we will see shortly, also enter in the decision. For most commonly used type styles and sizes, the use of either two or three columns to a standard magazine page is acceptable and common. As a matter of fact, many magazines use a two-column design for some sections and a three-column approach for others. To come up with a uniform type page in this instance, we might settle on the following for an 8½ by 11-inch trim size magazine:

Bottom margin: 5 picas
Outside margins: 4 picas
Top margin: 4 picas
Inside (gutter) margin: 3 picas
Column divider on a 3-column page: 1 pica

Column divider on a 2-column page: 2 picas
Type page dimension: 44 picas wide and 57 picas deep
Column width: 21 picas and 14 picas

Although this example is quite typical for an 8½ by 11-inch magazine, it is only one of countless possibilities for that size or any of the other common sizes. The important elements here are the relationships that should exist among the margins and column breaks so that the end result is a unified readable product, not the exact dimensions. Dimensions can vary considerably.

Establishing Typographical Policy

Traditional magazines, like books, are inclined to adhere to rather strict typographical guidelines. Body types are usually consistent for any magazine, being selected in a size and style that assures reading ease. Column widths, because they set line lengths for body type, have a bearing on size and style selection. The basic principles of body type selection are covered in chapter 13.

Along with newsmagazines, other magazines of traditional design often restrict display type to one or only a few styles used in patterns that also have little variety. Some, however, use all varieties of display type to tailor the type display to the content of individual articles.

There are a number of other minor but consequential visual devices that should be a matter of typographical policy. Decorative typographical devices, called *dingbats,* can serve some useful purposes. One of these, the large initial letter, can be an especially helpful device if properly used. If used indiscriminantly, it can contribute to a cluttered appearance. Misuse can be prevented by setting the policy that large initials will be used, but only to signal the start of the text of an article. Continuity can be achieved by deciding in advance on the sizes to be used and whether they are to be dropped into their text or ride above it. A "drop-in" initial letter (see figure 15.6, except top example) requires special marking on body copy so that more than one line is set to a shorter measure (or partially blank) to make room for the initial. A stand-up initial (see figure 15.6, top) needs room only at the beginning of the first line. Either is acceptable, but usage should be uniform.

It can also be helpful to readers if a graphic symbol is used to indicate the end of articles. Some kinds of typographical devices can become, through usage, recognized as an end mark to prevent readers from leaving an article when coincidence causes the end of a section of that article to fall at the end of a page, perhaps leading the readers to think the article has ended. A bullet (large dot), one or more stars, some asterisks, check marks, or other devices are used with considerable success. The selection of the device and provisions for its use in a way that ensures uniformity should be a policy decision.

Even as small a matter as the *folio* (page number) requires a policy decision because it is a continuing aspect of the magazine's typography. Should the folio be spelled out or used as a numeral? Should it be centered or flush to either side? Should the word *page* be used with the numeral? It is surprising how many questions can be asked about so minor a point, and uniformity demands that a decision be made and followed. The use of folios should be in keeping with the other typographical practices that are adopted. Although their placement on outside bottom corners seems practical from the standpoint of the reader's ability to locate them quickly, any folio policy, as long as it is consistent, seems to be acceptable.

Applying the Principles

Many magazines with a consistent traditional approach to design have created visual personalities that have developed and maintained reader loyalty for years. One of the best of these examples is *Smithsonian* magazine, whose booklike design has been welcomed and appreciated by readers for 20 years.

The original design for *Smithsonian* was worked out by Edward K. Thompson, the founding editor, and Bradbury Thompson, the noted designer. Editor Thompson wanted a magazine that was clean and straightforward and reasonably dignified, as a magazine representing the Smithsonian Institution would be expected to be. The success in meeting these basic goals can be seen in figures 15.7 through 15.11.

Nearly 200 years ago a group of statesmen met in Philadelphia, the principal city of British North America, to protest England's oppressive colonial policy.

At the same time the general mood of the colonists began

At its spacious, breezy headquarters beside the Amman airfield, the academy's classrooms are a 30-second walk from its fleet of Cherokees. There are six single-engined Cherokees, a twin-engine Piper and six full-time flight instructors, in addition to ground instructors. The

When Columbus pushed his vessels into the waters of the New World, almost 200 different Indian cultures were flourishing in Mexico. Countless others had come and gone by then, leaving towering and breathtaking records of their presence: mas-

Although some historians say Syria's capital is the oldest continually inhabited city in the world, the fragments of the city's walls still standing don't reflect this great antiquity. The most picturesque section of wall, a mile-long stretch of stone and clay fortification

Figure 15.6 Initial letters, raised and dropped. Note the special effects in the second and fourth examples.

From its cover to the single-page opening feature at the back of the magazine, *Smithsonian* shows conservatism, dignity, and class. Founding editor Thompson had been a longtime managing editor of *Life* and disliked rules, cookie-cutter graphics, "and other such razzmatazz," in the words of current editor Don Moser. Moser, who shares his predecessor's belief in letting good pictures speak for themselves, continues to guide *Smithsonian* in its traditional design. Moser gives these specifics about *Smithsonian* design:

The design is very simple. All the type (except on front and back matter) is 10/12 Baskerville. We use only two or three headline styles, and either a two- or three-column grid of 19.6 or 13.5 picas. There is a generous use of white space; wide margins, a sidehead breaking every full column, and a *Smithsonian* trademark, the "Thompson Corner," named after Brad Thompson. This is an 18-line block of white space in the upper

Figure 15.7 The traditional book design of *Smithsonian* starts with a cover devoted to nameplate and bleed illustration. One dignified block of type usually sells the main article of the issue. (Courtesy *Smithsonian Magazine.*)

Figure 15.8 White space opens up and gives plenty of air for the listings on the table of contents page, which resembles such pages in books. (Courtesy *Smithsonian Magazine.*)

Figure 15.9 Departments carry out the functional and tasteful use of traditional typography by using a working title along with a departmental label and ample white space. (Courtesy *Smithsonian Magazine.*)

Figure 15.10 The rectangle of white space dropped in at the upper left at intervals as articles develop has been a hallmark and tradition of *Smithsonian* design for years. (Courtesy *Smithsonian Magazine.*)

By Rudolph Chelminski

'What are we having
for little lunch?'

"Papa, what are we having for little lunch?"

There it was again, a picture-perfect example of the grammatical gibberish that has been driving me to distraction. For years now, the guard guardians of French linguistic virginity have been railing against the tidal wave of *Franglais* that has been invading their culture (everything from *le penalty* and *le footing* to *le software* and *le weekend*—which the more fanatically inclined are now Gallicizing into *le ouiquende*—and, of course, the inevitable *hambourg-air*). Little do they realize, or care, that there is another side to the coin. My little girl's little lunch was a splendid demonstration of it.

She was speaking "Frenglish" to me. I hope that Jack Lang, France's fire-eating Socialist minister of culture, will be happy to know that what he describes as cultural imperialism works both ways. What Stephane was inquiring about was the menu for *petit déjeuner*, which is the way the French say breakfast. Little lunch. Kids are smarter than I realized. I realized: if they happen to be brought up in a bilingual situation (I am employed as a cancan impostor at the *Folies Bergère*, and my wife, also American, is an ear-lobe model for Chanel Number 4), they naturally fall into the habit of migrating directly from one language to the other without paying the least attention to the grammatical stop signs that adults have erected at the frontiers between them. It seems to be an absolute rule: when they can't think of the word or the proper grammatical construction in one language, they simply borrow from the

other one and translate literally. Hence Stephane's little lunch for something she used to call "brefks" before she started "attending" a French school.

And here comes the second absolute rule of bilingualism: it is always the language of the school and the little friends that wins. If we lived in Tonga the kids would be speaking Polynesian, I guess, and if it were Baltimore, they'd pick up Baltimer, heaven forfend. My wife and I have an iron rule of speaking only American at home, but the kids (aged eight and nine) jabber back at us in French unless we resort to threats of corporal violence or TV deprivation. It is then, when they are in the American mode, that the Frenglish comes roaring at us.

"I have a blue."

"What did you said?"

"I got a big blue when I falled off the *balançoire*."

Is that all clear now?

This enlightening dialogue, carried on the other day between Stephane and Romy, succinctly described the travails encountered in any kid's normal working day, and my own in trying to teach them to distinguish between one language and the other: she got a bruise when she fell from the swing. Needless to say Franco-American children are very "fashed" (angry) when their mother "groonds" (scolds) them about Frenglish.

Weak and strong verbs are bedeviling for anyone who is not bathed in them 24 hours a day. "I gued," "I rassd" and "I winned" are so frequent they hardly even elicit shrieks of parental dismay anymore. Occasionally, I am moved to chagrined admiration at the creation of a whole new

class of verbal constructions, such as "You walk on'd it" and "It get oun like that." But the most consistent fomenters of Frenglish catastrophes are past participles and the simple, multipurpose French preposition *à*, which can mean "at," "to" or "in," depending on how you use it. How can you explain to a kid that English likes to complicate things, and that we are going to England to eat at Freddy's house in London? I'll tell you: you can't. Without *à*, they don't know where they're at.

As for the past participle, it is just supposed to be there, because that is what they have learned, and so the world is constructed that way. How can you explain that the magic addition of "did" in the verbal construction eliminates its need in English, as in did you go and did you are? Can't do that, either: kids will go on saying it their way, because it's more logical, dammit. That's why Stephane asked me: "Did you went at America?"

When I leave them to their own devices and simply observe, I realize that what they speak to each other is neither *Franglais* (French colonized by English) nor Frenglish (English colonized by French), but a mix of the two languages that is akin to French-Canadian. But in their case, the hybrid is further complicated by a dash of leftover baby talk.

"*Babou, tu m'as pas flushé le toolet?*" my boy recently exclaimed to his sister.

That may not be clear to all of you, but I'd be willing to bet that it is to every *maman* in Quebec. Now if I could only get the kids to stop correcting my French in front of company. . . .

152

Figure 15.11 Like many other magazines, *Smithsonian* takes care of readers who might start at the back of the magazine by using the first left-hand page for a short feature of high interest. The design of this page carries the visual personality started with the front cover and carried through to the end of each issue. (Courtesy *Smithsonian Magazine*.)

left-hand corner of a spread, and we usually use one to three of them in a story. I think that all of this gives the magazine an airy, inviting look, and although we run some pretty long pieces, I think that the appearance of the stories says to the reader: This isn't something you're going to have to slog through.

The magazine's design is so simple that we don't even have an art director in the conventional sense. Laying out an issue is essentially a matter of picture selection and placement; the job is done by the editor, the picture editor and a representative from a local design firm.

Although the design is certainly conservative, I find it significant that I have never received a single letter of criticism about it from our readers—and they are quick to complain about anything they don't like. And so we must be doing something right.

Look again at figures 15.7 through 15.11. The desired personality is evident on every page. Traditional framing of pictures is evident, but, when a full-page bleed is warranted, it is used, often as the climax to an article. Generous white space, strong photographs, and legible type make the *Smithsonian* both interesting and easy to read.

The Smithsonian Institution is unique, and the readers of the magazine are special, so what is successful there might not be so successful in other situations. It does illustrate the principle, however, that a magazine's design should be tailored to its editorial content and its reader interest.

Establishing a Page Grid: Nontraditional Approach

Magazines giving special emphasis to design often are inclined to create contemporary visual personalities, breaking away from the traditional book approach to design.

Page grids in these cases usually move away from standard column structure, often using half-columns, and create geometric patterns that are unusual but standardized enough to provide a continuing nature to the design. They usually divide the page into rectangles, often taking this division down to a small unit, such as those framed by horizontal lines that are one line of type apart and vertical lines that are the same or perhaps a pica apart. Larger rectangles are overlayed on these small units and provide compartments for the location of titles, illustrations, or other display units. White space can then be allocated in geometric patterns conforming to these compartments. These rectangles, or *mods* as they are sometimes called, reflect the design skills of the creator of the grid, with no real restrictions applying otherwise.

An example using a nontraditional grid and another example of a magazine's design personality being tailored to its editorial content and its readers' interests is *Enterprise* magazine of the Southwestern Bell Corporation. This public relations magazine is published quarterly for the company's employees and retirees. As a public relations magazine with goals to accomplish for the company, it must rely on design and graphics to generate interest among its readers.

Established in 1984 when the Bell companies were separated from AT&T, it is an excellent example of the planning and partnerships that are necessary for success of a corporate magazine. With the breakup of AT&T, the newly independent Southwestern Bell Corporation wanted to signal to employees the change in corporate identity through a new quarterly magazine replacing a monthly magazine called *Scene*. Editor Peter J. Faur's statement of objectives and procedures involved in creating a new visual personality for *Enterprise* best shows the planning that was involved:

The new magazine would help foster a sense among employees that they in fact are proprietors of the business and should treat their jobs accordingly. By encouraging this new, entrepreneurial attitude, the company hoped to provide a more rewarding workplace while simultaneously reaping the benefits of increased employee contributions to the business.

The magazine also wanted to signal to employees that, even though the company has been separated from AT&T, there is no reason to be seen as one of "Ma Bell's homeless, pitiful orphans." Instead, the magazine's design would help capture the truth that Southwestern Bell Corporation is a dynamic, powerful leader in telecommunications, residing in the top 50 of the Fortune 500 companies.

Enterprise, it was decided, had to be far different from its folksier predecessor.

Design planning began with the establishment of goals and objectives for the visual personality of the magazine:

The magazine's visual impact has to convey "controlled excellence," that is, it has to have a clearly stated appearance, consistent from page to page and structured to make the publication easy for the reader to follow. The concept has to be structured enough so that we can apply it consistently but not so rigid that it looks academic or literary. We want a look that will stand up to passing design fashions yet will consistently appear contemporary.

As shown in figures 5.12 through 5.14, the design was based on a three-column format with a floating half-column. Editor Faur cites these advantages of the grid:

The half-column offers tremendous flexibility. It can be used to carry art and cutlines. It can separate a sidebar from a main story. It can be coupled with a full column or multiple columns when art requires an unusual display area.

Hairline rules lend a structured, business-like look to the publication. Four-point rules accent the tops of all short columns and provide contrast to the hairline rules.

The more unusual or complicated a grid is, the less obvious the pattern is. There is no doubt that, for most magazines, a grid's restrictions tend to create order and standardization, which contribute to a magazine's visual personality.

For some audiences, however, there are factors working against an obvious grid of any kind. For younger audiences (MTV viewers), avant garde intellectuals, and visual sophisticates, design must be free from restriction. Skilled designers whose

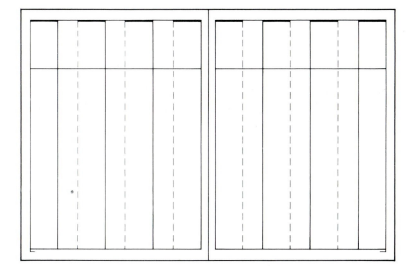

Figure 15.12 The *Enterprise* grid.

Figure 15.13 One of the key parts of the page grid developed for *Enterprise* is the half-column that can float according to the needs of any page or spread; another is the use of rules for column dividers. (Courtesy *Enterprise*, Southwestern Bell Corporation.)

Figure 15.14 These opening two pages of a four-page article show the use of a strong illustration to open the article, a half-column of white space, a large initial letter, vertical and horizontal lines, subheads, and an arrow to lead the reader on, all as elements of design interest. (Courtesy *Enterprise,* Southwestern Bell Corporation.)

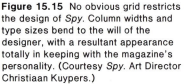

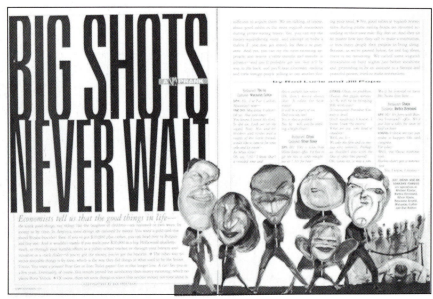

Figure 15.15 No obvious grid restricts the design of *Spy.* Column widths and type sizes bend to the will of the designer, with a resultant appearance totally in keeping with the magazine's personality. (Courtesy *Spy.* Art Director Christiaan Kuypers.)

talents and training enable them to present pages with organization that comes from apparent disorder are required to cater to these audiences. In many cases, they produce pages where design is more important than content, a concept that is heretical to most editorial journalists, but successful for appropriate magazines. What is obviously difficult-to-read typography adds to the alienation of some editors toward such design.

Designing Without a Grid

Look at the examples in figures 15.15 and 15.16. Each page seems to be designed as a separate work of art, not a subordinate part of a larger publication. The continuing characteristic of each is only the art director's skill rather than a geometric page pattern.

Some magazines, however, seem to be suited to this kind of design, and it is essential that editors appreciate the skills of designers in such instances. Artistic talent of the highest order is required to avoid total disorder and chaos while presenting pages for such audiences.

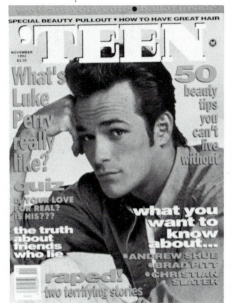

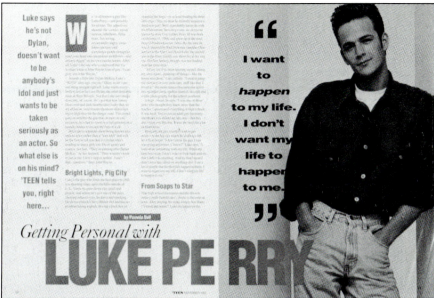

Figure 15.16 Magazines such as *'TEEN* may or may not use a grid, but they must have an appearance lively enough to appeal to the youth audience. Age demographics have a direct bearing on magazines, from *Ranger Rick* for kids to *Modern Maturity* for senior citizens. (Courtesy *'TEEN.*)

Spy magazine's art director exhibits such talent with each issue. Type is used in violation of every legibility principle, but with an artistry that creates a visual experience on each page.

For *Spy,* every page seems to be designed as much to create a visual sensation as it is intended to be read. Also, that kind of page design is as much a part of *Spy*'s personality as the irreverent treatment it gives to subjects of all kinds.

For those editors who are not skilled in design, copying of the work of *Spy*'s designer or any other talented designer is not possible or feasible. Instead, what is to be learned from them is an appreciation of their work and an understanding of its role for magazines.

Copying the work of a more traditionally designed magazine, such as *Smithsonian,* might be possible because it is so structured, but that is not feasible, either. The most important principle of magazine design is simply this: each magazine should be designed and edited with its audience in mind. *Smithsonian* is suitable for its audience and *Spy* is tailor-made for its readership.

Consider again the examples presented in figures 15.15 and 15.16. The cover and two pages from *'TEEN* are designed to create a personality befitting their audience. It could not conceivably be the same as the design for *Modern Maturity,* for example. It is just as important to match design with audience as to match it with content.

16 Layout

ONE of the most interesting and challenging aspects of magazine editing is the process of putting all the components of a magazine into an attractive, effective package. Layout of pages is the final stage in this process, and it requires both artistic and editorial skills and knowledge.

In the ideal situation, the staff includes a specialist, usually called an *art director,* who has primary responsibility for the creative aspects of design. In some larger operations, the art director is assisted by a fairly sizable staff. Often, however, because of budgetary or other considerations, the assistance of a free-lance designer on a part-time basis is the only help provided for an editor. There are also many instances in which the editor must operate without the assistance of an art director or artist. Unfortunately, this latter case is typical among the smaller magazines that so often provide the training ground for the newcomers in magazine editing.

Working with, and Without, an Art Director

There is no doubt that a talented art director is one of a magazine's most valuable assets. From art directors can come the innovation that lifts appearance out of the commonplace. Their visual presentations can add a vital dimension to editorial material. The history of contemporary magazines is full of examples of the impact art directors can have on their own publications and on magazines generally, as well. Alexey Brodovitch, the Russian-born designer who became art director of *Harper's Bazaar* in the early 1930s, gave his own publication a fresh visual appeal and influenced many of the people and magazines of his era. Willie Fleckhaus, from his office in Munich, designed the pages of *Twen* magazine so effectively that his new ideas set the pace for the design of other magazines all over the world, including some of those in the United States. Allen F. Hurlburt's work with *Look* magazine, Henry Wolf's and later Samuel Antupit's with *Esquire,* and Otto Storch's with *McCall's* set standards of excellence that have provided inspiration for other designers. They and others who provided new concepts of magazine design also established the art director as a top-level partner in the editorial-management team of consumer magazines.

The partnership of art director and editor was not an easy one to establish, nor is it an easy one to maintain. The relative importance of form and function provides ample fodder for continuing debate and potential antagonism. The excesses of "screaming graphics" that made some magazines almost impossible to read in the 1960s, though also deplored by many designers, unfortunately fueled the prejudices of editorial types who placed visual presentation at the bottom of their importance scale.

The de-emphasis of content by some designers to the point that they seem to be designing for the sake of design alone also presents some difficulty. So does the tendency of many to imitate the innovations of the creative pacesetters to the point that fads sweep through the magazine industry, making look-alikes of periodicals whose varied functions logically demand varied design approaches. Regardless of the difficulties, the maintenance of a partnership between editor and art director is essential if magazines are to be at their best.

Basically, the editor's job in working with an art director is to keep design within some limits of function. At the same time, the art director should be given the freedom to provide the creative spark that results in the bright and unique presentations needed to attract and hold readers despite the great competition for their reading time.

For editors who must work alone as they combine pictures, artwork, and white space to form magazine pages, it is best to let form follow function. Design that has been created expressly to carry out a communication function is usually acceptable. Attempts at spectacular design by the untrained or untalented can produce disastrous results. If, as editors lay out the pages of their magazines, they consider the editorial "why" of their actions, the design should at least be unobtrusive. At best, they may even give added visual appeal to their content.

It is beyond the scope of this book to attempt to provide the background for art direction of a magazine. For that matter, considerable additional reading is recommended to gain a full appreciation of the role of the art director of mass circulation magazines.

There is no doubt that the minimum for art direction should at least include establishing the visual personality as described in the previous chapter with the development of page grids. Beyond that, it may be necessary for editors to make design decisions on a day-to-day basis, applying sound editorial judgment and some basic layout principles as pages are laid out. Fortunately, there are some principles that, if applied well, result in functional and attractive page layout.

Working in Miniature

One of the most helpful aids in page layout is a miniature dummy. The miniature can show at a glance how an edition is shaping up visually. Checking on the issue's adherence to the magazine's visual personality and/or the need for changes of pace in layouts is easy to do in miniature. The availability of color and any other production requirements can also be shown on a mini.

Preprinted sheets with facing pages outlined in miniature can permit layout "doodling" that produces alternate ideas quickly and efficiently. While doodling miniatures, editors should be preparing to specify display type because ordinarily it is lettered on the final page layout and typeset from the layout, not from a typed sheet of paper. If design policy has not precluded it, the editorial content should be reflected in the title typography. A magazine ordinarily is intended as a storehouse of many different articles, each with its own flavor and substance. Titles, through their type dress, should convey these differences. As suggested in chapter 13, many typefaces seem especially suitable for certain subjects, feelings, and moods. The *tone* and approach of a magazine page can be matched by type also. A page that is heavy in design, with large pictures and strong lines, accommodates bold and heavy type styles. On the other hand, a page with a delicate and balanced group of components might call for just the opposite type selection. In any case, suitability should be a basis for type selection and use. Figure 16.1 illustrates this point well. The wild West flavor of the type, and the circular treatment of the illustration work together to give visual meaning to the layout. The special treatments given to type and illustration have definite design purposes. The use of type designs just for the sake of being different can have disastrous results; wild display and bizarre arrangements are as unsatisfactory as dullness and monotony.

Order and Structure

While trying for suitability of design, an editor or a designer of magazine pages is also concerned with order and structure because these are, in fact, the foundation of design. A primary determinant of order in design is *balance,* a relative feeling of

equilibrium with respect to a vertical axis in the center of the area. The easiest way to ensure this equilibrium is to place elements directly on the axis, just as if they were being placed directly over the fulcrum on a teeter-totter (figure 16.2). Complete symmetry is thus obtained, guaranteeing a feeling of stability. Absolute symmetry also can be obtained by placing equal elements at equal distances from the axis (figure 16.3). Relative symmetry can be obtained by varying the distance from the axis according to the weight of the elements. Heavy elements can be balanced by lighter elements by placing the heavier ones close to the axis and the lighter ones farther away (figure 16.4).

Another basic contributor to order on the magazine pages is *grouping*. Especially in situations involving several items—perhaps five photos, five captions, a title, and an author's blurb—grouping is essential. The smaller the number of display elements, the greater the chance for order. If the five photos can be grouped to form one visual element, and the captions are visually tied to the photos, the potential for order is increased and the tendency toward clutter and disorder is decreased.

Alignment

Alignment of elements can also be especially helpful in giving order to magazine pages. A good question to ask when placing any visual element on a layout is, What can this line up with? Instead of floating in space, captions should be lined up with the edges of photos, photos should line up with column dividers, title type should line up with an adjacent illustration, and so on. Figure 16.5 shows how alignment prevails between elements and within elements, such as titles. It also shows that alignment can sometimes aid a reader's movement as he or she views the page or spread.

Visual Syntax

The fact that a layout has order and structure does not mean that it is static. Some motion that correlates to normal reader eye movement can be a vital characteristic of well-designed pages. To make pages effective in this regard, two things must be considered: (1) which pattern readers' eye movement will take and (2) in which order elements should be placed along any eye movement path if readers are to be able to extract meaning from the presentation.

SYNCRUDE ON STREAM

The risk and reality of oil in the tar sands

BY GORDON DONALDSON

PHOTOGRAPHS BY ALEX MACDONALD

PHOTOGRAPHS BY BLAIR SEITZ

In the kitchen of the Massey house in Broomall, Pennsylvania, where he often does open-hearth cooking, food historian and writer William Woys Weaver uses historic utensils from his collection to prepare a wild squab casserole (the squab can be seen in the earthenware dish).

Historian at the Stove

A collector of cookbooks and utensils and no slouch in the kitchen himself,
William Woys Weaver is exploring the origins of Pennsylvania German cookery

by Ruth Hoover Seitz

In 1979 the proprietor of a Pennsylvania antiques shop, puzzled about the function of two dozen tin cups mounted on a metal square, casually pointed the contraption out to a customer. The customer recalled seeing a similar item in a nineteenth-century advertisement for a confection called moshey—a Pennsylvania German molasses taffy—and promptly bought the piece. Culinary historian and writer William Woys Weaver thus indulged his two passions: researching old cooking lore and collecting kitchen utensils used by

early Pennsylvania housewives.

Weaver, thirty-six, shares his Philadelphia-area home—part of which operated as a tavern from 1812 to 1865—with two large collections. One comprises some twenty-five thousand books, including more than a thousand cookbooks; the other contains hundreds of kitchen utensils.

Displayed on a Weaver ancestor's butcher's apron are (from right) an earthenware crock, iron fork and spoon, cleaver, sausage stuffer, spatula and spoon, meat tenderizer, meat scorner, lard can, and flour sprinkler.

AMERICANA 43

The people who dropped from heaven

The Miccosukees, a unique tribe of native Americans, are Exxon's neighbors in Florida's Big Cypress Swamp.

LONG AGO A PEOPLE dropped from heaven into a lake in northern Florida. They swam ashore and set up camp. And from them came the Miccosukees, an Indian tribe of no more than 550 people who now live in southern Florida some 40 miles west of Miami. They are a remarkable people. Like the beatific legend of their origin, they're a gentle group, friendly and hospitable. They don't hate anybody.

The nearest neighbors of the Miccosukees are the Seminoles, good friends who share most of their same beliefs and practices. Exxon Company, U.S.A. is another neighbor. The first company to find oil in Florida (in 1943), Exxon had a drilling program under way for many years in the Big Cypress Preserve nearby. In the past, Exxon has leased Miccosukee lands for oil and gas exploration and enjoys a good relationship with the tribe, although no lands are currently under lease.

In an age of hostilities, of picketing, shouting crowds, and violence, the soft-spoken Miccosukees comprehend the power of reasonableness and have used it to achieve their aims. Their leader, Buffalo Tiger, a big, handsome man of 63, is chairman of the corporation the tribe formed in 1962. Unlike most of the 500 other Indian tribes in the United States, the Miccosukees administer all their own funds without the presence of the Bureau of Indian Affairs as intermediary. In 1971, the Miccosukees took over from the BIA all programs and services, including health, education, and welfare.

Since few tribal members had formal training in accounting and other administrative skills, and conscious of the need for careful bookkeeping, the tribe brought in outside personnel for most jobs. Slowly, however, Miccosukees are replacing many of their non-Indian employees as tribal members gain the necessary skills and experience.

The tribe's achievements have been considerable. The tribal office is a splendid brick structure, air-conditioned and carpeted. Be-

A traditional Miccosukee village consists of thatched-roof houses called chickees built on hammocks of high ground and housing some 15 to 20 people, all closely related.

Figure 16.2 A feeling of equilibrium on a magazine page can be achieved automatically by placing the dominant elements on the center line. (Courtesy *Americana,* © Americana Magazine, Inc., all rights reserved; *Imperial Oil Review;* and *Exxon USA.*)

OUT IN THE COLD

Winter camping isn't for everyone. That's the beauty of it. If you can handle the weather, you'll be rewarded with views of sparkling, snow-washed scenery few people ever see.

BY TIM SMIGHT

I T WAS THE COLD THAT WOKE ME. The dull, aching kind of chill that slowly seeps into your bones on a winter night. Still half asleep, I tried curling up into a tight ball in the depths of my sleeping bag. No use. Warming up would require more clothing, motion, and hot food. But that meant getting up and going outside the tent, into the *real* cold. It seemed to be a losing proposition either way.

"Hey, rise and shine in there!" called a voice from outside. "How about some help with this stove?" It was Christine, the first one up and around on this stinging cold morning. Ken, Brian, and I stretched and groaned in unison. At least the dilemma had been resolved. Slowly I pushed my head and arms up out of the sleeping bag to grope around the tent for my boots. I found them at the foot of my bag, stiff as bronze, their insides lined with a thin layer of ice.

"Condensation," said Ken, chuckling at me. "You should have slept on them like I did. Mine are fine." I forced a smile. This was my first winter camping trip, and I hadn't yet picked up all the tricks.

Why did I come on this trip, anyway? I wondered as I pulled on my wool socks. I could have been snoozing the weekend away

in a warm bed or basking in the sun with the spring-break crowd at Daytona Beach. Instead I'm playing Jeremiah Johnson up in the Montana Rockies. It's 15 degrees out there, and I've got frozen boots.

Five minutes later, I unzipped the tent and stepped outside into a world I had never seen before. Immense, whitewashed mountains leaped up on three sides of our camp, standing watch over a forest of frosted pine. Lit up by the sun, the western peaks stood out sharply in the crisp, clean air, white jewels sparkling against the pale blue sky. The only sound in the valley was the gentle rippling of the creek nearby. There were no other human beings in sight. The thought sent a shivering surge of excitement up my spine, and I remembered why I'd come.

For a long time, friends had been urging me to pay a winter visit to Glacier National Park, a place I'd enjoyed camping in during the summer months but had never seen off-season. The idea of camping in the snow and cold—not to mention trudging through it with a backpack—just wasn't appealing to me. All I could think of when I envisioned winter camping was that Jack London story in which the guy freezes to death because his hands are too numb to light a fire. And be-

sides, I had zilch experience on snowshoes or cross-country skis.

"No problem," said my friend Mike, talking long-distance from his Montana home. "You can learn cross-country in a day. Of course, it *will* be cold. It's not like a summer stroll through the woods. But that's the whole point. In winter you can experience a completely different world up here."

I was sold. Two weeks later, I arrived in Whitefish, Montana, to join Mike and six friends he'd recruited for an overnight trip into Glacier. Our destination was Avalanche Lake—a mountain-rimmed pool accessible by trail from Going-to-the-Sun Road, the only highway through Glacier Park. We planned to drive in as far as possible (only the first 11 miles of Sun Road are kept open in winter), then ski five miles farther up the road to the trailhead, where we'd camp for the night. The next day, relieved of our bulky packs, we'd hike the 2.5-mile trail up to the lake on foot.

"We should have plenty of time to get up

Winter transforms Glacier's rock-gray peaks into gleaming white jewels, creating a spectacular landscape that's completely different from the summer scenery.

10 AMERICA

AMERICA 11

Figure 16.3 Relatively equal elements positioned on both sides of the center line also provide a feeling of equilibrium. (Courtesy *America* Magazine, reprinted with permission from the Fall 1982 *America,* © 1982 by 13–30 Corporation, 505 Market St., Knoxville, TN 37902.)

Figure 16.4 Placement of heavier (larger, darker) elements closer to the fulcrum to balance them with lighter elements placed farther from the center. (Reprinted from *NCR World* of NCR Corporation.)

Figure 16.5 Note the horizontal and vertical alignment that is evident among the elements on this spread. (Reprinted from *NCR World* of NCR Corporation.)

With regard to point one, some generally accepted assumptions are reasonably substantiated by research. For example, the upper left quadrant of a page or spread is considered the normal starting place, with readers tending to read to the right and then down. Two commonly accepted movement patterns are those that resemble a question mark or a letter *z*. Even if these patterns are valid, however, successful communication is not assured unless elements are placed in a sequence that is meaningful.

An analogy with verbal syntax is in order here. As a person reads a line of type from left to right, the words must be in proper order if they are to convey meaning. Journalists are taught that, for many basic news stories, simple declarative sentence with the standard order of subject, verb, and object can be most effective. Complicated sentences can fog meaning, and incorrect word order can give totally erroneous meaning. It seems reasonable to assume that the order of presentation for graphic or visual elements can have the same results. There is, in effect, good and poor visual syntax.

Armed with photos, title, captions, body copy, and white space, how can an editor place them in proper order for reader viewing? There is at least one technique that can help: the careful selection of a dominant element, such as one of the illus-

THE ALZHEIMER PUZZLE
Putting the pieces together

By Linda Hubbard

New technology such as PET scan allows scientists to "look" into the brain and measure chemical activity.

Figure 16.6 Sometimes obvious lines are used to bridge the gutter and help unify two pages. (Courtesy *Modern Maturity*.)

trations or the title. This element can then be given visual dominance, made to be the starting place for a reader. Placement of this element in the upper left takes advantage of the reader's normal inclination to start there. We can think of this as an analog of placing the subject first in a simple declarative sentence—in most cases, it is the easiest, most effective way to communicate. However, good writers don't use only simple declarative sentences, and good magazine designers don't always put the starting element in the upper left. As pointed out in the chapter on titles, there is nothing wrong with placing titles any place on a page or spread, provided they are given sufficient strength to get reader attention. In verbal syntax, when sentence structure becomes more unusual or more complicated, more care must be given to the arrangement if meaning is to remain clear. So it is with the visual; the more designers vary from the normal, the more careful they must be to make sure their graphic presentation is strong enough to guide readers through the layout in a meaningful order. The creation of lines through the placement of elements is perhaps the best way of directing reader eye movement.

Working with Spreads

Placement of elements to direct eye movement must be done with the realization that readers are ordinarily viewing two pages as a unit, not a single page. As a matter of fact, except when looking at the front cover or back cover, readers always have the horizontal area created by two pages spread out before them. Consequently, spreads, rather than single pages, should be the basic layout area.

As indicated in an earlier chapter, margins are usually set so the inside (gutter) margin is no more than half the size of the largest margin. This practice is intended to help hold the spread together, rather than let it visually become two separate page units. Other techniques are also used to maintain a horizontal directional flow that bridges the gutter and ties two pages together. An obvious and straightforward line can be used (figure 16.6). Placement of photos in horizontal groupings can also help. Titles can be designed to carry across the gutter too. Figures 16.7 and 16.8 show some of these page-linking devices at work.

Perhaps equally important is the necessity to give vertical eye movement to a page that must stand independently from the one facing it. An article that opens on a right page, for example, should be designed to be completely separated from the end of an article on the facing page. Placement of white space, vertical shapes

An Island affair

Why I'm in love with Hawaii

By Charles N. Barnard

Figure 16.7 The alignment of elements horizontally across a spread wipes out the normal division created by the gutter margins. (Courtesy *Modern Maturity* and *Imperial Oil Review.*)

Figure 16.8 Pictures, titles, and white spaces, jointly and separately, can unite two pages. (Courtesy *Sun* Magazine, Sun Company, Inc.)

for titles, vertical alignment of photos, and similar devices are helpful in this instance. Some pages designed to stand apart instead of forming a unit with the facing page are shown in figure 16.9.

This short discussion of white space is not included at the end of our discussion of layout because it is of least consequence. In fact, the reverse is true. Although we tend to think of the black type, the dark photos, or the color blocks as we create page layouts, the apportionment of white space that results from the positioning of other elements is of utmost importance.

For anyone who has worked with a camera, the importance of white space should be obvious, because we know that a camera sees only white space. Place a type proof in front of a camera and black type reflects no light to the film, but the white background fully exposes the film. Human eyesight relies on the reflection of light also, and this point should be remembered when any graphic design is created.

White space can be a powerful unifying factor. It can also destroy a design as effectively as huge black lines. For the beginner, there is this helpful maxim: *place excess white space to the outside of a layout.* If that is done, the effect will be to unify the spread or page. Interior white space can be destructive. In this context, it should be remembered that margins are only intended to be limits for type. The urge to push outward (thus, leaving inner white space) to form neat marginal lines should be resisted. In the placement of photos, however, the restriction of white space may be undesirable. Rather than confine the action of photos with borders of white, it is often better to bleed them to increase, rather than restrict, their magnitude.

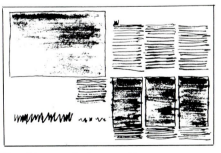

Possible page designs roughly sketched in miniature are a helpful first step in page layout. With little effort, several possible variations can be visualized before full-size layouts are started.

Mechanics of Page Layout

All of the attention to good design, the positioning of elements for maximum impact, and all the other factors of appearance go down the drain unless elements fit their designated locations and printers understand exactly where these locations are.

At some point, the content and the layout must be made to match. The length of the body copy, the words of a title, and the content of illustrations might be made to dictate layout; that is, the design would be forced to conform to material intended for use. On the other hand, an art director might design the page or spread, and the writers and illustrators must make their product fit the package. Even more likely, form and content are juggled simultaneously as page layouts are executed. The extent to which production stages are completed in-house or by outside specialists also complicates procedure.

Basic Steps in Page Layout

Starting with a miniature layout showing the number of pages and the rough apportionment of space among title, illustrations, and body copy, plus full-size grid sheets, these steps must be completed:

1. Determine exactly the amount of space that will be used by the text of the article.
2. Determine the amount of space for any illustrations.
3. Position body type and illustrations.
4. Design and position display type for title.
5. Place type specifications on layout for all display type.
6. Show in color all elements that are to be in color, or designate color usage.
7. Specify any typographical requirements that would not accompany the article manuscript, such as border rules or shaded areas.

After the preceding steps are completed, the final product should be a plan that a printer can follow precisely to create a finished page or spread that will be exactly as planned. The sequence of the steps just listed can vary considerably, and they also tend to blend together, but this sequence can work in most situations.

Casting body copy (determining how much space the manuscript will occupy) often is done first because the text tends to be least flexible of the elements. Type size, leading between lines, and line length are usually constants that cannot be changed, thus making expansion or contraction of edited copy impossible. Using the technique described in the next chapter, it is relatively easy to determine the total depth of type, in picas, of any article.

Assume for example, that we have decided two facing pages will be needed for an article, have made the calculations, and know that the article (when set in our type specifications) will use 64 picas of space. That is too long for a single column in a standard magazine, so we have the choice of dividing it into two, three, or whatever larger number of columns would be available.

In making this allocation of column space to the body type, we must have in mind which illustrations are available, which shapes they are, and how strong they are. We might, for example, want to use one as a full-page bleed to open a two-page spread, or we could be aware of the fact that three photos are vertical rectangles that could be lined up to form a horizontal panel across one full page.

To create a working example here, let's say we have four photos and we can use one of them (a horizontal shape) to dominate the left page, and we can use the other three together or independently. After some doodling, we came up with the miniature in figure 16.10. By dividing our 64 picas of body type into three columns, the copy will go across the top of the second page (figure 16.11), and the three pictures line up across the bottom with captions directly under each.

These three photos, plus the one we position on the left page, must go through a process called *scaling,* or *proportioning,* so that we know their dimensions after enlargement or reduction for use on our spread. The specifics of illustration scaling are presented in chapter 18. It suffices here to say that our dominant photo occupies space as shown in figure 16.11, and the other three are placed as shown there. The remaining open space accommodates the title.

After some rough lettering on scratch paper, we might present our title, MEDICARE, Its Pluses and Minuses, as lettered in position in figure 16.11. We know the title will fit there because we have lettered it by tracing from a type book, and our type specs for it are from the book. Techniques for fitting display type to space are explained in the next chapter.

Figure 16.11 now represents a blueprint for the printer to follow in putting these pages together. If we have typesetting facilities in our own offices, we could set the type and paste photocopy proofs in position, or, as shown in figure 16.11, we can use bogus type to show the location of body type. Note that photos are indicated by tone sheets in figure 16.11. We might just draw rectangles with *X*s to show the location of photos, numbering each to ensure proper placement, but the use of tone sheets and bogus type permits good visualization of what final pages will look like. A contrasting bogus type has been used for captions. Bogus type and tone sheets can be purchased at art stores or made to order.

Figure 16.10 One miniature of the many that may be tried is selected as the basis for a single page layout.

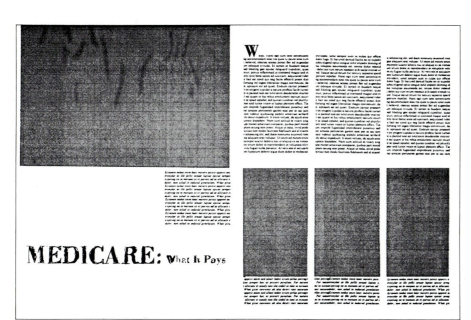

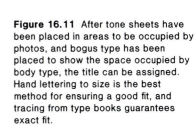

Figure 16.11 After tone sheets have been placed in areas to be occupied by photos, and bogus type has been placed to show the space occupied by body type, the title can be assigned. Hand lettering to size is the best method for ensuring a good fit, and tracing from type books guarantees exact fit.

Figure 16.12 In addition to the dummy as executed in figure 16.11, or as a substitute for it, a pasteup using the actual type proofs may be required. The letters and numbers on the type proofs on this page from *Printing Management* identify the type that should be positioned there. (Courtesy *Printing Management*.)

Note that there are no instructions on the layout for body type; the person setting this type never sees the layout and must have full specifications on the typewritten sheets. Note, however, that the display type specs are here; usually display type is set from the layout, thus permitting the setter to follow any special spacing that might be desired and shown on the layout.

The layout shown in figure 16.11 may be the only one needed. If properly done, positioning of the elements is exact, and each is placed exactly as shown. In some situations, a layout is not made until the type has been set, and the type proofs are in position, instead of bogus type (figure 16.12).

Assuming that we might want our key title word (MEDICARE) to be set in red, lettering it in red on the layout communicates that fact to the printer. Verbal designations of color are also acceptable, but they do not permit visualization in advance of the effect the use of the color will have.

Regardless of variations in procedures that prevail, these functions must be accomplished by a layout:

1. Show the locations of all visual elements exactly.
2. Guarantee that each block of body type, each word of display type, and each illustration fits as placed on the layout.

Page Layout by Computer

Because computers are ideally suited for layout of magazine pages, they are increasingly being put to work for this task. As described in chapter 12, both desktop and proprietary computer systems are miraculous tools for accomplishing this function. With the ability to see on a screen all elements in place exactly as they will appear in print, editors and art directors can make countless changes as they search for excellent page layouts.

For many magazine staffs, total computer pagination is still in the future. For some, their systems permit the creation of partial pages on their computer screens with what is called *area composition.* In area composition, display and body type are joined to form rectangles that cover major sections of a page, thus reducing to a minimum the number of elements to be pasted in position. Artwork must be handled independently, but, for many magazine staffs, all body type, display type, and drawings must be pasted in page form for photographing and platemaking.

Magazines without the capability of pagination by computer are involved directly or indirectly with preparation of mechanicals (finished, camera-ready pasteups of pages). Traditionally the domain of the printer, the preparation of mechanicals is now more likely the responsibility of magazine staffs. Even if mechanicals are prepared by printers, however, the knowledge of the basic techniques involved is essential for editorial and production staff members.

Function of a Mechanical

The word *mechanical* is short for *photomechanical,* the term that properly identifies the camera-ready pasteup as the first step in the photochemical printing process.

As the beginning phase of production, preparation of mechanicals requires mechanical skills and strict attention to detail. A good mechanical reduces to a minimum the work that follows; incomplete or sloppy mechanicals cause additional work when negatives are made or stripped into a mask for platemaking.

If a mechanical is incomplete, extra stripping is required, and it is much more difficult to fasten negatives into a mask than it is to apply paper proofs to grid sheets. Any blemishes require extra brush work when opaquing negatives. Fortunately, such blemishes can be removed from the negative, but, again, the time and cost involved for opaquing are greater than what is involved in keeping mechanicals clean.

A good mechanical also has all elements positioned exactly, and absolutely square and true. In addition, it contains any instructions necessary for later production steps.

A separate mechanical is needed for each color involved in printing, and sometimes extra ones are needed even if only one color is involved. Overprinting of type or line illustrations over photographs may involve separate mechanicals, for example. In any case, one of the mechanicals is considered the *key* and is usually made on board or paper; the others are called *overlays* and are usually made on transparent or translucent film.

Positioning of elements is controlled by *register marks,* small marks with a cross enclosed in a circle, much like a gunsight. With transparent overlays placed so their register marks fall exactly over the register marks on the key, exact positioning is assured from that point on.

Register marks are, therefore, a part of the communication from the preparer of the mechanical to the stripper who must take the negatives made from mechanicals and strip them into position in a mask.

Content of Mechanicals

One must know the difference between what printers call *line copy* and what they label as *continuous tone copy* to know what can be placed on a mechanical. Line copy is any copy composed of only pure whites and pure blacks, such as body type, display type, and line drawings. Continuous tone copy is all material that contains images ranging in tones continuously from light to dark, such as photographs, watercolor paintings, and oil paintings. For best results, continuous tone copy is handled separately, going through the halftone screening process and then being stripped into a separate mask. The process of exposing light through a second mask onto a plate is called *double burning*.

To avoid double burning, it is possible to convert continuous tone copy into screened photoprints that can become a part of the basic mechanical containing line copy. Screened photoprints, often called Veloxes because of the brand of paper used in making them, suffer some slight loss of quality in the converting step, but they are used by many magazines.

Tools and Materials Needed

To prepare mechanicals, the tools needed include

1. A grid sheet, preprinted with all critical lines in place
2. Cutting tools, such as X-acto knives or razor blades, for precise cutting of proofs
3. Adhesives, such as rubber cement or adhesive wax, for fastening proofs in position. Glues that cause paper to wrinkle are not satisfactory.
4. Guides for alignment, such as drawing boards, T-square, and triangles
5. Red, blue, and black pencils and pens for drawing lines and writing instructions
6. Paste-down borders, rules, and other typographical symbols
7. Transparent red film with adhesive backing for designating continuous tone areas
8. A light table that provides lighting from underneath
9. Masking tape for fastening sheets to table surface

Preparing the Mechanical

The first step in preparing a mechanical is to fasten the grid sheet to the working surface with masking tape, using a T-square and triangle to be certain that margins and columns are lined up.

Lines are blue on the grid sheet because, for the lithographic film used by printers, blue is the same as white; it exposes film totally when light is reflected

The first step in preparing a mechanical is to fasten grid sheets into a squared off position on the drawing board or light table.

from it. On the other hand, red lines are just like black lines, and do not expose the film because they absorb the rays of light. You should remember that lines that do not reflect light to film remain clear on the film and, therefore, allow light through to a plate, resulting in the line being printed.

A nonreproducing blue pencil is essential for working with mechanicals; using it to draw lines can provide guidelines that will not show up in print. Care must be taken not to use dark blue lines; the darkness comes from black within the blue, which can cause such lines to reproduce.

By reserving black lines for material that is to be reproduced, and red lines for material that is to carry through to the negative but then be blacked out, some confusion can be avoided. Red lines reproduce as well as black, but, if their use conveys the notice that the material should not be in the final reproduction, they can provide very helpful placement lines for the stripper.

The second step usually is the drawing or placement of any rules, borders, or other lines that are to print. Most borders or rules are available in rolls of pressure-sensitive tape that can be easily positioned and cut. Drawing of these lines is best avoided; good ruling pens and undercut line guides are absolutely necessary if that is to be done.

Next, trim all type proofs and illustrations, including screened Velox prints, usually leaving about ⅛ inch of space around them. The fact that the proof is raised above the surface can cause a shadow, and the edge allowance usually causes any shadow to be far enough from the image that it is hidden behind the mask after stripping.

This edge allowance interferes with the accurate alignment of type columns, but this difficulty can be eliminated by cutting a slit about ¼ inch long at the top left edge of the proof and another at the bottom left. The cut then forms small tabs that can be lifted up to permit lining up the proofs with the grid line below.

Illustrations can be most accurately placed if they are positioned before final trimming. Crop marks or grid lines can be followed for the final trimming.

Preparing Overlays

An overlay is usually required for each color, in addition to black and/or for any double burning that is required. It is possible, however, that printers prefer to break for color from a single mechanical. For example, if everything on a page is to be black except a title line in green, one mechanical, including the title as well as other

Working at a light table with T-square and ruling devices, a staff member pastes proofs in exact position to create a usable mechanical.

Border tape is used to form column rules or outlines for boxed areas. It is available in various styles and is pressure sensitive.

Type proofs, coated with adhesive wax or rubber cement, are positioned on the grid sheet.

An overlay is used with a key pasteup to assure the correct positioning of material that is to be in any additional plate burning. The key and the overlay are photographed separately, put into separate masks, and exposed to separate plates if they are to be printed in separate colors. They are exposed on the same plate when the overlay is used only to get precise positioning of elements for printing in black only.

Areas being set off for halftones are covered with pressure-sensitive red transparent film. The red film results in a clear window on the negative, thus permitting the placement of a screened negative beneath it. Screened Velox prints may be used on the mechanical instead of the film.

elements, could be used to make two negatives. By blocking out the title on the one negative, the black plate can be made. Then, by blocking out everything but the title in the other negative, the color plate can be made for applying the green ink.

When starting the preparation of an overlay, the register marks must be placed to coincide exactly with the marks on the key mechanical under the overlay. Then any material positioned on the overlay is as exactly located as it would be if it were being placed on the key.

Double Burning

To get the highest quality of reproduction, photographs are separately exposed on a printing plate. The technique used for positioning them on the key mechanical is to cut and position transparent red film in their place. Pressure-sensitive red tone sheets are available from art stores for this purpose. The result is a clear window in the negative made from the key mechanical. The halftone negative can then be stripped exactly into position in a separate mask that will be double burned on the same plate with the material from the key.

The best and most positive means for identifying illustrations for a stripper is to use a photostat of the illustration behind the red tone sheet; it will not appear in the negative, but it will be seen there on the mechanical as the stripper fastens half-tone negatives in the mask.

Tint Screens and Special Illustrations

Tint screens and special finishes for illustrations can be handled on mechanicals, but in general it is wiser to let printers do this work at the negative stage.

A tint screen glued to a mechanical can be distorted or marred before the mechanical is photographed, but, if a negative for a tint screen is stripped in position, quality of reproduction is guaranteed. The same is true of using red film to form a mask to outline a shape in a photo or to get a reversal of tones. Unless a staff is especially skilled in mechanical preparation, all these techniques are best left to the printer and his or her strippers.

Copy Processing: Editing for Production

AS editors apply their creative talents to improving words and pictures and putting them together as functional and attractive pages, they must be constantly aware of production-related aspects of editing.

They are creating a product that must be manufactured, and the limitations or capabilities of the manufacturing process (and the personnel involved) cannot be forgotten or ignored. Open communication, always in the language of the producers (printers), is essential through all the steps of copy processing.

These steps include marking instructions for typesetting, ensuring that all material is properly positioned, correcting the typesetting, and making certain that all material fits into the allocated position.

In some circumstances, the preparation of pages for the creation of negatives and plates by the printer is also an editorial responsibility.

Marking Instructions for Typesetting

The copyediting symbols presented in chapter 7 are used to tell printers of any changes in typewritten copy. They represent an efficient shorthand for deleting, inserting, and changing typewritten copy. On video terminals, the cursor and keystrokes provide even more efficiency in copy changing.

Specifications indicating how the body type is to be set are usually placed at the top of the manuscript, and the instructions for display type are usually put on the layout. There are many variables in typesetting, and absolute understanding between printer and editor is necessary if the printer is to deliver an acceptable product. Specifying all these variables would be somewhat complicated except for the fact that many of them, because they are the norm, can be assumed.

For example, a printer really needs eight specific bits of information before typesetting can begin, but most of these can be skipped under normal circumstances. Complete type specifications would include

1. Size of type (such as 8-point)
2. If there is to be additional white space between lines (usually created by adding space to make lines taller than the size of type, such as 8-point type set on a 10-point line)
3. Family name of the style, such as Bodoni, Baskerville, or Vogue
4. The particular variation within the family, such as bold or condensed
5. The posture of the type (roman [upright] or italic [slanted])
6. Letter composition (all capitals, capitals and lowercase, capitals and small capitals, etc.)
7. Appointment of space (flush left and right, centered, letter spacing, etc.)
8. Length of line (usually expressed in picas)

Although rarely are all these items included, a full set of instructions might be written in this fashion: *8/10 Bodoni Bold ital. c/lc, flush left and right × 18 picas.* The expression of the type size (8 pt.) and the thickness of line (10 pt.) as a fraction is a common short form, as are the abbreviations for italic and capitals and lowercase. The "× 18 picas" is also an accepted brief way of denoting line length; some editors designate line length as the bottom element of a fraction:

$$\frac{\text{8/10 Bodoni Bold Italic}}{\text{18 picas}}$$

Because of mutually accepted assumptions, only a few of these specifications need to be written on each piece of magazine copy. For body copy, it is assumed that there is no difference between type size and line thickness unless specified, the family version is standard, posture is upright, letter composition is as typed, appointment of space is flush left and right, and letter spacing is normal. A more typical set of instructions might simply be *8 pt Bodoni × 18 picas.* The more "unwritten" (but clearly understood) communication that exists between editor and printer, the more efficient the operation. In some in-house operations (the print shop is operated by the magazine's publisher), it may even be possible that no instructions are needed for most copy. If type specifications, including column width, are standard, only exceptions, such as cutlines, need to be marked.

Type specifications should be clearly written at the top of each piece of copy; they usually are circled to indicate that they are not part of the material to be set in type.

Computer Specifications

Computer video terminals can handle type specifications very efficiently. Terminals usually are on-line (wired directly) to a typesetter, and instructions can be keyboarded to the typesetter.

To avoid the necessity of transmitting the preceding eight points of specific information, computer systems are usually programmed to designate fonts by number, a font being the specific designation of one size of one branch of one family of type. Font 1 might be 8-point Century Condensed, for example. Other details, such as leading and line length, are usually programmed into *format* keys. In this case, *formatting* is the term describing the use of a single keystroke to specify complicated typesetting instructions. By prior programming, one keystroke might designate the specifics of display type to be used as a headline, as well as all necessary specifics for body type that goes with it.

Keying Copy for Location

No article is fully marked with instructions until it contains the information necessary to get it (1) to the proper publication when it is set in type and (2) to the correct location within the publication.

A *slug,* or guide, is necessary, usually including the name of the magazine, issue date, and page number. This information is set into type and becomes the first line or two on the type proof. In figure 17.1, "Printing Management" (PTG MGT) tells the printer which magazine the copy was set for, "November" indicates the issue, and "News National" tells the department where it is to be included. The same slugging systems prevail when working at computer terminals. The first line of type on the screen should identify the story; the page layout then shows where the story is to be placed.

Reading Type Proofs

Printers are responsible for the errors of their typesetters and correct such errors free of charge, provided they are detected and clearly marked on a galley proof. They also correct any author's errors at any time but charge for the labor time involved.

9755 — PTG MGT lh18

NEWS NATIONAL ....
NOV DRAHOS ....

Polychrome purchases plant to expand plate production

Polychrome Corporation, manufacturer and distributor of lithographic printing products, announces the purchase from Celanese Corporation of a manufacturing plant on a 10½ acre site in Clark, N.J.

Purchase of the recently constructed plant will enable the company to increase lithographic plate manufacturing to augment its present production facilities in Yonkers, N.Y. The new plant also will enable Polychrome to expand both production and research and development activities of many printing products the company markets including a new photopolymer relief plate for flexography, letterpress and dry offset.

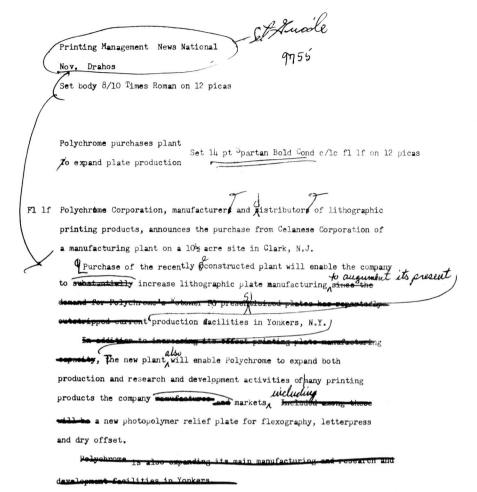

Figure 17.1 The typewritten sheet of copy as edited produced the accompanying galley proof. Note the typesetting instructions on the copy, plus slug (guide) lines. (Courtesy *Printing Management*.)

Corrections on type proofs are made with a uniform set of proofreading symbols (figure 17.2). Application of these symbols involves marking the error at the point it occurs in a line of type, sometimes drawing a guideline to the nearest margin, but always writing the proper symbol in the margin. A sample of corrected proof is shown in figure 17.3.

The admonition is worth repeating here that *all* type corrections should be detected and marked at the earliest possible stage of the type checking cycle. Corrections missed on galleys become costly as they are made on page proofs because they require undoing work already done.

When working with a computerized system, editors should make all corrections before type is *dumped* into the typesetter. Corrections made after proofs are made tend to lead to considerable resetting or sloppy work. Patching-in small sections of columns of type, once the type is exposed on the photopaper, can result in misalignment or shifting of the patches. Obviously, all errors cannot be avoided even with constant vigilance, but proofing copy while it is still on the screen must be as thorough as possible.

Fitting Body Copy to Space

As in the case of the proverbial two pounds of sugar that won't fit into a one-pound bag, it should be obvious that only so much copy in a given type size fits into a column, page, signature, or magazine. It should also be obvious that the feeling that would arise when an editor discovers he or she had underestimated the material would be dismal indeed. Blank pages, or pages with gaping white holes that should have been filled, just don't sell magazines or give editors satisfaction. The consequences of having too much copy are just as bad, although they may not be quite as obvious to the beginner. In either instance, quality and cost are both likely to be

Figure 17.2 Proofreading symbols.

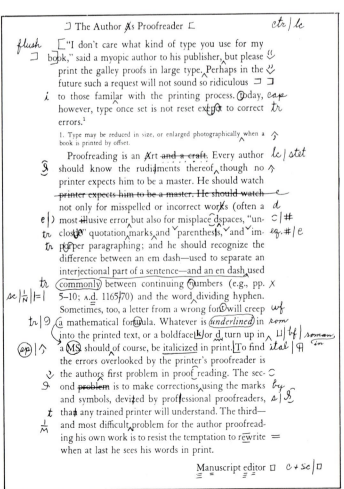

Figure 17.3 A corrected proof. Note that the correction symbols are in the margin.

```
LT(2)   STATUS  INSERT           LO(08) CW(10) FT(OPBOLC)   RT(2)
over a year ago offering to repair the public timepiece the commissioners did
not accept his offer at the time because the clock tower was pollutted with
pidgeon droppings a possible health hazzzard. But earlier this year the tower
was cleanled and the commisioners' approved Bartol's repair project although
he had to wait untill the whether was coll enought to allow him to work
comfortably in the tower.<<
'He quietly started repairing the clock Friday morning, examining the gigantic
faces and internal gizmos.  He discovered several twisted screws, but the only
other attention the North sand south clockfaces needed was a good kerosene
soaking, which cleaned and lubricated the delicate inner parts.<
'Bartol discovered the clock almost qualified as an antique, although he
couldn't give its exact age.<
'''A lot of people would like to get their hands on one of these he said.<
'By late afternoon, Bartol was redy to align the hands of the two working
sides with the accurate time.  Sheriff Robert Allen loaned him two sheriffs'
department walkie-talkies.  Bartol had Tammy Presley, a graduate
photojournalism student who was photographing the operation, stay in the tower
and operate one radio. A start time later, Bartols daughter joined her father
and Ms. Presley.<
'County Commissioner      Roxanne Groff ws elected to descend to street level
with the second radio as Bartol adjusted the gigantec hands.<
'Bartolsaidhe will return some Saturday to repair the eat and west faces.  He
also will attempt to fix the bell, which rang in the tower yeterday but
couldn't be heard on the street.<
```

In a computerized system, proofreading is done on a video screen. Here the cursor is placed in the fourth line to delete a character. The fact that the editor is actually serving as a typesetter places greater responsibility at this stage of correcting copy in computerized systems.

affected. Under-writing can destroy appearance, and rushing to fill unwanted holes at the last minute often adds overtime costs or causes delay. Over-writing also can destroy appearance, and there is a direct and measurable cost that comes from *overset,* type set by the printer but not used. Printing contracts are based on a normal amount of typesetting, and printers rightfully charge for excessive overset.

Careful planning during copyediting is necessary, therefore, to have material fit space that has been allotted to it or to allot sufficient space for material that has already been processed. Most magazines try to fit copy with an accuracy that permits no more than a line or two of variation in a column; they also like to have a system that is as simple as possible in its computations. With only a line or two of variations, a shortage can be compensated for with slight additional white space between paragraphs. On the other hand, a line or two of extra length can usually be squeezed into an area without destroying page design; at least any resetting would be minimal. Some magazines, such as *Life* and others that copied it during its lifetime as a weekly, carried copyfitting to an extreme by insisting that the last line in a block of copy fill out to the right in spite of the fact that some resetting was often needed.

The copyfitting system used for body copy by virtually all magazines is based on the number of characters in a specific typeface that fit into a given line length. A character is any letter, space, number, or piece of punctuation; no allowance is made for obvious variations in width among characters. In small type sizes and relatively large copy blocks, variations in character width are expected to average out.

The character count system does take into account the variations resulting from design differences in typefaces and, consequently, is much more precise than systems based on average type designs or on words rather than characters. To use the system, an editor must be provided with information about the typeface he or she is using. This information is furnished by the printer or type manufacturer, either in the form of figures denoting the number of characters in a pica of line length (figure 17.4) or the number in a given line length, such as 20 picas (figure 17.5).

When working with information presented as it is in figure 17.5, the line length (in picas) must be multiplied by the number of characters in a pica to find the number of characters in a line. For example, a line of 10-point Baskerville that is 20 picas long would contain 52.8 characters (20 × 2.64). For ease in computation, this figure can be rounded off, preferably to the lower whole number, 52. It is better to be slightly short of copy than over because type cannot be squeezed into a smaller space, but it can be spaced out without difficulty.

A magazine operating with columns that are 20 picas wide would therefore be copyfitted on the basis of 52 characters in each line of type if the face chosen was 10-point Baskerville. To facilitate copyfitting, most magazines would then standardize manuscript typing to 52 characters per line so a line of typewritten material would be, on the average, equivalent to a line of type. The printing of ruled copy paper with the space between rules accommodating the desired number of characters is a common aid for copyfitting. Manuscripts typed on the ruled paper, if lines are typed so that those that go beyond the right margin are balanced out by those that are short of the right margin, contain lines each the equivalent of a line of type.

When the number of characters per line is known, the only other dimensions involved in copyfitting are the number of lines and the thickness of lines. For an example, let's assume that our magazine uses 10-point Baskerville leaded two points (10/12 Baskerville) in columns that are 20 picas wide. A manuscript that has been typed with 52 characters per line contains a total of 36 lines. We would know immediately to allow 36 picas of space in a column for the manuscript because each typewritten line is the equivalent of a line of type, and each line of type is 12 points (one pica) thick.

Eliminating the shortcuts taken in the previous example, the procedure for finding the amount of space an article will occupy involves

1. Finding the number of characters that fit into a line of type (from printer's information)
2. Finding the number of characters in the manuscript being edited (facilitated by typing manuscripts in standard fashion)
3. Dividing the number of characters per line into the number of characters in the manuscript to find the number of lines of type needed
4. Multiplying the number of lines of type needed by the thickness of the line to find how many points of column depth the article will occupy. Because dummying is ordinarily done in picas, divide the points by 12 to find the number of picas of depth.

Although at first glance copyfitting seems to be complicated, for magazine editors it really is not. The fact that type styles and sizes and column width are standardized takes care of much of it for them. After fitting a few articles to space, it becomes a matter of simple routine. For the beginner, practice can bring the same skill and confidence. Figure 17.6 shows the steps involved "by the numbers" as an aid for practice.

Copyfitting with computer systems can be virtually effortless, depending on the sophistication of the system. Major news weeklies have systems that instantly show the equivalent of a type proof on a screen permitting additions or deletions by keyboard to make the copy fit a space. Other systems may require input of basic type instructions and font specifications before computing the length of the column that would be formed by the copy.

Face	Point Sizes				
	8	9	10	11	12
Baskerville	3.22	2.96	2.64	2.46	2.3
Caledonia	3.12	2.87	2.63	2.44	2.26
Caslon	3.39	3.27	3.16	2.76	2.38

Figure 17.4 Characters per pica.

Face: 10-point Bodoni

Length of line in picas:	12	14	16	18	20	22	24	26	28	30
Characters per line	37	43	49	55	61	67	73	79	85	91

Face: 10-point Bernhard Modern Roman

Length of line in picas:	12	14	16	18	20	22	24	26	28	30
Characters per line	43	50	57	64	71	78	85	92	99	106

Figure 17.5 Characters per line.

Figuring to determine depth of space needed on layout:

1. Find characters per pica or characters in line from printer's type catalog. If using characters per pica, multiply by picas in line of type to get characters per line.
2. Determine total characters in article by multiplying characters in a typewritten line times number of lines in article. All lines count as full lines.
3. Divide total characters in article by the characters in line of type to find the number of lines of type that will be produced when article is set in type. Round up to next line if answer is in fraction.
4. Multiply the lines of type by thickness of lines (type size plus leading if any) to find the space needed (in points). Convert to picas by dividing by 12 points in a pica. You can now mark off that total depth on your layout knowing the article will fit.

Finding how many characters to write to fill space on layout:

1. Find characters per pica or characters in line from printer's type catalog. If using characters per pica, multiply by picas in line to get characters in line of type.
2. Measure depth of area on layout in picas and convert to points by multiplying by 12 points in a pica.
3. Determine number of lines of type that will fit in area by dividing points of depth by thickness of type line (type size plus leading if there is any). Round down to lower number if answer is in a fraction.
4. Multiply the lines of type by the number of characters in a line of type to find the total number of characters to write. You can now proceed to write an article of that length knowing that it will fit the layout.

Figure 17.6 Copyfitting at a glance.

Fitting Display Type to Space

Computerized systems also make fitting of display type relatively effortless. After the words or lines are on the screen, input of the type specifications via the keyboard results in the computer's determining the number of picas per line needed for the material as specified.

In traditional copy processing, the common procedure for fitting titles is to write and design the title and to specify an appropriate type that fits the space. Hand lettering of the type to correct size (often called *comp* lettering) reveals which size or sizes to specify. Some trial-and-error effort may be involved, but, if a type catalog with complete fonts is available, tracing of letters guarantees an absolute fit.

When specifying size based on hand lettering, the novice must remember to allow for descending strokes. Figure 17.7 shows how guidelines for the center body letters (such as *a, c,* and *e*) and the tips of the ascenders assure accurate sizing and fitting to space. Remember, no letter ever measures out to be the point size needed, not even capitals. Size of type is based on the body, which includes space for descenders on letters such as *y* and *p,* even if all capitals are used.

In some instances, the use of transfer or paste-down letters can be the most efficient method of all. With only reasonable care, the title can be presented on a layout exactly as it will be when it appears on a finished page.

If a means for enlarging or reducing is available, such as a photostat machine or process camera, manipulation of title sizes is easier than by trial-and-error. Also, sophisticated typesetting that permits reverse leading, letter distortion, and limitless size with its internal enlargement or reduction makes title design much more flexible.

Newsmagazines and other magazines with book-style design usually simplify title design and type fitting through the use of *headlines* and *headline schedules.*

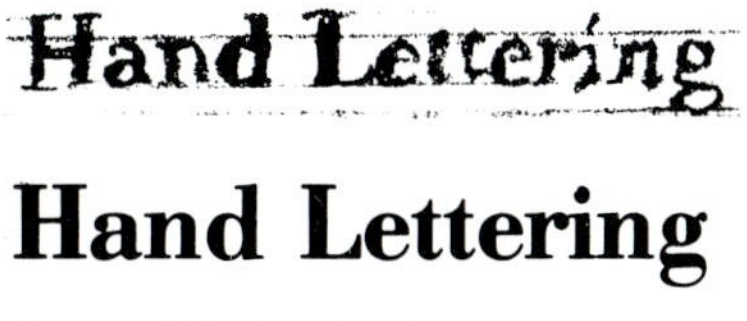

Hand Lettering

Hand Lettering

Figure 17.7 The best way to assure the fit of display type in most magazine situations is to letter the type exactly to size by hand, as shown here. To have the type set in the size as lettered, one must be certain to allow for descending letters, even if there are none in the line.

```
Many Men Want
Equality Also
```

**Many Men Want
Equality Also**

Figure 17.8 The top lines were typed at a typewriter without proportional spacing and appear to be equal. When set in type, the lines are quite different in length.

Use of a Headline Schedule

Headlines and headline schedules are really a product of newspapers, but they have a natural application to magazines with standardized title treatments. Assuming that one, two, or at most, three type families are to be used, it is relatively easy to establish acceptable size, depth, and width restrictions for a variety of headline patterns.

First, the typefaces to be used must be determined, including the number of sizes and family variations to be available. Second, the display patterns must be selected; flush left and/or right lines are common. The third and last step is to establish a headline schedule that is based on these selections and provides the method for fitting the headlines to space.

The first and second steps just outlined are really design considerations and should be a part of the creation of a personality for the layout and page grid of the magazine. Selection of conservative, old-style typefaces or new, modern faces obviously help establish the visual character of any publication.

The mechanics of setting maximum or minimum lengths for headlines are relatively simple. We should recall here that typography is based on variable letter spacing, not equal spacing as with typewriters (figure 17.8). This variable letter spacing, plus the fact that there are only a few letters, each with large size, in most headlines makes the use of character counting too inaccurate for fitting headlines to space. Instead, we would have to make allowances for thin letters, such as *Iliftjr* and wide letters such as *m, w,* and capitals. A *unit count* system with reasonable allowances for such variations is usually needed.

Unit Count System

In order to simplify the fitting of headlines to space, a simple unit count system with only four variations is usually used, considering letters to fall into one of these four categories: thin, medium, fat, and superfat. With one unit for medium, the thin letters are considered to be one-half, the fats one and one-half, and the superfats two. The task then is to determine which characters should be in each of the four divisions, with these assignments often being accepted:

> One unit: All normal letters, such as *a, b, c, d, e, g, h, k, n, o, p, q, r, s, u, v, x, y, z,* spaces between words, all numbers except one (1)
> One-half unit: Narrow letters *I, l, i, f, t* and perhaps *j, r,* depending on the particular typeface being used
> One and one-half units: All capitals plus the lowercase *x, m,* and *w*
> Two units: Capital *M* and *W*

Note that the unit assignments made in determining counts for the headline schedule must be used as the headlines are fitted to space. If *j* and *r* are normal letters in the original count, they must be given a full count as headlines are written.

For every specific headline included in a schedule, a sample should first be set. One example here should suffice to show the procedure. Assuming that we have a headline to be formed by flush-left lines of 36-point Bodoni stretching across two 13.5 pica columns with one pica of white space between them, we can set lines with a random assortment of letters to fit that space, 28 picas. Figure 17.9 shows such a line, along with the assignment of unit values for each character. It indicates that the maximum number of units possible for such lines is 21. Figure 17.10 shows a line from a headline written to conform to that maximum, with the unit count conforming to the one used for the sample. Unit counting assures that this line of 20 units fits the space allowed for it.

It is possible to establish a much more accurate counting system for display type based, for example, on the subdivisions of the *em* that prevail in many display typesetters. Most typesetters divide the em (the unit of measure equal to the square in the type size, or what usually is the width of a lowercase *m*) into 18 units, thus allowing much wider variations, with separate values for *i* and *f*, for example. However, such a system would make counting headlines too complicated and time consuming. The "half to one and one-half" variations provide sufficient accuracy, so headlines, properly counted, seldom fail to fit.

Because type families vary according to their manufacturers, it is best to use the output of the typesetters that will be used for production as a basis for a headline schedule. Using paste-down letters in creating a schedule when a phototypesetter will be used for production puts unnecessary inaccuracies into the system.

Mdlirep Cen witf Ghitile

2   1   ½ ½ 1   1   1   1   1½   1   1   1½   ½ ½ ½ 1   1½   1   ½ ½ ½ ½   1 (21)

Figure 17.9 An assortment of letters in 36-point Bodoni by 28 picas.

Roads Suffer Damage

1½   1   1   1   1 1 1½   1   ½ ½   1   1 1   1½   1   1½   1   1   1   (20)

Figure 17.10 A line written to conform to maximum for 28 picas.

18 Processing Illustrations for Production

GETTING original illustrations ready for production is even more involved than the marking, correcting, and fitting to space of body copy. The steps are fundamentally the same—illustrations must be marked for the printer, errors must be corrected, and art must fit the space allocated to it—but the fact that the illustrations must be rephotographed compounds the procedures.

Any illustration, from a bar chart to a full-color photo, can be enlarged or reduced for reproduction, and the figuring involved for these enlargements and reductions is puzzling to some beginners in editing. Part of the problem stems from the fact that this figuring does not take place in a vacuum; the content of the photo or other illustration is an important and ever-present consideration. To make the process as clear as possible, let's consider it step-by-step and in terms relating directly to magazine usage.

Marking Printers' Instructions

No illustration is ready for production until it contains four crop marks to set its original dimensions and provide the printer with reproduction dimensions. In special circumstances, special descriptions of the reproduction techniques must be given.

Let's look at the photo in figure 18.1. You may recognize it as the same picture used in chapter 14 to show how it was cropped to emphasize the main subject. Note that there are four crop marks; the two across the top are establishing the original width, and the two on the right side are establishing the original depth. Any additional crop marks would be confusing and misleading for printers, but these four are essential. The top pair could be used across the bottom, and the side pair could be moved to the right side, but in no case would we use more than those four. As far as printers are concerned, the photo has now been cut off at those marks, just as much as if it had been cut with scissors or a razor blade.

Look also at the weather map in figure 18.2; it also contains the four crop marks. Without the crop marks, the dimensions are not established, as far as a printer is concerned. In this case, the marks allow the full outline of the map to be included in the reproduction.

It is best to keep all dimensions or other marks off the front of the photo; they would only create confusion. Crop marks also should be in the border, if possible, and made with a china marker (grease pencil) so they can be rubbed off if need be. Any lines drawn on the face of the illustration are a source of potential production problems, often finding their way into the reproduction at some points.

With crop marks placed, the next step is to give the printer directions for making the reproduction. This can be written on the back (preferably on a sticker, so the writing does not press into the photo) in terms of inches (for example, 4 × 3 inches) or picas (24 by 18 picas), with the width always expressed first. For the photo in figure 18.1, we would also have to specify a screen to be used in the reproduction.

Figure 18.1 This photograph, used in chapter 14 to illustrate cropping to improve a photograph, shows the crop marks necessary for a printer: two to set the width and two to set the depth.

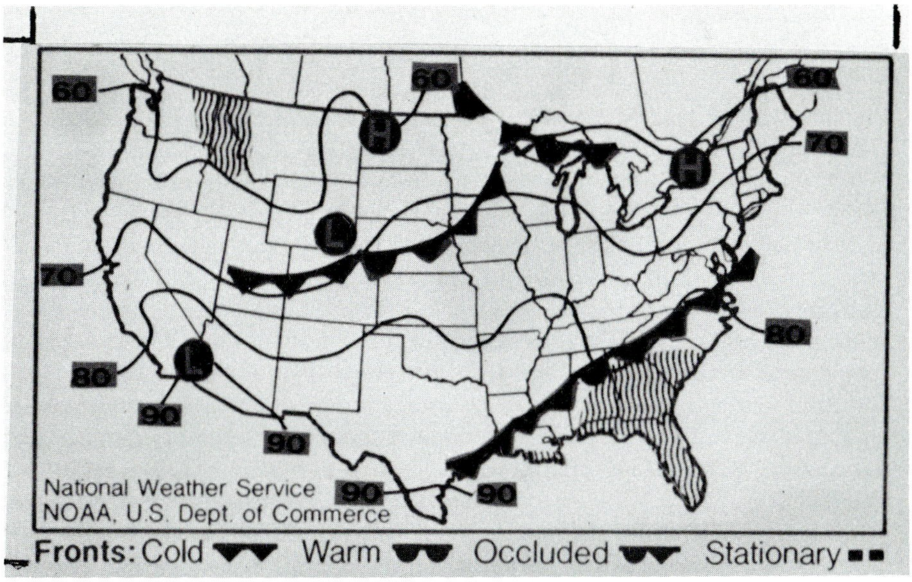

Figure 18.2 No illustration, including line drawings like this weather map, is ready for production without the four crop marks as shown.

Continuous tone illustrations are reproduced in printing by being rephotographed through a screen in a large *process* camera, a camera equipped with a vacuum back to hold a film screen tightly over film as light is reflected from the copy board to the film, as shown in chapter 11. The screen is made of intersecting black lines, and the areas between the lines form small openings for light to go through to the film and expose dots. The formation of these dots provides the means for capturing the various tones of the original on film and then on the printing plate.

The more intersecting lines per linear inch of a screen, the finer the dots are and, generally, the finer the reproduction that is possible. The common screens for magazines contain 110, 120, 133, or 150 lines per inch, all of which provide reasonable fidelity of reproduction, but one of them must be specified. Therefore, to complete our marking for the photo in figure 18.1, we might order (on the back of this photo) a 4-by-3-inch, 150-line halftone reproduction.

For the map in figure 18.2, the marking could be complete with dimensions (such as 4 inches by 3 inches) and *line illustration* as to the type of reproduction desired.

Marking of illustrations, therefore, seems simple enough—just set the dimensions of the original with four crop marks and specify reproduction dimensions and the type of reproduction desired. There are several complications, however. If drawings are to be reproduced in more than one color, overlays should be made containing the portion of the drawing to be done in each color. If special treatments, such as silhouetting a portion of the photo, are required, an overlay containing visual and verbal instructions to show exactly which portion is to be outlined must be included. The biggest complication is related to the enlargement and reduction of the originals.

Enlargements and reductions are made photographically, and reproduction dimensions *must* relate to the original dimensions. The fact that we ordered a 4 × 3 inch reproduction in figure 18.1 does not guarantee that a printer can deliver a reproduction in those dimensions. As a matter of fact, that would be impossible because the original shape is a vertical, and 4 × 3 is horizontal. The work involved in relating original shapes and sizes to reproduction dimensions is called either *proportioning* or *scaling*. Photographs rarely come from photographers with the same dimensions an editor eventually sets for them. If such is the case, they can be cropped and marked to be reproduced *same size* (SS). Otherwise, some proportioning or scaling must be done.

Proportioning and Scaling

Although this aspect of illustration processing is relatively simple, it seems to be difficult for some beginners to grasp; rather than understand the procedure, they attempt to learn a handy formula only to find that their lack of understanding often makes the formula, or any other helpful device, useless.

To clarify, let's look at this technique from two directions, each suggested by one of two names given to it. Proportioning, for example, refers to shape, and shape is set by the relationship of the sides of a rectangle. A rectangle that is 4 inches wide and 4 inches deep is a square shape; one that is 4 inches wide by 8 inches deep is a vertical shape; and one that is 10 inches wide and 5 inches deep is a horizontal shape (refer to figure 18.3). In processing illustrations, we must remember only that the enlarged or reduced shape has the same proportions as those of the original. Therefore, our square (4 × 4) can be enlarged or reduced to any other square (2 × 2, 8 × 8, 1.5 × 1.5, and so on) because the relationship of 4/4 equals 2/2, 4/4 equals 8/8, and 4/4 equals 1.5/1.5.

Our vertical rectangle (4 × 8) reduces and enlarges only to other vertical shapes with the same relationship of sides, such as 2 × 4, 3 × 6, and 5 × 10. For all these rectangles, the width is one-half the depth.

The horizontal rectangle can enlarge or reduce only to shapes with the same proportion of 10 to 5 (such as 4 to 2, 12 to 6, and so on).

The proportions in these examples are deliberately obvious, and the potential enlargements or reductions can be seen without any computation. For shapes that are not obvious, computation can be carried out in this fashion:

$$\frac{\text{Original width}}{\text{Original depth}} \text{ equals } \frac{\text{Reproduction width}}{\text{Reproduction depth}}$$

When three of the dimensions are known, the fourth can be found quickly:

$$\frac{8}{10} \text{ equals } \frac{4}{x}$$

In this case, our photo is 8 inches wide and 10 inches deep and is being reduced so it is 4 inches wide, but we do not know the depth. By cross-multiplying, we find that $8x$ equals 40. Dividing both sides by 8 then tells us that x equals 5. We then know that an 8 × 10 reduces to a 4 × 5. Any problem in which editors know three dimensions and must find the fourth can be solved in this manner. They are simply finding dimensions of a rectangle that has the same proportion as another rectangle, the dimensions of which they already have.

On the other hand, if one thinks of this process as *scaling*, one is concerned with an area being enlarged or reduced so that it is *to scale* with the original, just as maps are to scale (i.e., 1 inch equals 10 miles). Now we must keep in mind the fact that, if one side of a rectangle is reduced, the other side is reduced to the same degree. Therefore, if we consider our 4 × 4 square on this basis, we think of the width, 4 inches, being reduced to 2 inches, and the depth being subjected to the same reduction, 4 inches to 2 inches. For our earlier example of a vertical rectangle, if the 4-inch width is reduced to 2 inches, the 8-inch width must also be reduced to half its dimensions, 4 inches.

Figure 18.3 Understanding the figuring of proportions of photo enlargement or reduction involves an appreciation of the basic rectangular shapes: vertical, horizontal, and square.

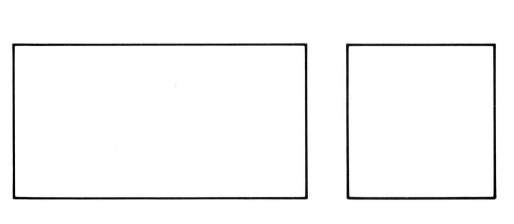

Setting these up as we did before, we see that the original width reduces to a reproduction width as the original depth is reducing at the same rate to a reproduction depth:

$$\frac{\text{Original width}}{\text{Reproduction width}} \text{ equals } \frac{\text{Original depth}}{\text{Reproduction depth}}$$

All problems that an editor might have can easily be computed in this manner. For example, if the 4 × 8 rectangle is going to be reduced to a reproduction that is 2 inches deep, the editor wants to know the width of the reproduction:

$$\frac{4}{x} \text{ equals } \frac{8}{2}$$
$$8x \text{ equals } 8$$
$$x \text{ equals } 1$$

The reproduction of the 4 × 8 photo therefore will be 1 × 2.

Whether one thinks in terms of illustration proportions or their scaling is relatively immaterial. Because their camera settings are based on the percentage of reduction, printers are concerned with scaling. For them, the preceding problem is simply a matter of the 8-inch depth being reduced to one-fourth of its original size, a 25 percent reduction (meaning that it is reduced to 25 percent of its original size). The important point for beginners here is simply that they should understand either method of computation.

Editors who must figure enlargements or reductions for scores of illustrations for each issue would do almost anything to avoid figuring their problems as just shown, and rightly so. They are interested in speed and accuracy for getting the job done. Note, however, that ability to make the arithmetical computations is necessary for emergencies, and for an understanding of how any device operates.

The most common scaling tool (figure 18.4) contains a rotating circle that is calibrated in fractions of inches on its edge. This circle is matched on the fixed background surface by another circle calibrated in the same fashion. The figures on the outer (fixed) circle line up with the figures on the rotating circle and represent fractions, all of which are equal around the circle. The scaler shown in figure 18.4 has been set so the 8-inch original width is across from the 10-inch original depth. By looking to the left on the outer circle until we find the new width (4), we can locate the new depth (5) because it is directly across from the 4.

This scaler can also be used to figure the percentage of reduction involved in any problem. When either original dimension on the inner scale is lined up against the reproduction size of that dimension, the percentage of reduction shows under the arrow. In figure 18.4, because the 10 is lined up with the 8, the arrow points to 80 percent. With the circular scaler, pictures can be proportioned or percentage of reduction can be figured in only a second or two.

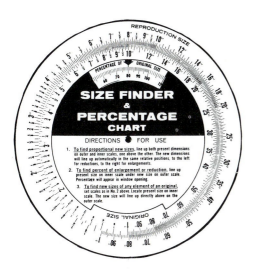

Figure 18.4 This circular scaling device contains a stationary outer circle and a rotating inner circle. By turning the inner circle, you can line up original dimensions, one over the other (8 over 10 in this case), and all ratios around the wheel are of that shape. If the reproduction width is to be 4 inches, we can tell that the depth is 5 because it is directly under the 4. As shown later, the wheel can also be used to find percentage of reduction.

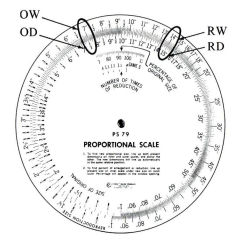

Figure 18.5 When the 7-inch original width is lined up over the 7.5-inch original depth, we can look to the right for 14 and find that the depth is 15 picas. The fact that one set of numbers is in inches and the other in picas is immaterial to the scaling wheel.

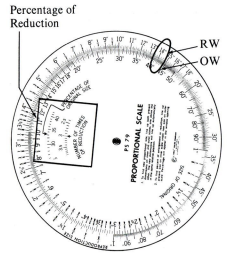

Figure 18.6 To figure percentage of reduction, one original dimension is divided into its counterpart reproduction dimension, and the wheel will figure this by having the original dimension below the reproduction dimension. If 42 picas is to reduce to 14 picas, we put the 42 picas beneath 14 and look into the opening in the scaler for the percentage (33⅓).

Some Typical Examples

Now let's get back to some examples that are typical of the normal day's routine for magazine editorial staffs. In one of them, we first crop the photo and then do the proportioning. In the other, we have to make the proportions of the original conform to the shape of the reproduction.

Let's start with the easier example. We'll use an 8 × 10-inch original glossy photograph of the head and shoulders of a man. As we look at the image of the man, we place two crop marks across the top, cutting off a little unnecessary background as we do so. Those crop marks measure 7 inches between them, and that is now our original width. Next we place two crop marks at the left, one slightly below the top and the other up a bit from the bottom. The distance between these crop marks is 7.5 inches and that is now our original depth. This picture must reduce to fit into our column width, which is only 14 picas. With three dimensions known, it is easy for us to do our figuring based on proportioning:

$$\frac{\text{Original width}}{\text{Original depth}} \text{ equals } \frac{\text{Reproduction width}}{\text{Reproduction depth}} \text{ or } \frac{7}{7.5} \text{ equals } \frac{14}{x}$$
$$7x \text{ equals } 105$$
$$x \text{ equals } 15 \text{ picas}$$

Notice two things of importance here: the fact that the original started out as an 8 × 10-inch photo does not enter the figuring because (1) the original dimensions are always within the crop marks and (2) we did not bother to convert picas to inches or vice versa because that would be wasted effort. As we do the figuring, we are concerned merely with figures (ratios) that set shapes. We assign picas to our answer of 15 after the figuring. The only trick is to know if the answer in such problems is in picas or inches. The fact that photos are often measured in inches, and layouts are always designed in picas, makes it handy to be able to figure as we have here, without converting dimensions. It works with the wheel too (see figure 18.5).

If, however, we want to figure percentage of reduction, we must divide one original dimension into its counterpart reproduction dimension, and both figures must be in the same unit of measure, either inches or picas. We could convert the 7 inches into 42 picas (remember: 6 picas to an inch) and divide that into 14 to find that the percentage of reduction would be 33⅓ percent, as we can see in figure 18.6.

It is important to understand that in this example we are concerned with ratios that set shapes; 7 by 7.5 is slightly vertical, as the reproduction must also be, and 14 by 15 does represent the same shape. Incorrect answers are readily discernible if this correlation of shapes is kept in mind.

This example is probably the most typical proportioning problem facing magazine editors, and it is by far the simplest. Cropping is dictated totally by content, and the one reproduction dimension is dictated by the column width.

Cropping for Shape

Sometimes cropping must be done to change the shape of a photo, hopefully without weakening the content, and preferably also improving it. The situation arises when layouts are completed, and content is made to adhere to the layout. In such cases, the dimensions of the reproduction of a photo are set, and the photo must be made to conform to them. Any of the preceding proportioning and scaling methods must then be used to determine how much to crop from the original photo to get it to the right proportions. Such problems merely involve taking one of the original dimensions as the unknown; the other photo dimension joins the two reproduction dimensions as known figures. The visualizing of shapes tells an editor which original dimension becomes the unknown; if a horizontal is to be reduced to a vertical, the width becomes the unknown and, if a vertical is to be reduced to a horizontal, the depth becomes the unknown. If the change in shape is not obvious, it is more difficult to visualize.

Such is often the case with the most common instance involving cropping to shape: the marking of a photo to become a full-page bleed reproduction. In some respects, this also represents the most difficult problem for students to understand.

One of the complications is the fact that photos that bleed off the edge of a page must be reproduced slightly larger than the page, so when the page is trimmed the chance of any irregularity with the edge is eliminated. The *bleed allowance,* as it is called, is usually 1/8th inch or 1 pica; this is sufficient to compensate for irregular folding or binding that otherwise might leave a sliver of white along a portion of an outside edge. Bleed allowance prevails *only* for the *trimmed* edges, so a full-page bleed would be trimmed top, bottom, and outside. For an 8½″ × 11″ magazine, we would add 2 picas to the depth and 1 to the width, making it 52 × 68 picas.

Suppose, then, that we have an excellent photo of basketball action for the cover of a sports magazine and it is, before cropping, 8 inches wide and 10 inches deep. Can an 8 × 10″ photo be reproduced as a 52 × 68-pica photo?

$$\text{Does } \frac{8}{10} \text{ equal } \frac{52}{68} \text{ ?}$$
$$10 \times 52 = 520, \text{ and } 8 \times 68 = 544$$

Obviously, 520 does not equal 544, but they are reasonably close. Some cropping must be done to make the photo's shape exactly the same as 52 × 68 picas without weakening the photo. The simplest way to do that is to crop the photo's width slightly, so the product of original width × reproduction depth drops from 544 to 520. Our ratios would be

$$\frac{x}{10} \text{ equals } \frac{52}{68}$$
$$68x \text{ equals } 520$$
$$x \text{ equals } 7.64$$

This figuring and the wheel in figure 18.7 tell us that we must crop the 8-inch width to 7.64 inches and, by studying the photo's content again, we determine that such cropping would do no damage to the picture. What would happen if we wanted to get rid of some of the depth of the photo? The amount to crop from the width would increase, and that could be troublesome.

Finding the percentage of reduction or enlargement in the previous example could be done most simply by dividing the original depth in picas (60) into the reproduction depth (68); we find that the reproduction would be a 113 percent enlargement.

The use of a circular scaler eliminates all the calculations in these examples, but practice is essential before newcomers can know with certainty which way the wheel is to be set, and where the pertinent ratios are located.

Production Techniques for Illustrations

Our examples of the photograph and the map illustrated the two common divisions of reproductions for illustrations: halftones and line. There are many variations possible for both of these reproduction divisions, as well as combinations of the two. Let's look at all these possibilities, starting with the simplest line illustration and working through combination reproductions. All have some value for magazines and should be understood by anyone responsible for processing illustrations for any printing process.

Line Drawings

The simplest form of illustration is a line drawing (figure 18.8). An artist creates a line drawing, usually with pen but perhaps with pencil or brush, without any middle tones. Where a pen makes a mark, the full tone (black) is created; the background (nonprinting areas) carries no tone.

For offset or rotogravure reproduction, the drawing can be pasted in position on its page layout, unless it has been prepared so that the special enlargement or reduction is required. If enlargement or reduction is needed, the lithographer makes a special *line negative* to be put into position in a mask, along with other elements on the page.

There is no charge for line illustrations in offset lithography or rotogravure unless a special negative is needed.

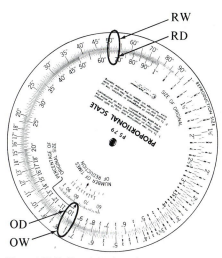

Figure 18.7 If a photo is to be reproduced as a full-page bleed (52 picas by 68 picas) we can set that ratio and look across from our known original dimension (10 inches) and find the missing original dimension (7.64 inches). Remember, in this and other similar cases, the reproduction dimensions are absolute and one of the photo's dimensions must be changed.

Figure 18.8 The simplest reproduction is called a line reproduction; it has no middle tones, only the extremes of light and dark.

Reverse Line Drawings

Printers can convert line drawings so the background becomes the printing area, and the drawing becomes the nonprinting area. In other words, the black areas in the drawing become the white areas and vice versa. This necessitates the making of a second negative by the exposure of light through the original line negative onto another piece of film. Figure 18.9 shows a reverse line illustration.

Benday Shading

The impression of middle tones in a line drawing can be created by artificially applying shading to the desired areas, as in figure 18.10. Although printers can apply the shading patterns as they etch a plate, it is now much more common for the artist to apply patterns directly to the drawings. At any rate, the production of a bendayed line illustration is no different than that of a standard line illustration in offset lithography.

Benday patterns are available in many varieties, including dots, stippled effects, slashes, and hashmarks. Transparent patterned sheets, with adhesive backing, are usually used by the artist for applying the shading to drawings. Any art supply store can provide them.

Continuous Tone Illustrations: Halftones

Photographs, oil paintings, watercolors, and any other original illustrations containing continuous tones require special production handling. As pointed out earlier, illustrations of these types must be photographed through a screen to produce a negative that, when transferred to a metal surface, produces an image that reproduces the various shades of tone. Figure 18.11 shows a photo reproduced with an 85-line screen, a 133-line screen, and a 150-line screen for comparison. The reproduction as shown is referred to as a *square-finish halftone,* the basic rectangular presentation for a continuous tone illustration.

Many special finishes are available, each involving some added cost because of added production time. Any halftone illustration in letterpress is somewhat expensive because of the need to etch a zinc or copper plate. There is an added halftone

Figure 18.9 A reverse line illustration produces tones opposite from the original.

Figure 18.10 The appearance of middle tones can be added to line illustrations by applying screen patterns where desired. This process is called Benday.

cost in offset lithography also because the special screened negative must be prepared in exactly the same fashion as for letterpress printing. However, it is a considerably smaller cost than for letterpress because no special plate is etched.

Silhouettes

Any halftone can be given a *silhouette* (outline) treatment (figure 18.12). Even a standard mug shot (head and shoulders picture) can be made so the subject is silhouetted against the white background of the paper it is printed on. The treatment is especially effective in emphasizing the central subject of a photo; elimination of the background provides maximum contrast. Partial silhouette treatment also is effective in such instances as an athlete in action silhouetted from the feet upward but with the turf given square finish at the bottom. A building with a distinctive roof line may be silhouetted at the top but squared off at the bottom to retain a well-landscaped foreground. To get a silhouette finish, an editor usually uses a tissue overlay as a diagram specifying the background to be eliminated. The engraver or lithographer eliminates the dot structure from the appropriate background by painting that area on the negative with an opaque fluid. The extra charge depends on the time involved in opaquing the background; the reproduction dimensions are those of the rectangle that would have included the opaqued background.

Vignettes

To create a feeling of age, beauty, or softness, a halftone may be given a *vignette* finish (figure 18.13). Rather than have the subject silhouetted or on a square-finished background, it is given an irregular border that simply fades into the paper. Portraits of delicate beauties, old-time subjects, or any scene calling for a soft or sentimental treatment are often vignetted.

The vignette effect is achieved by gradually eliminating dots from the background area of a negative in an irregular border surrounding the subject. It, too, involves a time charge beyond the normal price of a square-finish halftone.

Ovals and Other Special Shapes

Another standard way of creating an old-time impression for a portrait is to present it in oval shape (figure 18.14). Any geometric shape can be reproduced, provided only that an overlay sheet shows the engraver or lithographer how the treatment is to be carried out. It is also helpful to provide him or her with line artwork that can be made into a line negative serving as a mask to create the special shape.

Figure 18.12 A silhouette or an outline halftone.

(a) (b) (c)

Figure 18.11 These halftones were made with (a) an 85-line screen, (b) a 133-line screen, and (c) a 150-line screen.

Figure 18.13 A vignette finish on a halftone.

Figure 18.14 An oval is only one of unlimited special shapes that can be ordered for halftones.

Do you know where your children are?

Figure 18.15 A mortised halftone.

Mortises and Notches

Areas within the border of halftones, or areas from the outer edge of halftones, may be eliminated to provide open space for type or other material. A cut-out within the halftone is a *mortise* (figure 18.15), and a cut-out from the outer edge inward is a *notch* (figure 18.16). The shape and dimensions of mortises and notches are shown on tissue overlays. Beginners must remember to allow for any enlargement or reduction of the photograph as they note the mortise or notch on the overlay. For letterpress printing, the areas are literally sawed out of the metal surface and wood mounting of the engraving plate. For lithography, the area need only be masked out when the negative is stripped into a mask.

Mortise and notch areas can be handy for inserting captions or titles; they also are sometimes used to make a spot for insertion of another illustration. Their added cost is usually negligible.

Fending for oneself has its drawbacks!

Figure 18.16 A notched halftone.

Combination Plates

The opportunity to have a line illustration and halftone in the same area without running a sheet through a press two times is provided by *combination* plates. As the name implies, these plates combine halftone and line material on the same plate surface. Because the reproduction of type constitutes line material, combination plates provide the opportunity to run titles or legends across a halftone surface.

If the line material is to appear in black on the surface of a halftone printing in black, the treatment is called a *surprint* or *double-print* combination (figure 18.17). The name comes from the fact that two photographic exposures (printings) are needed to get the two images on one plate surface. To get a surprint combination finish, an editor must provide the halftone copy (usually a photo) and the line illustration (often a proof of type). An overlay must be used to show the location for the line illustration on the face of the halftone. The production steps involved include the making of a normal halftone negative and line negative. The halftone negative is then exposed on the plate surface; when it is removed, the line negative is exposed in position. When the plate is then developed, the line illustration is in position on the halftone.

It should be obvious that, if a page is being printed in more than one color, the halftone can be printed in black and the line illustration can be printed in another color over it without the use of a combination plate.

Should it be desirable to have the line illustration appear in white on the halftone surface, a *reverse combination* treatment is required (figure 18.18). In addition to the line and halftone negatives required for a surprint combination, a reverse line negative must be made for this treatment. The halftone and reverse line negatives can be exposed on a plate simultaneously because the background area of a reverse negative is transparent.

Some Special Effects

Interesting and unusual special effects can be given to illustrations through what might be called *gimmickry.* Especially during the late 1960s and early 1970s, designers were making maximum effective use of such techniques as *line conversions, magnified screens, special screens,* and *posterization.* Most of these effects are best shown in multicolor reproduction, but a few can be illustrated here in black-and-white.

A line conversion is the reproduction of a continuous tone illustration as a line illustration (figure 18.19). It is designed to create an impression similar to a pen or brush drawing of the subject. Addition of color and combination with tone reproduction produce dramatic effects.

Magnified screen illustrations result from another distorting device for the reproduction of continuous tone illustrations. The dot pattern that is normally present in halftone reproductions is so magnified that the pattern becomes an integral part of the illustration (figure 18.20).

Special screens, in which the pattern may be made by straight lines, wavy lines, circles, pebble grains, wood grains, mezzotints or any custom design that might be wanted, are available and can be used in similar fashion. They are intended to add style or a mood to a continuous tone illustration. Some special screens are shown in figure 18.21.

In posterization, negatives made from a continuous tone illustration are manipulated to get the solid applications of color that create a poster look.

These special treatments are only a few of those available; there is virtually no limit to the design effects that can be obtained. Combinations of these treatments also present different and interesting results.

The talent and imagination of the art director, the skill of the lithographer or engraver, and editorial judgment of the editor, if mixed in proper dosages, can produce striking and effective results.

Figure 18.17 A surprint combination places line copy on the face of a halftone.

Figure 18.18 A reverse combination places line copy in reverse on the face of a halftone.

Figure 18.19 A continuous tone illustration reproduced as a line illustration is called a line conversion.

Figure 18.20 As shown here, halftone dots can be enlarged for special effects.

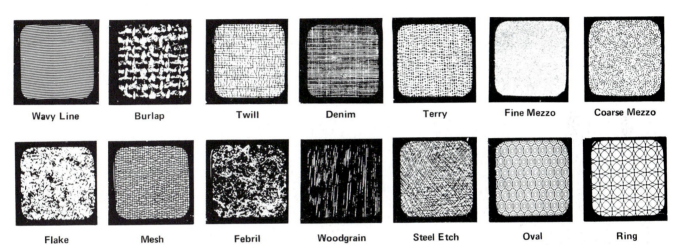

| Wavy Line | Burlap | Twill | Denim | Terry | Fine Mezzo | Coarse Mezzo |

| Flake | Mesh | Febril | Woodgrain | Steel Etch | Oval | Ring |

Figure 18.21 Special screens of many kinds are available to create special "mood" effects when reproducing photographs.

19 Magazine Circulation

MAKING it easy for readers to get their favorite magazines, whether at the newsstand or by mail, isn't as simple as one may imagine. A large magazine's circulation department may be the most complex operation within the organization.

Circulation means the distribution of periodicals to readers and also the number of copies of a given issue sold or distributed. Some editors believe in separation of editorial from other departments to the extent that they are unconcerned with circulation, but many find that sharing information with the circulation department can help them in the editing process.[1]

All magazines make basic policy decisions about circulation at the outset of their publishing venture and then review these from time to time as they continue publication.

Circulation Policy

The editorial idea for starting a magazine is itself a circulation policy decision. A plan to edit a magazine for working mothers about money management, meal preparation, child care, child health, personal health and beauty, and about balancing their careers with their families has implicit in it a policy of circulating to mothers pursuing careers who are interested in this mix of content. The target audience may have to be defined more specifically, but this is a starting point.

In the business magazine field, basic circulation and editorial policies are determined when a publisher decides, for example, to begin a magazine for computer network operators.

Sometimes the general policy may be specific enough. A travel magazine may want to reach *everyone* interested enough in travel to pay the subscription or single-copy rate. Another travel magazine may want to restrict its circulation to people who travel frequently to elegant destinations, another to consumers of resorts and tours.

A business magazine may want to restrict its audience to a field limited by certain criteria, such as job title, number of employees supervised, annual budget administered, size of company in which the subscriber is employed, or whether the subscriber is licensed within the field. *Purchasing,* for example, considers as qualified recipients "vice-presidents in charge of purchasing, purchasing directors, purchasing managers, purchasing agents, assistant purchasing agents, procurement managers, buyers, material directors and/or managers, plus a limited number of titled individuals who perform the purchasing function."

Some consumer magazines zero in on targets, such as people who live in the zip code areas with the highest family incomes (*Time*'s Top Zips edition), but most consumer magazines are not selective about who can subscribe.

Base circulation policy to be determined includes decisions about whether circulation will be primarily paid, primarily controlled, or a mixture of paid and controlled; whether it will be audited; and its desired demographic qualities.

Paid Circulation

Consumer magazines usually are distributed by paid circulation, which is one criterion for determining who is sufficiently interested in the magazine to receive it. Basic standards for paid circulation have been established by the Audit Bureau of Circulations (ABC). The ABC regulations are complex, but the two principal factors are that at least 70 percent of a magazine's circulation must be paid to qualify it as a paid magazine, and a purchaser must pay at least 50 percent of the basic price for a copy or subscription and not buy it for resale. A magazine with an $18-a-year subscription price can count as paid subscriptions all that are sold for $9 or more. A magazine with a $3 single-copy price similarly can count as paid all copies sold for $1.50 or more. Special offers and the number sold must be reported on the publisher's ABC statement.

Paid circulation has some advantages besides determining who will receive the magazine:

1. Paid circulation periodicals qualify for second-class postal rates, which are lower than other rates.
2. Paid subscriptions provide revenue to the publisher in addition to advertising revenue.
3. Paid lists can be "cleaner" because nonrenewals and cancellations are eliminated from the list. Under ABC rules, however, a nonrenewal can be carried up to three months beyond expiration and still be counted as part of the circulation.
4. Subscription renewal can be measured and is an indication of the reader's interest in the magazine. ABC does not require renewal percentages in its magazine reports, and most large consumer magazines do not report their renewal percentages. ABC defines a renewal as any subscription "received within six months after its expiration and paid for within seven months following receipt."

Controlled Circulation

The majority of business magazines are distributed by controlled circulation, which refers to setting specific qualifications and sending the publication to anyone who requests it and meets those qualifications. Qualifications usually are specified in terms of the field served and the types of persons who receive the publication.

Magazines with controlled circulation save much of the cost of promoting and selling subscriptions that paid publications must undertake and, although they must annually check on readers' qualifications, they save the cost of promoting renewals. This is especially beneficial in the business publications field where the definition of the target audience severely limits the number of persons eligible to be subscribers.

Advantages of controlled circulation include

1. Controlled publications can reach all the significant personnel in a field.
2. Broader coverage of the field can come to paid publications only through the time-consuming process of building circulation by selling subscriptions. Controlled publications can build rapidly.
3. Paid circulation may be developed through promotional devices such as discounts, premiums, aggressive subscription sales personnel, or low rates. A subscription does not necessarily mean interest.
4. Controlled publications avoid the high cost of promoting subscriptions and the extra record-keeping and collection problems involved.

Controlled circulation usually is linked to business publications, but some consumer magazines are distributed in this method. Other nonpaid magazines include the airline inflight magazines and magazines distributed in rooms by hotel chains.

Combination Paid and Controlled

Many magazines have some paid and some controlled circulation but are predominantly one or the other. A few approach a 50–50 split. The mixture of paid and controlled may change for a given magazine as conditions change. Natural expansion of its field made it advisable for *Automotive Industries* to increase its circulation to 30,000 from 20,000. The publisher made careful estimates and decided the advertiser would be best served by going part paid and part free, building the additional circulation on a tailor-made basis. It would have been too costly and time consuming to add 10,000 paid subscriptions on a quality-controlled basis. As time passed and the field expanded further, *Automotive Industries* became a totally controlled circulation magazine, its 93,000 circulation all nonpaid. Another Chilton publication, *Motor/Age,* has a circulation of 136,000, which is 39 percent paid and 61 percent nonpaid.

Auditing Circulation

Verification of circulation figures became a crucial issue in the early 1900s. Advertising rates were based on circulation, and exaggerated or false circulation claims were widespread. At that time, advertising agencies were mainly space brokers, buying space in publications and selling it at huge profits. Unscrupulous operators had an unfair advantage over honest publishers.

The Audit Bureau of Circulations was established in 1914 to set standards of definition and reporting for paid circulation. Growth of controlled circulation, primarily in the business publication field, eventually resulted in formation of the Controlled Circulation Audit in 1931, renamed in 1954 the Business Publications Audit of Circulation, Inc., or BPA.

Both ABC and BPA are tripartite organizations with voting power divided among advertisers, advertising agencies, and publishers. They audit only member publications. Membership dues vary according to class of membership and other characteristics of the member firm. In addition to membership dues, publishers pay the full cost of their audits based on a uniform hourly rate for the field auditor's time.[2]

A third auditing agency, the Verified Audit Circulation Corporation (VAC) is a profit-making organization that audits all types of publications, regardless of field served or method of distribution, and verifies the validity of circulation by surveys to random samples of subscribers.

For a magazine that sells advertising, the value of being audited is apparent. The standards established by the auditing agencies and verification of figures through the audit itself certify to advertisers the exact circulation, permitting advertisers to make more meaningful comparisons in selecting their media.

Auditing may be more important to magazines with large circulations. Most reported circulation is audited even though most magazines are not. An ABC circulation study found that 3,379 magazines, farm publications, and business publications in the United States reported circulation and that 454 did not report their circulations. Of these publications, 1,489 were audited and 716 ABC members accounted for 69 percent of the total reported circulation.[3]

The large-circulation magazines are paid, audited, and members of ABC. ABC lists 73 consumer magazine and farm publication members with circulations exceeding 1 million, not including comic books and magazine groups.

One also can sense that a subscriber to one magazine is not necessarily equal, in the eyes of the advertiser, to a subscriber to another magazine. The fact that hundreds of magazines can sell advertising without reporting circulation figures suggests that even an unknown quantity of readers in a given field has value to certain advertisers.

For many years, there was a significant separation between paid and controlled circulation publishers and auditing groups. As promotion and renewal costs increased, fields grew, and magazines wanted to reach them quickly and at low cost, multiple publishers issued some paid and some controlled magazines, and the situation changed.

BPA audited only controlled circulation until 1947. It now audits controlled, paid, and any combination of the two. ABC audited only paid circulation publications until 1970, when it changed its rules to admit business publications whose circulations were at least 70 percent request circulation in the field served, or a combination of paid and direct request totaling 70 percent of total distribution. The minimum for paid and direct request circulation is now 50 percent.

Auditing standards and definitions help standardize classifications to facilitate comparisons, even though no two publications or their audiences are identical. Besides total circulation, reports tell advertisers where the readers are and, for business publications, something about their dispersion within the field served.

Both ABC and BPA publisher's reports list thorough breakdowns of the average circulation per issue for a six-month period. Total qualified circulation is shown by paid and nonpaid and is broken down by subscriptions, single-copy sales, and subscriptions paid for out of association dues. They also list circulation for one issue by nine geographic regions, by individual states, and in Canada by provinces. For business publications, circulation also is shown by type of firms and persons served within the industry.

Publisher's reports also indicate the duration of subscriptions sold, prices for which they were sold, whether sold with premiums or not, and channels of subscription sales—mail, salespeople, association memberships, and other channels. Supplemental Data Reports may list circulation by county.

A large number of magazines that are not audited report their circulations on sworn (notarized) statements. For these, Standard Rate and Data Service defines the terms *paid, nonpaid* and *unpaid* or *nonqualified* the same as ABC and BPA to standardize figures reported in its publications. Many respected publications use sworn statements rather than audit reports.

Quality of Circulation

In the business magazine field, some readers are more valuable than others to advertisers. A purchasing director of a company with hundreds of outlets obviously is more important to an advertiser than is a buyer for a single retail store in a small city. Beyond circulation figures themselves, publishers attempt to demonstrate that their readers are more valuable to advertisers than readers of similar magazines. This is done through the use of demographics.

Inflight magazines have developed from small issues with substantial public relations objectives into thick, advertising-laden issues targeted to business and executive passengers. Delta's *Sky* distributes more than 400,000 copies a month. (Courtesy Delta Air Lines *SKY* Magazine.)

Demography is the statistical study of human populations, especially with reference to size and density, distribution, and vital statistics. Magazines spend much time and money to gather demographic data about their readers in many areas: income; marital status; ownership of property, automobiles, or other durable goods; consumption of goods; occupational status; and the like.[4]

Demographic data for constructing reader profiles often come from group studies supported by several magazines. All the magazines get the data, then each can emphasize the facts that look best in selling its advertising space. In effect, each can counter the others' arguments, and each knows the strengths and weaknesses of all the magazines in the study.

Delta's *Sky* advertises that it has the largest monthly audience of any inflight magazine and is #1 in households earning $50,000+, buyers of personal computers for business, and purchasers of mainframes and minicomputers for their companies, based on Mediamark and Simmons research. It also advertises that its percentage of readers is comparable to *Time, Forbes,* and *Inc.* in the professional/managerial, top management, and median personal income categories while its CPM is the lowest of all four. This way, it takes on the direct competition and indirect competition by showing itself as a good buy.

Sky also promotes the affluence of its readers, whose household incomes average $135,628. Their median age is 47.7, 58 percent fly more than seven round trips annually, 79 percent spent 11 or more nights in hotels or motels in the last year, 77 percent rented a car in the last year, 30 percent took a cruise in the last three years, and 99 percent own credit cards.

Parents advertises that its readers' median age is 31.6, a decade younger than the women's service magazine readers, that 63 percent work, and that their median household income of $35,083 is well above the national average. It is "more efficient than the Seven Sisters in reaching mothers 18–34 who in recent months have purchased a car, a new camera, a VCR, a microwave or 'other appliance,' or who have shopped in department stores for fashion and 'other items.' "

Automotive News advertises that 73 percent of all new car dealers read one or more of its last four issues and 58.4 percent of all dealers said *Automotive News* is the most useful trade publication they read. Compared to the competition, it is better read among dealers by "almost 2 to 1. And almost 10 to 1 more useful." The figures come from an Erdos & Morgan study. It adds that it is the only 100 percent paid subscription publication in the industry and its 79 percent renewal rate is "proof positive that our readers certainly believe we're filling their editorial needs."

Based on a Readex study, *Telephone Engineer & Management* advertises that it is the "most useful" of five business publications in its field. From Research USA data it adds that more telco professionals read it regularly than two other publications. Its circulation to carriers is highest of the five, and its CPM is the lowest. In competition, *Telephony* advertises that it is the "publication most widely and regularly read by the Bell Operating Company and Carrier Market," according to Exhibit Surveys, Inc.; that it carries far more advertising than *TE & M,* 2,338 pages to 1,258; and that more qualified subscribers pay for it than for *TE & M,* 17,958 to 6,449. Both are controlled circulation publications, *Telephony* with 29,813 non-paid and 17,958 paid subscribers and *TE & M* with 36,132 nonpaid and 6,449 paid subscribers.

Flying, a consumer magazine, buys a duplicate listing in *Business Publication Rates and Data* and advertises that, of its readers, 44 percent are entrepreneurs, 39 percent are top executives, 20 percent are owners/partners, 11 percent are CEOs/presidents, and 24 percent are presently evaluating aircraft or plan to within 24 months.

The competition is keen, and each magazine must make its best case to potential and current advertisers.

Business publishers' reports give a business analysis of circulation by classifications agreed on by member publications within that field. These can be very detailed. *ENR,* for example, reports circulation by 19 classifications within the construction industry, then by seven levels of personnel within each classification for a total of 133 separate circulation categories.

A simpler example is *Discount Store News,* which reports circulation in six classifications: (1) retailers; (2) multi-unit independent headquarters executive corporate officers, merchandising and buying personnel, regional/district managers and supervisors; (3) chain store management personnel, store managers, and other supervisory personnel; (4) wholesalers, jobbers, and distributors; (5) manufacturers and manufacturers' representatives; (6) others allied to the field (including financial institutions, investment firms, and industry associations).

These reports give the advertiser important information (especially when it measures the data against the size of the industry as a whole) about both the sizes of the businesses reached and the position within the firms. These figures can also remind editors of some characteristics of their audiences.

Coverage of the firms within the industry is called horizontal coverage. Horizontal coverage can also refer to coverage of a given position or function across several industries—purchasing agents, for instance, regardless of the specific industry in which they are employed. Vertical coverage refers to coverage of persons at various levels within a firm or field. In a retail field, vertical coverage may reach executives in headquarters offices, corporate buyers, departmental buyers, and sales and promotion personnel.

Probably no magazine could achieve or survive 100 percent coverage of a field; there is a point of diminishing returns. One axiom business magazine people use is that 20 percent of the firms in a given field do 80 percent of the business in that field. Advertisers are interested in reaching the major firms that do most of the business because they constitute the most profitable audience from a business-producing standpoint.

One business publication developed a marketing brochure pointing out that there were 35,647 retail outlets in its field but that 21 percent of the stores did 71 percent of the total sales volume. Obviously, these 7,483 stores were more valuable to the advertiser and to the publication than the other 28,164.

Limiting horizontal coverage, therefore, can maximize efficiency and economy in reaching the most important units in a field. Controlled circulation publications with broad horizontal coverage can sell subscriptions at a price that approximates printing and postage costs to smaller units that do not represent good prospects for the advertiser. One business publication with 63 percent controlled circulation charges the 37 percent paid subscribers $70 a year; another with 84 percent controlled circulation charges its paid subscribers $50 a year. Those figures are not unusual for fully paid circulation business publications.

Relationship of Circulation to Advertising Rates

There is a direct relationship between circulation and advertising rates, expressed as cost per thousand, or CPM. It refers to the cost of one page of advertising in 1,000 copies of the magazine and is calculated by dividing the advertising rate for one page by the circulation and multiplying by 1,000. A magazine having a page rate of $500 and a circulation of 100,000 has a CPM of $5, for example ($500/ 100,000 $\times$ 1,000 = $5).

Separate CPMs can be figured for black-and-white advertising pages, four-color advertising pages, and even the cost of reaching consumers interested in a specific product. In the last case, the advertiser can use Simmons or other market and readership data to determine how many readers of a given magazine are prospective automobile buyers, for example, and the cost of reaching each 1,000 of them. This figure is much more meaningful than the gross cost of reaching 1,000 readers, most of whom are not interested in buying a given product.

The burden on the circulation department in relation to advertising is to maintain the circulation guarantee on which advertising rates are based. Subscriptions are expiring daily, and new ones must be sold to maintain the needed number. Selling too many new subscriptions can be bad, too, because the magazine is not receiving advertising revenue for the bonus circulation beyond the guarantee but has the expense of printing and delivering it. Some leeway is allowed in setting advertising rates, of course, because the magazine does not want to fall short of its guarantee. Circulation promotion and sales must be a continuous operation to avoid an erratic circulation pattern.

Because CPM is not the same for all magazines, demographic or other reader data are important. Each magazine needs to use demographic or psychographic information to show prospective advertisers how it differs from other magazines in its field. The advertiser wants to know if its target market exists in the circulation to a sufficient extent to make the magazine an efficient buy. In other words, advertisers are looking at the quality of circulation, not just the quantity.

The CPMs for 32 consumer magazines in 1992 are listed in table 19.1. Several women's magazines are closely bunched in CPM and each would use demographic and other data about its readers to convince advertisers that they can reach their target markets through its magazine. This table illustrates that some magazines' audiences are more valuable to advertisers than others, but it also shows a problem with CPM. An advertiser usually will place enough advertising to earn discounted rates, and the real CPM would be based on the rate earned and would be lower. Further, advertisers are interested only in readers in their target market, so the weighted CPM based on only those readers could be several times the CPM based on all circulation.

Each copy of a magazine is read by more than one person. Because research firms report projected numbers of readers as well as circulation, magazines often will use that figure, because it is lower, if they mention their CPM. Research firms also calculate and report the CPM for reaching purchasers of specific products. Even then, other factors often enter into decisions about where to advertise.

CPM is even less useful in business publications. As table 19.2 shows, CPMs vary widely, even though the cost of an advertising page costs much less than in a consumer magazine. The smaller circulations drive up the CPM, but each reader of a business publication is worth far more to an advertiser than a reader of a consumer magazine. Also, the actual cost per ad page is relatively inexpensive when compared with large-circulation consumer magazines.

TABLE 19.1
Cost per Thousand of One-Page, Four-Color Ad in Selected Consumer Magazines

Magazine	CPM	One-Page Rate*
Town & Country	$76.07	$34,555
Los Angeles	68.39	11,770
Texas Monthly	64.13	19,730
Mirabella	62.08	34,800
Vanity Fair	52.96	52,490
Lear's	51.06	23,680
Harper's Bazaar	49.29	36,105
Working Woman	43.15	38,100
Entertainment Weekly	40.35	29,985
Working Mother	40.24	30,725
Vogue	39.12	49,000
Sports Illustrated	38.70	127,600
Self	36.63	44,010
Atlantic	35.07	16,090
Mademoiselle	34.36	41,440
Time	32.99	134,400
Essence	32.76	28,450
Glamour	30.27	63,000
People	28.72	97,090
YM	26.97	27,480
Smithsonian	26.25	56,180
Cosmopolitan	25.23	69,170
Seventeen	24.48	45,320
Good Housekeeping	23.52	122,035
Ebony	20.78	38,103
Family Circle	19.15	96,990
Better Homes and Gardens	18.43	147,500
Woman's Day	18.25	84,320
Ladies' Home Journal	18.18	92,100
Redbook	18.07	69,755
McCall's	16.44	83,315
Modern Maturity	10.11	226,970

*Undiscounted.

Source of rates: *Consumer Magazine and Agri-Media Rates and Data*, September 1992.

TABLE 19.2
Cost per Thousand of One-Page, Four-Color Ad in Selected Business Magazines

Magazine	CPM	One-Page Rate*
Tobacco International	$843.69	$2,850
Folio:	460.50	4,745
Magazine Design & Production	349.62	4,915
Meetings & Conventions	171.72	13,825
Editor & Publisher	156.51	4,000
Architecture	150.42	9,910
Successful Meetings	150.04	11,520
Appliance Manufacturer	145.44	4,950
ENR	100.68	9,430
Restaurants & Institutions	97.57	13,840
Aviation Week & Space Technology	85.13	12,075
Industry Week	65.85	18,970

*Undiscounted.

Source of rates: *Business Publication Rates and Data,* July 1992.

Circulation of Public Relations Magazines

Public relations magazines, because they are circulated to advance the sponsoring company or institution, have a different approach to circulation. First, they must determine who will receive the magazine. Second, they must determine the most effective way to deliver it.

Audience

The nature of a magazine selects much of the audience. An employee magazine usually attempts 100 percent coverage of a company's employees. A customer magazine, though, may restrict its coverage to customers who do a certain amount of business with the company or to those who have made purchases recently, say within the last two years. The cost of printing and distributing the magazine is substantial, so copies should not be wasted.

Auto manufacturers generally require their dealers to pay the cost of distributing their magazines to customers. This keeps the lists up-to-date, because a dealer who is paying for the magazine is less likely to keep a poor prospect or former customer on that list.

The magnitude of waste also is illustrated by the experience of *Cascades,* award-winning magazine of Pacific Northwest Bell Telephone Company in Seattle, Washington. Offering its readers some of the most beautiful color photography found anywhere, with articles about the Pacific Northwest, its free distribution grew to more than 50,000. However, nearly half the circulation was outside the company's territory of Oregon, Washington, and northern Idaho; those readers received this letter:

> We're sorry to disappoint you, but we can no longer offer CASCADES to readers outside the Pacific Northwest.
>
> Ten years ago, CASCADES began publication as a regional magazine for readers in Oregon, Washington and northern Idaho, the area Pacific Northwest Bell serves. Today, the magazine has subscribers throughout the United States and in a great many foreign countries. The number of readers has doubled from 25,000 to more than 50,000.
>
> The increase in circulation has been flattering, but rising production costs and our budget limitations dictate a change in our policy.
>
> We hope you'll understand.

A public relations magazine needs to define its audience so that it will achieve adequate coverage with minimum waste circulation. Besides its primary audience—employees, customers, or stockholders—it should select other recipients who may benefit from the magazine and from whom the sponsoring company may benefit. Examples of this latter group are

1. Employees on leave—military leave, sick leave, educational leave. Employees temporarily away from their employment like to keep in touch.
2. Potential employees—students in professional schools (engineering, pharmacy, journalism), college libraries, and other places where potential employees can be reached.

3. Retired employees—people who like to talk about their former place of employment and will do a good job of presenting its story if kept well informed.
4. Business publications in the company's industry—occasionally will produce valuable publicity for the company through reprints of articles and condensation of news items.
5. Other company publications—because editors like to see each other's work, get ideas, and keep each other apprised of what they are doing.
6. Civic and political leaders—to keep key persons in company communities in touch with what the company is doing.
7. Doctors and dentists—to make the company's message available in waiting rooms of professional persons. Employees also may take some pride in seeing their company's publication on display in these places. The size of the community and the nature of the publication determine whether such circulation is desirable.

Mail Distribution

An International Association of Business Communicators survey, although it does not represent all public relations magazine distribution, reported that 58 percent of the participating magazines' distribution is by mail, 7 percent in-house, and 35 percent a combination of the two.

Advantages of mail distribution include

1. Family readership—there is greater potential for other members of the family to read the magazine if it is mailed to the home, and many editors are particularly interested in reaching the employee's spouse with the company story, knowing that, if the spouse is satisfied, the employee tends to be satisfied also.
2. Leisurely reading—the reader is likely to be more relaxed and willing to read the magazine at home after a day's work.
3. Certainty of coverage—by mailing to each recipient, the company can be sure that each person in the intended audience is receiving a copy.
4. Reasonable cost—although in-house distribution has no postage expense, it often requires larger press runs to offset waste from extra copies employees pick up and copies sent out in bulk to cover a number of distribution points within the company, so the cost difference is not as great as one may originally estimate.

In-house Distribution

Advantages of in-house distribution also tend to be disadvantages of mail distribution. They include

1. Less competition with other magazines—the public relations magazine won't arrive in the mail with *Time, Newsweek, Sports Illustrated, McCall's, Better Homes and Gardens,* or other consumer magazines.
2. Reader receptiveness—because employees are thinking about the company at work, it is better for them to receive the magazine at work than at home, where they may prefer to forget the day's work. Reader receptiveness probably varies from company to company and with type of work, so no single generalization appears to be applicable. Research into the most receptive time and place may be beneficial to an editor.
3. Reaches home anyway—most employees who are at all interested will take the magazine home, and those who are not probably would throw away a mailed copy. Mail distribution is not automatically more effective at reaching the family than in-house distribution.
4. Low cost—in many businesses, distribution can be inexpensively handled by distributing magazines with pay checks, at the time clock when employees punch out, or through supervisors who hand them out. The nature of the sponsoring organization as well as the audience determine which is the most effective and least expensive method.

An editor or a public relations director designing an efficient distribution system analyzes all the aspects of the company and the magazine's objectives as well as factors about distribution effectiveness. Editors have contended that in-house distribution gives a check on reader acceptance, because, the more copies that are thrown away at work, the less well accepted is that issue. However, they don't know whether the employee reads the issue before discarding it, and they don't know the discard rate of mailed copies, so they are still estimating.

Especially with stockholder and other external magazines, a business reply postcard can be inserted every year or two, asking recipients if they want to continue to receive the magazine. External magazines often tell the reader they will discontinue mailing it if the card is not returned. Others simply ask whether they should continue sending it without mentioning cancellation. The approach may depend on budget and whether the company is willing to pay to reach marginally interested readers.

Although the public relations magazine has a different circulation situation than paid and controlled circulation consumer and business magazines, its circulation should be handled just as professionally and carefully if the magazine is to be effective in achieving its objectives.

Selling Circulation

Consumer magazines need to screen out some potential subscribers, just as do business magazines. The criteria may not be so readily obvious nor so vigorously applied, but there are ways magazines can be selective in reaching households of above-average income and with heavy users and heavy buyers of products and services. Selling circulation is a very specialized facet of the magazine industry.

Considerations in circulation strategy include the magazine's circulation guarantee to advertisers, its desired demographic makeup, the economics of selling subscriptions by direct mail, and the feasibility of selling single copies on newsstands.

Single-Copy Sales

Magazines that successfully sell the majority of their copies on newsstands claim superiority of circulation because they say it proves the reader is willing to pay the full single-copy price and is making the decision every issue, unlike some subscribers who buy a discounted subscription and do not read the magazine when it arrives.

Few magazines are outstandingly successful at single-copy sales. Two are *First for Women* and *Woman's World,* both of which sell only single copies, 1.6 million and 1.2 million per issue, respectively. *Cosmopolitan,* long having required subscribers to pay as much as if they bought each issue at the newsstand, sells 76 percent of its circulation as single copies. *TV Guide* doesn't sell more than one-half of its copies singly, but it sells 6.1 million single copies each week of its total 14.9 million circulation.

Other magazines that sell a high percentage of their total circulation as single copies include *Bridal Guide* (99 percent), *National Enquirer* (89 percent), *Country Folk Art* (88 percent), *Guitar School* (86 percent), *Modern Bride* (78 percent), *Muscle & Fitness* (78 percent), *Penthouse* (76 percent), *Beckett Baseball Card Monthly* (73 percent), *Easyriders* (71 percent), *Woman's Day* (69 percent), and *Soap Opera Digest* (62 percent).[5]

Most magazines, however, rely mainly on subscriptions, and Karyl Van points to a danger in overselling a concept:

Sometimes circulation and advertising people, in a desire to promote current advantage, wake up a few months later to find that exploited advantage no longer exists and that we have burned our bridges behind us. . . .

As an example, newsstand sales soared at the close of World War II. Almost all of us sold this great voluntary circulation like crazy. It was, we said, a great demonstration of voluntary purchases by readers. Newsstand circulations declined, and we went back to looking for that bridge to get across on safe ground. It wasn't there.[6]

As an example of changes in newsstand sales, *Life* was selling 2.5 million single copies per issue in 1947 and only 210,000 in 1971. *Look* sold 1.4 million single copies per issue in 1947 and 240,000 in 1971.[7] The monthly *Life* in 1988 was selling 666,000 single copies, 35 percent of its circulation.

Another consideration in single-copy sales is the logistics of getting the right number on each of the 138,000 newsstands each issue. Paul Young, then in charge of single-copy sales for Time Inc., once said, "No newsstand man ever sold a copy of a magazine. It is circulation's job to get the right number of magazines in the right place at the right time, properly displayed. The magazine must sell itself."[8]

H. Carlisle Estes says that the "only salesman for single copies is the editor," and "most important to sales is the proper cover." The magazine is an impulse item, and the customer makes the decision on which magazine to buy at the newsstand. The magazine needs an attractive cover to get attention, then cover lines that describe the contents "in such a way as to grab the customer's interest. . . . I don't think anything is as important as choosing the proper cover lines."[9]

Estes pointed to the need for minimizing waste in a print order. He noted that a copy of one magazine cost 147 percent of its cover price just for printing, paper, and distribution. After giving the normal markup to retailers and wholesalers, the publisher got 53 percent of the cover price, so each copy costs nearly one and one-half times the cover price, whether or not it is sold, and must generate more than twice its cover price to break even.[10] If a wholesaler gets too many copies and returns proof of the unsold copies, the publisher refunds the money and absorbs the loss. The same thing happens if the wholesaler does not distribute the copies properly and move them around from slow-selling outlets to those approaching sell-outs during the sales period.

A certain number of unsold copies (*returns*), though, is desirable. Estes calls them "growth allowance." If the magazine sells out, the opportunity for growth is restricted, especially if it's a hot issue that might induce some new buyers to come back issue after issue. A newsstand with an average volume of 100 copies an issue may be given 120 to allow it to build up an increase in sales. A small dealer averaging two copies per issue may be given three to allow for growth. These figures represent 20 and 50 percent growth allowances, showing that dealers must be watched so copies are not wasted. Although growth is needed, the cost of growth must be controlled.[11]

Dealers, too, don't want sell-outs; they want merchandise on hand to sell. Many stores have established several points of purchase for magazines. *TV Guide* may have as many as 20 displays in one store, *Reader's Digest* 10, and *Newsweek* 3. This added factor of multiple displays affects the return or growth allowance policy.[12]

Publishers' growth allowances vary. One large-circulation magazine operated on a 12 percent allowance; other magazines have as much as 40 percent. Each publisher's economic structure determines the return rate.[13] The statement of ownership, management, and circulation published each October gives a clue to growth and returns. *Field & Stream* in 1992 reported an average monthly press run of 2,365,096 and average returns from news dealers of 199,680. Its paid circulation was 2,006,573. The remaining copies were distributed free (157,462) or not distributed (1,361). *Time*'s returns exceed 250,000 a week.

Contrast with this a controlled circulation business magazine that has no returns from news dealers. *Modern Office Technology,* a Penton publication, in 1992 reported an average monthly press run of 155,445, requested mail subscription of 151,856, free distribution of sample and complimentary copies of 2,048, and 1,541 copies not distributed. Its press run and total circulation were less than *Field & Stream*'s monthly returns.

The rapid turnover in magazines makes them a profitable item for the retailer. A study of drug stores in five metropolitan areas by Wholesalers Project Development found that, for every $100 worth of inventory in the average drugstore magazine department, $732 worth of gross profit is produced in a year. Turnover amounts to 24.4 times a year.[14]

Single-copy sales are important to the consumer magazine publisher. Even though the publisher receives only 50 to 55 percent of the cover price from a newsstand sale, that is far more than the 10 percent received from a subscription sale by a direct-mail subscription agency. A $2 monthly magazine yields $1. Over a year, that is $12 compared with $1.80 if it is sold as an $18 subscription by a direct-mail agency.

A controlled circulation business magazine like *Modern Office Technology* can reach its target audience economically with almost no waste circulation and with no returns from news dealers. (Courtesy *Modern Office Technology* and copyright 1992 by Penton Publishing, subsidiary of Pittway Corporation.)

Magazines usually use one of the dozen national distributors to reach the 550 wholesalers who service the 138,000 retailers. A few publishers bypass a distributor and work directly with the 550 wholesalers.

The distributor instructs the printer, who ships copies to the wholesalers. That takes about a week to 10 days. Another week is required for the wholesaler to get the magazines to the retail outlets.

Nearly all magazines are sold on consignment. A monthly magazine is kept on sale for 30 days; then unsold copies are returned to the wholesaler for credit. Eventually reports from all wholesalers are combined by the national distributor into a record of sale for each issue. This record, which may be several months old, is used by the publisher's single-copy sales manager and the national distributor's account executive to determine the number of copies of the next issue to distribute.

The distributor generally advances 10 to 25 percent to the publisher after shipping an issue. On a 25 percent advance contract of a 200,000 draw magazine with a $3 cover price, the publisher gets $82,500 ($1.65 $\times$ 50,000 copies). The distributor also advances shipping costs to the wholesaler.

Final settlement for an issue usually comes 90 days after off-sale. The November issue, placed on sale October 15, is collected for about February 15. If the magazine sold 50 percent, which is the average in the industry, there would be 150,000 returns, which would be destroyed or recycled by the wholesalers, and the publisher would receive a second payment of $82,500 less shipping charges and special allowances. The national distributor's share runs 6 to 8 percent of the cover price of sold copies.

The new publisher often is at a disadvantage in single-copy sales. A small dealer with a poor credit rating, for example, may deal with the wholesaler on a cash basis. Such a dealer may reject new magazines for which there is no sales experience, or the dealer may return them for credit before the sales period has ended.

The national distributor bills the wholesaler for the copies sold (draw less returns) at 36 to 40 percent off the cover price. The discount usually is split with the retail dealer.

There are about 2,000 newsstand magazines, but even large retailers display only about 200. Most display only a small portion of the cover, hiding the cover lines. The largest, most aggressive magazines with large field staffs get full display at checkouts—*Family Circle, Woman's Day, TV Guide, People,* and *National Enquirer,* for example.

New magazines often pay dealers special allowances for full display, usually 10 percent of the cover price, but not all dealers live up to the agreement, and it is difficult and costly to police.

The date on an issue usually indicates when it goes off sale. A monthly magazine that goes on sale September 15 for one month, for example, is dated October. A weekly magazine, such as *Newsweek* or *Time,* published April 9, is dated April 16.

Business magazines, of course, generally do not want single-copy sales because it would dilute their control over the audience they sell to advertisers.

Subscriptions

Most magazines do not lend themselves to single-copy sales. Only 15 of the 50 top circulation magazines sell more single copies than subscriptions, so the circulation department must obtain subscriptions to meet the circulation guarantee on which advertising rates are based and keep it there or continue to increase it. However, it also must avoid too rapid growth, which pushes the cost of printing and distributing the magazine up more rapidly than advertising rates can be increased to cover it.

Two basic areas of subscription sales are new business and renewals. Decisions about new business include the number of new readers wanted, the number wanted through commissionable sources (agents, salespersonnel, etc.), space advertising, and promotion, such as Christmas gifts. Rates, terms, types of readers desired, how much can be spent on achieving the circulation goal, and how fast the readers must be added also are major considerations.[15]

Renewal business justifies the money spent on getting new subscribers if the reader continues reading and paying for the magazine long after the trial subscription expires. Often a magazine loses money promoting new subscriptions and attempts to make it back through renewals of those subscriptions.

Each magazine, depending on the audience it is attempting to build, finds its own best sources of prospects and promotion techniques. Women's magazines obviously have different successful strategies than men's magazines, confession magazines different than *haute couture* magazines. Some generalizations apply to most paid circulation magazines, though.

Direct Mail Strategy.   List brokers specialize in maintaining and selling names and complete addresses of people who can be approached by direct-mail advertising. They can provide numerous *mail-order lists* of people who have already responded to someone's mail-order solicitation, either by making a purchase or requesting information. They also can supply *compiled lists* of people who share some common interest or description, such as PTA, campers, physicians, boat owners, florists, and teachers. Compiled lists don't identify who has responded to direct mail and, generally, are less productive than the mail-order lists. The cost of mailing to compiled lists is likely to exceed total income from all the subscriptions they buy.[16]

Mail-order lists are not always preferable to compiled lists, but they usually are preferred and are in plentiful supply for consumer magazine use. A business magazine, on the other hand, having defined its field of service, is restricted to the equivalent of compiled lists of people in its field, such as building contractors, architects, engineers, and building material dealers. Lists should be keyed so their productiveness can be measured in terms of subscriptions, deadbeats, cancellations, and renewals.

Some things are so essential in selling new subscriptions that they are almost axiomatic:

1. A reduced price or introductory price is essential to significant production of new readers. The editor abhors those reduced-price offers, but they are essential to really significant production.
2. If your offer includes significant savings, then emphasize these savings within the copy. Give them dramatic position. For example, "half-price offer," abhorrent as it may be to an editor, is good for extra subscription orders.
3. Credit privileges are most important today for a maximum return.
4. Emphasis in mailings should be on short terms to encourage the prospects to try the magazine without a long-term commitment. Certainly, you have your crack at those people for renewals on a long-term basis, but, at first, offer modest terms.[17]

Subscriptions expire every day and new ones must be sold, but there are better times of the year for renewals than others. Experience among magazines varies, but some publishers say January, February, July, and August are the four best months to obtain new subscribers by mail.[18]

In selling new subscriptions, a 10 percent rate reduction may bring in more dollars, but a 50 percent or half-price offer is dramatic and easy to grasp and usually brings in many more subscriptions, opening the way to potentially more renewals.[19]

Because direct-mail promotion is so extensive and expensive, it is imperative to test the mailing piece and its approach. *Reader's Digest* test mails 10,000 pieces to reach decisions about mailing 20 million pieces.[20]

Cost is an important factor in direct mail. The direct-mail package that sells the most subscriptions may be uneconomical because of its higher production cost than the one it is tested against. In a two-way test where package A pulls 20 orders per thousand (2.0 percent) and package B pulls 24 orders per thousand (2.4 percent), B pulled better, but, if B is more elaborate and costs 50 percent more, B's orders cost 25 percent more than A's. If cost per order is the important factor, A is the choice. If total orders regardless of cost is the major consideration, B is the choice.

Subscription Agencies.   Subscription agencies are a tremendous source of new readers. Orders cleared through agencies originate from numerous sources: individual agents, catalog agencies, department stores, telephone solicitation, mail agencies, cash field selling, sponsored sales, newspaper agencies, school plans, and paid-during-service (PDS).

Individual agents are salespersons who report directly to the magazine publisher, sometimes selling for premiums or prizes rather than cash commissions. Catalog agencies are similar, but the agent has a catalog of many magazines—maybe hundreds—and clears orders through the one agency rather than directly with individual publishers.[21] Two or three catalog agencies sell to 30,000 libraries of schools, government agencies, and large corporations. The publisher receives 10 to 15 percent, plus a good source of renewals and very large pass-along readership.

Department stores have sold subscriptions for years in the store and through inserts with billings, mailings separate from billings, and telephone solicitation. Telephone solicitation also is used by publishers and agents.

The WATS (Wide Area Telephone Service) line has made it economical to solicit from a single city, such as New York, across time zones from a single location (called a *boiler room*). For example, solicitors can call from 9 A.M. New York time through 10 P.M., which is 7 P.M. in California, keeping the line in use 13 hours a day. This is especially useful for business publications that call subscribers at work. Consumer magazines and agencies representing them will make more calls to subscribers' homes in the evening.

Mail agencies were developed when the high cost of mailing made it desirable to offer several magazines in one mailing piece. The first attempts were through department stores, and some are still handled that way. Other agencies have been started, including a huge one that offers 40 to 99 magazines at a special introductory price that must be at least as good as any offer the publisher makes directly. Because these offers usually are for shorter terms as well as lower prices, some major publishers do not use this source. Sweepstakes often are used to promote response to these offers.

Direct-mail agencies pay publishers in advance for subscriptions, even though that is only 10 percent of the subscription price. Publishers can pinpoint when they want to receive their subscriptions. The cancellation rate is comparatively small, but renewals are a problem because the customer wants a good deal again and another chance to win the sweepstakes. The demographics of readers buying this way usually are lower than those gained through the magazine's own direct-mail efforts.

Cash field selling is done by trained professionals who work in crews traveling from city to city. They collect the full subscription price in cash before transmitting the order. They may collect only a down payment at the time of the sale, but their agencies do not transmit orders to the publisher until they are paid in full.

Sponsored sales were developed to overcome some of the problems of fly-by-night magazine solicitors during and following the economic depression. A local organization, such as a church, volunteer fire department, or hospital organization, is booked to sponsor the sales drive and provide local identification for a professional crew or even individual agents, for which the organization gets a commission from each sale.

Newspaper agencies sell one form of paid-during-service subscriptions. The usual approach is an annual sales campaign that permits a newspaper subscriber to receive three or four magazines for a small weekly charge added to the price of the newspaper. This is a good source of quality business at a moderate cost, and the subscription term usually is two years or more.

School plans involve student sales of subscriptions from lists of 150 or so magazines to provide commissions to the school for activities, projects, or materials. Individual or team prizes may be awarded to student salespersons as incentives in the campaign, which normally lasts a week to 10 days. The fact that a subscriber chooses from a list of 150 magazines indicates significant interest in that magazine and its editorial content.

Paid-during-service (PDS) operations are much like the newspaper agency, but without the newspaper. Typically, salespersons are residents of the community and offer a choice of magazines from a card for a weekly amount that is payable monthly. A contract is signed, and, after the sale is reported, the branch office verifies it by telephone, mail, or personal visit before the order is processed. Subscribers usually mail the monthly payments to the agency. PDS is a relatively low-cost source of new business. Most PDS agencies block out certain groups or areas in a community where they do not operate because experience has shown an unacceptable rate of collection. PDS subscriptions have a greater tendency to be canceled before expiration than those paid in advance.[22]

Renewals. Magazines generally make more money on renewals than on new subscriptions, and renewals provide some stability to circulation. Circulation managers analyze circulation on an annual basis, considering two six-month introductory subscriptions as one circulation (or *circ,* pronounced sirk) and one two-year subscription as two circs.[23]

In overall circulation strategy, renewals are tremendously important. By analyzing the number of cancellations (both by subscribers themselves and by the magazine for failure of subscribers to pay) and the percentage of first renewals, second renewals, third renewals, fourth renewals, and so on, a circulation manager can form a basis for algebraically determining the number of new subscriptions needed and the renewal promotion techniques likely to be successful.[24]

An introductory offer may result in 10 percent cancellations and 30 percent renewals after the 10 percent shrink, but those 30 percent renewals the second time around may be good for 65 percent renewals and only 5 percent cancellations, and it may continue at about a constant rate for the second, third, fourth, and subsequent renewals.[25]

Renewals are less expensive to sell because the list used is live customers who have already purchased. Even the 30 percent renewals for an introductory offer is very good compared with the 2 percent or so subscription rate from a direct mailing to prospective new subscribers. Also, renewals are more likely than new subscribers to send cash with their orders, cutting down billing costs. Obviously, editorial content is tremendously important in securing renewals.

Curtis Circulation Company reports that more than one-half (54 percent) of all single copies of magazines are sold in supermarkets and grocery stores, 20 percent in transportation outlets and newsstands, 10 percent in convenience stores, 9 percent in pharmacies, and 7 percent in bookstores.[26]

Using a different approach, a 1990 study found that most magazine buyers (59 percent) bought both subscriptions and single copies during the year. Twenty-four percent bought subscriptions exclusively and 17 percent bought only single copies.[27] In this study, purchasers mentioned buying their copies at supermarkets (70 percent), drug stores (13 percent), convenience stores (11 percent), and newsstands (11 percent). This study asked purchasers where they bought magazines. The one mentioned previously counted where single copies were actually sold.

The 1990 study reported that magazine insert cards and clearinghouse stamp sheets accounted for 51 percent of initial subscriptions. Publisher mailings accounted for 54 percent of renewals. The average subscriber bought 4.6 subscriptions a year. Seven of 10 subscription purchases and 82 percent of publisher mailings' purchases were considered planned. Only 45 percent of stamp sheet subscriptions were planned and 51 percent were spur-of-the-moment.[28]

Specific sources of current subscriptions were publisher mailings (43 percent), insert cards (22 percent), stamp sheets (12 percent), school/school drive (4 percent), telephone (3 percent), television offers (1 percent), door-to-door (1 percent), gifts (6 percent), other (4 percent), and don't know (4 percent).[29]

Subscribers recalled reduced prices in 56 percent of recently entered subscriptions. Stamp sheet subscribers remembered reduced prices for 80 percent of their purchases.[30] Magazines were read to the same extent regardless of whether they are spur-of-the-moment single-copy purchases or planned subscription purchases. Magazines purchased either way were read for an hour, they were looked at 3.3 to 3.6 times, and 53 to 55 percent of their pages were opened on the last reading occasion.[31]

Magazine buyers 18 to 34 years old said they were buying more magazines than five years ago. Buyers over 55 years old reported a definite decline in their buying, especially of single copies.[32]

Advertising

Publishers often trade off advertising on a circulation basis. If one magazine has 600,000 circulation and another 300,000, the second runs twice as much advertising for the first as the first runs for the second. Newer magazines making concerted efforts to increase circulation are more likely to trade off than are more established magazines.

Television commercials are an effective way to sell magazine subscriptions when placed in low-cost time slots and using toll-free numbers to take orders that are charged to credit cards at the time of ordering. Otherwise, nonpayment followed by cancellation is common. Radio and television commercials are effective at promoting newsstand sales.

Fulfillment and Records

Essentially, fulfillment is getting the magazine to the reader for the term of the subscription, including promptly placing the name on the mailing list when the order is entered and making address changes as they are necessary. Fulfillment involves record keeping and adequate staff and machinery to maintain the services to keep records up-to-date. Most large-circulation magazines contract with one of the large fulfillment houses to handle this for them.

Circulation records may be classified by three types: working records, forecasting and projection records, and budgeting and planning records. The editor need not be thoroughly familiar with these but should understand their necessity.

Working records include renewal results, billing results, bind-in results, agency production, direct-mail results, other miscellaneous promotion results (such as clubs and reader service inquiries) and the single-copy draw and sales results.[33]

Examples of forecasting and projection records are renewal percentage and trend, billing percentage and trend, expire inventory and its structure, and agency production and renewability. The direct-mail potential with lists, pull of lists, list record forms, and single-copy sales promotion test results also relate to forecasting and projection.[34]

Budgeting records include the expire inventory by source, renewability of expires by source, record of direct-mail pull by volume mailed, extension percentages in direct mail, extension percentages in agency production, and single-copy sales history of draw and sale.

The forecasting and projection records grow out of and are refinements of the working records. Budgeting records are refinements of the forecasting and projection records. By using the history of various subscriber groups, lists, promotion strategies, payment records, and the like, the circulation department can forecast trends and establish budgets to provide for growth in subscriptions and single-copy sales.[35]

Magazine publishing is a tripartite operation—editorial, advertising, and circulation. Some magazines get along without advertising, but none exists without some kind of circulation operation.

Notes

1. See, for example, John Mack Carter, "Reader Profiles—One Dimension or Two?" in *Modern Circulation Methods*, ed. S. Arthur Dembner and William E. Massee (New York: McGraw-Hill Book Company, 1968), p. 11.
2. *ABC Bylaws and Rules*, 1992.
3. Analysis based on *United States and Canada Periodical Circulation Study* (Schaumburg, Ill.: Audit Bureau of Circulations, 16 December 1980).
4. Richard Loyer, "Specialized Subscription Sales," in Dembner and Massee, *Modern Circulation Methods*, p. 85.
5. Based on *ABC Fas-Fax: United States and Canadian Periodicals*, 30 June 1992.
6. Karyl Van, "Audited Circulation and Advertising Sales Business," in Dembner and Massee, p. 14.

7. Chris Welles, "Can Mass Magazines Survive?" *Columbia Journalism Review* (July–August 1971): 13; "ABC Magazines," *ABC Fas-Fax: United States and Canadian Periodicals,* 30 June 1988, p. 12.
8. H. Carlisle Estes, "Single-copy Sales," in Dembner and Massee, p. 74.
9. Estes, pp. 76–77.
10. Ibid., p. 79.
11. Ibid.
12. Ibid., p. 81.
13. Ibid., p. 79.
14. "Mags Earn Big Profit on Investment," *American Druggist* (14 July 1971): 75.
15. John Millington, "Circulation: Strategy and Tactics," in Dembner and Massee, p. 7.
16. William S. Campbell, "Prospecting by Direct Mail," in Dembner and Massee, p. 19.
17. Ibid., p. 20.
18. Ibid., p. 23.
19. Ibid.
20. Gordon Grossman, "Direct-mail Testing," in Dembner and Massee, p. 27.
21. Robert M. Goshorn and William A. Eyerly, "Magazine Subscription Agencies," in Dembner and Massee, pp. 100–101.
22. Ibid., pp. 109–12.
23. Halbert F. Speer, "Renewal Analysis," in Dembner and Massee, pp. 115–16.
24. Speer, "Renewal Analysis," pp. 116–23.
25. Ibid., pp. 116–18.
26. *The Magazine Handbook, 1990–1991 (MPA Research Newsletter No. 59),* p. 10.
27. *The Study of Magazine Buying Patterns* (Publishers Clearing House, 1991), p. 14.
28. Ibid., p. 17.
29. Ibid., p. 38.
30. Ibid., p. 17.
31. Ibid., p. 15.
32. Ibid., p. 16.
33. Walter Mills, "Circulation Records," in Dembner and Massee, pp. 142–51.
34. Ibid., pp. 150–51.
35. Ibid., pp. 153–54.

20 Pressures and Responsibilities

ETHICS has been a major concern among American journalism organizations and professors in recent years. Probably more has been published on journalism ethics in the last 6 years than in the preceding 60. Nearly every professional meeting has a session or two on ethical issues. Ethics in journalism, as in any profession, is a serious matter. Even if all of these discussions will not eliminate ethical lapses by professional journalists, they will help reduce the number of them.

Ethics is not a code that someone else hands down or some group votes into existence, but a working framework of principles that help one make decisions when difficult situations arise. One suggestion has been to consider to whom one's loyalties are owed *after* having defined the problem, examined the operative values, and considered principles that could be applied. Developed by Ralph Potter of the Harvard Divinity School, this approach is used as the basis for Christians, Rotzoll, and Fackler's *Media Ethics: Cases & Moral Reasoning*. It may sound simple until one considers how many groups can be owed moral duty: ourselves, our readers, our magazine, professional colleagues, society. When these conflict, to whom do we owe the greatest moral duty or loyalty?

Pressures on editors come from many directions: special interest groups, individual readers, staff members, business, government, and advertisers. Editorial integrity is a prized attribute that is not easily earned but can be easily eroded.

Social Responsibility

Freedom of the press is guaranteed by the First Amendment to the United States Constitution and by articles in or amendments to the states' constitutions. This establishes what is called the libertarian philosophy, that there shall be no prior restraints on what people may publish in periodicals. Over the last 40 years, dating particularly from the 1947 report *A Free and Responsible Press* by the Commission on Freedom of the Press, a concept called social responsibility has developed. The report insists that the press should publish balanced reports that reveal the truth about the fact as well as the fact itself, that significance should be indicated, and that meaning should be stated to flesh out the reporting of the facts.

Because costs today prohibit everyone from starting his or her own publication, some insist that all readers have a right to space in established publications to express their ideas or views. As a practical matter, access cannot be guaranteed to everyone because there just is not enough space in periodicals for everything readers would like to have published. A guarantee like this to readers would infringe on a free press, forcing editors to publish items that their editorial judgment says should not be published. In other words, a guarantee to readers abridges the publishers' and editors' freedom of the press. However, the social responsibility concept emphasizes to editors that their readers' broad interests must be carefully considered as items are accepted for or rejected from publication, that there is a responsibility to the public interest beyond what will sell.

Balance does not always mean giving equal play to two or more sides of an issue. When it becomes known that Vietnamese prisoners were placed in tiger cages during the war, there should be no compulsion to find someone who favors that action. If mistreatment of mental patients is uncovered, one needn't find a spokesperson who favors such mistreatment. The social responsibility in these and similar cases requires the editors to stand for what is right for society as they see it.

Photographs

The vast majority of magazines use *photo illustrations* rather than *photojournalism.* They are obviously posed or set up, and nearly everyone has little concern about that. When a photo of a real object is altered, however, outcries are heard. Does a magazine have an obligation to label its altered pictures to make them totally clear to its readers? Do readers understand what a credit line "Photo illustration by Joe Doakes" means?

Readers are not oblivious to how pictures are made. They understand how food layouts and home and garden magazine photos are created. They realize that there is no spontaneous action in posed photos of people being profiled in magazines. Usually these people look so perfect one wonders how long it took to get them that way.

Most readers probably don't care if a cola can is airbrushed or digitally removed from an image of a Pulitzer Prize–winning photographer and his wife. They may accept a cover photo of altered pyramids on a scientific society's multimillion circulation magazine. What should magazines tell their readers about their photographs?

Several discussions in this book have emphasized that there is a bond between the editor and the reader and between the writer and the reader. Some editors and writing coaches recommend that writers keep the reader in mind, rather than the subject being written about. The reader is more important than the topic. That can also apply to photography.

Editors are readers and should constantly think as readers. Several ethicists have said the Golden Rule is no longer appropriate. It is not sufficient to treat people the way you would want to be treated, but treat them the way *they want to be treated.* Instead of thinking "a little airbrushing won't hurt anything," think "how do my readers want this photo handled?" If editors don't know, they should take steps to find out.

Editors who came up as writers instead of photographers should make distinctions about different types of photos and analyze how they should be handled.

Set-Up Photos 1: Still Life

These are photos of food, room arrangements, draperies and decorating items, furniture, home workshop projects, model building, and the like. Since they are set up, is it acceptable to alter them? They are of contrived reality, so does it matter if they are further contrived?

Set-Up Photos 2: People

The new mayor profiled in the city magazine, the World Series Most Valuable Player modeling men's clothing in a gentleman's magazine, President and Mrs. Clinton, Chelsea, and Socks: since they are set up, is it acceptable to alter them, by removing a McDonald's coffee cup or a can showing the brand name of a cat food? Maybe we can touch up the mayor's hair and remove a few wrinkles from her face, even though it is not a portrait.

On its cover, *TV Guide* placed an artist's rendering of a photograph of Oprah Winfrey on Ann-Margret's body from an 11-year-old picture of her. Is this serious journalism or merely a clever way to create a cover that becomes a conversation piece?

Real-Situation Photos

A photo taken for *Woman's Day,* a Hachette magazine, in Times Square captures a *New York Times* delivery truck with a *Family Circle* poster on the side. Is it OK, mandatory, or unacceptable to remove the lettering and poster from the side of the truck? It's not a photo of real news, so does it need to meet a standard a news journalist would apply?

News Photos

A photographer captures a mother, father, and brother sobbing beside a dead child. Should the body be retouched to soften the effect? Should the photo be cropped to show only the grieving? Should the photo be published? Is it a matter of ethics, taste, or sensitivity?

Cropping Versus Image Altering

Almost no one cries foul when part of an image is cropped away and not published. Photos also can be altered by removing the background (outlining, silhouetting, or stick-outs). Many people object to altering an image that is published—to improve it, of course—after it has been cropped. Is there a difference between altering a photo by cropping it and altering a photo by changing the image that is printed?

One answer was provided several years ago by William Rivers and Wilbur Schramm. A photographer looking for scenic pictures in a state park noticed an interesting pattern of leaves and rocks along a stream but thought it would be more attractive if he were to move two leaves and add another. A class of 30 graduate students considered the situation and decided the picture was artistic and would not preclude arranging leaves. They were unanimous, though, in criticizing a veteran news photographer who recommended that photographers carry a broken tricycle in their car trunks to provide foreground interest when covering fatal accidents involving children. Rivers and Schramm observed: "One of the most damaging aspects of photojournalism is that too many of the men who make pictures for the mass media treat the truth casually. They become accustomed to arranging pictures and do not know when to stop. The time to stop is at the beginning—with the innocuous little scene of the leaves."[1] Generally supporting this view, Hiley Ward writes, "Picture are supposed to reflect a real world, so most editors and photographers are not happy with 'doctoring' procedures."[2]

Magazine Diversity

The photo analogy of the leaves extends to other areas of editing and writing, although it is more difficult to avoid arranging words, because all writing is arranging words. With such variety in the magazine field, an argument can be made that diversity among magazines makes slanted reports, one-sided reports, and advocacy pieces desirable. In the typical community, there may be two or three daily newspapers, counting ones that come in from neighboring cities, a dozen or so radio stations, and numerous television channels, mostly on cable. A newsstand, however, may have 150 to 200 different magazines on hand at any time. There readers have much greater selection and may choose what serves them best.

Some may find it tempting to insist on a prescribed ethic for everyone, but ethics and social responsibility are largely matters of individual integrity, honor, and choice. Journalists are not licensed and cannot be disbarred, so individuals operating with support and pressure from colleagues ultimately make their own decisions.

Inaccuracy

News reports sometimes become garbled in newsmagazines and on wire services. More often than not, the mistakes are made by an editor who had not covered the event and who was not given a clear enough report of it by the writer. Sometimes it occurs when tightening writing. The conventional advice is to avoid making mistakes by carefully checking everything but, when mistakes are made, to publish clear, carefully worded corrections. The belief that printing corrections creates suspicions about everything else in the publication has given way to one that corrections create a greater feeling of credibility, that when errors are made they will be acknowledged. Also, legal studies have shown that most people wronged by a serious inaccuracy prefer a retraction or correction to a lawsuit. Corrections are a fact of editorial life.

Plagiarism and Attribution

Plagiarism often results from innocent or careless failure to attribute one's source. Editors need to be especially careful in evaluating submissions, as the following California case illustrates.

Jamie Cackler, a reporter for the *Contra Costa Times,* received a news release from the International Education Forum (IEF) that plagiarized her story and attributed quotes she had obtained from several other sources to IEF's president. The incident was compounded when the *Walnut Creek Journal,* owned by the same company as the *Times,* used the release in a story under a byline of its reporter. The quotes attributed to the IEF president were used without further checking. Three days after receiving the release, Cackler settled with the IEF for a retraction, $1,800, and a letter of apology. Cackler said, "It's totally unethical to borrow from someone else's work for your article," and donated $1,300 of the settlement to a journalism department for an investigative reporting scholarship.[3]

An editor at *Time* said that he once caught a file from a correspondent as having been taken directly from a newspaper report, because he had read a clipping from that newspaper in gathering information for his story.[4]

Many editors, particularly of smaller magazines, tell about the brilliantly written articles they have received from writers in various prisons, only to find out—before publication or from the original author after publication—that they were plagiarized. Caution is a key word here.

While words spoken on a nationally televised news conference or before 2,000 people at a national convention or a news conference attended by a dozen reporters at the local university might safely be picked up and quoted from an Associated Press dispatch or a local news report, attribution is the safeguard that tells our readers where we got our information. We obviously should check to confirm it. If it turns out to be incorrect, we can at least point out that we had identified our source.

Hiley Ward advises writers, "Plagiarism is a sign of an amoral, if not perverse personality. No thinking person should descend to plagiarism. Plagiarists—who almost always get caught—have to live with guilt all their lives."[5]

Media Events: Image or Reality?

When news was conceived largely as an unusual event, editorial judgment was relatively simple. Significance, importance, intellectual stimulation, and worth have long since complicated the matter. The staged event, publicity stunt, press conference, and news release have made it tougher to distinguish material of legitimate public interest from self-serving promotion. Historian Daniel Boorstin discusses this at some length in his book, *The Image.*

The pseudo-event, Boorstin writes, "is not spontaneous, but comes about because someone planned, planted, or incited it. Typically it is not a train wreck or an earthquake, but an interview." The objective of a pseudo-event is to be reported. "Usually it is intended to be a self-fulfilling prophecy," leading to the general belief that something said to be true is true.[6]

Walt Disney World invited 5,250 media representatives to a three-day party to celebrate its 15th anniversary, and each could bring a personal guest. Disney, airlines, Orlando-area hotels, convention bureaus, and state and local government agencies underwrote the cost of about $8 million. Christians, Rotzoll, and Fackler in *Media Ethics* point out that "Disney's management made no effort to shape the reporting but, given their expertise at generating publicity, it correctly presumed that the results would be overwhelmingly positive."[7]

Experience and research tend to indicate that you can't fool all of the people all of the time in regard to truth about events and product performance. The realm of ideas is more difficult to assess. An individual may develop a favorable attitude toward a company or candidate based on inadequate or one-sided information and hold that attitude until strong contradictory data alter it. Packaging ideas and persuading people are more challenging than reporting an observable event. Social security was attacked as socialism in the 1930s but accepted as a normal governmental program within 20 years. Socialized medicine was vehemently fought in the 1950s, but partially accepted as Medicare for the aged in the late 1960s. Others insist that proper health care is a human right that should be made available to everyone by the federal government, and health care has become a major national issue.

Public relations practitioners will continue to advance their interests, whether they are pseudo-events, one-sided position statements, or idea pieces offered as balanced presentations with a hope that readers may side with the advocates' interests.

Identifying Ghostwriters

All these issues tie into another problem editors frequently face: ghostwriting. Prominent persons—from the president of the United States through cabinet officers, corporation executives, university presidents, and even university professors—have writers who "know" what the employer wants to say, who offer some additional ideas, and who mix them together into speeches that can be given and articles that can be published.

We usually can assume that the person whose byline appears on the piece has at least approved it, but we don't know who wrote it or whose ideas really are being expressed. In many cases, neither the editor nor the readers can judge a public figure by what is published under his or her name.

One step toward honesty is the use of *with* or *as told to* in addition to the principal's name: "My Fight for Baby M" by Mary Beth Whitehead with Loretta Schwartz-Nobel (*Family Circle*), "Sex Secrets Wives Keep" by Ken Druck with Kathleen Duey (*Reader's Digest*), "How to Break Par on the Greens" by Gary Player with Desmond Tolhurst (*Golf Digest*), or "A Strong Silken Thread" by Nien Cheng, Washington, D.C., as told to Mary Ann O'Roark (*Guideposts*). This at least suggests to the reader that the principal's ideas were used but refined or expressed more clearly by the writer. Writers frequently find that they must submit questions in writing before an interview and limit themselves closely to the questions and prepared answers. This may irritate writers, but it may be the only way to get answers. Also, the answers may be better researched and more factually accurate as well as better stated. The writer prepares and researches and should expect some research by the interviewee.

Reporting Techniques and Checkbook Journalism

Magazines that deal in news and reportage face the same ethical questions as news-gathering organizations in other media. They must decide whether to obtain information by deception or misrepresentation in some cases, whether to permit sources to remain anonymous, whether to use composite characters in articles, and whether to let interviewees check an article before publication. The answers to these vary according to the specific situation, the field the magazine serves, the principals involved, and the ethical standards by which they operate. All of these ethical problems are discussed at much greater length in other works, as they deserve to be.

Editors frequently pay sources for information. Many journalists oppose all such "checkbook journalism," but many others accept it as long as convicted criminals are not paid for their stories and are not given undue publicity. The National News Council found that *Life* fell short of the highest professional standards in paying $8,000 for pictures ($1,000 each) of Bernard Welch, the burglar accused of killing Dr. Michael Halberstam, for an article on the careers of both men in the February

1981 issue. *Life* obtained pictures of Halberstam from his family and the Harvard University Archives. The National News Council reiterated its 1975 position on checkbook journalism:

If compensation beyond actual expense is made to any person for news in the form of an interview (published or broadcast), or for information to be used in a news story or broadcast, or for an article by a person in the news, that fact should be disclosed. A prefatory note or on-the-air statement immediately preceding the article or program should be published or broadcast.

Such notification to the reader or viewer is not intended for the publication of articles or photographs or radio and television productions actually written or produced by an individual or supplier and marketed to the news organization through commonly accredited practices that do not deceive the public.

The council further recommended that news organizations not pay criminals for news materials.[8]

Two excellent books on media ethics that discuss these and other issues in detail are *Media Ethics: Cases & Moral Reasoning* by Clifford G. Christians, Kim B. Rotzoll, and Mark Fackler (Longman) and *Ethics in Media Communications: Cases and Controversies* by Louis A. Day (Wadsworth).

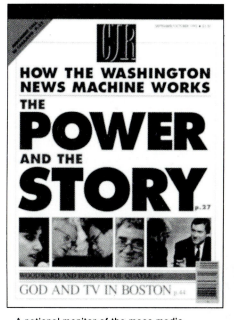

A national monitor of the mass media, *Columbia Journalism Review* frequently deals with ethical issues in major articles and in its Darts and Laurels department. (Courtesy *Columbia Journalism Review.*)

Gifts and Junkets

Whether a journalist should accept small gifts, favors, junkets, and positions on boards of public bodies will forever be debated. The best answer is to avoid all offers that may influence *or be construed by readers to influence* any writer or editor, or that may undermine the magazine's credibility with its readers. Publishers, editors, and writers don't always see it that simply.

Many writers, of course, are working on several manuscripts at a time, offering them to different magazines or publishers. Their editors need to know more about the circumstances than the manuscript includes. Is the writer also being paid by a company mentioned in the article or performing public relations duties for a company or its public relations agency? Did the writer accept a trip to the site of the article or interview? Has anything been involved in researching and writing the piece that readers might construe as influence on the writer or the magazine? If the writer does not make full disclosure, the editor should ask about the circumstances.

If an editor believes a writer's work is so good that it must be published in spite of entanglements, allegiances, or obvious business connections, the least the editor can do is to be totally fair to all ideas and sides, to make the piece balanced, and to have researchers check it for both factual inaccuracies and omissions. Also, an editor's note with the piece should state that the writer does public relations for the firm involved or that the writer once worked for this candidate, as the case may be. Readers never should be surprised to learn later, from another source, that the article they enjoyed was written by a person with a vested interest in the subject.

It may seem petty to insist that media pay their writers' way wherever they go, but it may be the small difference between editorial independence and perceived allegiance.

Some media organizations won't let editorial employees accept anything, not even a cup of coffee. Others allow a meal or anything that can be eaten at one sitting. Some use the 24-hour rule, anything one can consume in 24 hours, so a bottle of wine may be acceptable but not a case. For gifts that cannot be consumed, some, such as *Newsweek,* use the $25 rule, which is the maximum Internal Revenue Service permits businesses to deduct from their taxes for a gift. These rules tend to beg the question. No experienced journalist can be corrupted by a free meal or a $25 gift, but, if readers think they can, there is a problem. The appearance of such influence to readers is as much a concern as any real influence. If it is a free trip to a theme park or another travel destination, the amount is considerably greater. Although they do not issue an absolute rule, Christians, Rotzoll, and Fackler in *Media Ethics* point out that "the acceptance of free trips may involve a conflict of interest whereas their refusal does not."[9]

Some editorial staff members may not always follow a magazine's policy. A corporate vice-president for public relations was awaiting the arrival of a magazine writer. He asked an assistant to be sure to take the writer to dinner and offer to pay his hotel bill. "The last magazine writer who was here," he said, "opened by telling me it was against his magazine's policy to accept favors, entertainment, or travel expenses. Then in the next breath he said 'Do you belong to a private club where we could have dinner tonight?' " That writer was wined and dined as he requested.

Business/Social Class Pressures

The company editors keep often is not typical of their magazine's readership, and most realize it. In all media of communication, the people at the top are well paid and move in a social circle higher than the typical reader's or viewer's. Editors socialize with publishers, businesspeople, entertainers, and prominent people in many walks of life. William Allen White called it the "country club complex" and noted that persons in these positions "get the unconscious arrogance of conscious wealth."

Concerns of business probably come across clearest to editors because they have more contact with businesspeople in their professional and social activities. Magazines, too, are a business, and editors can be expected to think like businesspeople.

Editors of public relations magazines have the added burden of being advocates of business and part of management. If their magazines are effective, they must remember the needs and interests of their readers and strongly identify with them. The overzealous advocate of management's viewpoint may have an unread magazine and do no one any good.

Simply recognizing the existence of class bias does not eliminate it, but it is a start. An editor who consciously considers personal biases when choosing content, angles, and play usually arrives at better decisions than one who does not. Think of the reader first and above all other considerations. What best serves the reader? What would the reader want you to do as editor? Keep in touch with readers so you will know what best serves them and what they want you to do.

Some ethicists have recommended a strong feeling of professionalism, the desire to do a job that will be respected by one's peers. Journalism reviews with their published criticism have had a salutary effect. The criticism, even if it is answered, nudges the editor to better or more professional performance.

Advertiser Influence

Advertisers' influence on editorial decisions goes along with social class pressures. The threat seldom has to be made directly and overtly; pressure is more subtle than that. It may permeate the editorial office. "They are long-time advertisers; let's jump a good article next to their ad," has been heard even from seasoned editors. This kind of influence is virtually impossible to pin down and prove. One staff member may insist it exists, while the person at the next desk believes there is nothing but fair play involved.

Advertisers and their agencies attempt to select the most effective media for their messages. When one advertiser is obviously favored, others are justifiably irate, and there can be a backlash against the favored advertiser, because a competitor might insist on a better deal. Editors tell how *Collier's* and *Saturday Evening Post* sold editorial favoritism to advertisers before going out of business.

Editor Ben Hibbs of *Saturday Evening Post* said of *Collier's:* "Someone from the business office was always looking over their [editors'] shoulders. Things often were done editorially solely to attract advertising—always a vain procedure and usually a fatal mistake."[10]

Otto Friedrich tells how Martin Ackerman promised advertising executives at Ford Motor Company that Henry Ford's picture would be on the cover of the October 5, 1968, *Saturday Evening Post* to save $400,000 worth of Ford advertising in that issue, but editorial employees insisted that the other auto makers would object and that immense damage would result. Because Ford had not been offered exclusive display on the cover, someone suggested featuring the heads of all four auto makers.[11] The obvious problem arising if the magazine sells out to one advertiser is that there is no stopping as the word gets around.

Editorial integrity is much easier to maintain if the book is in solid financial condition and does not desperately need to woo advertisers. However, the long-term price of selling one's integrity is more likely to be loss of advertising pages rather than gain.

The question of whether editorial content, especially bold content, will lose advertisers from the magazine frequently arises. John H. Johnson said *Ebony* has to have advertising, and in some cases he thought the magazine was going so far that advertisers would reject it. He was fearful of the possible consequences of publishing "Was Abraham Lincoln a Segregationist?" and later an entire issue devoted to the "white problem" in America. In each case, however, after thinking about it and weighing the circumstances, he said, "I've got to go forward with this."[12]

Articles that relate directly to advertisers are no different, as Herbert Mayes, former editor of *McCall's* and *Good Housekeeping,* noted:

To set out deliberately to antagonize advertisers would be senseless. But when there was reason to investigate and expose, there was no hesitation. Disclosures of unfair airline practices ("Going to Fly? Another Look at the Airlines"), or of the diamond monopoly ("Diamonds Are a Girl's Most Overpriced Friend"), or life insurance sales methods ("Let's See What the Insurance Companies Offer"), meant we might never get the advertising of the companies named; such possibility never deterred us.[13]

In the history of American journalism, honesty and integrity have been proved necessary for economic survival. Dishonesty in advertising and circulation claims around the turn of the century led to the formation of a number of professional associations to ensure the truthfulness of these claims. Editorial integrity and strong independence from advertisers also have been found to be sound business practices.

A magazine in financial difficulty often finds it impossible to maintain a sufficient level of advertising revenue. The psychology of this situation is summed up by an old advertising agency executive saying: "No one wants his ad to appear in the last issue of a magazine." When rumors are spread about a magazine's problems, ad pages decline, hastening the magazine's demise.

Separation of Advertising from Editorial

One long-standing principle of editing decrees that advertisements be clearly differentiated and separated from editorial matter. Postal regulations require that ads that do not clearly look different from editorial matter be labeled "Advertisement." Many ads that copy a magazine's page layout style and use its editorial typefaces have found their way into print. The policy of differentiation is an overall publishing policy and an advertising policy, and the advertising department has the option of rejecting ads that look like part of the magazine's editorial content. Ads that have come under fire for being virtually indistinguishable from editorial content have included a Delta Air Lines ad in *People,* and ads for Oil of Olay in *Reader's Digest, Saturday Evening Post,* and several other magazines.

Another criticism of advertisements is lack of taste. Although the editorial and advertising departments should be completely separate, an editor certainly is concerned with whether the advertising department accepts ads that may be objectionable to some readers or that may promote dangerous products or services. Does advertising policy permit the acceptance of advertisements for products and services that have not been checked? Magazine historians John Tebbel and Mary Ellen Zuckerman have written that business publications' "reliability was guaranteed by the separation of editorial services from advertising."[14]

Magazines that usually have handsome ads run a sprinkling of ads with intentionally cheap and cluttered-looking layouts. These ads, with their unsophisticated, irritating appearance, jump out at the reader and diminish the reader's overall impression of the magazine. A magazine has the right to reject any ad, and the advertising department should consider enforcing a standard of visual taste in keeping with the visual appearance of the rest of the magazine.

Undue advertiser influence may be implied when the magazine publishes an article written by an advertiser's public relations department or the ad agency's PR department. The line of demarcation is thin, almost invisible. It is more dangerous if the reader is not informed that the article was written by a PR agency and is left with the impression that it is a staff-written piece.

Magazines frequently create special sections, even special editions, to generate additional advertising. The advertising staff often prepares the nonadvertising copy that accompanies the advertisements and clearly labels the entire section "Advertisement" or "Special Advertising Section." At other times, the editorial staff may be expected to provide related features that are informative, helpful, or entertaining to readers. As long as the staff maintains its editorial integrity and standards of quality, there should be no problem. If the magazine publishes transparent puffery of advertisers' products or services, there is disservice to both readers and advertisers.

Editorial Viewpoint (Bias)

Bias within the magazine staff itself is frequent and not always bad. A denominational religious magazine can be expected to support its sponsor's positions on moral issues, although it may find the occasional offer of contradictory ideas by other writers to be advantageous. A magazine of critical opinion, such as *The Nation,* may well make clear its own position. As mentioned earlier, balance does not always mean giving the other side or sides equal space or impact. If something is obviously wrong, there is no need to publish material advocating the wrongdoing.

Stopping short of sensationalism is recommended, although opinions vary about where that point is. Robert Root told of a National Health Forum where a physician asked why *Look* had used a sensational heading, "Why Hospitals Lock Out Doctors." The *Look* editor replied, "What is sensational about that? They are colorful words. . . . We are competing for [the reader's] attention." An emotionally involved reader, or a reader within the industry or profession being discussed is usually more sensitive and more critical than the average reader. Editors must make their best judgment and prepare to take the flak that comes their way from readers.

Government

Government seldom exerts a direct threat to magazines, but the people who operate its many bureaus often hinder the free flow of information, and public officials use the press for their trial balloons. Writers and editors often sense that they are being used to advance proposals that are not being made whole-heartedly, and that can easily be shot down by public reaction. Whether to permit such use of a periodical is a decision that the editor must make by individual case. In a free marketplace of ideas, a cabinet officer's article on a proposed new federal program, the revision of an existing agency, or the elimination of an ineffective one can add greatly to public discussion, which is part of the legislative and administrative process. Editors are delighted to publish pieces of articulate cabinet officers, senators, and other officials, especially if they might add prestige or readership to the magazine.

The Reader's Perception

An editor may believe that he or she is wholly fair and involved in no conflicts of interest, but the *appearance* of such to the reader is as damaging to the credibility of the magazine as is the reality. To protect the integrity of their magazine, editors need to avoid being perceived as being unfair or being involved in conflicts of interest. That holds true down the line to writers, who themselves may be involved in insider trading or other breaches of reader trust.

Relations with Outside Writers (Free-lancers)

Editors maintain a trust with outside writers that is enhanced by complete communication. Occasionally, a writer simultaneously submits an article to two or more magazines. Writers who admit this to each editor run the risk of immediate rejection. An established writer may get immediate attention and a quick offer, start a bidding war, or be rejected by all editors involved. If the writer does not admit the simultaneous submission, two or more editors may schedule the piece for an upcoming issue until the writer informs them of the problem.

Because editors recognize that their magazines seldom can be any better than their writers, they temper their reactions to a writer who has simultaneously submitted an article to several magazines. While the first reaction may be to reject the writer and ban him or her from the magazine, that writer may develop into a first-rate source of material for the magazine. Editors cannot dictate the ethics of all their free-lance writers. They can be open and honest in their communication with them and encourage the same in return.

Writers sometimes use the same material but write it from different angles for different magazines. Editors generally appreciate knowing that an article with a different angle and with no or very little duplicated information has been submitted elsewhere. The editor wants a unique article and does not want to be surprised by a nearly identical article by the same writer in a competitor. Editors may find it advisable to tell writers this when contracting with them for articles.

Editors usually edit an article as much as necessary to make it meet the magazine's requirements. It is generally accepted that the editor should make no substantive changes to the article, as the work of the bylined writer, without permission of the writer. Changes for purposes of style, grammar, conciseness, or arrangement may be made by the editor as long as they do not change the intent or sense of the article.

A writer may be obliged to rewrite a piece on an editor's request, according to the code of the American Society of Journalists and Authors, but the writer also is entitled to withdraw the manuscript and offer it elsewhere. A writer also may consent to have the piece rewritten by someone else. Staff writers may have to adhere to other practices. As employees, they are expected to write to the employer's standards and practices.

Codes of Ethics

Journalists have long debated whether codes are of real value, citing their vagueness and lack of enforceability as major weaknesses and their usefulness as general guidelines as a strength. Journalistic codes generally stand for and discuss truth, accuracy, responsibility, independence, impartiality, fair play, and freedom of the press. The definition and application of these precepts are left largely to individual journalists and especially to editors. When the codes are specific, as in the Society of Professional Journalists' statement that "nothing of value should be accepted" or that journalists should protect themselves "from conflict of interest, real or apparent," large numbers of journalists disagree. Nevertheless, codes are useful guides to most journalists, who need to be reminded of basic precepts and of what others in the profession say about them.

Although created by and for writers, the ASJA Code of Ethics and Fair Practices gives editors the viewpoint of this group of organized writers.

The Society of Professional Journalists Code of Ethics is frequently cited and debated. Dealing primarily with news gathering and reporting, it is a guide worth noting.

The American Business Press has both a Code of Professional Research Ethics and Practices and a Code of Publishing Practice.

American Society of Journalists and Authors
Code of Ethics and Fair Practices

Preamble

Over the years, an unwritten code governing editor-writer relationships has arisen. The American Society of Journalists and Authors has compiled the major principles and practices of that code that are generally recognized as fair and equitable.

The ASJA has also established a Committee on Editor-Writer Relations to investigate and mediate disagreements brought before it, either by members or by editors. In its activity this committee shall rely on the following guidelines.

1. Truthfulness, Accuracy, Editing

The writer shall at all times perform professionally and to the best of his or her ability, assuming primary responsibility for truth and accuracy. No writer shall deliberately write into an article a dishonest, distorted or inaccurate statement.

Editors may correct or delete copy for purposes of style, grammar, conciseness or arrangement, but may not change the intent or sense without the writer's permission.

2. Sources

A writer shall be prepared to support all statements made in his or her manuscripts, if requested. It is understood, however, that the publisher shall respect any and all promises of confidentiality made by the writer in obtaining information.

3. Ideas and Proposals

An idea shall be defined not as a subject alone but as a subject combined with an approach.

A proposal of an idea ("query") by a professional writer shall receive a personal response within three weeks. If such a communication is in writing, it is properly viewed and treated as business correspondence, with no return postage or other materials required for reply.

A writer shall be considered to have a proprietary right to an idea suggested to an editor.

4. Acceptance of an Assignment

A request from an editor that the writer proceed with an idea, however worded and whether oral or written, shall be considered an assignment. (The word "assignment" here is understood to mean a definite order for an article.) It shall be the obligation of the writer to proceed as rapidly as possible toward the completion of an assignment, to meet a deadline mutually agreed upon, and not to agree to unreasonable deadlines.

5. Conflict of Interest

The writer shall reveal to the editor, before acceptance of an assignment, any actual or potential conflict of interest, including but not limited to any financial interest in any product, firm, or commercial venture relating to the subject of the article.

6. Report on Assignment

If in the course of research or during the writing of the article, the writer concludes that the assignment will not result in a satisfactory article, he or she shall be obliged to so inform the editor.

7. Withdrawal

Should a disagreement arise between the editor and writer as to the merit or handling of an assignment, the editor may remove the writer on payment of mutually satisfactory compensation for the effort already expanded, or the writer may withdraw without compensation and, if the idea for the assignment originated with the writer, may take the idea elsewhere without penalty.

8. Agreements

The practice of written confirmation of all agreements between editors and writers is strongly recommended, and such confirmation may originate with the editor, the writer, or an agent. Such a memorandum of confirmation should list all aspects of the assignment including subject, approach, length, special instructions, payments, deadline, and guarantee (if any). Failing prompt contradictory response to such a memorandum, both parties are entitled to assume that the terms set forth therein are binding.

All terms and conditions should be agreed upon at the time of assignment, with no changes permitted except by written agreement signed by both parties.

9. Rewriting

No writer's work shall be rewritten without his or her advance consent. If an editor requests a writer to rewrite a manuscript, the writer shall be obliged to do so but shall alternatively be entitled to withdraw the manuscript and offer it elsewhere.

Continued

10. Bylines

Lacking any stipulation to the contrary, a byline is the author's unquestioned right. All advertisements of the article should also carry the author's name. If an author's byline is omitted from a published article, no matter what the cause or reason, the publisher shall be liable to compensate the author financially for the omission.

11. Updating

If delay in publication necessitates extensive updating of an article, such updating shall be done by the author, to whom additional compensation shall be paid.

12. Reversion of Rights

A writer is not paid by money alone. Part of the writer's compensation is the intangible value of timely publication. Consequently, reasonable and good-faith efforts should be made to schedule an article within six months and publish it within twelve months. In the event that circumstances prevent such timely publication, the writer should be informed within twelve months as to the publication's continued interest in the article and plans to publish it. If publication is unlikely, the manuscript and all rights therein should revert to the author without penalty or cost to the author.

13. Payment for Assignments

An assignment presumes an obligation upon the publisher to pay for the writer's work upon satisfactory completion of the assignment, according to the agreed terms. Should a manuscript that has been accepted, orally or in writing, by a publisher or any representative or employee of the publisher, later be deemed unacceptable, the publisher shall nevertheless be obliged to pay the writer in full according to the agreed terms.

If an editor withdraws or terminates an assignment, due to no fault of the writer, after work has begun but prior to completion of a manuscript, the writer is entitled to compensation for work already put in; such compensation shall be negotiated between editor and author and shall be commensurate with the amount of work already completed. If a completed assignment is not acceptable, due to no fault of the writer, the writer is nevertheless entitled to payment; such payment, in common practice, has varied from half the agreed-upon price to the full amount of that price.

14. Time of Payments

The writer is entitled to full payment for an accepted article within 30 days of delivery. No article payment, or any portion thereof, should ever be subject to publication or to scheduling for publication.

15. Expenses

Unless otherwise stipulated by the editor at the time of an assignment, a writer shall assume that normal, out-of-pocket expenses will be reimbursed by the publisher. Any extraordinary expenses anticipated by the writer shall be discussed with the editor prior to incurring them.

16. Insurance

A magazine that gives a writer an assignment involving any extraordinary hazard shall insure the writer against death or disability during the course of travel or the hazard, or, failing that, shall honor the cost of such temporary insurance as an expense account item.

17. Loss of Personal Belongings

If, as a result of circumstances or events directly connected with a perilous assignment and due to no fault of the writer, a writer suffers loss of personal belongings or professional equipment or incurs bodily injury, the publisher shall compensate the writer in full.

18. Copyright, Additional Rights

It shall be understood, unless otherwise stipulated in writing, that sale of an article manuscript entitles the purchaser to first North American publication rights only, and that all other rights are retained by the author. Under no circumstances shall an independent writer be required to sign a so-called "all rights transferred" or "work made for hire" agreement as a condition of assignment, of payment, or of publication.

19. Reprints

All revenues from reprints shall revert to the author exclusively, and it is incumbent upon a publication to refer all requests for reprint to the author. The author has a right to charge for such reprints and must request that the original publication be credited.

20. Agents

An agent may not represent editors or publishers. In the absence of any agreement to the contrary, a writer shall not be obliged to pay an agent a fee on work negotiated, accomplished and paid for without the assistance of the agent. An agent should not charge a client a separate fee covering "legal" review of a contract for a book or other project.

21. TV and Radio Promotion

The writer is entitled to be paid for personal participation in TV or radio programs promoting periodicals in which the writer's work appears.

Continued

22. Indemnity

No writer should be obliged to indemnify any magazine or book publisher against any claim, actions, or proceedings arising from an article or book, except where there are valid claims of plagiarism or copyright violation.

23. Proofs

The editor shall submit edited proofs of the author's work to the author for approval, sufficiently in advance of publication that any errors may be brought to the editor's attention. If for any reason a publication is unable to so deliver or transmit proofs to the author, the author is entitled to review the proofs in the publication's office.

Rev. 5/77, 9/79, 2/82, 7/86, 4/89, 6/91, 10/91

Reprinted by permission of the American Society of Journalists and Authors; from the ASJA Handbook: *A Writer's Guide to Ethical and Economic Issues.* Copies are $12.95, available from ASJA, 1501 Broadway, #302, New York City 10036.

Society of Professional Journalists
Code of Ethics

SOCIETY of Professional Journalists, believes the duty of journalists is to serve the truth.

We BELIEVE the agencies of mass communication are carriers of public discussion and information, acting on their Constitutional mandate and freedom to learn and report the facts.

We BELIEVE in public enlightenment as the forerunner of justice, and in our Constitutional role to seek the truth as part of the public's right to know the truth.

We BELIEVE those responsibilities carry obligations that require journalists to perform with intelligence, objectivity, accuracy, and fairness.

To these ends, we declare acceptance of the standards of practice here set forth:

I. RESPONSIBILITY:

The public's right to know of events of public importance and interest is the overriding mission of the mass media. The purpose of distributing news and enlightened opinion is to serve the general welfare. Journalists who use their professional status as representatives of the public for selfish or other unworthy motives violate a high trust.

II. FREEDOM OF THE PRESS:

Freedom of the press is to be guarded as an inalienable right of people in a free society. It carries with it the freedom and the responsibility to discuss, question, and challenge actions and utterances of our government and of our public and private institutions. Journalists uphold the right to speak unpopular opinions and the privilege to agree with the majority.

III. ETHICS:

Journalists must be free of obligation to any interest other than the public's right to know the truth.

1. Gifts, favors, free travel, special treatment or privileges can compromise the integrity of journalists and their employers. Nothing of value should be accepted.

2. Secondary employment, political involvement, holding public office, and service in community organizations should be avoided if it compromises the integrity of journalists and their employers. Journalists and their employers should conduct their personal lives in a manner that protects them from conflict of interest, real or apparent. Their responsibilities to the public are paramount. That is the nature of their profession.

3. So-called news communications from private sources should not be published or broadcast without substantiation of their claims to news values.

4. Journalists will seek news that serves the public interest, despite the obstacles. They will make constant efforts to assure that the public's business is conducted in public and that public records are open to public inspection.

5. Journalists acknowledge the newsman's ethic of protecting confidential sources of information.

6. Plagiarism is dishonest and unacceptable.

IV. ACCURACY AND OBJECTIVITY:

Good faith with the public is the foundation of all worthy journalism.

1. Truth is our ultimate goal.

2. Objectivity in reporting the news is another goal that serves as the mark of an experienced professional. It is a standard of performance toward which we strive. We honor those who achieve it.

Continued

3. There is no excuse for inaccuracies or lack of thoroughness.

4. Newspaper headlines should be fully warranted by the contents of the articles they accompany. Photographs and telecasts should give an accurate picture of an event and not highlight an incident out of context.

5. Sound practice makes clear distinction between news reports and expressions of opinion. News reports should be free of opinion or bias and represent all sides of an issue.

6. Partisanship in editorial comment that knowingly departs from the truth violates the spirit of American journalism.

7. Journalists recognize their responsibility for offering informed analysis, comment, and editorial opinion on public events and issues. They accept the obligation to present such material by individuals whose competence, experience, and judgment qualify them for it.

8. Special articles or presentations devoted to advocacy or the writer's own conclusions and interpretations should be labeled as such.

V. FAIR PLAY:

Journalists at all times will show respect for the dignity, privacy, rights, and well-being of people encountered in the course of gathering and presenting the news.

1. The news media should not communicate unofficial charges affecting reputation or moral character without giving the accused a chance to reply.

2. The news media must guard against invading a person's right to privacy.

3. The media should not pander to morbid curiosity about details of vice and crime.

4. It is the duty of news media to make prompt and complete correction of their errors.

5. Journalists should be accountable to the public for their reports and the public should be encouraged to voice its grievances against the media. Open dialogue with our readers, viewers, and listeners should be fostered.

VI. MUTUAL TRUST:

Adherence to this code is intended to preserve and strengthen the bond of mutual trust and respect between American journalists and the American people.

The Society shall—by programs of education and other means—encourage individual journalists to adhere to these tenets, and shall encourage journalistic publications and broadcasters to recognize their responsibility to frame codes of ethics in concert with their employees to serve as guidelines in furthering these goals.

CODE OF ETHICS

(Adopted 1926; revised 1973, 1984, 1987)

Copyright © Society of Professional Journalists.

The ABP Code of Publishing Practice

As a condition precedent to membership and as a condition for the continuation of membership, each member of the American Business Press, Inc., agrees:

1. To hold uppermost the interest of its readers, firm in the knowledge that devoted service to readers is the key to effective service to advertisers.

2. To publish no editorial material either as a consideration for advertising or in return for monetary or other consideration; and further to publish no advertising material which simulates the publication's editorial content without clearly and conspicuously identifying such material as a message paid for by an advertiser.

3. To maintain absolute editorial independence from advertisers, from government, or from sources other than the publisher.

4. To vigilantly and forcefully fight for the constitutional right of freedom of the press.

5. To practice and encourage the highest standards of journalistic and publishing ethics; to strive constantly for honest and effective presentation of all news and articles; to refrain from infringement of the trademarks and copyrights of others.

6. To submit each publication to regular circulation audits conducted by an independent, nonprofit, tripartite auditing organization, and to encourage similar auditing practices by all publications of whatever type.

7. To make available to advertisers, advertising agencies and other interested persons or organizations, a complete listing of all the prices which a publication charges for all units of space, including but not limited to preferred or specified positions, colors, bleed, inserts, etc., as well as the terms of payment thereof; and to afford no advertiser an opportunity to purchase such space at a rate more advantageous than is available to any other advertiser.

Continued

8. To refuse knowingly to accept advertising which is untruthful, misleading, deceptive or in bad taste, or which unfairly disparages or attacks the goods, prices, services or advertising of any competitor or any other industry.
9. To promote and sell its own publications solely on their merits.
10. To employ no advertising or personal selling methods on its behalf which are untruthful, misleading or deceptive, or which unfairly disparage other publications or advertising media.

Courtesy American Business Press.

Notes

1. William L. Rivers and Wilbur Schramm, *Responsibility in Mass Communication,* rev. ed. (New York: Harper & Row, 1969), p. 141.
2. Hiley Ward, *Magazine and Feature Writing* (Mountain View, Cal.: Mayfield, 1993), p. 315.
3. Mary Schaefer, "Press Release Plagiarism," *The Quill* (November/December 1991): 31–32.
4. Ward, p. 316.
5. Ward, p. 317.
6. Daniel Boorstin, *The Image* (New York: Atheneum, 1962), pp. 10–11.
7. Clifford G. Christians, Kim B. Rotzoll, and Mark Fackler, *Media Ethics: Cases & Moral Reasoning,* 3d ed. (New York: Longman, 1991), p. 47.
8. " 'Life' Criticized for Paying Accused Killer," *Columbia Journalism Review* (May–June 1981): 91.
9. Clifford G. Christians, Kim B. Rotzoll, and Mark Fackler, *Media Ethics: Cases & Moral Reasoning,* 2d ed. (New York: Longman, 1987), p. 40.
10. *Advertising Age* (16 February 1959): 8.
11. Otto Friedrich, *Decline and Fall* (New York: Harper & Row, 1970), p. 374.
12. " 'Failure Is a Word I Don't Accept,' an Interview with John H Johnson," *Harvard Business Review* (March–April 1976): 88.
13. Herbert R. Mayes, *The Magazine Maze* (Garden City, N.Y.: Doubleday & Company, 1980), p. 102.
14. John Tebbel and Mary Ellen Zuckerman, *The Magazine in America 1741–1990* (New York: Oxford University Press, 1991), p. 348.

The Editor and the Law

L EGAL problems that confront a magazine editor usually stem from inadequacies in editing—failure to check accuracy or authenticity, acceptance of facts
from untrustworthy sources, or reckless disregard for the truth in a rush to publish.
Libel is not a great threat to a magazine that is carefully edited. Nevertheless, magazines of any size should budget for legal counsel and be prepared to be sued.

It should be pointed out that anyone can file a civil suit against anyone else, so
even the most carefully edited magazine needs a libel lawyer. The big cost may be
attorney fees rather than court judgments. Also, congested court dockets, delays,
and appeals can extend the duration of a suit to unbelievable lengths.

Libel

Communication that exposes persons to hatred, ridicule, or contempt; lowers them
in the esteem of others; causes them to be shunned; or injures them in their business
or calling is defamation. Printed, written, or broadcast defamation is called libel,
and spoken words of limited reach are slander. Courts also recognize personal humiliation, and mental anguish and suffering, widely termed "infliction of emotional
distress."[1]

Don Pember in *Mass Media Law* points out

To be actionable defamation, the words must actually damage a reputation. There must be
some harm done to the individual's reputation. Without proof of this harm, the party who
claims injury should not be able to recover damages for injury. But the awarding of
damages by juries is hardly a science and often a plaintiff is compensated for suffering
emotional harm or loss of self-esteem. Such awards should only be possible if the suffering
or loss of esteem is a direct result from the actual harm to the reputation.[2]

One of the major magazine cases stems from the article "Story of a College
Football Fix" in the 23 March 1963 issue of the weekly *Saturday Evening Post*. It
accused Wallace Butts, University of Georgia athletic director, of conspiring to fix
a football game between Georgia and Alabama by giving information to Alabama
coach Paul "Bear" Bryant. The article was based on information from George Burnett, an insurance man who said that he had been cut in on a long distance conversation between Butts and Bryant.

Butts immediately sued for $10 million in Atlanta Federal Court, claiming the
Post had "willfully, maliciously and falsely" libeled him. Bryant sued for $5 million
in Montgomery Federal Court.

The Butts case came to trial, and on 20 August the jury awarded $60,000 in
general damages as compensation for his loss of reputation and $3 million punitive
damages for callous disregard of the injured party. The *Post* filed for both a new
trial and reduction of judgment. The federal judge in Atlanta ruled the punitive
damages excessive and gave Butts the choice of accepting a reduced judgment totaling $460,000 or going through a new trial. On the advice of his lawyers, he ac-
cepted the reduced judgment. However, the *Post* again filed for a new trial, and
Butts' lawyers countered with a motion to restore the original judgment.

Finally, the judgment was affirmed by the United States Supreme Court in 1967. Justice John Harlan wrote in the court's opinion

The evidence showed that the Butts story was in no sense "hot news" and the editors of the magazine recognized the need for a thorough investigation of the serious charges. Elementary precautions were, nevertheless, ignored. The *Saturday Evening Post* knew that Burnett had been placed on probation in connection with bad check charges, but proceeded to publish the story on the basis of his affidavit without substantial independent support. Burnett's notes were not even viewed by any of the magazine's personnel prior to publication. John Carmichael who was supposed to have been with Burnett when the phone call was overheard was not interviewed. No attempt was made to screen the films of the game to see if Burnett's information was accurate, and no attempt was made to find out whether Alabama had adjusted its plans after the alleged divulgence of information.

The *Post* writer assigned to the story was not a football expert and no attempt was made to check the story with someone knowledgeable in the sport. At trial such experts indicated that the information in the Burnett notes was either such that it would be evident to any opposing coach from game films regularly exchanged or valueless. Those assisting the *Post* writer in his investigation were already deeply involved in another libel action, based on a different article, brought against Curtis Publishing Co. by the Alabama coach and unlikely to be the source of a complete and objective investigation. The *Saturday Evening Post* was anxious to change its image by instituting a policy of "sophisticated muckraking," and the pressure to produce a successful expose might have induced a stretching of standards. In short, the evidence is ample to support a finding of highly unreasonable conduct constituting an extreme departure from the standards of investigation and reporting ordinarily adhered to by responsible publishers.[3]

This case was decided in the same decision with *Associated Press v. Walker.* Retired Major General Edwin A. Walker opposed the integration of the University of Mississippi and appeared there in 1962, when rioting accompanied the enrollment of James H. Meredith, an African American. An Associated Press dispatch said that Walker had taken command of a violent crowd and had personally led a charge against federal marshals. It also described Walker as encouraging rioters to use violence.

The court delivered four opinions. All agreed that Butts and Walker were "public figures," Walker, wrote Justice John Harlan, "by his purposeful activity amounting to a thrusting of his personality into the 'vortex' of an important public controversy." This definition of *public figure* is frequently cited in subsequent decisions. Chief Justice Earl Warren wrote that "under any reasoning, General Walker was a public man" in whose conduct society had a "substantial interest." After examining AP's coverage, Justice Harlan found no "extreme departure from the standards of investigation and reporting ordinarily adhered to by responsible publishers." The AP story was news that required immediate dissemination, the correspondent was competent, and his dispatches were internally consistent with a single exception.[4] These cases illustrate that magazines are held to a higher standard of accuracy and care in verification of the statements to be published than are the media publishing "hot news" on tight deadlines.

Bryant previously had sued the *Post* for $500,000 over an article that linked him with college football brutality. On 3 February 1964, he settled both suits out of court with the *Saturday Evening Post* for $300,000. The Butts and Bryant cases show how much time litigation requires. It took four years for Butts to conclude his case, while Bryant, by settling out of court, concluded his action within one year.

A libel judgment against *Look* won by former San Francisco mayor Joseph Alioto over an article published in 1969 was upheld by the U.S. Supreme Court in 1981. "The Web That Links San Francisco's Mayor Alioto and the Mafia" was published with reckless disregard for the truth because, according to the Court of Appeals (9th Circuit), there were "obvious reasons to doubt the veracity" of the source who had supplied the authors with much of the information for their article.[5] Four trials were conducted over eight years before the former mayor won the judgment.[6] *Look* ceased publication in 1971 and Cowles Communications, which had pursued the suits, was held responsible.

Defenses

When an editor is sued for libel, several defenses are available.

The **constitutional defense** originated with *New York Times v. Sullivan* in 1964 and has been used more frequently than any other defense in libel cases since 1964.

Under it, a public official or public figure must prove that the publisher published the defamatory statement with knowledge that it was false or with reckless disregard for the truth (actual malice).[7]

The defense does not necessarily apply to every case involving a public official. Public officials are required to prove actual malice only "when the defamatory comments or statements concern (1) their *official conduct,* that is, actions taken in an official capacity or actions while they undertake their public official role and (2) their general fitness for public office."[8]

The *Rosenbloom v. Metromedia* decision (1971) extended the public figures portion of this defense for a while to all public or private persons who were libeled in a discussion of an event of interest to the public. However, that was narrowed in 1974 to two types of persons who are "public figures" in *Gertz v. Welch.* Although an attorney active in civil rights disputes in Chicago, Gertz was ruled not a public figure in this case, which did not involve civil rights. The Supreme Court, in the opinion by Justice Lewis Powell, described two kinds of public figures:

In some instances an individual may achieve such pervasive fame or notoriety that he becomes a public figure for all purposes and in all contexts. . . . More commonly, an individual voluntarily injects himself or he is drawn into a particular public controversy and thereby becomes a public figure for a limited range of issues.[9]

We should note that the *Gertz* case involved a magazine, and *Rosenbloom* involved radio, a spot news medium, giving us one of many indications that magazines have less leeway than spot news media.

The question of whether the material is in the public interest or is of interest only to the magazine personnel, possibly arbitrarily selected by them for publication, arose in the *Gertz* case. Gertz was an attorney who represented the family of a young man who was slain by a Chicago policeman in a civil action for damages after the policeman was convicted of murder. *American Opinion* magazine, published by Robert Welch, attacked Gertz, falsely charging that he was a Communist fronter, a Leninist, and an architect of the frame-up against the police officer, and the magazine alleged that he had a criminal record. Gertz had been only a peripheral figure in the circumstances surrounding the death and the murder trial and, having been found not a public figure, did not have to prove actual malice. The controversy existed before Gertz was ever involved; therefore, he did not cause the controversy, and the court ruled that the mere fact that he was an attorney in a case that had attracted some attention did not make him a public figure.

In the *Gertz* decision, the Court also ruled that a plaintiff cannot win punitive damages in a libel suit unless there is negligence on the part of the publication in not discovering the falsity of the published statements.[10] The U.S. Supreme Court took no libel case until *Sullivan* (1964). Negligence was a common standard in civil law prior to 1964.

In *Firestone v. Time, Inc.* (1976), the court affirmed *Gertz* and pointed out that a controversy of interest to the public, in this case a divorce proceeding, is not the same as the "public controversy" cited in the *Gertz* opinion, even though the plaintiff was a prominent member of Palm Beach society and held several press conferences during the 17-month legal proceeding. The ruling in *Firestone* was that the plaintiff was not a public figure for purposes of *Time* magazine, although she probably was for the Palm Beach newspaper. A person may be a public figure locally, in the state, and in a profession, but not in a broader context, such as nationally. Firestone withdrew her claim for harm to reputation before the trial. She won a judgment for $100,000 for emotional anguish.[11]

A person on a public payroll or who receives public funds is not necessarily a public official or public figure. The director of research of a state mental hospital who had successfully applied for nearly a half-million dollars in federal funds for research on aggression in animals was ruled not to be a public figure in *Hutchinson v. Proxmire* (1979). "Hutchinson did not thrust himself or his views into public controversy to influence others," and his position did not invite public scrutiny.

Fabricated quotations were considered by the U.S. Supreme Court in *Masson v. New Yorker Magazine* (1991). *The New Yorker* in December of 1983 ran a two-part profile by Janet Malcolm on Jeffrey Masson, a psychoanalyst who was projects director of the Sigmund Freud Archives in London. He later sued, claiming many quotations were fabricated by Malcolm and had damaged his reputation. Malcolm denied altering Masson's statements, and her legal defense argued that quotations—fabricated or otherwise—are entitled to First Amendment protection if the modified quotes are rational interpretations of the original statements. The California Federal District Court and subsequently the Court of Appeals agreed. However, the U.S. Supreme Court disagreed, ruling that the case should go to trial.

"It's important to point out that the U.S. Supreme Court's decision was surprisingly sensitive to the practical realities of journalism and news gathering, and did not penalize journalists because they failed to quote a source verbatim," Robert N. Landes, McGraw-Hill executive vice-president and legal counsel, said. In fact, the court acknowledged that, in most cases, it would be impractical for a reporter to use exact quotes. "The key factors, as the court saw them, are whether a material alteration took place—an alteration that changed the meaning of a statement—and whether that alteration damaged the plaintiff's reputation," he continued. "If both factors are met, then reporters may run the risk of a libel judgment against them."[12]

Based on the 1991 U.S. Supreme Court ruling, California's Ninth Circuit Court of Appeals reversed itself in April 1992 and confirmed that Masson could proceed with his libel action against Malcolm and *The New Yorker.* Judge Alex Kozinski said Malcolm could be sued, since Masson claims Malcolm deliberately or recklessly fabricated quotations and thereby damaged his reputation. *The New Yorker* could be sued because it has a fact-checking process and, if Masson could prove he complained about lack of accuracy during that process, the magazine had an obligation to double-check against notes or tapes. Masson's suit against Alfred A. Knopf, which later published the profile as a book, *In the Freud Archives,* was rejected because Knopf was entitled to rely on "the magazine's sterling reputation for accuracy and the existence of its fabled fact-checking department."[13] In June 1993, a federal jury found that Malcolm had misquoted and libeled Masson but deadlocked on damages, ending the trial inconclusively. The jury's separate decision said *The New Yorker* was not responsible. In September 1993, the federal district judge granted Masson a retrial of the suit against Malcolm and removed *The New Yorker* from the case because the evidence indicated that its editors "neither knew the quotations were false, nor acted with reckless disregard as to falsity." Masson can appeal the dismissal of the magazine after his case with Malcolm has been resolved.

New York magazine called Tex Maule the worst writer on *Sports Illustrated* and said most of his stories were rewritten. The court determined him to be a public figure because he had taken an affirmative step to attract attention through publication of his books and articles (*Maule v. New York Magazine,* 1980). The criticism was directed toward Maule's writing, the area to which he had attracted attention to himself.

Carol Burnett won a libel suit against the *National Enquirer* for a four-sentence item in the weekly's 2 March 1976 gossip column, based on information from a freelance tipster. Headlined "Carol Burnett and Henry K. in Row," it said Burnett was drunk and quarreled with former Secretary of State Henry Kissinger at a Washington restaurant in January 1976. She sued for $10 million.[14] As a public figure, she had to show that publication was made with knowledge that it was false or with reckless disregard for the truth.

The trial judge ruled that the *National Enquirer* is a magazine rather than a weekly newspaper and, therefore, is not protected by a California statute that limits libel judgments against newspapers that print retractions. At Burnett's request, a retraction had been published. The jury's award of $300,000 in general and $1.3 million in punitive damages to Burnett was cut by the judge to $50,000 in general and $750,000 in punitive damages. The *Enquirer* announced it would appeal.[15] The District Court of Appeals retained the $50,000 general damages verdict but cut punitive damages to $150,000. Burnett finally settled in December 1984 for an undisclosed sum rather than exercise her option to seek a new trial. Burnett recovered damages almost entirely for emotional distress.[16]

Miss Wyoming of 1978 alleged that a *Penthouse* article falsely implied that she was sexually promiscuous and immoral and in 1981 won a jury award of $1.5 million in compensatory damages and $25 million in punitive damages. The federal district court judge quickly reduced the figure by one-half but said the reduced figure must exceed *Penthouse*'s libel insurance protection of $10 million if it were to punish the magazine. *Penthouse* appealed and after another year received a new judgment: the article could be reasonably understood by readers as only "pure fantasy," not as defamation of the plaintiff (*Pring v. Penthouse, 1982*).

Pring was not mentioned by name, but it was ruled that the use of Miss Wyoming plus the fact that she was described as wearing a purple bathing suit in the swimsuit competition constituted identification. Magazine editors need to recognize that verbal descriptions can constitute identification even when a name is not used.

Plaintiffs often lose their cases or have them dismissed. In dismissing a libel suit filed by a biochemist against *Consumer Reports,* the court stated that he had not demonstrated actual malice and further stated, "It is clear that *Consumer Reports* made a thorough investigation of the facts. . . . The unquestioned methodology of the preparation of the article exemplifies the very highest order of responsible journalism."[17]

The threat of an emerging separate tort of infliction of mental injury was lessened in 1988 by the U.S. Supreme Court's decision in *Hustler v. Falwell,* which held that the First Amendment protects parodies, even *Hustler*'s mock ad that said Reverend Jerry Falwell's first sexual experience had been in an outhouse with his mother while she was drunk. The ad had a fine-print disclaimer: "ad parody—not to be taken seriously." Reverend Falwell sued *Hustler* and publisher Larry Flynt for libel plus invasion of privacy plus intentional infliction of emotional distress.

A U.S. District Court jury found that Falwell had not been libeled because "no reasonable person would believe that the parody was describing actual facts about Falwell" and that his privacy had not been invaded; however, the court did find infliction of mental injury and awarded him $200,000—$100,000 in compensatory damages plus $50,000 in punitive damages against Flynt and $50,000 against his magazine. The Court of Appeals, Fourth Circuit, affirmed the ruling. The U.S. Supreme Court unanimously disagreed.

Chief Justice William Rehnquist wrote that Reverend Falwell was a public figure involved "in the world of debate about public affairs [where] many things done with motives that are less than admirable are protected by the First Amendment." Chief Justice Rehnquist declared that any system of civil damages that might teach Flynt a lesson would also endanger a long and valued tradition of caustic American political caricatures—verbal and visual—and cartoons.[18] He wrote

The appeal of the political cartoon or caricature is often based on exploration of unfortunate physical traits or politically embarrassing events—an exploration often calculated to injure the feelings of the subject of the portrayal. The art of the cartoonist is often not reasoned or evenhanded, but slashing and one-sided.[19]

Rehnquist conceded that "*Hustler* is at best a distant cousin of . . . political cartoons . . . and a rather poor relation at that." David A. Anderson, a University of Texas law professor, observed that this decision "cuts off the main avenues of the emotional distress claim."[20] Lyle Denniston of the *Baltimore Sun* and other authorities believe that this ruling leaves little chance for public figures to win emotional distress claims for even the most outrageous parody.[21] At the Supreme Court level, the case makes the same point that was ultimately made in *Pring v. Penthouse* with regard to satire and outrageous statements.

Three traditional defenses are truth, qualified privilege, and opinion and fair comment. If the **truth** of the published statement can be proved to the satisfaction of the court and, in some states, that it was published with good motives and justifiable ends, the editor has a complete defense. This defense has very limited application because most libel suits are filed by public persons who have to show known falsity or negligence. Further, the U.S. Supreme Court has ruled that it is unconstitutional to put the burden of proving truth on a media defendant when the issue involved is a "matter of public concern" (*Philadelphia Newspapers v. Hepps, 1986*). Truth is still considered by many state courts and in matters that are not of public concern or that do not involve public officials or public figures.

Qualified privilege is based on the assumption that, under a republic form of government, free and open discussion in *public and official* bodies must be protected. Statutes vary widely from state to state over what is both public and official, and journalists often are mistaken in thinking some information they have procured from a government agency, such as facts from a police blotter, is privileged. Further, because the journalist is not publishing the full text of courtroom testimony or a legislative session, the defense becomes qualified privilege, qualified by the publication of a fair and accurate summary of the proceedings.

In some cases, **opinion and fair comment** may be an effective defense. The test for fair comment revolves around an honest expression of opinion on a public person or a matter of legitimate public interest based on observed fact and lacking malicious intent. An article stating opinion should give the reader the facts on which the opinion was based or examples of those facts. A critical movie review, for example, should report some of the scenes, dialogue, or acting characteristics that led to the reviewer's opinion of the movie. Courts disagree whether the opinion and fair comment defense has been absorbed into the First Amendment through the *Gertz* decision. This opinion defense seems to have been diluted substantially by the U.S. Supreme Court in *Milkovich v. Lorain Journal* (1990).

Chief Justice William H. Rehnquist wrote "we do not think this passage from *Gertz* was intended to create a wholesale defamation exemption for anything that might be labeled 'opinion.' " Further, "even if the speaker states the facts upon which he bases his opinion, if those facts are either incorrect or incomplete, or if his assessment of them is erroneous, the statement may still imply a false assertion of fact. Simply couching such statements in terms of opinion does not dispel these implications." Also, "*Hepps* ensures that a statement of opinion relating to matters of public concern which does not contain a provably false factual connotation will receive full constitutional protection" (*Milkovich v. Lorain Journal,* 1990).

Dwight Teeter, Jr., and Don Le Duc write that the *Milkovich* decision suggests that journalists should look to their ethics and "repress the desire to clobber reputations, especially *private* reputations, with opinion statements if the underlying facts are squishy."[22]

Occasionally, an error slips past everyone into print. In these cases, a retraction is in order. If a suit is filed, the retraction tends to decrease the amount of damages by showing lack of actual malice. A libeled person often accepts a properly worded retraction as sufficient settlement, especially since few people want to expend the time, funds, and energy to undergo the rigors of a trial and its attendant publicity.

A study of almost 1,000 libel and privacy suits filed between 1974 and 1984 found that about three-fourths of all plaintiffs said they would have been satisfied with a published or broadcast correction, retraction, or apology. Most plaintiffs bring lawsuits not so much to win monetary damages but out of frustration by their treatment by the mass media.[23] Editors can help reduce the increasing number of suits by trying to resolve the situation before it gets to that stage.

Statute of Limitations

A suit for libel must be filed within the statute of limitations, which varies from one to six years and in most states is one or two years. About half the states accept a later sale of the magazine issue in question as an additional publication that reactivates the beginning of the the time period covered by the statute. The other states have ruled that each entire edition is a single publication, and subsequent sales do not constitute republication.[24]

The date on a magazine usually is not the date it was published but an off-sale date. Courts have ruled that the statute of limitations begins on the date the magazine is distributed to a substantial portion of the public. *Time,* which is published a week before the date on its cover, was sued in New Jersey on 17 February 1981 over an article in the 18 February 1980 issue. Because a substantial portion of that issue's circulation had been distributed to subscribers and newsstands before 18 February 1980, the United States district court ruled that the statute of limitations had expired (*MacDonald v. Time,* 1981). A similar suit by Donald Wildmon, a minister, over an article in the November 1978 *Hustler* magazine was dismissed because the 9 October 1979 filing date was more than one year after the issue went on sale, 3 October 1978 (*Wildmon v. Hustler,* 1979).

It is possible for a plaintiff who has not filed a libel suit within the statute of limitations in his or her home state to file an action in another state that has a longer statute of limitations if the libel has been circulated in this other state. New Hampshire has a six-year statute of limitations. In 1984, the U.S. Supreme Court ruled that a resident of New York could sue a magazine based in Ohio in the state of New Hampshire. Associate Justice William Rehnquist wrote, "False statements of fact harm both the subject of the falsehood and the readers of the statement: New Hampshire may rightly employ its libel laws to discourage the deception of its citizens." The state may extend its concern to the injury that in-state libel causes within New Hampshire to a nonresident, he added (*Keeton v. Hustler,* 1984).

The U.S. Supreme Court also has ruled that writers can be required to appear in courts in remote locations if they have written about and caused injury to people who live in those locations in publications circulated in those locations. The case involved a suit filed in California by a Californian against Florida-based *National Enquirer* writers (*Calder v. Jones,* 1984).

Right of Privacy

A person's right to be left alone, to keep his or her name and picture out of the mass media, is the right of privacy. This right varies from state to state and is judged by the court in each case. Privacy has been recognized in federal courts in the District of Columbia and all of the states except Minnesota.[25]

When newsworthiness can be proved, a person generally cannot collect damages for invasion of privacy, but, if the material in question was used without his or her consent for advertising or commercial purposes or in fiction, a person's privacy generally has been invaded. Part of an opinion by Justice Shientag of the New York Supreme Court gives useful guidelines, even though it is based on the New York statute:

The rules applicable to unauthorized publication of photographs in a single issue of a newspaper may be summarized generally as follows:

1. Recovery may be had under the statute if the photograph is published in or as part of an advertisement, or for advertising purposes. . . .
2. There may be no recovery under the statute for publication of a photograph in connection with an article of current news or immediate public interest.
3. Newspapers publish articles which are neither strictly news items nor strictly fictional in character. They are not the responses to an event of peculiarly immediate interest but, though based on fact, are used to satisfy an ever-present educational need. Such articles include, among others, travel stories, stories of distant places, tales of historic personages and events, the reproduction of items of past news, and surveys of social conditions. These are articles educational and informative in character. As a general rule, such cases are not within the purview of the statute.[26]

In a 1950 opinion, Justice Van Voorhis wrote, "These classifications apply, with some possible distinctions, to books and magazines."[27]

Photographs

Although newsworthiness is broadly construed, it is advisable to obtain the consent of persons depicted in photographs. Most cases involving the right of privacy have centered on misused photographs.

A 10-year-old girl was knocked down by a careless motorist, and a news photographer got a picture of a woman helping the girl to her feet. Publication of the photo in the newspaper was not actionable; it was a news picture used to convey a news event. Twenty months later, the *Saturday Evening Post* used the picture to illustrate an article titled "They Ask to Be Killed." The photo caption included "unpredictable darting through traffic still takes its sobering toll" and a box by the headline said, "Do you invite massacre by your own carelessness? Here's how to keep them alive." A Federal Court of Appeals wrote, "The legitimate subject for publicity for one particular accident, now becomes a pictorial, frightful example of pedestrian carelessness. This, we think exceeds the bounds of privilege."[28]

Teeter and Le Duc write

The lesson, for photo editors, should be plain: if a picture is not taken in a public place or if that picture—or its caption—places someone in a false light, don't use it. The exception, of course, would be when you have received permission, in the form of a signed release, from the person pictured.[29]

When a picture or an account of an event ceases to be news and becomes a symbolic but false illustration, entertainment, or commercial in nature, it may become the subject of successful litigation by the person pictured or described.

Magazines should insist on written consent for the use of pictures that may not be deemed newsworthy. Public relations magazines vary in their practice about getting releases from employees. Some insist on signed releases from everyone pictured; others assume that the employee implied consent when he or she had the picture taken, knowing the use to which it would be put.

Permission to use a photograph does not automatically include permission to use a person's name. That must be specified in the same or a different release, or the magazine will be open to suit for invading a person's privacy for using his or her name without consent.

A model release gives written consent of the persons pictured to use the photograph for specified purposes. From the editor's viewpoint, a blanket release permitting all uses is desirable. From the model's viewpoint, a more restricted use may be better. A sample release is

The undersigned hereby irrevocably consents to the unrestricted use by [photographer's name], advertisers, customers, successors and assigns of my name, portrait, or picture for advertising purposes or purposes of trade, and I waive the right to inspect or approve such completed portraits, pictures, or advertising matter used in connection therewith.

Some caution should be taken in using pictures, even with unrestricted releases. In one case, the model sued because the photo had been retouched to suggest a completely different situation than had originally been photographed. She won.[30] In Louisiana, a man agreed to "before" and "after" photos for a health studio's body-building course. However, when the photos were used in an ad 10 years later, the court held that his privacy had been invaded.[31]

The real danger lurks in picture files because the conditions under which the picture was taken and the nature of the agreement may not be with the picture. Its first use usually poses no problem, but the second use does, such as in the *Saturday Evening Post* example previously described.

When you buy a photo from an agency or a photographer, you buy the right to publish it in your magazine one time. It is possible to buy exclusive rights, but you need a written agreement covering those rights. Magazines in competitive markets generally want exclusive rights. Smaller or more specialized magazines may not.

Photos taken by a magazine's staff are no problem beyond the routine of getting written releases because the magazine has exclusive rights and can sell or assign any or all of them.

Four classifications of right of privacy have evolved from decided cases: (1) intrusion, (2) appropriation of one's name or likeness, (3) publicity that places the person in a false light before the public, and (4) publicity that discloses private facts.

Intrusion is the acquisition of information from or about a person by physical trespass or other means from which an ordinary person could expect a reporter to be excluded. In one case, reporters posed as patients to gain admittance to the home-office of an alleged medical quack and, once there, surreptitiously took photographs and made sound recordings. This was found to be an invasion of privacy, and the fact that the ruse was undertaken to gather news was not accepted as a defense. Privacy was invaded when the intrusion took place and existed whether or not the information was published. Electronic eavesdropping, wire-tapping, harassment, and conversion of another's personal documents have been alleged to be intrusive invasions of privacy.[32]

Appropriation involves using a person's photograph or name for advertising purposes or in trade without written consent. Use of a living person's name or likeness in an intentionally fictionalized version of a topic of news or general interest may be a case of appropriation. In one case in 1966, Warren Spahn, a well-known baseball pitcher, won a privacy suit over publication of an unauthorized biography because there were significant amounts of intentionally fictionalized material in the book.[33]

Much promotional material is published as editorial content, but the determination of whether it is informational or commercial is carefully made by a court. One teenage woman who was featured in *Seventeen* magazine's "make-over" section inadvertently did not sign the routine permission forms and release. Teenagers featured in this section are paid and are given clothing, cosmetics, and advice on how to improve their appearances. The article includes before-and-after pictures and mentions brand names of products in discussing the make-over. The teenager sued, contending that her name and likeness had been appropriated for trade purposes. She lost when the court ruled that the article about grooming, makeup, and clothing was newsworthy to the teenage audience at which it was aimed (*Lopez v. Triangle Communications,* 1979).

Family Circle bought the rights to publish portions of the revised book *Your Baby's Sex: Now You Can Choose It.* It contained an unsolicited letter from a woman who had successfully used the techniques recommended in the first edition. The woman sued *Family Circle,* contending publication of her letter was an advertisement for the book and that the entire article was an advertisement for the book, using her name for trade purposes. The Appellate Division of the New York Supreme Court noted that the book's publisher, Dodd, Mead & Company, had not paid for the publication but that *Family Circle* had purchased the rights to the material (*Heller v. Family Circle*).

A magazine may, however, use editorial material from previous issues in its own advertising. In *Booth v. Curtis Publishing Company* (1962), the court held that a *Holiday* magazine ad reproducing a photograph of actress Shirley Booth from an article that had appeared earlier in editorial pages was not an invasion of privacy.[34] In *Namath v. Time, Inc.* (1976), New York State's highest court upheld lower court decisions that the use of a picture of Joe Namath in the 1969 Super Bowl game and his name in an ad promoting *Sports Illustrated* did not invade his privacy. However, had the ad contained words that implied that Namath endorsed the magazine, "a completely different issue would have been presented," wrote an appeals judge whose decision was upheld. Namath had sued for $2.5 million.[35]

Under both these New York State court decisions, as long as the names and likenesses have been previously published editorially and are used in advertising to illustrate the quality and content of the publication, written consent is not required and appropriation has not taken place.

Forum magazine used a picture of Cher, the entertainer, to promote an edition of the magazine, stating that Cher endorsed the magazine, which was not true. A United States district court in California ruled that use of Cher's name and picture went much further than establishing the news content and quality of the magazine. The advertising was not merely incidental to the original publication of an interview with Cher (*Cher v. Forum International,* 1982).

False light deals with publication of untrue information that is not defamatory but which places the individual in a false light before the public and therefore invades the person's privacy. In the *Time, Inc. v. Hill* case (1967), the U.S. Supreme Court ruled that damages for a false light invasion of privacy could not be awarded unless the untrue material was published "with knowledge of falsity or reckless disregard for the truth."

In *Cantrell v. Forest City Publishing Co.* (1974), the court found that the plaintiff had been portrayed in a false light through knowing or reckless untruth ("calculated falsehoods") in an article that falsely implied that she had been present during the reporter's visit to the family home, that he had observed her facial expression, and that she was reluctant to talk about the tragedy of a widely publicized bridge collapse in which her husband had been killed.[36] There are two qualifications for false light: (1) the published false information must be highly offensive to a reasonable person, and (2) the plaintiff must prove that the publisher knew the information was false when it was published, or acted with reckless disregard for the truth of the information.[37]

"Fictionalizing" was a factor in the first privacy case to reach the United States Supreme Court. The 28 February 1955 issue of *Life* carried an article titled "True Crime Inspires Tense Play," relating how the James Hill family of Whitemarsh, Pennsylvania, near Philadelphia, had been held captive in its own home in 1952, and that this had been used as the basis for a novel by Joseph Hayes titled *The Desperate Hours*. The article said, "Now they [Americans] can see the story re-enacted in Hayes's Broadway play based on the book, and next year will see it in his movie." In the next paragraph, it said, "LIFE photographed the play during its Philadelphia tryout, transported some of the actors to the actual house where the Hills were besieged. On the next page scenes from the play are re-enacted on the site of the crime."[38]

The play and novel, though, did not match the "true crime." The Hills, called Hilliards in the fiction, had not been harmed by the convicts in any way, but in the novel and play father and son were beaten and the daughter subjected to "a verbal sexual assault." Hill, who had moved to Connecticut to avoid public scrutiny, sued for invasion of privacy under the New York statute on the grounds that the *Life* article "was intended to, and did, give the impression that the play mirrored the Hill family's experience, which, to the knowledge of the defendant . . . was false and untrue."

Time Inc. in its defense contended that the subject of the article was "a subject of legitimate news interest," "a subject of general interest and of value and concern to the public" at the time of publication, and that it was published "in good faith without any malice."

The trial court jury awarded $50,000 compensatory and $25,000 punitive damages to the Hills. On appeal, a new trial on the question of damages was ordered but the finding that *Life* had invaded the Hills' privacy was upheld. A jury was waived, and the court awarded $30,000 compensatory and no punitive damages.

Writing the opinion on the appeal to the U.S. Supreme Court, Justice William Brennan noted that truth was a complete defense under the statute but that Hill was entitled to sue to the extent that *Life* "fictionalized" and "exploited for the defendant's commercial benefit." He also noted that Hill was a newsworthy person substantially without a right to privacy as far as his hostage experience was involved. He then brought in the *New York Times v. Sullivan* libel case:

Material and substantial falsification is the test. However, it is not clear whether proof of knowledge of the falsity or that the article was prepared with reckless disregard for the truth is also required. In *New York Times Co. v. Sullivan*, 376 U.S. 254, we held that the Constitution delimits a State's power to award damages for libel in actions brought by public officials against critics of their official conduct. Factual error, content defamatory of official reputation, or both, are insufficient to an award of damages for the false statements unless actual malice—knowledge that the statements are false or in reckless disregard of the truth—is alleged and proved. . . .

We hold that the Constitutional protections for speech and press preclude the application of the New York statute to redress false reports of matters of public interest in the absence of proof that the defendant published the report with knowledge of its falsity or in reckless disregard of the truth.[39]

Although five justices voted for *Life,* they were split in their reasons, three agreeing on use of the *New York Times* rule, and two concurring in the decision on other grounds. The Chief Justice joined two other justices in a dissenting opinion. The Brennan opinion did not establish truth as a dependable defense in invasion of privacy suits. His majority opinion placed the benefits of freedom of the press to society ahead of an individual's right to privacy and allowed for incidental, non-malicious error to creep into an article as part of the risk of freedom:

We create grave risk of serious impairment of the indispensable services of a free press in a free society if we saddle the press with the impossible burden of verifying to a certainty the acts associated in news articles with a person's name, picture or portrait, particularly as related to nondefamatory matter. Even negligence would be a most elusive standard. . . . A negligence test would place on the press the intolerable burden of guessing how a jury might assess the reasonableness of steps taken by it to verify the accuracy of every reference to a name, portrait or picture.[40]

Although the lower courts had found that the *Life* article was not legitimate news but fictionalized entertainment for purposes of trade, Justice Brennan wrote, "We have no doubt that the subject of the *Life* article, the opening of a new play linked to an actual incident, is a matter of public interest. 'The line between the informing and the entertaining is too elusive.' "[41]

Author Hayes had said the Hill incident triggered his writing of the book and the play, but that he had not attempted to portray the Hill family's experience and that he had used incidents from California, New York, Detroit, and other places in shaping his story. Brennan rejected the question of commercial exploitation by quoting a 1952 Supreme Court decision:

That books, newspapers, and magazines are published and sold for profit does not prevent them from being a form of expression whose liberty is safeguarded by the First Amendment.[42]

Future courts may find differently, and the split in the court in this decision muddles the question, but this decision did bring to bear on an invasion of privacy suit many aspects of press freedom and protection that had been established, including nonmalicious error, difficulty of attributing commercial exploitation, and the element of newsworthiness.[43] Note that this was a 1955 case not settled until 1967 and that a 1964 decision, nine years after the article was published, was cited in the Supreme Court decision. The law changed though the facts did not.

Public disclosure of private and embarrassing facts is much less of a problem; publishers have won most of the cases filed against them so far.

William J. Sidis was an 11-year-old mathematical prodigy in 1910. He graduated from Harvard at age 16 and received much publicity. An article about him in the 14 August 1937 issue of the *New Yorker* was accompanied by a cartoon with the captions "Where Are They Now?" and "April Fool." The article told how Sidis lived in a "hall bedroom of Boston's shabby south end" and worked at a routine clerical job. He sued for invasion of privacy, but the court held that, although the *New Yorker* had published "a ruthless exposure of a once public character, who has since sought and has now been deprived of the seclusion of private life," it found "The article in the *New Yorker* sketched the life of an unusual personality and it possessed considerable popular news interest." The court would not comment on whether newsworthiness would always constitute a complete defense. It further observed

Revelations may be so intimate and so unwarranted in view of the victim's position as to outrage the community's notions of decency, but when focused upon public characters, truthful comments upon dress, speech, habits, and the ordinary aspects of personality will usually not transgress this line. Regrettably or not, the misfortunes and frailties of neighbors and "public figures" are subjects of considerable interest and discussion to the rest of the population. And when such are the mores of the community, it would be unwise for a court to bar their expression in the newspapers, books, and magazines of the day.[44]

"Who Let This Doctor in the O.R.? The Story of a Fatal Breakdown in Medical Policing" in *Medical Economics* described an anesthesiologist's patients who suffered disabling or fatal injuries in the operating room, focusing on the lack of self-policing by physicians. In documenting his allegations, the writer discussed the anesthesiologist's psychiatric and related personal problems. Her name and picture were included in the article. She conceded the story was newsworthy but argued that publication of her photograph, name, and private facts revealing her psychiatric and marital histories added nothing to the story and was an invasion of her privacy. The court ruled otherwise, stating that the inclusion of the name and photograph strengthened the impact and credibility of the article. "They obviate any impression that the problems raised in the article are remote or hypothetical, thus providing an aura of immediacy and even urgency that might not exist had plaintiff's name and photograph been suppressed." Her psychiatric and marital problems were connected to the newsworthy topic by the rational inference that her personal problems were the underlying causes of the acts of alleged malpractice (*Gilbert v. Medical Economics*, 1981).

A *Sports Illustrated* article about a bodysurfer included alleged private and embarrassing facts, such as that the surfer extinguished cigarettes in his mouth to impress women, intentionally injured himself so he could collect unemployment and have time for surfing, and ate insects. He had told the reporter these but claimed that prior to publication of the article he forbade publication of them. The federal district court said that to lose First Amendment protection the offensive facts must first be highly offensive as a matter of community mores and, second, the revelation must be for its own sake. These facts, however, were not sufficiently offensive and were revealed in "a legitimate journalistic attempt to explain his extremely daring and dangerous style of bodysurfing" (*Virgil v. Time, Inc.*).[45]

People close to public figures sometimes lose some of their privacy. *Saturday Evening Post* published names of the children of "Tiger Lil" Corabi in an article that said she was accused of planning a complex burglary. The Pennsylvania high court ruled that she was a public figure, and anyone could publish her biography without her consent and could include names of family members (*Corabi v. Curtis Publishing Co.*, 1971).

Reader's Digest published a story about the tremendous number of truck hijackings nationally and mentioned, only as a detail, an incident in which Marvin Briscoe hijacked a truck. It did not mention that this had taken place 11 years earlier. Briscoe asserted that he had served his time in jail and had led an exemplary life since he was freed. The story revealed to friends, neighbors, and family part of his life he had hidden. The California Supreme Court questioned the value of re-telling this story, which negated the state's rehabilitation of him. The suit was sent back to the state court for trial, but *Reader's Digest* had it removed to a federal district court, and a federal judge granted a motion for summary judgment for the magazine (*Briscoe v. Reader's Digest Association*, 1971).

Copyright

Editors should be certain the material they are buying is original with the author. Brilliant articles often are accepted, later to be found as having been cribbed from other publications.

Copyright in the United States protects a work for the life of the author plus 50 years or, in the case of a work made for hire or an anonymous or pseudonymous work, the lesser of 75 years after publication or 100 years after creation. Federal copyright protection begins as soon as a work is created, even though a notice of copyright is not required until the work is published. Publication is defined as "the distribution of copies or phono-records of a work to the public by sale or other transfer of ownership, or by rental, lease, or lending."[46]

One cannot tell from a copyright notice exactly what is covered. In many instances, authors retain the copyright to their articles or photographs, and the notice does not tell that. When you contact the permissions department of the publication, you may find you have to contact someone else who owns the rights. A copyrighted publication also can contain material that is in the public domain, but the publication does not tell you what is and what is not.

When a person creates a work while employed by a corporate publisher, unless there is a written agreement to the contrary, the employer is considered to be the author and the actual author (employee) is considered to have produced the "work for hire." If a publisher expects to use material produced by contributors who are not employees as works for hire, he or she must have a written agreement to that effect with the contributors.

Any transfer of copyright greater than a nonexclusive license is valid only if in writing and signed by the owner of the rights conveyed. In other words, a publication wanting to buy exclusive rights to an article, photographs, or illustrations must have a written agreement specifying exclusive rights with the copyright owner of the article, photographs, or illustrations. A magazine intending to use material in a book or as a reprint or to protect itself from having the piece turn up elsewhere must enter a signed agreement with the contributor.[47]

Copyright registration of an issue of a magazine protects all editorial content and those advertisements on behalf of the magazine's owner. No separate notice is required to protect an individual contributor's work. All other advertisements have to bear their own copyright notice to be protected.

Before the current copyright law took effect 1 January 1978, copyright in the United States was for a term of 28 years, with one renewal permitted to extend the total period to 56 years. After that, material was in the public domain and could be reprinted with impunity. However, in this transition period from the former law to the current law, further checking is required to determine whether a copyright has expired. The current law extended the copyright of works in their second term of copyright in 1978 to 75 years from their first publication and provided that works in their first term can receive a second term of 47 years.

Copyright protects the actual expression of the piece, not the ideas or facts contained in it. Further, if copyright is infringed, it is necessary for the copyright

---

AUTHOR'S/ARTIST'S RELEASE

The undersigned hereby grants to _____ one-time magazine publication rights in the article/art work tentatively entitled _____ .
The undersigned acknowledges receipt of full payment for such rights.
The undersigned warrants originality, authorship, and ownership of the aforesaid article/art work, that it has not been heretofore published, and that its publication will not infringe upon any copyright, proprietary, or other right.

The undersigned further grants to _____ the exclusive right to negotiate and to sell reuse of the above titled article/art work for one-time use in foreign publications including, but not limited to, those with which _____ may have a regular working relationship. It is understood that the undersigned will be entitled to 50% of the gross amount paid to, and actually received by, _____ for such foreign reuse. _____ agrees to pay all transaction costs (including, but not limited to, cable fees, reproduction of negatives and film, shipping, insurance where appropriate, telephone calls, etc.) involved in negotiating such reuse.

This purchase also gives _____ the right to select and republish your material as part of any of _____ anthological collections. For this reuse you will receive your pro-rata share of 5% of the gross sales of such special edition which is reserved for distribution among all contributors. Such payments will be made in two parts: the first, at the time of off-sale of such publication and the second at approximately 90 to 120 days off-sale. The first payment to be publisher's estimate of anticipated sale. It is further understood that if the above titled article/art work is the acknowledged collaborative product of more than one author and/or artist, then the author/artist's share described above shall be distributed among such authors and/or artists on a pro rata basis.

SIGNED: _____ DATE: _____

ADDRESS: _____
                (Street)   (City)   (State)   (Zip)

PHONE: Home (   )   Business (   ) _____
                area code   area code

SOCIAL SECURITY or ID No.: _____

owner to file suit to recover damages. The Copyright Office in the Library of Congress merely registers copyright claims; it does not grant copyrights. Most consumer and business magazines are copyrighted to protect material that could be used advantageously by competing magazines. Magazines of associations and those with public relations objectives often are not copyrighted and often contain instead of a copyright notice a statement like this one from *Dodge Adventurer:* "Other media are invited to use all content, partially or full, of this publication, with or without credit." An association or public relations magazine sees this as a possibility for extra publicity for its sponsor.

Whether to copyright a magazine is a policy decision that must be made in the light of a magazine's competition, purposes, proprietary interest in its articles and photographs, and similar factors. It might suffice to ask whether the magazine would go to court to collect damages if its material were reprinted without permission, and if the magazine expects to sell reprint rights. If the answer is yes in either case, the magazine should be copyrighted.

To obtain a postpublication copyright, one must (1) produce copies with a copyright notice, (2) publish the work, and (3) register the claim with the Copyright Office. The first step is accomplished by placing copyright notice, the year of publication, and the name of the copyright owner on the title page or the first page of text. The second is completed when copies are placed on sale, sold, or publicly distributed by the copyright owner. The third is done by sending two copies of the work and a completed application form to the Register of Copyrights, Library of Congress, with payment for the copyright fee. Full information and necessary forms are available from the Register of Copyrights, Library of Congress, Washington, DC, 20559.

Omission of the copyright notice or an error in it can be remedied by registering within five years with the Register of Copyrights and making a reasonable attempt to add notice to all copies that are distributed to the public after the omission or error has been discovered. In the meantime, an innocent infringer would not be liable.

The Nation was found to have infringed copyright in publishing a 2,000-word excerpt from the copyrighted memoirs of former President Gerald Ford. The memoirs were soon to be published in book form by Harper and Row and the Reader's Digest Association. *Time* magazine had purchased the right to publish excerpts before publication of the book. *The Nation* published a section of the memoirs without permission and argued in defense against Harper and Row's suit that the material it published was newsworthy and should be protected by the fair use doctrine. *Time* abandoned its agreement to publish excerpts, costing Harper and Row the fee *Time* had agreed to pay for prepublication rights (*Harper and Row v. Nation,* 1983, 1985).

In an ad promoting its new TV magazine, the *Miami Herald* showed copyrighted covers of *TV Guide*. The Fifth United States Court of Appeals ruled that it was fair use of copyrighted material, that the use of the covers in the ad had no effect on the potential market or value of the *TV Guide* covers. The ad might hurt sales of *TV Guide,* but that would be the effect of the advertisement, not the copyrighted covers. The court also said that the effect of the use on the market for the copyrighted work "is widely accepted to be the most important factor" (*Triangle Publications v. Knight-Ridder Newspapers, Inc.* 1980).

Trademarks

Magazine editors quickly find that trademarks are valuable company property and must be protected. If you misuse a trademark, by not capitalizing it, for example, you are likely to get a letter from a company attorney warning that it must be capitalized and should be followed by the generic term of the product: Scotch Brand cellophane tape, L'eggs pantyhose, Magnavox color television receiver.

The danger to a company is that, if a trademark is accepted into everyday use in place of the generic term and the company has not protested such use, it is likely to lose its legal claim to the trademark. Aspirin, cellophane, escalator, shredded wheat, milk of magnesia, linoleum, and lanolin once were trademarks, but all lost their protection when they came to designate the item rather than a brand name of the item. An irony is that a company may spend millions of dollars to get the public to think of its brand synonymously with the product but that it must protect the distinctiveness or identity of its trademark independent of the item.

When you use a trademark in place of a generic name, you may receive a letter from a trademark lawyer politely and firmly reprimanding you. The important thing to the lawyer is to have on record a copy of the complaint so that, if there is litigation involving the trademark, it can be introduced as evidence that the company did attempt to protect the trademark from falling into generic use. Most stylebooks suggest using generic terms in place of trademarks.

Lack of evidence in protesting misuse of trademarks can cause courts to find that the trademark has lost its distinctiveness and the company has lost its exclusive right to use it. An unusual case of this type was legal action the King-Seeley Thermos Company took against Aladdin Industries for calling its vacuum bottles "thermos." The court found that the company not only had not protested the use of "thermos" in place of "vacuum bottle" but had mildly encouraged that use. It ruled that Aladdin could call its vacuum bottles "thermos" but that King-Seeley Thermos retained the right to the "Thermos" trademark.[48]

Coca-Cola has succeeded in protecting "Coke" as a trademark even though it has been used generically by Americans for at least a half-century. This illustrates what diligence in protecting a trademark will do, in sharp contrast to what happened with Thermos.

Editors of company-sponsored publications become keenly aware of ways to protect trademarks, and many company magazines use the encircled R (®) after every company-owned trademark in editorial copy as well as in advertising.

Names of magazines cannot be copyrighted but they can be registered as trademarks. Intent to register a trademark is indicated by the small letters "TM" after the trademark. A trademark applies to the class of goods on which it is used as long as it continues to be used. In other words, a magazine cannot prevent a manufacturer from using its name on pet food, clothing, or furniture. In some cases, however, courts have broadly interpreted the law and have ruled that a business, such as a restaurant, was using the good reputation of a publication's name to promote its business and must cease using the name.

When a magazine discontinues publication, its owners lose the right to its name because it is no longer being used in commerce. Some publishers protect names by incorporating them into other magazines they issue, such as *Redbook, incorporating American Home.* At a later date, the publisher may revive the defunct magazine or sell its name to another publisher.

Even though magazines lose their names when they cease publication, publishers planning to use the name of a defunct magazine generally buy the name from the previous publisher to ensure that no lawsuit will be filed. For large publishers, this is an economical form of protection.

Postal Regulations and Obscenity

Most magazines distribute a substantial amount of their circulation by mail and must be aware of postal regulations, which provide that obscene, filthy, lewd, or lascivious publications may be barred from the United States mails. The knowledgeable violation of this provision can result in a fine, imprisonment, or both. The fine or imprisonment would not necessarily be imposed unless copies containing the nonmailable matter were deposited in the mails after determination by the Postal Service that the copies were nonmailable under the statute.

Also nonmailable are material about lotteries, except state-approved ones, fraudulent matter relating to obtaining money under false pretenses, and matter deemed disloyal to the United States or advocating or urging treason, including insurrection or forcible resistance to any law of the United States.

Obscenity has been an issue in magazine problems with the U.S. Postal Service. Ralph Ginsburg ran afoul of the liberal interpretations of obscenity of the mid-1960s by promoting his publications, which did not appear to be obscene under the law, as if they actually were. Ginsburg's three products were *Eros*, a hardcover magazine devoted to sophisticated sexual themes; *Liaison,* biweekly newsletter; and *the Housewife's Handbook on Selective Promiscuity,* a short book. According to Justice William Brennan's opinion for the Supreme Court, evidence showed

that each of the accused publications was originated or sold as stock in trade of the sordid business of pandering—"the business of purveying textual or graphic matter openly advertised to appeal to the erotic interest of their customers." EROS early sought mailing privileges from the postmasters of Intercourse and Blue Ball, Pennsylvania. The trial court found the obvious, that those hamlets were chosen only for the value their names would have in furthering petitioners' efforts to sell their publications on the basis of salacious appeal; the facilities of the post offices were inadequate to handle the anticipated volume of mail, and the privileges were denied. Mailing privileges were then obtained from the postmaster of Middlesex, New Jersey. EROS and Liaison thereafter mailed several million circulars soliciting subscriptions from the post office; over 5,500 copies of the *Handbook* were mailed.

The "leer of the sensualist" also permeates the advertising for the three publications.[49]

Four of the nine justices dissented. Ginsburg appeared to be taking advantage of the landmark 1957 *Roth* decision, in which Justice William J. Brennan wrote that the test of obscenity is

whether to the average person, applying contemporary community standards, the dominant theme of the material taken as a whole appeals to prurient interest.[50]

The work as a whole and its effect on the "average" person were to be the considerations, not the effect of selected passages on a susceptible person. The *Roth* decision also reaffirmed that obscenity is not protected by the First Amendment:

All ideas having even the slightest redeeming social importance—unorthodox ideas, controversial ideas, even ideas hateful to the prevailing climate of opinion—have the full protection of the guaranties, unless excludable because they encroach upon the limited area of more important interests. But implicit in the history of the First Amendment is the rejection of obscenity as utterly without redeeming social importance.[51]

Chief Justice Earl Warren's concurring opinion helped change the focus of future obscenity actions. He suggested that the conduct of the defendant should be the central issue. Nine years later, the *Ginsburg* decision revolved on this point, that Ginsburg had commercially exploited the prurient interest even though his publications in themselves apparently were not obscene. The Supreme Court decision upheld a $28,000 fine and five-year prison sentence. Ginsburg finally went to prison in 1972 and was paroled after eight months.

In 1973, another 5–4 decision involving an unsolicited, sexually explicit advertising mailer changed the obscenity situation a bit, but not as much as some people thought. In *Miller v. California,* the court ruled that states could regulate obscene materials, but only those that depict or describe sexual conduct that is clearly defined in the applicable state statute. Chief Justice Warren Burger wrote the decision, which said in part,

State statutes designed to regulate obscene materials must be carefully limited. As a result, we now confine the permissible scope of such regulations to works which depict or describe sexual conduct.

That conduct must be specifically defined by the applicable state law, as written or authoritatively construed. A state offense must also be limited to works, which, taken as a whole, appeal to the prurient interest in sex, which portray sexual conduct in a patently offensive way, and which, taken as a whole, do not have serious literary, artistic, political, or scientific value.

The basic guidelines for the trier of fact must be (a) whether "the average person applying contemporary community standards" would find that the work, taken as a whole, appeals to the prurient interest, (b) whether the work depicts or describes, in a patently offensive way, sexual conduct specifically defined by law, and (c) whether the work, taken as a whole, lacks serious literary, artistic, political, or scientific value.[52]

Although local police and other officials in several communities cleared *Playboy, Penthouse, Oui,* and similar magazines from newsstands,[53] such action was not covered by the ruling and the magazines soon reappeared.

In fact, the Supreme Court decision had stated,

Under the holdings announced today, no one will be subjected to prosecution for the sale or exposure of obscene material unless these materials depict or describe patently offensive "hard core" sexual conduct specifically defined by the regulatory state law, as written or construed. We are satisfied that these specific prerequisites will provide fair notice to a dealer in such materials that his public and commercial activities may bring prosecution.[54]

Hamling v. U.S. (1974) clarified that jurors may rely on their own knowledge of standards in their community; however, they are not to use their own standards but rather to draw on their knowledge of the standards of the average person in that community so that the "material is judged neither on the basis of each juror's personal opinion nor by its effect on a particular sensitive or insensitive person or group."[55]

The U.S. Supreme Court tried to clarify the obscenity law in 1987 by declaring that a "reasonable person" test should be applied to judging the value of a work accused of obscenity instead of a "community standards" test (*Pope v. Illinois,* 1987). Justice Byron White wrote,

. . . Smith v. United States, 431 U.S. 291 (1977) held that, in a federal prosecution for mailing obscene materials, the first and second prongs of the *Miller* test—appeal to prurient interest and patent offensiveness—are issues of fact for the jury to determine applying contemporary community standards. The Court then observed that unlike prurient appeal or patent offensiveness, "[L]iterary, artistic, political, or scientific value . . . is not discussed in *Miller* in terms of contemporary community standards. . . . Just as the ideas a work represents need not obtain majority approval to merit protection, neither, insofar as the First Amendment is concerned, does the value of a work vary from community to community based on the degree of local acceptance it has won. The proper inquiry is . . . whether a reasonable person would find such value in the material, taken as a whole.

The U.S. Supreme Court has been generous in what it accepts as definitions of "patently offensive 'hard-core' sexual conduct," but overall there has been a decline in arrests, prosecutions, and convictions since *Hamling* and *Miller.*[56]

Ideas, then, remain absolutely protected by the First Amendment. Obscenity continues not to be protected, and state laws can regulate only that obscenity which describes or depicts sexual acts specifically defined in those laws.

Although it does not affect the vast majority of magazines or even books, the Pandering Advertisement Act of 1968 permits the individual to define obscenity for himself or herself. He or she can have the Postal Service order the sender of unsolicited mail to strike his or her name from their mailing lists by swearing that he or she has been sexually aroused by their mail. Complaints under this act have been filed, among others, against advertisements for the *Christian Herald,* an electronics magazine, and auto seat covers.

Another act permits an individual to protect himself or herself and his or her children under age 19 for a five-year period from receiving sexually oriented advertisements in the mail by filing form 2201 at the post office.

Other Legal Matters

Legal considerations of lesser magnitude that arise occasionally include the law that applies to confidential sources, reproduction of currency, lotteries, labor law, and advertising.

Confidentiality

In *Cohen v. Cowles Media Company* (1987), the U.S. Supreme Court held that promises of confidentiality by a reporter are enforceable contracts and remanded this Minnesota case back to a state court. Kenneth M. Vittor, McGraw-Hill vice-president and associate legal counsel, cautioned that "the U.S. Supreme Court is saying that any alleged editorial promise, and not just a promise of confidentiality, represents a potentially binding contract." Therefore, failure to fulfill an alleged oral promise made to a source to write a favorable article, publish a piece as a cover story, provide final photo selection, or grant final editorial approval can serve as a breach of contract claim against a publisher.

Journalists should be very selective in making unconditional promises of confidentiality, or any oral promises, to their sources. Robert N. Landes, McGraw-Hill executive vice-president and general counsel, said, "If possible, a reporter should only grant confidentiality status to a news source in connection with publication of an article. Broader promises of confidentiality for all purposes (i.e., disclosure of name for litigation) should be extremely limited."[57]

Reproducing Currency

Federal law forbids publication of illustrations of U.S. currency or uncanceled stamps unless the illustrations are for historical, educational, or numismatic purposes. Then the illustrations must be in black-and-white and either less than three-quarters (75 percent) or more than one and one-half times (150 percent) the size of the original currency or uncanceled stamp.[58]

Lottery

Lotteries authorized by state law can be advertised in matter sent through the mail, under the Charity Games Advertising Clarification Act of 1988.[59] Many states allow nonprofit groups to have lotteries, bingo, and other games of chance and these can be advertised. Because this is a state law, editors need to confirm whether the applicable state has authorized such advertising.

A lottery exists when there are three elements—prize, chance, and consideration. Generally, a prize is an award of greater value than any or all of the other participants receive. Most contests have this element of lottery. Chance means that the outcome is beyond the control of the participants and is not based on skill, talent, or persistence. Most contests also have this element. Consideration is not as easily defined, but it involves payment to enter, buying a specific product, or being present when prize winners are announced. The most common technique for eliminating consideration is to permit a brand name to be written in block letters on a 3″ × 5″ piece of paper in place of submitting a wrapper or proof of purchase from the sponsor's product.

Because *all three* elements must be present to constitute a lottery, elimination of any one makes the material publishable in all editorial or advertising content. Apparently innocent items often are lotteries: a door prize when one pays to enter an event, an auto raffle or turkey raffle, or a bingo party when one pays to play. The absolute prohibition against material about lotteries was softened in 1947, when the Post Office ruled that lotteries may be mentioned if "the element of lottery is only incidental to a newsworthy event." Few publications are harassed by postal authorities for mentioning lotteries.

Labor Law and Employee Magazines

Editors of company-sponsored magazines for employees must be aware of actions of the National Labor Relations Board under the Taft-Hartley Act. Employers often convey information about employee benefits and contract negotiations and offers in their employee publications. They are free to do this as long as the material does not threaten the employee or promise benefits for adopting the employer's position. Section 8(c) of the Taft-Hartley Act specifies the conditions:

The expressing of any views, argument, or opinion, or the dissemination thereof, whether in written, printed, or graphic, or visual form, shall not constitute or be evidence of an unfair labor practice under any provisions of this Act, if such expression contains no threat of reprisal or force or promise of benefit.

Material that affects labor relations usually comes from the company personnel department and is checked routinely with its legal counsel, so the main point here is that the editor be aware of the potentially damaging situation. An employer, for example, may campaign against a union seeking to represent employees, indicate a preference for one union over another, urge employees to change unions or start a new one or have none at all, or tell employees it does not like to deal with unions.

An employer may not threaten employees with economic reprisal for participating in union activities, promise benefits to employees if they reject the union or choose a union the employer prefers, or give financial support or other assistance to a union or to employees who are opposing or supporting a union.

Advertising

Although primarily concerned with editorial content, the editor is interested in advertisements and what they look like and say in the publication. A McGraw-Hill attorney recommends that every advertising rate card have a provision giving the publisher the right to reject any advertising believed to be inappropriate and a protective clause that makes the advertiser and advertising agency totally responsible to the publisher for the content of any advertisement published in the magazine. At McGraw-Hill, each magazine sets it own criteria for accepting or rejecting ads.[60]

Avoiding Legal Problems

The preceding discussions of potential legal problems suggest some ways to avoid those problems. An editor can reduce the possibility of being subjected to legal action if he or she

1. Attains a reasonable knowledge of federal and state law affecting publications and especially court decisions involving publications. Knowledge of potential dangers can help one consider ways to avoid or overcome them.
2. Consults routinely with counsel before entering danger areas. A courageous editor must be willing to risk litigation in serving readers or society at large. However, he or she should not take unnecessary risks that leave the magazine open to unnecessary suits. McGraw-Hill's general counsel told a company legal seminar

   Our job as lawyers is to counsel you on how to avoid litigation or defend yourself against it. Your obligation is to identify a potential legal problem and let us know, as soon as possible, when you have one. We are not censors; we don't want to kill articles. We want to get your stories published by working with you on reducing the possibilities of legal risks.[61]

3. Insists on careful editing that makes every effort to avoid error. A substantial number of lawsuits against magazines originate from error rather than intent.

Editors should know their writers well and insist on careful fact checking by magazine staff members. Free-lance writers routinely are required to assure the accuracy of their work and to assume the costs of litigation stemming from it in the contract used to buy rights to their articles. This is a good way to impress responsibility on writers, but the magazine must also accept responsibility. It nearly always has greater resources than free-lancers and should take proper precautions to make sure its articles have been verified. Many magazines' editors and staff members insist that it is impossible to check all facts that will be published. A few magazines say their staffs *do* verify *every* fact. For every magazine, consultation with legal counsel and careful checking of anything that may become a legal problem, even a fictitious name that happens to be a real person's name in the local phone book or the address of a person of the same name who becomes libeled by the publication, is imperative. Careful editing will prevent most litigation.

Notes

1. Dwight L. Teeter, Jr., and Don R. Le Duc, *Law of Mass Communication,* 7th ed. (Westbury, N.Y.: Foundation, 1992), pp. 100, 128.
2. Don R. Pember, *Mass Media Law,* 6th ed. (Dubuque, Iowa: Wm. C. Brown Publishers, 1993), p. 119.
3. *Curtis Publishing Co. v. Butts* and *Associated Press v. Walker* 388 U.S. 130 157–58 (1967).
4. Teeter and Le Duc, pp. 155–57.
5. *The News Media & The Law* (February–March 1981): 21.
6. Teeter and Le Duc, p. 142.
7. Teeter and Le Duc, p. 146.

8. Pember, p. 142.
9. 418 U.S. 351 (1974).
10. Harry Johnston III, "Libel and the Magazine Publisher," *Folio:* (December 1976): 34.
11. Teeter and Le Duc, p. 128.
12. *McGraw-Hill World* (25 July 1991): 4.
13. *ASJA Newsletter* (June 1992): 7.
14. UPI dispatch from Washington, D.C., *Baton Rouge, La., Morning Advocate,* 22 February 1984, p. 5-B.
15. *The News Media & The Law* (June/July 1981): 26–27.
16. Teeter and Le Duc, p. 128.
17. *The News Media & The Law* (February–March, 1981): 24.
18. Teeter and Le Duc, pp. 129–131, and Pember, p. 200.
19. Pember, p. 200.
20. Margaret G. Carter, "Press Breathes Sigh of Relief after the Falwell Decision," *Presstime* (April 1988): 34.
21. Pember, p. 201.
22. Teeter and Le Duc, p. 241.
23. Don R. Pember, *Mass Media Law,* 5th ed. (Dubuque, Iowa: Wm. C. Brown Publishers, 1990), p. 102.
24. Pember, 6th ed., pp. 170–71.
25. Teeter and Le Duc, p. 253.
26. *Lahiri v. Daily Mirror, Inc.,* 162 Misc. 776, 295 N.Y. Supp. 382 (1937).
27. *Molony v. Boy Comics Publishers, Inc.,* 277 App. Div. 166, 98 N.Y.S. 2d 119 (1950).
28. *Leverton v. Curtis Publishing Co.,* 192 F.2d 974 (1951).
29. Teeter and Le Duc, p. 291.
30. *Russell v. Marboro Books, Inc.,* 13 Misc. 2d 166, 183 N.Y.S. 2d 888 (1955).
31. *McAndrews v. Roy,* 131 So. 2d 256 (1961).
32. Harry M. Johnston III, "Invasion of Privacy," *Folio:* (February 1977): 66.
33. Ibid., pp. 66–67.
34. Ibid., p. 67.
35. *Advertising Age* (14 June 1976): 88.
36. Johnston, "Invasion of Privacy," p. 68.
37. Pember, 6th ed. p. 250.
38. 385 U.S. 374, 377, (1967).
39. 385 U.S. 374, 386–88 (1967).
40. 385 U.S. 374, 389, (1967).
41. 385 U.S. 374, 388, (1967), quoting *Winters v. New York,* 333 U.S. 507, 510 (1948).
42. Quoting *Joseph Burstyn, Inc. v. Wilson,* 343 U.S. 495, 501–2, (1952).
43. In an earlier stage of the Hill case, Presiding Judge Bernard Botein had held that "showing that a noteworthy item has been published solely to increase circulation injects an unrealistic ingredient into the complex of the right to privacy and would abridge dangerously the people's right to know. In the final analysis, the reading public, not the publisher, determines what is newsworthy, and what is newsworthy will perforce tend to increase circulation." [*Hill v. Hayes,* 18 A.D. 2d 485, 240 N.Y.S. 2d 286, 293 (1963)]
44. *Sidis v. F-R Publishing Corp.,* 113 F. 2d 806 (C.C.A.N.Y. 1940).
45. Pember, 6th ed., p. 244.
46. Public Law 94–553 (19 October 1976), Sections 302, 401, and 101.
47. Harry M. Johnston III, "What the New Copyright Law Means to You," *Folio:* (June 1977): 30.
48. Judge Robert P. Anderson ruled in June 1962 that "thermos" is generic and in the public domain as a synonym for "vacuum insulated" and as an "adjectival noun meaning a vacuum insulated container." Aladdin was permitted to use "thermos" only when the word "Aladdin" preceded it and only in all lowercase letters. [*Advertising Age* (2 July 1962): 2, and (13 January 1964): 16.]
49. 383 U.S. 463, 467–68, (1966).
50. 354 U.S. 476, 489, (1957).
51. 354 U.S. 484 (1957).
52. 413 U.S. 23–24 (1973).
53. *The Quill* (October 1973): 9.
54. 413 U.S. 27 (1973).
55. Pember, 6th ed., p. 418.
56. Ibid., pp. 423–25.
57. *McGraw-Hill World* (25 July 1992): 4.
58. *McGraw-Hill News* (12 July 1979): 2, reporting a company seminar on "Magazines and the Law."
59. Pub. L. No. 100–625, 102 Stat. 3205, amending 18 U.S.C. 1307.
60. *McGraw-Hill News* (12 July 1979): 2.
61. Ibid., p. 1.

Appendix
National Magazine Awards, 1966–1992

The National Magazine Awards

General Excellence
1973 Business Week
1981 ARTnews
     Audubon
     Business Week
     Glamour
1982 Camera Arts
     Newsweek
     Rocky Mountain Magazine
     Science81
1983 Harper's
     Life
     Louisiana Life
     Science82
1984 The American Lawyer
     House & Garden
     National Geographic
     Outside
1985 American Health
     American Heritage
     Manhattan, inc.
     Time
1986 Discover
     Money
     New England Monthly
     3-2-1-Contact
1987 Common Cause
     Elle
     New England Monthly
     People Weekly
1988 Fortune
     Hippocrates
     Parents
     The Sciences
1989 American Heritage
     Sports Illustrated
     The Sciences
     Vanity Fair
1990 Metropolitan Home
     7 Days
     Sports Illustrated
     Texas Monthly
1991 Condé Nast Traveler
     Glamour
     Interview
     The New Republic
1992 Mirabella
     National Geographic
     The New Republic
     Texas Monthly

Personal Service
1986 Farm Journal
1987 Consumer Reports
1988 Money
1989 Good Housekeeping
1990 Consumer Reports
1991 New York
1992 Creative Classroom

Special Interests
1986 Popular Mechanics
1987 Sports Afield
1988 Condé Nast Traveler
1989 Condé Nast Traveler
1990 Art & Antiques
1991 New York
1992 Sports Afield

Reporting
1970 The New Yorker
1971 The Atlantic Monthly
1972 The Atlantic Monthly
1973 New York
1974 The New Yorker
1975 The New Yorker
1976 Audubon
1977 Audubon
1978 The New Yorker
1979 Texas Monthly
1980 Mother Jones
1981 National Journal
1982 The Washingtonian
1983 Institutional Investor
1984 Vanity Fair
1985 Texas Monthly
1986 Rolling Stone
1987 Life
1988 The Washingtonian and
     Baltimore Magazine
1989 The New Yorker
1990 The New Yorker
1991 The New Yorker
1992 The New Republic

Feature Writing
1988 The Atlantic
1989 Esquire
1990 The Washingtonian
1991 U. S. News & World Report
1992 Sports Illustrated

Public Interest
1970 Life
1971 The Nation
1972 Philadelphia
1974 Scientific American
1975 Consumer Reports
1976 Business Week
1977 Philadelphia
1978 Mother Jones
1979 New West
1980 Texas Monthly
1981 Reader's Digest
1982 The Atlantic
1983 Foreign Affairs
1984 The New Yorker
1985 The Washingtonian
1986 Science85
1987 Money
1988 The Atlantic
1989 California
1990 Southern Exposure
1991 Family Circle
1992 Glamour

Design
1980 Geo
1981 Attenzione
1982 Nautical Quarterly
1983 New York
1984 House & Garden
1985 Forbes
1986 Time
1987 Elle
1988 Life
1989 Rolling Stone
1990 Esquire
1991 Condé Nast Traveler
1992 Vanity Fair

Photography
1985 Life
1986 Vogue
1987 National Geographic
1988 Rolling Stone
1989 National Geographic
1990 Texas Monthly
1991 National Geographic
1992 National Geographic

Fiction
1978 The New Yorker
1979 The Atlantic Monthly
1980 Antæus
1981 The North American Review
1982 The New Yorker
1983 The North American Review
1984 Seventeen
1985 Playboy
1986 The Georgia Review
1987 Esquire
1988 The Atlantic
1989 The New Yorker
1990 The New Yorker
1991 Esquire
1992 Story

Essays & Criticism
1978 Esquire
1979 Life
1980 Natural History
1981 Time
1982 The Atlantic
1983 The American Lawyer
1984 The New Republic
1985 Boston Magazine
1986 The Sciences
1987 Outside
1988 Harper's Magazine
1989 Harper's Magazine
1990 Vanity Fair
1991 The Sciences
1992 The Nation

Single-topic Issue
1979 Progressive Architecture
1980 Scientific American
1981 Business Week
1982 Newsweek
1983 IEEE Spectrum
1984 Esquire
1985 American Heritage
1986 IEEE Spectrum
1987 Bulletin of the Atomic Scientists
1988 Life
1989 Hippocrates
1990 National Geographic
1991 The American Lawyer
1992 Business Week

Single Award
1966 Look
1967 Life
1968 Newsweek
1969 American Machinist

Special Award
1976 Time
1989 Robert E. Kenyon, Jr.

Specialized Journalism
1970 Philadelphia
1971 Rolling Stone
1972 Architectural Record
1973 Psychology Today
1974 Texas Monthly
1975 Medical Economics
1976 United Mine Workers Journal
1977 Architectural Record
1978 Scientific American
1979 National Journal
1980 IEEE Spectrum

Visual Excellence
1970 Look
1971 Vogue
1972 Esquire
1973 Horizon
1974 Newsweek
1975 Country Journal
     National Lampoon
1976 Horticulture
1977 Rolling Stone
1978 Architectural Digest
1979 Audubon

Fiction and Belles Lettres
1970 Redbook
1971 Esquire
1972 Mademoiselle
1973 The Atlantic Monthly
1974 The New Yorker
1975 Redbook
1976 Essence
1977 Mother Jones

Service to the Individual
1974 Sports Illustrated
1975 Esquire
1976 Modern Medicine
1977 Harper's
1978 Newsweek
1979 The American Journal of Nursing
1980 Saturday Review
1982 Philadelphia
1983 Sunset
1984 New York
1985 The Washingtonian

Glossary

Alignment Design device to create order by lining up visual elements.

Appropriation Using a person's name or likeness for commercial purposes, usually in advertising, without that person's written permission; an invasion of privacy.

Area composition Sophisticated typesetting, with the output placed in several columns to fill a desired rectangular area rather than in one long column.

Ascender In a typeface, a stroke that rises above the center body of a letter.

Backbone Binding edge of a magazine.

Backleading Capability of modern typesetting machines to back up after setting type, thus permitting the reduction of space between lines, overlapping, or the setting of type in several columns under one headline.

Backward readers Those who peruse a magazine from the back to the front.

Balance Feeling of equilibrium created in layout by placing elements of equal or similar weights on both sides of an axis.

Bar graph Explanatory illustration relying on differences in the length of bars to show statistical differences.

Benday Process for artificially adding shading to a line illustration.

Bleed allowance An extra pica or 1/8 inch allowed for illustration reproduction dimensions on outside edges where the allowance will be trimmed off before binding.

Bleed Extension of an illustration beyond the edge of a page.

Blueline Paper proofs in offset lithography, so-called because the printing areas show in blue. Also called *blueprint*.

Body type Type of the smaller sizes (13-point and smaller) used to present the main text (body) of a message.

Body Part of a piece of type that holds the face at the right height for printing. The main text of a message.

Book Trade term for magazine.

Break-of-the-book Process of deciding what goes on each page of an issue.

Brownline In offset lithography, paper page proof on which the printing image shows in brown. Also called *brownprint*.

Budget Plan for a business for a stated period, usually one year. Budgets are expressed in pages as well as dollars. Budgets for different issues vary according to the size of the issue and its revenue.

Business publication or magazine One published to serve readers in their business, industry, profession, or other vocation.

Byte Set of binary digits (bits) sufficient to represent a verbal piece of information, such as a character or a number. Usually eight or six bits represent one byte.

Camera ready Type and/or illustrations ready to be photographed to print by offset lithography.

Charter subscription Sale of a periodical when publication is started or on special terms with a guarantee that the subscription price will not be increased provided renewal is made regularly at expiration.

Checkbook journalism Paying a source for an interview or for information.

Clicking Calling for action on a computer screen by pressing the click button on a mouse.

Clip art Stock drawings of common subjects now available on microcomputer disks for desktop publishing applications.

Cold type Any type not set with hot metal.

Combination internal-external circulation Circulation both within and outside the sponsoring organization, such as employees and investors.

Command In computerized printing production, a string of bytes of information that forces an action by the computer.

Commission Reduction in revenue allowed to agency for placing advertising, usually 15 percent of gross. Also called *agency commission*.

Company magazine One published by a company to promote its own interests. Also *public relations magazine*.

Contributing editor Usually a person not on the staff, who writes a regular column, who consults with the editorial staff, or whose name is used to lend credibility to the magazine. If a consultant, often called an *advisory editor*.

Controlled circulation Circulation to qualified readers only, usually free or at a token price.

Copy control form Editorial record of the status of all articles and other elements of an issue.

Copyediting Process of reading and correcting copy.

Copyfitting Computation of space requirements for copy.

Copyright Protection of original written, visual, or design works for a period of time from their creation or publication.

Cost per thousand (CPM) Cost of one full page of advertising in 1,000 copies of the magazine. Also can be calculated per thousand readers or per thousand of an advertiser's prime prospects (target market). Indicates cost but not quality of circulation.

Crop marks On illustrations to be printed, marks that set the width and depth dimensions of the original.

Crop Figurative removal of a portion of either dimension of a photo.

Cursive Type group with letters resembling hand lettering.

Cursor Blinking light on a video terminal screen that is used to locate any text changes as they are made on the screen.

Demographics Social and economic characteristics of individuals and households, such as age, income, education, sex, occupation, home ownership.

Demographic edition Version of a magazine issue distributed to a portion of the total circulation according to demographic characteristics, such as income or profession. Most demographic editions differ only in advertising content, not editorial content.

Department Category of editorial content in a magazine. Often used to describe a specific column or continuing feature. Also a staff organization unit, such as the Food Department.

Descender Vertical stroke extending below the center body of a letter.

Descriptive titles Those that quickly answer the question, What is this article about?

Desktop publishing Microcomputer-based publishing systems with capabilities ranging from typesetting to pagination, with output to laser printers or to digital typesetters.

Diagram Drawing showing a process or the method of accomplishing a task.

Dingbat Decorative typographical device such as a star, circle, or check mark.

Discount Reduction in advertising rate allowed for placing larger amounts of advertising. *Volume discounts* are based on the total number of pages or amount of space bought during the contract period, usually one year. *Frequency discounts* are based on the number of issues ads are placed in during the contract period. *Multiple-page* and other discounts may be available.

Display type Larger sizes of type, from 14-point up.

Dots per inch (dpi) Number of dots in each inch of image production. The greater the dpi, the better the quality of reproduction.

Double burn In offset, the exposure of light through each of two flats onto one plate to get close positioning of elements.

Draw programs Object-oriented software for creating graphic images that can be enlarged, reduced, or altered in other ways without a loss of quality in reproduction.

Dumping Clearing material from a computer into a typesetter.

Duotone Reproduction of a halftone in two colors from two plates.

Editorial calendar List of special topics, content, and themes by date of publication. Used to sell advertising.

Editorial formula Specific content and types of content that establish the magazine's editorial personality and appeal to its target audience and that differentiate it from its competitors.

Editorial objective Specific, measurable result that the magazine editorial staff intends to achieve.

Em A measure of quantity in type. A square in the type size being used. Common amount of indentation for a paragraph.

External circulation Circulation outside the sponsoring organization.

External Public relations magazine prepared for and circulated to a group of readers outside the organizational structure, such as customers, investors, or community leaders.

Face Printing image of type.

False light Publication of untrue information that is not defamatory but places a person in a false light before the public; an invasion of privacy.

Family variations In typography, the variations in weight, width, posture, and size with a family classification, such as Melior Light, Melior Bold, Melior Italic, Melior Extended, Melior Condensed.

Family In typography, a collection of types so similar as to be from the same family and carry the same family name, such as Melior.

Floppy disk Data storage device for microcomputers in 5¼″ and 3½″ diameter formats.

Font One size of one branch of one family of type in sufficient quantity to do normal typesetting.

Format Size, shape, and other characteristics giving identity to a periodical. In typesetting, the instructions as to type size, etc., that are fed into an automated typesetter.

Formatting In computerized typesetting, the capability of calling for a set of markup instructions for a piece of typesetting with one keystroke.

Free-lance Nonstaff: free-lance writer, free-lance manuscript.

Fulfillment In circulation, the activities necessary to deliver the magazine to the subscriber, including start date, billing, address file maintenance, and cut-off on expiration.

Galley proof Type proof taken before the type has been put into page form.

Ghostwriting Writing a speech or an article for someone else, who delivers it or gets the byline.

Gothic A basic group of typefaces that are skeletal and monotonal.

Graphics Charts, graphs, and other artwork.

Grid Pattern for page layout.

Gridding Design technique in which space is divided into rectangles and elements are confined in those rectangles, thus creating a Mondrian-like geometric design.

Group In typography, one of five basic classes of type: Text, Roman, Gothic, Script and Cursive, or Novelty.

Halftone Illustration that reproduces continuous tones; also the plate needed to reproduce such illustrations.

Hot type Type cast with molten metal.

House organ Public relations or company periodical.

Humanizing Writing technique involving the use of human references and anecdotes instead of statistics.

Imposition Arrangement of pages in a printing form so that, when the sheet they are printed on is folded, the pages are in proper sequence.

In-house From within the publishing firm, as distinguished from an outside supplier.

Industrial magazine Long-used term for *company* or *public relations* magazine. Also used to designate a business or trade magazine for manufacturing industries—therefore, a confusing term.

Insert Sheet of printing containing fewer pages than the normal signature and added to a magazine during binding.

Internal Public relations magazine prepared for and circulated to a group of readers within the organizational structure of the sponsor, such as employees.

Internal circulation Circulation within the sponsoring organization, such as employees.

Intrusion Acquiring information from or about a person by physical trespass or deception; an invasion of privacy.

Italic Slanted posture version of a type family.

Justified Type lines made flush to the right as well as to the left.

Kerning Typesetting capability of moving one letter into another letter's space, such as the letter *a* under the roof of a capital *T*.

Kill fee Fee paid to a free-lance writer when an assigned article or a previously accepted article is not published.

Leading Pronounced "ledding," the addition of white space between type lines. Also called *linespacing*.

Letterpress System of printing that uses a raised surface to carry ink to paper.

Letterspacing Space between letters, which can be specified as normal, loose, or tight.

Libel Printed, written, or broadcast communication that exposes persons to hatred, ridicule, or contempt; lowers them in the esteem of others; causes them to be shunned; or injures them in their business or calling. Also personal humiliation, and mental anguish and suffering, widely termed "infliction of emotional distress."

Line graph Chart showing trends over time.

Lottery A prize awarded by chance (not skill) after payment of consideration.

Lowercase Small letters, as contrasted with capitals.

Magapaper Periodical designed to look like a tabloid or pony tab newspaper, usually using high-quality printing on high-quality paper stock. Combines magazine content with newspaper design.

Magazine Experts have avoided defining the term. Generally, a variety of content presented periodically to recipients. Can be printed, electronic, or in another form.

Manuscript receipt record Form used to keep track of free-lance manuscripts as they are received and processed.

Mask Vehicle, usually a sheet of opaque paper, that holds negatives in position so offset plates can be exposed. Also called a *flat*.

Mechanical Layout or dummy, with all type and line illustrations pasted in position, ready to be photographed and transferred to a printing plate.

Media event An event that does not naturally occur but is staged to receive media attention; often called a pseudo-event.

Modem Device that permits the use of telephones to transmit digital information.

Modern Roman Division of the Roman type group, featuring straight, thin serifs and variation among width of strokes.

Mortise Illustration with a portion removed from within its outer borders.

Mouse Device for dragging the cursor to any location on a monitor screen.

Nonpaid circulation In controlled circulation publications, circulation that meets the requirements of qualified circulation and which is sent free to the recipients in the field served.

Nonpaid distribution Term used in ABC paid circulation report for copies distributed at shows and conventions; checking copies and promotional copies sent to advertisers and ad agencies; and miscellaneous, including staff copies; not included in reported total circulation (rate base or circulation guarantee).

Notch Illustration with a portion cut away from one or more of its outer dimensions.

Obscenity Depiction or description of sexual conduct, as defined by state law, in a patently offensive way, which, taken as a whole, appeals to the prurient interest of the average person and lacks serious literary, artistic, political, or scientific value.

Offset System of printing that is chemical, planographic, and indirect. An inked image on a flat plate is transferred to a rubber surface before being pressed to paper; the plate surface is treated to accept greasy ink in image areas, which resist water, and to accept water in nonimage areas, which resist the ink.

Oldstyle Roman Division of the Roman type group, featuring bracketed serifs and moderate difference in width of strokes.

On line In computerized systems, being hooked together by wire.

On the board Display of the pages of an article or issue on a wall or bulletin board so editors can evaluate their final form and placement.

One-shot magazine Special magazine issued only one time on a subject or an event not likely to warrant succeeding issues.

Organizational magazine One sponsored by an organization, usually issued to advance the organization and its purposes.

Over the transom Unsolicited, as in freelance material that was not solicited.

Overlay Transparent sheet placed over the face of an illustration or a layout to position material to be printed in color or to provide instructions for preparation.

Pagination Creating or numbering pages in a publication. Creating full-page layouts on computer terminal screens.

Paid circulation Circulation to paid subscribers and single-copy buyers, including circulation that is paid by part of an association's dues.

Paint programs Bit-map-oriented software that permits the editing of images pixel by pixel.

Pass-along audience Persons other than addressees who are exposed to part of the content of a publication.

Paste-down type Fonts of type with adhesive backing so letters can be cut from sheets and fastened in position on mechanicals.

Perfect binding Binding system using flexible glue to serve as a backbone of a publication.

Perfecting press One that prints on both sides of a sheet or web at one impression.

Pica Basic unit of printers' measurement. One-sixth of an inch, or 12 points.

Pictograph Bar graph using objects to form the bars.

Pie chart Explanatory illustration using a circle split into segments to show relationship of quantities.

Pixels Picture elements. The dots that form a computerized image.

Plagiarism Use of another's work without attribution to the original source.

Point Unit of printers' measurement equal to 1/72d of an inch, 1/12th of a pica.

Posterization Reproduction of a continuous tone illustration so there will be only three tones, making the reproduction appear like a poster.

Posture In typography, either the upright or the italic version of a face.

Preliminary planning Earliest work done to set theme or generate general ideas for an issue.

Private facts Facts about a person that are not of public interest or relevant to a published article of public interest, publication of which invades one's privacy.

Privilege Protection of untruths uttered in *public and official governmental proceedings* from action for libel or slander; to be protected, the proceeding must be defined by law as both *public* and *offficial*. Publications are afforded *qualified privilege* if their report of such proceedings is a *fair and accurate summary* of the proceedings.

Process color Lifelike color that is achieved by printing from four plates created by separating the primary colors plus black.

Progressive margins System of margins in which the bottom is largest, and the others are progressively smaller in this order: outside, top, gutter.

Proofreading symbols Marks for correcting errors made by a printer in setting type.

Proportioning Process of computing the proportions of enlargements or reductions of illustrations.

Proprietary systems Computerized systems designed specifically for high-quality publishing.

Public domain Works for which the copyright period has expired are in the *public domain* and can be reprinted without permission.

Public relations magazine One issued by a company or another organization to advance one or more of its public relations purposes. Also called *company magazine, organizational magazine,* or *house organ.*

Publisher Chief executive of a magazine, ultimately responsible for all decisions (editorial, business, advertising, circulation), usually the owner's representative or the owner.

Publishers Editorial Profile Capsule statement in Standard Rate and Data advertising rate directories that describes to advertisers how a magazine attempts to appeal to its target audience. Often describes the editorial formula.

Qualified recipients Individuals who meet the publisher's definition of recipient qualification within the field served.

Readability research Measurement of the ease of reading writing by considering word choice, sentence length, and other factors.

Reader Object of magazine editing. Each magazine is read by one reader at a time. Editors need to develop a relationship or involvement with their readers.

Readership studies Research into when, how, where, and the extent to which readers read magazines and the demographic and life-style characteristics of those readers.

Regional edition Version of a magazine issue distributed to a portion of the total circulation in a defined geographic area. Most regional editions differ only in advertising content, not editorial content.

Register Positioning of elements in printing so their images are located exactly as desired on the printed sheet, or web, especially with reference to applying additional colors on the sheet.

Renewal Subscription that is renewed within six months after expiration.

Reverse In illustrations, to reproduce blacks as whites and whites as blacks.

Right of privacy Right to restrict the use of one's name and likeness in published materials; generally applies only to uses in advertisements and editorial material on subjects not of public interest.

Roman Basic type group characterized by serifs and variation in thickness among basic strokes and upright posture as opposed to italic.

Rotogravure Printing from depressed (engraved) areas on a rotating cylinder.

Saddle-wire Type of binding to which sections of a magazine are inserted rather than stacked and staples are driven through the fold from the outside. Also called *saddle-stitch*.

Sans serif Type without serifs, the small strokes that run counter to main strokes in some type designs.

Scaling Computation of the dimensions of illustrations after enlargement or reduction.

Scanner Device that scans printed material and digitizes it for entry into a computer.

Screen Sheet of film, containing intersecting opaque lines, that is placed over the film in an engraver's camera, which breaks a continuous tone image into dots as it exposes the film. The dots are the vehicle for reproducing the various tones present in photographs.

Script Basic group of type styles resembling handwriting.

Self-cover Magazine whose cover is part of a large sheet that folds into a section of the magazine (the outside signature).

Sheetfed Type of press that prints on sheets of paper rather than rolls.

Sheetwise System of imposing half the pages of a magazine section in a printing form so that, when the sheet is printed with the remaining pages on the other side and folded into a magazine section, the pages are in proper sequence.

Side-wire Binding system in which staples are driven through stacked magazine sections about 1/8 inch from the backbone. Also called *side-stitch*.

Signature Section of a magazine—usually 8, 16, or 32 pages—formed when a press sheet is folded to format size.

Silhouette Illustration treatment that eliminates all background to permit the subject to stand in outline against the paper.

Slant Approach or direction taken in developing an article.

Slug A word or two used to identify a piece of copy.

Special magazine One issued infrequently, such as a Christmas ideas special, or only once, as a one-shot, on a subject or an event that does not warrant frequent issues.

Specific planning session Meeting of staff members to translate general ideas into specific articles and assignments for an issue.

Split roller Printing technique in which ink rollers and fountains are split so a different color can be rolled over a form from each segment.

SS Same size, the designation telling a printer to reproduce an illustration the same size as the original.

Statute of limitations Time in which a suit must be filed.

Strike-on Type composition by way of a typewriterlike device through which the alphanumeric characters are placed on paper with the striking of keys.

Subhead Heading between paragraphs, usually in boldface or other type variation used to break up gray areas.

Subtitle Secondary title used to elaborate on a concise main title.

Surprint combination Illustration that combines continuous tone and line images in one area; created by exposing continuous tone and line negatives in sequence to the same plate area. Also called *double print*.

Tabazine Periodical in tabloid newspaper format. Usually similar to a *magapaper*.

Templates Computerized patterns establishing style and location of visual elements on pages.

Text Body of an article. Also an ornate type group appropriate for religious and ceremonial subjects.

Tint block Flat tonal area or the plate used to create it.

Tip-in One-sheet insertion glued into the binding of a magazine or book.

Trade journal or magazine Same as *business publication*, which is the preferred term of the professional association.

Trademark Name, sign, or logo used in trade to identify a product or company. May be registered with the U.S. Patent Office and renewed every 10 years.

Type page Image of a page. The page exclusive of margins.

Typo Typographical error.

Unit count In headlines, a counting system using one unit for normal width letters, one-half unit for narrow ones such as *i* and *l*, one and one-half for capitals or wide letters such as *m* and *w*, and two units for capital *M* and *W*.

Velox Screened photoprint that can be reproduced as a line illustration.

Visual syntax Arrangement of visual elements so a message is presented logically according to the placement of the elements.

Web fed Printing press fed from a roll of paper rather than sheets.

Work-and-turn Same as work-and-tumble, except that, after one side is printed, the sheet is turned over sideways so the same front edge is retained.

Wrap Four-page insert wrapped around a signature for binding.

Selected Bibliography

Abramson, Howard S. *National Geographic: Behind America's Lens on the World*. New York: Crown, 1987.

Anderson, Elliott, and Mary Kinsie. *The Little Magazine in America*. Yonkers, N.Y.: Pushcart Press, 1978.

Backstrom, Charles H., and Gerald D. Hursch-Cesar. *Survey Research*. 2d ed. Evanston, Ill.: Northwestern University Press, 1981.

Baird, Russell N., Duncan McDonald, A. T. Turnbull, and Ronald H. Pittman. *The Graphics of Communication*. 6th ed. New York: Harcourt Brace Jovanovich, 1993.

Byron, Christopher M. *The Fanciest Dive*. New York: Plume/New American Library, 1987.

Christians, Clifford G., Kim B. Rotzoll, and Mark Fackler. *Media Ethics: Cases & Moral Reasoning*. 3d ed. New York: Longman, 1991.

Cohn, Jan. *Creating America: George Horace Lorimer and the Saturday Evening Post*. Pittsburgh: University of Pittsburgh Press, 1989.

Compaigne, Benjamin M. *The Business of Consumer Magazines*. White Plains, N.Y.: Knowledge Industry Publications, 1982.

Cousins, Norman. *Present Tense*. New York: McGraw-Hill, 1967.

Day, Louis A. *Ethics in Media Communications: Cases and Controversies*. Belmont, Cal.: Wadsworth, 1991.

Dembner, S. Arthur, and William E. Massee, eds. *Modern Circulation Methods*. New York: McGraw-Hill, 1968.

Donovan, Hedley. *Right Places, Right Times*. New York: Simon & Schuster, 1991.

Elfenbein, Julien. *Business Journalism*. 2d ed. New York: Harper & Bros., 1960.

————, ed. *Businesspaper Publishing Practice*. New York: Harper & Bros., 1952.

Ford, James L. C. *Magazines for Millions*. Carbondale, Ill.: Southern Illinois University Press, 1969.

Gillmor, Donald M., and Jerome A. Barron. *Mass Communication Law*. 5th ed. St. Paul, Minn.: West, 1990.

Greco, Albert N. *Business Journalism, Management Cases & Notes*. New York: New York University Press, 1988.

Gunning, Robert. *The Technique of Clear Writing*. Rev. ed. New York: McGraw-Hill, 1968.

Gussow, Don. *The New Business Journalism*. New York: Harcourt Brace Jovanovich, 1984.

Hamblin, Dora Jane. *That Was the LIFE*. New York: W. W. Norton, 1977.

Hubbard, J. T. W. *Magazine Editing for Professionals*. Rev. ed. Syracuse, N.Y.: Syracuse University Press, 1989.

Humphries, Nancy K. *American Women's Magazines: An Annotated Historical Guide*. New York: Garland, 1989.

Kahn, E. J., Jr. *Year of Change: More About the New Yorker and Me*. New York: Viking Penguin, 1988.

Kobler, John. *Luce: His Time, Life and Fortune*. New York: Doubleday, 1968.

Koff, Richard M. *Strategic Planning for Magazine Executives: How to Take the Guesswork Out of Magazine Publishing Decisions*. 2d ed. Stamford, Conn.: Folio Magazine Publishing, 1987.

Kunhardt, Philip B., Jr. *Life: The First Fifty Years, 1936–1986*. Boston: Little, Brown, 1986.

Lynn, Peter. *Success Story: The Life and Times of S. S. McClure*. New York: Charles Scribners Sons, 1963.

Mahon, Gigi. *The Last Days of The New Yorker*. New York: McGraw-Hill, 1988.

Mayes, Herbert R. *The Magazine Maze*. Garden City, N.Y.: Doubleday, 1980.

Meyer, Philip. *The New Precision Journalism*. Bloomington, Ind.: Indiana University Press, 1991.

Nelson, Roy Paul. *Publication Design*. 5th ed. Dubuque, Iowa: Wm. C. Brown, 1991.

Nourie, Alan, and Barbara Nourie, eds. *American Mass-Market Magazines of the United States*. Westport, Conn.: Greenwood, 1990.

Paine, Fred K., and Nancy E. Paine. *Magazines: A Bibliography for Their Analysis, with Annotations and Study Guide*. Metuchen, N.J.: Scarecrow Press, 1987.

Pember, Don R. *Mass Media Law*. 6th ed. Dubuque, Iowa: Brown & Benchmark, 1993.

Peterson, Theodore. *Magazines in the Twentieth Century*. 2d ed. Urbana: University of Illinois Press, 1964.

Prendergast, Curtis, with Geoffrey Colvin. *The World of Time Inc.: The Intimate History of a Changing Enterprise, 1960–1980*. New York: Atheneum, 1986.

Riley, Sam G., and Gary W. Selnow, eds. *Index to City and Regional Magazines of the United States*. Westport, Conn.: Greenwood, 1989.

———. *Regional Interest Magazines of the United States*. Westport, Conn.: Greenwood, 1991.

Rivers, William L. *Free-Lancer and Staff Writer: Newspaper Features and Magazine Articles*. 5th ed. Belmont, Cal.: Wadsworth Publishing Co., 1992.

Stempel, Guido H. III, and Bruce H. Westley, eds. *Research Methods in Mass Communication*. 2d ed. Englewood Cliffs, N.J.: Prentice Hall, 1989.

Taft, William H. *American Magazines for the 1980s*. New York: Hastings House, 1982.

Taylor, Frank C., and Albert N. Greco, eds. *Editorial Excellence in Business Press Publishing*. New York: New York University Press, 1988.

Tebbel, John, and Mary Ellen Zuckerman. *The Magazine in America, 1731–1990*. New York: Oxford University Press, 1991.

Teeter, Dwight L., Jr., and Don R. Le Duc. *Law of Mass Communication*. 7th ed. Westbury, N.Y.: Foundation, 1992.

Thurber, James. *The Years with Ross*. New York: Grosset & Dunlap, 1959.

Wainwright, Loudon. *The Great American Magazine: An Inside History of Life*. New York: Alfred A. Knopf, 1986.

Ward, Hiley H. *Magazine and Feature Writing*. Mountain View, Cal.: Mayfield Publishing Co., 1993.

White, Jan V. *Designing Covers, Contents, Flash Forms, Departments, Editorials, Openers, Products for Magazines*. New York: R. R. Bowker, 1976.

———. *Designing for Magazines*. New York: R. R. Bowker, 1982.

———. *Editing by Design*. 2d ed. New York: R. R. Bowker, 1982.

———. *Graphic Idea Notebook*. Rockport, Mass.: Rockport Publications, 1990.

———. *Great Color: Making Pages Sparkle, Type Talk & Diagrams Sing*. El Segundo, Cal.: Serif Publications, 1992.

———. *Mastering Graphics*. New York: R. R. Bowker, 1983.

———. *Using Charts and Graphs*. New York: R. R. Bowker, 1984.

Wolseley, Roland E. *The Changing Magazine*. New York: Hastings House, 1973.

———. *The Magazine World*. New York: Prentice Hall, 1951.

———. *Understanding Magazines*. 2d ed. Ames, Iowa: Iowa State University Press, 1969.

Index